BOOK LOAN

Please RETURN or RENEW it no later
than the last date shown below

Spatial Representation and Behavior Across the Life Span

Theory and Application

DEVELOPMENTAL PSYCHOLOGY SERIES

SERIES EDITOR
Harry Beilin

Developmental Psychology Program
City University of New York Graduate School
New York, New York

LYNN S. LIBEN. *Deaf Children: Developmental Perspectives*

JONAS LANGER. *The Origins of Logic*: *Six to Twelve Months*

GILBERTE PIERAUT-LE BONNIEC. *The Development of Modal Reasoning*: *Genesis of Necessity and Possibility Notions*

TIFFANY MARTINI FIELD, SUSAN GOLDBERG, DANIEL STERN, and ANITA MILLER SOSTEK. (Editors). *High-Risk Infants and Children*: *Adult and Peer Interactions*

BARRY GHOLSON. *The Cognitive-Developmental Basis of Human Learning*: *Studies in Hypothesis Testing*

ROBERT L. SELMAN. *The Growth of Interpersonal Understanding: Developmental and Clinical Analyses*

RAINER H. KLUWE and HANS SPADA. (Editors). *Developmental Models of Thinking*

HARBEN BOUTOURLINE YOUNG and LUCY RAU FERGUSON. *Puberty to Manhood in Italy and America*

SARAH L. FRIEDMAN and MARIAN SIGMAN. (Editors). *Preterm Birth and Psychological Development*

LYNN S. LIBEN, ARTHUR H. PATTERSON, and NORA NEWCOMBE. (Editors). *Spatial Representation and Behavior Across the Life Span: Theory and Application*

In Preparation

W. PATRICK DICKSON. (Editor). *Children's Oral Communication Skills*

EUGENE S. GOLLIN. (Editor). *Developmental Plasticity: Behavioral and Biological Aspects of Variations in Development*

Spatial Representation and Behavior Across the Life Span

Theory and Application

Edited by

LYNN S. LIBEN

Department of Psychology
University of Pittsburgh
Pittsburgh, Pennsylvania

ARTHUR H. PATTERSON

Division of Man-Environment Relations
College of Human Development
The Pennsylvania State University
University Park, Pennsylvania

NORA NEWCOMBE

Department of Psychology
The Pennsylvania State University
University Park, Pennsylvania

ACADEMIC PRESS   1981

A Subsidiary of Harcourt Brace Jovanovich, Publishers

New York   London   Toronto   Sydney   San Francisco

ACADEMIC PRESS, INC.
111 Fifth Avenue, New York, New York 10003

United Kingdom Edition published by
ACADEMIC PRESS, INC. (LONDON) LTD.
24/28 Oval Road, London NW1 7DX

Library of Congress Cataloging in Publication Data
Main entry under title:

Spatial representation and behavior across the life span.

    (Developmental psychology)
    Includes bibliographies.
    Includes index.
    1. Spatial behavior. 2. Developmental psychology.
I. Liben, Lynn S. II. Patterson, Arthur H.
III. Newcombe, Nora. IV. Series.
BF469.S68   155   80–1105
ISBN 0–12–447980–4

PRINTED IN THE UNITED STATES OF AMERICA

81 82 83 84   9 8 7 6 5 4 3 2 1

Contents

I Introduction

II Developmental and Individual Differences

v

III Production and Comprehension of Spatial Representations

Commentary on Part III

IV Conceptualizing and Designing Spatial Environments

11 A Cross-Cultural and Dialetic Analysis of Homes   283

IRWIN ALTMAN AND MARY GAUVAIN

12 Spatial Ability, Environmental Knowledge, and Environmental Use: The Elderly   321

DAVID A. WALSH, ISELI K. KRAUSS, AND VICTOR A. REGNIER

Commentary on Part IV

13 Spatial Representation and the Environment: Some Applied and Not Very Applied Implications   361

ARTHUR H. PATTERSON

 **Conclusions**

List of Contributors

Numbers in parentheses indicate the pages on which the authors' contributions begin.

LINDA P. ACREDOLO (63), Department of Psychology, University of California, Davis, Davis, California 95616

IRWIN ALTMAN (283), Department of Psychology, University of Utah, Salt Lake City, Utah 84112

ROBERT CIOTTONE (251), Department of Psychology, Clark University, Worcester, Massachusetts 01610

ROGER M. DOWNS (145, 237), Department of Geography, The Pennsylvania State University, University Park, Pennsylvania 16802

MARY GAUVAIN (283), Department of Psychology, University of Utah, Salt Lake City, Utah 84112

LAUREN JULIUS HARRIS (83), Department of Psychology, Michigan State University, East Lansing, Michigan 48824

ROGER A. HART (195), The Graduate School and University Center, City University of New York, New York, New York 10036

BERNARD KAPLAN (251), Department of Psychology, Clark University, Worcester, Massachusetts 01610

ISELI K. KRAUSS (321), Department of Psychology, University of Southern California, Los Angeles, California 90007

LYNN S. LIBEN ° (3), Division of Individual and Family Studies, College of Human Development, The Pennsylvania State University, University Park, Pennsylvania 16802

JEFFREY J. LOCKMAN (39), Institute of Child Development, University of Minnesota, Minneapolis, Minnesota 55455

* *Present address:* Department of Psychology, University of Pittsburgh, Pittsburgh, Pennsylvania 15260

NORA NEWCOMBE (373), Department of Psychology, The Pennsylvania State University, University Park, Pennsylvania 16802

ARTHUR H. PATTERSON (361), Division of Man-Environment Relations, College of Human Development, The Pennsylvania State University, University Park, Pennsylvania 16802

HERBERT L. PICK, JR. (39), Institute of Child Development, University of Minnesota, Minneapolis, Minnesota 55455

VICTOR A. REGNIER (321), Housing Research and Development, Department of Architecture, University of Illinois, Urbana-Champaign, Urbana, Illinois 61801

ALEXANDER W. SIEGEL (167, 237) Department of Psychology, University of Houston, Houston, Texas 77004

DAVID A. WALSH* (321), Department of Psychology, University of Southern California, Los Angeles, California 90007

SEYMOUR WAPNER (251), Department of Psychology, Clark University, Worcester, Massachusetts 01610

JOACHIM F. WOHLWILL (129), Division of Man-Environment Relations and Division of Individual and Family Studies, College of Human Development, The Pennsylvania State University, University Park, Pennsylvania 16802

* *Present address:* Andrus Gerontology Center, University of Southern California, Los Angeles, California 90007

Preface

The perception, representation, design, and use of space concern scholars and practitioners in a variety of disciplines. Cognitive psychologists, for example, have been interested in how individuals represent their spatial environments and how they manipulate these representations. Developmental psychologists have been concerned with identifying and explaining how these representations and manipulative skills change across the life span. Behavioral geographers are interested in how people construct internal representations of their environments, and how people interpret and use various kinds of prepared maps. Environmental psychologists are concerned with how people perceive their environments and how these perceptions affect individuals' behaviors in space, including where they choose to live, shop, and travel. Professionals, such as urban planners and architects, who are concerned with the actual design of spatial environments, are becoming increasingly aware of the need for knowledge about psychological factors that influence the way in which space is used.

Unfortunately, there have been only limited opportunities for interaction among scholars and practitioners from these and related disciplines. As a consequence, many of the conceptualizations and research methodologies that are well-known to members of one discipline must be reinvented by members of another. This volume was designed to provide an opportunity for integration across a variety of perspectives on space, and to suggest potentially fruitful avenues for further collaboration.

To facilitate meaningful communication among scholars, and thereby avoid publishing a collection of isolated papers, the contributors to this book (representing fields of developmental psychology, environmental psychology, social psychology, geography, gerontology, and architecture) participated in a conference on "Spatial Representation and Behavior Across the Life Span: Theory and Application," held at The Pennsylvania State University in May of 1979. The conference was sponsored jointly by the Division of Individual and Family Studies and the Division of Man-Environment Relations (both of the College of Human Development) and by the Department of Psychology (of the College of Liberal Arts). Throughout the conference and this volume, an effort has been made to integrate concepts and methods across disciplines, and to consider both theoretical and applied concerns. In addition, the contributions to this book have been selected to emphasize the utility of taking a life-span developmental approach to the study of space. This means that there is attention first, to changes in individuals as they move from infancy to childhood to adulthood to old age, and second, to changes in the broader context in which individuals develop, such as changes in physical environments and cultures.

In a further attempt to provide the kind of integration outlined above, the book begins and ends with integrative chapters. In addition, each of the three major sections, "Developmental and Individual Differences," "Production and Comprehension of Spatial Representations," and "Conceptualizing and Designing Spatial Environments," contains a section commentary. With this organizational structure, the book serves not only to provide "state of the art" reviews, but also to integrate diverse disciplines and methods and to suggest avenues for reformulating and expanding past conceptualizations. As such, the book should be a useful resource for graduate students, scholars, and practitioners concerned with space in any way, including its psychological representation, its design, and its influences on behavior.

Acknowledgments

The credit for producing this volume belongs not only to the authors, but to many other individuals and institutions as well. Although we cannot possibly name all of them here, we would like to acknowledge several who have been particularly important. First, we are grateful for the intellectual support and financial commitments made at the initiation of this project by the administrative heads of the participating departments, specifically, Paul Baltes (Individual and Family Studies), Sidney Cohn (Man-Environment Relations), and Robert Stern (Psychology). We also thank Fred Vondracek (current head of Individual and Family Studies) for continued administrative support. In addition, we are indebted to colleagues and graduate students in each of these programs for their interest in the substance of the conference and for their willingness to perform some of the tedious tasks such a venture necessitates. The secretarial staffs of all three departments provided endless help in the preparation of manuscripts, publicity, and other details. We are also grateful to the staff on the Keller Conference Center at The Pennsylvania State University that handled administrative details of the conference and left us free to attend to substantive issues. The substance of the conference itself was enhanced significantly by presentations by Sidney Cohn, William Ittelson, Leon Pastalan, and Peter Pufall. Their comments have influenced many of the contributions to this book. The book has also profited from the outstanding staff at Academic Press, and from the support of Harry Beilin, editor of the Developmental Psychology Series. Finally, we would like to thank our respective spouses—Richard Nowell, Nancy Chiswick, and Jeffrey Lerner—for their intellectual and personal support throughout this project.

I

Introduction

1 Spatial Representation and Behavior: Multiple Perspectives

LYNN S. LIBEN

A book concerned with spatial representation and behavior should begin with a concise definition of space. Unfortunately, space, like time, is a concept that we seem to understand intuitively, but that becomes uncomfortably elusive when we try to define it. Since antiquity, many definitions have been offered, and innumerable volumes have been written to explicate them. It would be unrealistic to attempt to provide a comprehensive review of these in a single chapter. Instead, the major themes that underlie various definitions are highlighted here, and major positions concerning the development and functions of individuals' spatial concepts are reviewed (see section entitled "Space").

This overview of the general concept of space is followed by a discussion of spatial representation and spatial behavior, with emphasis on the ways in which these have been interpreted and investigated by developmental and environmental psychologists (see section entitled "Spatial Behavior and Spatial Representation"). It is argued that a failure to recognize very fundamental differences in definitions and questions has led to considerable confusion in interpreting past research and theory.

In the section entitled "Influences on Spatial Activity and Representation," a framework is presented for examining influences on individuals' spatial representations and behavior. Considered are cultural and individual histories; physical, cognitive, and socioemotional characteristics of individuals; and characteristics of physical environments. Finally, the section entitled "Conclusions" contains a discussion of possible links between theory and application, and provides an overview of the organization of this book.

3

SPATIAL REPRESENTATION AND BEHAVIOR
ACROSS THE LIFE SPAN

Space

Definitions of Space

Several issues arise in response to the seemingly simple question "What is space?" The most fundamental concerns the distinction between defining space as _absolute_ versus _relative_.[1] In the former, space is understood as a framework that exists independently of anything contained within it. Material objects are located at particular places within the framework, but even when all objects are removed, the space exists unchanged. Implied in this concept of absolute space is the irrelevance of the observer's perspective.

In contrast, the second view defines space in relative terms; that is, as an expression of a set of relationships among objects. Under this view, space changes with alterations in the position of objects and of the observer. The term "empty space" has no meaning. In philosophy, the concept of absolute space is represented in the work of Plato and Clarke; the concept of relative space, by Leibnitz and Kant. In physics, both concepts have also been evident, with a historical shift from absolute (Newtonian) to relative (Einsteinian) notions.

Just as there has been a shift from absolute to relative spatial concepts in physics, there has also been a shift from an exclusively *Euclidean*, three-dimensional model of space, to *non-Euclidean* models of space with the possibility of more than three dimensions. Euclidean versus non-Euclidean space, then, forms a second major distinction within which definitions of space may be categorized (see Cassirer, 1950; Jammer, 1954; O'Keefe & Nadel, 1978). It is interesting that despite this conceptual pluralism within physics and philosophy, much of the psychological work on spatial concepts (e.g., Piaget & Inhelder, 1956) seems to assume implicitly that the mature concept of space is (and should be) an absolute, three-dimensional Euclidean model.

In the course of defining relative space, an additional distinction arises between *place* and *space*.

> Now as to the concept of space, it seems that this was preceded by the psychologically simpler concept of place. Place is first of all a (small) portion of the earth's surface identified by a name [Einstein, 1953, p. xiii, in Jammer, 1954].

> I will here show how Men come to form to themselves the Notion of Space. They consider that many things exist at once, and they observe in them a certain Order of Co-existence, according to which the relation of one thing to another is more or

---

[1] Only a brief review of this and other dichotomies concerning space is presented here. For a more comprehensive review of relevant philosophical and psychological positions as well as a review of empirical data, see O'Keefe and Nadel (1978). A more extensive historical review of the concept of space may be found in Jammer (1954).

less simple. This Order is their Situation or Distance. When it happens that one of those Co-existent Things changes its Relation to a Multitude of others, which do not change their Relation among themselves; and that another Thing, newly come, acquires the same Relation to the others, as the former had; we then say it is come into the Place of the former . . . then we may say, that Those which have such a Relation to those fixed Existents, as Others had to them before, have now the same Place which those others had. And That which comprehends all those Places, is called Space [Leibnitz, 1717, cited in Jammer, 1954, p. 115].

The distinctions between place and space found in both of these quotations foreshadow a distinction drawn later in this chapter between "environment" and "spatial abstraction," that is, a distinction between locations or places in particular, and spatial concepts or abstractions in general. As noted in the later discussion, the failure to recognize this distinction has caused considerable confusion.

A final issue concerns the distinction between psychological space and physical space. O'Keefe and Nadel define (1978) *psychological space* as "any space which is attributed to the mind . . . and which would not exist if minds did not exist. . . . In contrast, *physical space* is any space attributed to the external world independent of the existence of minds [pp. 6-7]." Although they suggest that the former is of interest to psychologists and physiologists, whereas the latter is of interest to physicists, it must be recognized that the study of physical space *is* relevant to psychologists who believe that psychological space is learned directly from physical space. However, since physical space can never be measured independently of a mind, the distinction becomes blurred. (Indeed, philosophers such as Berkeley deny the existence of physical space altogether.) In any case, the focus on "spatial representation and behavior" evident in this book necessitates a focus on psychological space. Thus, the derivations or origins of psychological space are discussed next.

Origins of Psychological Space

As in virtually any other substantive area of cognition, three radically different epistemological positions concerning the ontogeny of psychological space may be identified. One is the empiricist position referred to previously, in which psychological space is hypothesized to be derived directly from experience with physical space. In the purest a posteriori view, psychological space is thought to be a copy of—and hence isomorphic with—physical space.

The sharpest contrast to this view is the nativist position in which the development of psychological space is thought to be determined by the inherited endowment of the organism. This nativist view has taken a variety of forms, ranging from the notion that the human mind is genetically equipped with very broad structures with which to organize spatial experience (e.g., the a priori categories of Kant; the predisposition of the hippocampus for a Euclidean framework, see O'Keefe & Nadel, 1978); to the notion that individuals are genetically equipped with highly specialized sensory mechanisms that lead to particular spatial perceptions (e.g., visual receptors specialized for lines in particular orientations, see Hubel & Weisel, 1959).

A third position holds that psychological space is actively constructed by the individual. Inherited and experiential factors interact to produce these constructions: Biological endowment permits certain types of activities and sensations, while experience permits the exercise and extension of these. But, the ultimate structure of psychological space is constructed by the individual in the process of these interactions. Thus, rather than proposing that structures used to organize spatial experiences are provided innately (Kant), the constructivist position holds that these structures are formulated de novo by the individual.[2] Various constructivist positions are found in developmental psychology, among them, that formulated by Piaget and Inhelder (1956). Reviews of related developmental positions may be found in Siegel and White (1975), Hart and Moore (1973), and are discussed briefly throughout this book (see, in particular, Chapter 7 by Siegel and Chapter 8 by Hart).

Although a discussion as brief as this cannot provide a comprehensive review of the relevant theories and empirical data, it does demonstrate the diversity of conceptualizations of space. Diversity is also evident in the varied functions served by psychological space, reviewed next.

Functions of Psychological Space

There are many possible ways to organize a discussion of the functions of psychological space. The one used here is taken from the formulation given by Cassirer, largely because of its unusually broad scope. Cassirer proposes three general functions of human consciousness: expressive, representative, and conceptual. Each function is associated with a different symbol system: myth, language, and science.

Mythic space represents feeling—hence serving an "expressive" function. Locations and directions are emotionally charged and ordered on a sacred-profane dimension, with no separation between thing and place, or between subject and object.[3]

[2] It should be recognized, however, that in contrast to the stance taken here, some argue or imply that positions labeled "constructivistic" are ultimately reducible to additive combinations of empiricistic and nativistic views (see Liben, 1981 for a discussion of these interpretations).

[3] Indeed, from certain perspectives including Piaget's (e.g., see Piaget, 1970b), the lack of subject-object differentiation means that mythic space is not strictly "symbolic" since true symbols require a separation between the signifier and significant.

> Throughout its spatial orientation myth clings to the primary and primitive modes of mythical world-feeling. The spatial intuition that myth achieves does not conceal or destroy this world feeling but is rather the decisive instrument for its expression. Myth arrives at spatial determinations and differentiations only by lending a peculiar mythical accent to each "region" in space . . . The near and far, the high and low, the right and left—all have their uniqueness, their special mode of magical significance. Not only is the basic opposition of sacred and profane interwoven with all these spatial oppositions; it actually constitutes and produces them [Cassirer, 1957, p. 150].

Particularly striking examples may be found in tribal cultures in which places are endowed with spiritual meaning (see Cassirer, 1955, for a wide range of illustrations), as well as in more familiar Western culture and religion (e.g., the artistic equation of space to the right of Christ's right arm as sacred, that to the left, profane). The expressive nature of space may even affect the design and decoration of homes across diverse cultures, as discussed by Altman and Gauvain (Chapter 11 of this volume).

The representative function is concerned with the empirical-perceptual nature of space, or what Cassirer refers to as "sensory space." What is represented and labeled through language is space as it "is," as in the extension or arrangements of individual objects. It must be recognized, however, that the simplicity of sensory space is illusory, given the very fundamental, unresolved issue of how one comes to sense or perceive objects in space in the first place. As Cassirer (1944) remarks, perceptual space

> is not a simple sense datum; it is of a very complex nature, containing elements of all the different kinds of sense experience—optical, tactual, acoustic, and kinesthetic. The manner in which all these elements coöperate in the construction of perceptual space has proved to be one of the most difficult questions of the modern psychology of sensation [p. 43].

And, one might add, of philsosphy as well (see especially Cassirer, 1957, Chapter 3).

Despite the elusiveness of the representative function, it may be easily contrasted to the third conceptual function of space, constituted through science, and abstracted beyond the empirical world. Laws or rules of arrangement order this mathematical space.

> The determinations of mathematical space do not follow simply from those of sensory space . . . on the contrary, we require a peculiar reversal of perspective, a *negation* of what seems immediately given in sensory perception, before we can arrive at the "logical space" of pure mathematics. Particularly, a comparison between "physiological" space and the "metric" space upon which Euclidean geometry bases its constructions shows this antithetical relationship . . . Euclidean space is characterized by the three basic attributes of continuity, infinity, and uniformity. But all these attributes run counter to the character of sensory perception. Perception does not know the concept of infinity . . . [nor] homogenity [Cassirer, 1955, p. 83].

It should be apparent that as one progresses from the expressive/myth through representative/language, to conceptual/science levels, the separation between subject and object (or knower and physical world) increases. Cassirer suggests that human consciousness grows increasingly differentiated as one moves from primitive to industrial societies, thus paralleling Heinz Werner's differentiation hypothesis with respect to ontogenetic development (see Wapner, Kaplan, & Ciottone, Chapter 10 of this volume). These formulations are useful in identifying a variety of functions of psychological space across cultures and age groups.

Summary

Major issues concerning definitions, origins, and functions of space have been highlighted here. Although these issues have been discussed independently, many interesting links exist. For example, the distinctions between place and space suggested in the passages by Einstein and Leibnitz are paralleled by Cassirer's distinction between the representative and conceptual functions of space. Although the preceding review is far from complete, either with respect to the issues taken individually or with respect to the relationships among them, it does indicate the diversity of the subject of "space." Space is not simply location (or, in the terminology used by Wapner *et al.*, Chapter 10 of this volume, the *scene* of action). It also is the expression of feeling; a conceptual abstraction; a tool for memory and problem solving (e.g., see Yates, 1966; Huttenlocher, 1968; Trabasso, Riley, & Wilson, 1975) and more. (See Downs, Chapter 6 of this volume, for additional examples of "spatialized" problem solving; Wapner *et al.*, Chapter 10 of this volume for further discussion of the myriad uses of space more generally.)

Having recognized that there is no universally acceptable definition of space, there remains yet another problematic issue that underlies virtually all theoretical and empirical work related to space and, in turn, the conceptualization of this book. That is, what do we mean by spatial representation and spatial behavior, and what is the relationship between them? These issues are discussed in the following section.

Spatial Behavior and Spatial Representation

Meanings and Methods

There is probably general agreement that when we talk about "spatial behavior" we are referring to behavior in space, that is, to sensorimotor activity in the environment, such as the manipulation of objects in space, or the locomotion of the self through the environment. (More specific classifications of relevant activities and discussions of their ontogenesis are given by Pick & Lockman, Chapter 2 of this volume.)

Unfortunately, there is considerably less agreement with respect to "spatial representation." Traditionally, psychologists have used paper-and-pencil tests, sketch maps, and tabletop models to assess individuals' spatial abilities and representations (e.g., see reviews by Fruchter, 1954; Hart & Moore, 1973; Siegel & White, 1975). Some have argued that these methodologies are inappropriate for children, however. For example, Siegel (Chapter 7 of this volume) notes that even kindergartners who were unable to build a tabletop model of their classroom from memory (Siegel & Schadler, 1977) "were never seen bumping into walls in their classroom." Thus he concludes that the source of poor performance on the modeling task is not in the "internal representation of the classroom, but rather in the technique used to externalize the children's spatial knowledge (i.e., their cognitive maps) [this volume, p. 172]."

The argument that young children have particular difficulty in externalizing internal representations has led many researchers to replace traditional measures with tasks in which children are asked to move through real environments. (Various methodologies of this kind are described elsewhere in this volume, see, in particular, Chapter 2 by Pick & Lockman; Chapter 3 by Acredolo; Chapter 7 by Siegel; and Chapter 8 by Hart.) The finding that young children typically perform far more competently on these locomotion tasks than on traditional tabletop measures has led some to conclude that young children actually have far more sophisticated spatial representations than had been originally thought.

It must be recognized, however, that this conclusion rests on the assumption that behavior in space taps spatial representation, an assumption that some would reject. Piaget, for example, argues that the two—that is, behavior in space and representation of space—are actually very different (Piaget & Inhelder, 1956). Specifically, Piaget distinguishes between "practical" space, which concerns the capacity to *act* in space, and "conceptual" space, which concerns the capacity to *represent* space. Piaget (1970a) draws this distinction in *Genetic Epistemology*, in explaining the contrasts between sensorimotor and operational knowing in general:

Similarly we can see the beginnings of reversibility in the understanding of spatial positions and changes of position, that is, in the understanding of movement in space within which the child moves at the time of the culmination of sensory-motor intelligence. At the beginning of the second year children have a practical notion of space which includes what geometers call the group of displacements, that is, the understanding that a movement in one direction can be canceled by a movement in the other direction—that one point in space can be reached by one of a number of different routes. This of course is the detour behavior that psychologists have studied in such detail in chimpanzees and infants.

> So this is again practical intelligence. It is not at the level of thought, and it is not at all in the child's representation, but he can act in space with this amount of intelligence [Piaget, 1970a, p. 44].

In other words, in Piaget's view, the fact that young children can locomote intelligently through space does not necessarily imply that they have a *representational* system for such space, any more than the fact that young children can maintain a vertical position when standing up or a horizontal position when lying down implies that they possess conceptual notions of horizontal and vertical axes, or that "From the fact that the child breathes, digests, and possesses a heart that beats . . . that he has any idea of alimentary metabolism or the circulatory system [Piaget & Inhelder, 1956, p. 378]."[4] Whereas the particular analogy might be strained, the general point is not: Particular action tasks (such as avoiding classroom walls) may be solved by perceptual, sensorimotor means (see Newcombe, Chapter 14 of this volume, for a more extensive discussion of this issue), and do not necessarily require spatial representation.

In summary, some investigators have suggested that traditional tasks underestimate children's spatial representations because they require irrelevant (i.e., nonspatial) skills, and thus that these tasks should be replaced by "action" tasks. However, the legitimacy of this methodological revision rests on the assumption that it is possible to infer spatial representation from spatial behavior; this assumption is specifically rejected by others. Although this discrepancy may, indeed, reflect two fundamentally different positions concerning the link between behavior and representation, it may instead reflect two different interpretations of what is meant by "spatial representation." In other words, what at first glance appear to be disagreements concerning the best methods for tapping spatial representation, might actually be disagreements with respect to what one is trying to tap. The latter possibility is discussed next by considering various interpretations of "spatial representation."

Specifically, three *types* of spatial representation—spatial products, spatial thought, and spatial storage—and two *contents* of spatial representation—specific and abstract—are identified. These are shown in Figure 1.1. Although it is difficult to discuss the figure as a whole prior to defining each of

---

[4] To suggest that practical and representational space are distinct does not imply that they are entirely independent. Indeed, Piaget argues that activity in space is a prerequisite for spatial representation, consonant with his general position that sensorimotor activity underlies intellectual activity at higher conceptual levels. Furthermore, individuals' spatial concepts may well influence their behavior in space. For example, when one emerges from a subway station exit that is not habitually used, the ability to reorient oneself correctly would presumably draw upon the individual's projective spatial concepts.

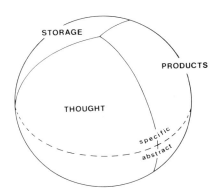

FIGURE 1.1. *Types and contents of spatial representation.*

the components, several introductory comments concerning the choice of this particular graphic representation are needed.

First, a sphere is used to accentuate the notion of rotation. Any particular researcher might study the sphere from a different angle. Thus, one investigator might be concerned primarily with spatial thought about abstract spatial concepts, whereas a second investigator might be concerned primarily with spatial storage of information about a specific space (environment). Second, the types and contents are given equal sections to avoid any suggestion that one type or content of spatial representation is more important or more legitimate than another. Third, the representation is unrestrictive with respect to pathways. For example, to go from spatial storage to spatial products it would be possible to go directly, or to pass through (be mediated by) spatial thought. Fourth, the intersections of latitudinal and longitudinal divisions are meant to suggest that each type of representation can be crossed with each content. Finally, boundaries should be thought of as permeable. These types and contents of spatial representation are discussed more fully in the following two sections.

Types of Spatial Representation

Spatial products refer to the external products that represent space in some way. This term is meant to encompass any kind of external representation, regardless of medium; it includes, for example, sketch maps, miniature models, and verbal descriptions.[5]

Probably the clearest examples of research focused on this type of spatial representation are found in the literatures concerning particular representa-

---

[5] The intended pluralism with respect to representational mode underlies the choice of the term "spatial products" rather than the perhaps more elegant "spatial models," because the latter typically engenders the notion of a small scale physical model that is fully isomorphic with the referent, as in an architect's model.

tional modes per se, such as graphic and semantic representation. In the former, investigators are concerned with how spatial relationships are represented in drawings, as in the work of Freeman and colleagues (Freeman, Eiser, & Sayers, 1977; Freeman & Janikoun, 1972), Cox (1978), and Willats (1977). In the latter, investigators are concerned with how spatial relationships are represented linguistically, as in the work of Olson (1975) and Clark (1973). In research of this kind there is an unabashed concern with the representational medium itself. If the ability to represent in some medium—graphics, words, models—is defined as a necessary part of representational ability, the various "externalization" components of tasks such as mapping are *not* superfluous performance variables, but rather, are central components of competence. As Downs (Chapter 6 of this volume) and Downs and Siegel (Chapter 9 of this volume) discuss, there is a need to look more closely at the use of various media and processes (e.g., mapping) in their own right.

The second type of spatial representation—*spatial thought*—refers to thinking that concerns or makes use of space in some way. Spatial thought is knowledge that individuals have access to, can reflect upon, or can manipulate, as in spatial problem solving or spatial imagery. (The terms *spatial consciousness* or *spatial reflectivity* suggest the essence of this type of spatial representation.) Examples of spatial thought include remembering the shape of one's living room and the arrangement of the furniture contained within it, or mentally manipulating an image of a motor part to determine where it will fit in the motor. Thus, many of the standardized spatial abilities measures tap spatial thought, as for example, the mental paper folding task of the Differential Aptitude Test or the rotating alarm clock task of the Guilford-Zimmerman Aptitude Survey (e.g., see Fruchter, 1954).

Also falling within the category of spatial thought are phenomena under the rubric of mental imagery. Although many investigations of mental imagery may be discounted because of their highly introspective nature, recent studies use methodologies that provide convincing data. Included in this latter category, for example, is the program of research developed by Shepard, Cooper, and their colleagues to study adult cognition (e.g., Cooper & Shepard, 1973; Shepard, 1978; Shepard & Metzler, 1971) and subsequently extended to children by Marmor (1977). In these studies, subjects are shown some configuration (e.g., a line-drawn picture of a three-dimensional block design), and are then asked to determine whether a second, rotated configuration is identical to the first. The time taken to give correct "same" judgments has been found to vary linearly with the degree of rotation of the original configuration. For example, once a constant has been subtracted out, subjects take twice as long to establish the identity between a model and its 180° rotation than between the same model and its 90° rotation. Methods such as these (see Kosslyn, 1978 for a review) are used to suggest how spatial images are manipulated internally, although barring a futuristic device that can externalize what the "mind's eye" sees (such as that fantasized by Shepard, 1978), it is, of course, impossible to ensure correspondence between the overt performance and the inferred internal image.

The third type of spatial representation—*spatial storage*—refers to any information about space contained "in the head" (and hence necessarily "represented" in some way, as in neurophysiological structures). This information may be stored as truth propositions, pure relations, stimulus-response bonds, or in any other format, isolated or integrated. The individual is not cognizant of this information, however. Once the individual becomes cognizant, or reflects upon this information, it becomes spatial thought. Research on spatial storage is perhaps best illustrated in the animal literature. On the basis of animals' intelligent, efficient movement through real environments (see Olton, 1979), it is possible to conclude that animals have internally stored (i.e., represented) extensive information about space. This does not, however, imply that these animals are cognizant of this information, or that they can imagine cartographic maps of their environments, for example. The concept of spatial storage is further clarified by analogy to linguistic competence. Language users must have information about their language stored to enable them to produce grammatical utterances (linguistic competence). However, the fact that a linguist can represent that underlying knowledge with a formal grammar does not imply that the language *user* is similarly aware of, or able to produce that grammar. Similarly, spatial storage is implicit or tacit knowledge (see also Downs, Chapter 6 of this volume).

Considerable confusion has been engendered by a failure to distinguish between spatial thought and spatial storage. Investigators observe subjects' systematic behaviors (e.g., nonrandom way-finding), and infer that the subject must "have" something (i.e., spatial representation). What is confused is the manner in which the subject is thought to "have" this internal representation, that is, the *type* of spatial representation.

A good example of this issue is provided by a study by Kosslyn, Pick, and Fariello (1974). Preschoolers and adults first learned the location of 10 objects (toys) in a 17 ft² space that had been divided into quadrants by one transparent barrier and one opaque barrier. Subjects were then asked to rank order the distances between all pairs of objects from memory, and these data were subjected to multidimensional scaling techniques to derive the best-fitting spatial structure given a particular program, number of dimensions, and metric. Both Euclidean and city-block solutions were attempted; the former were found to "more effectively capture the Ss' spatial representations [p. 713]."

However, to say that a Euclidean solution "captures" the subject's spatial representation is only to say that a subject's knowledge about the space can be modeled by this particular solution (among others), *not* that the subject's internal representation of the space is necessarily isomorphic with that solution. The inappropriate inference that the derived model is found internally is similar to the inference made by many with respect to Piagetian theory that because adolescents' thought can be modeled by the 16 binary operations, adolescents are therefore fully conversant with formal propositional logic (see Downs & Siegel, Chapter 9 of this volume, for additional discussion of these issues).

If, as suggested above, the distinction between spatial thought and spatial storage is a critical one, it is obviously important to specify the dimensions on which they differ. One candidate might be the format of representation, for example, propositional versus analogue representation (see Anderson, 1978; Kosslyn & Pomerantz, 1977), or enactive versus iconic versus symbolic representation (Bruner, 1964). This criterion is unacceptable here, however, since as stated earlier both spatial thought and spatial storage are meant to be pluralistic with respect to mode. For example, cognizance of a series of metric distances between sets of cities or an image of a cartographic map would both be exemplars of spatial thought; information in either form could be stored at the neurological level. Furthermore, even if format of representation were the distinguishing feature, Anderson (1978) has argued convincingly that this distinction is empirically unknowable.

A second possible dimension that *is* consistent with the earlier discussions is that thought and storage may be distinguished with respect to the subject's cognizance of the representation, assuming that one does not discard phenomenological consciousness as epiphenomenal. (See Kosslyn & Pomerantz, 1977 in defense of this position; see also Piaget, 1976 for a discussion of the development of cognizance or reflectivity.) Although subjects' intuitions alone are untrustworthy (see Anderson, 1978), corroborative data bolster their credibility (see Kosslyn & Pomerantz, 1977). From this perspective, spatial storage may be inferred simply on the basis of activity (e.g., way finding), but spatial thought requires additional evidence (e.g., sketch maps, models, verbal descriptions). (See Newcombe, Chapter 14 of this volume, for additional discussion of this distinction.)

Although it is difficult—perhaps impossible—to distinguish spatial thought and spatial storage definitively, the conceptual distinction remains important for its heuristic value. In particular, it sheds light on the question raised initially concerning the inference of representation from action. Action alone may be appropriate when the type of representation of interest is spatial storage, as it appears to be in questions like: "What is the nature of the knowledge system that permits you to solve the problem [of figuring out] alternative routes to work? [Siegel, Chapter 7 of this volume, p. 167]." However, converging operations are needed if the representation of interest is spatial thought, as it is in research on spatial concepts by Piaget and Inhelder (1956).[6] In summary, positions that appear to be different with respect to methodologies or with respect to the hypothesized link between representation and action appear to be more readily understood and reconciled by recognizing that there are differences with respect to the construct (type of representation) of interest, that is, with respect to the questions being asked.

Contents of Spatial Representation

As noted earlier, in addition to examining types of spatial representation, it is also necessary to consider the *content* of those representations, that is, what is being represented. There seems to be a generally unacknowledged assumption that everyone working in the area that might be called "spatial cognition" is ultimately interested in the same thing. On the contrary, however, two different concerns may be identified. Some investigators are interested in determining what information people have about space that enables them to maneuver in their environments, that is, individuals' knowledge about *specific* spaces, or what might be called *environmental cognition*. In this volume, the contribution by Hart (Chapter 8) provides an excellent illustration of work focused on environmental cognition, since it addresses "the development of children's knowledge of their everyday surrounding environment [p. 195]."

Alternatively, some investigators are interested in individuals' notions about space in the *abstract*, or what might be called *spatial abstraction*. Included in this domain, for example, are Piaget's interests in individuals' understanding of projective relationships, alternative and conflicting frames of reference, and continuity (see Piaget & Inhelder, 1956). Parallel distinctions have been noted elsewhere, as in the distinction between "place" and "space" (see pp. 4-5), the difference between environmental and developmental psychologists' approaches to space (see Acredolo, Chapter 3 of this volume), and the distinction between environmental cognition and fundamental spatial relations (see Downs, Chapter 6 of this volume).

It is important to recognize that two investigators with different research agenda—one interested in environmental cognition, the other in spatial

---

[6] Piaget is, of course, also concerned with practical space in infancy; see *The Construction of Reality in the Child*, Piaget, 1954.

abstractions—might nevertheless use identical tasks. Thus, for example, both Hart (Chapter 8 of this volume) and Piaget (Piaget *et al.*, 1960) ask children to produce external representations of their school, home, and playgrounds. But, whereas Hart is primarily interested in what these representations indicate about children's knowledge of their hometown, Piaget primarily is interested in what these representations imply about children's abstract spatial concepts such as the ability to use reference systems, conserve distances, comprehend topological relationships, and so on.

It is equally important to recognize that even when a task is developed specifically to assess environmental cognition or spatial abstraction, the task almost invariably taps both contents. A good example of the mixture may be found in tasks developed by Piaget and Inhelder (1956) to assess children's ability to use a coordinated reference frame of horizontal and vertical axes. Children were asked to show the position of horizontals and verticals of the physical world; specifically, they were told to indicate the position of water and plumb lines in the context of oblique baselines (e.g., to draw liquid in a tipped bottle, or to draw trees on the side of a mountain). Young children's inaccuracies on such tasks (e.g., drawing liquid as parallel to the base of the bottle, and drawing trees as perpendicular to the inclined ground) were taken as an indication that they had not yet constructed a Cartesian coordinate system.

Although Piaget and Inhelder developed these tasks to tap underlying coordinate systems (and hence spatial abstraction), these tasks also tap environmental cognition; that is, the knowledge that on earth, water stays horizontal and plumb lines remain vertical due to the effects of gravity. Indeed, it has been demonstrated that the difficulty that individuals have on these horizontality and verticality tasks are in part (but *only* in part), attributable to inadequate knowledge about the relevant physical phenomena (Liben & Golbeck, 1980).

It should be emphasized that, as in the case of the theoretical separation of spatial representation and behavior, the argument made here with respect to environmental cognition and spatial abstraction is meant to suggest that the two are different, but *not* that the two are unrelated. Indeed, one of the major purposes of this book is to demonstrate that individuals' abstract notions of space affect their use of their environments, and similarly, that their use of environments affect their abstract spatial concepts. These relationships are discussed in the next section of this chapter.

Summary

The research in spatial cognition contains diverse foci, methods, and theoretical positions. It has been argued that: (a) there are important differences among investigators with respect to the types of spatial representation of interest, including external spatial representational products, spatial thought, and spatial storage; (b) different methodologies may be needed to tap these different types of spatial representation; and (c) there are often unacknowledged differences with respect to the content of interest: Whereas some investigators are ultimately concerned with individuals' environmental cognitions, others are concerned with individuals' spatial abstractions.

The purpose of pointing out these issues in an introductory chapter is not with the expectation of resolving them here. Rather, the purpose is to alert the reader to the possibility that the questions and assumptions that underlie the subsequent chapters vary along the dimensions discussed, and that it is, therefore, important to proceed cautiously in interpreting and integrating these contributions.

Despite these differences in approach, however, there is universal agreement that there are important, reciprocal interactions among the various pieces of the spatial puzzle, and that these components and relationships vary significantly with development. In the next section of this chapter, spatial representation and behavior are considered in relation to the developmental, individual, and cultural factors that affect them.

Influences on Spatial Activity and Representation

Overview

Whatever we mean by spatial representation and behavior, and whatever the relationship between them, it is clear that there are many influences on their development and expression. The major factors of importance are shown in Figure 1.2. Before discussing this figure in detail, however, several preliminary comments are necessary. First, it should be noted that the construct labeled as "spatial activity <——> representation" refers to all components discussed in the previous section of this chapter, and that possible differences with respect to the antecedents of the various types and contents are intentionally skirted here. Second, although all constructs should be understood as related, and all relationships understood as reciprocal, only major relationships are indicated by arrows in order to maintain visual clarity. Third, it should be recognized that the entire system is moving through, and changing with, time. There are changes at the level of individual characteristics (e.g., cognitive level), of cultural heritage (e.g., societal practices that affect males' versus females' freedom to explore the environment), and in physical space (e.g., the urbanization of rural environments). Finally, it should be noted that the present discussion is designed to organize and illustrate major influences, not to provide exhaustive reviews. Additional explications of these constructs and the relationships among them are included in later chapters of this book.

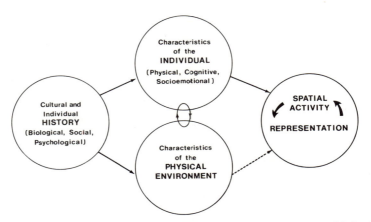

FIGURE 1.2. *Influences on the development of spatial representation and behavior.*

As suggested in Figure 1.2, characteristics of the individual and characteristics of the physical environment are of central importance. The following discussion, therefore, is focused on these, both with respect to their qualities per se and with respect to how they, in turn, are influenced by biosocial histories at both macro (cultural) and micro (individual) levels.

Characteristics of the Individual

The qualities of individuals relevant to spatial behavior and representation may be grouped into three major categories: physical, cognitive, and socioemotional. Within the *physical* dimension, the most striking differences are those associated with age. The different physical characteristics of infants, children, adults, and the elderly necessarily affect activities in space and representations of space. For example, viewing position (eye level) varies with age: Infants usually view the world from a prone or supine position; young children, although upright, are unable to see over objects such as tables that pose no visual obstacle for older children and adults. These differences affect the quantity and quality of the spatial environment that can be perceived (in this volume see Chapter 2 by Pick & Lockman; and Chapter 5 by Wohlwill).

Also important are changes in the way individuals move through the environment as they become older. First, the methods of locomotion change (e.g., from crawling to walking to driving). In addition, the locus of control of locomotion shifts. For example, there is a change from being carried around passively in a caretaker's arms or being wheeled in a stroller during infancy to walking independently during adulthood. (In some cases, the passive-to-active trend may reverse in old age, as for victims of stroke or severe

arthritis.) Empirical data demonstrate the importance of the mode of locomotion for environmental cognition. Appleyard (1970), for example, found
that people who traveled to and from a city by car drew more coherent
sketch maps of the urban road system than those who traveled by bus. Extended discussions of the effects of modes of locomotion (ranging from walking to sailing to traveling by space ship) are contained elsewhere in this
volume (see, in particular, Chapter 2 by Pick & Lockman; Chapter 8 by
Hart; Chapter 12 by Walsh, Krauss, & Regnier).

Variations in visual perspective, means and control of locomotion, and
similar skills may be expected to have important effects on the amount,
diversity, and quality of space that is encountered. In turn, these differences
may be expected to affect the development of representation as well, particularly if one assumes (e.g., as does Piaget) that sensorimotor activities provide the foundation for conceptual skills.

Relevant physical characteristics also vary *within* particular chronological
ages. The most dramatic illustrations of these variations may be found by
considering individuals with physical and sensory handicaps. Individuals with
limited motor skills, such as people with cerebral palsy or orthopedic handicaps, and people with impaired sensory skills, such as blind people or deaf
people, interact with their environments very differently than those without
such impairments. Importantly, variations in sensory and motor skills may
affect not only actual activity in the environment (spatial behavior), but also
the way that the environment is represented. For example, given the same
tactual experience with a set of objects, or the same opportunity to walk
through the room, two individuals—one congenitally blind, the other blindfolded but normally sighted—would be likely to represent the objects or environment differently (see Pick & Lockman, Chapter 2, and Wapner *et al.*,
Chapter 10 for relevant empirical data).

In the domain of *cognitive* characteristics, it is again possible to identify
qualities that differ both across and within portions of the life span. Among
the most important of the former are qualitative changes in logical thought
processes that occur as the individual moves from sensorimotor to preoperational to concrete operational to formal operational stages (e.g., Piaget,
1970).[7] The qualitative variations in these stages have important implications
for spatial conceptualization. For example, the egocentric nature of preoperational children's thinking interferes with their ability to represent
another's visual perspective accurately in tasks on projective space (see
Flavell, 1978 for a review and critique of recent work in this area).

A second change with age concerns the store of relevant knowledge.
Older individuals have typically had more opportunity to gather information

---

[7] This statement reflects a particular theoretical orientation to which not everyone would
subscribe (see Overton & Reese, 1973).

about space, both specific and abstract. For example, repeated experiences within a particular environment enhance the ability to represent that environment (e.g., see Appleyard, 1970, 1976; Devlin, 1976; Moore, 1974; in this volume see Chapter 2 by Pick & Lockman; Chapter 5 by Wohlwill; Chapter 7 by Siegel; and Chapter 10 by Wapner *et al.*), while exposure to many different instances of particular types of settings (e.g., different cities) add to the individual's generalized concepts of what is contained in these settings and how they should be arranged (see Nagy & Baird, 1978). In addition, formal instruction (as in science and mathematics classes) may add to the individual's knowledge about abstract spatial concepts.

Again, there are also important cognitive differences within particular ages, including, for example, differences in general intelligence or spatial abilities (see Harris, Chapter 4 of this volume), and in cognitive styles. Some of these individual difference variables have been studied in relation to performance on particular spatial tasks (e.g., the relationships between field dependence and performance on Piagetian horizontality and verticality tasks, see Hyde, Geiringer, & Yen, 1975; Liben, 1978; Pascual-Leone, 1967), but many more remain unexamined. Indeed, one of the themes arising repeatedly in this volume is the need for systematic, extensive investigations of individual differences. (For extended discussion of this theme, see Chapter 6 by Downs; Chapter 9 by Downs & Siegel; Chapter 14 by Newcombe; and Chapter 5 by Wohlwill. Empirical illustrations are found in virtually every chapter.)

Finally, *socioemotional* factors play an important role in individuals' spatial activities and representations. Variations in individuals' confidence to roam from well-known sites (such as home) are no less real than variations in physical skills in influencing the amount and diversity of the space encountered. There are empirical data to suggest that rich experiences in space are related to the development of both environmental cognition and spatial abstraction (e.g., Conner & Serbin, 1977; Hart, Chapter 8 of this volume; Herman, 1980). In addition, individuals' self-concepts about their spatial abilities may also be presumed to affect performance on space-related tasks, be they standardized tests of spatial aptitude, performance in geometry classes, map reading, or way finding.

It seems likely that people who avoid or worry about the exploration or manipulations of space or about working on spatial problems would have underdeveloped skills and knowledge—thereby leading to still greater anxiety and avoidance. Empirical evidence for at least part of this cycle is provided by a study by Kaplan (1976) in which junior high school students were given various tasks in a natural environment. Students who had been given prior preparation (e.g., through contour maps and aerial photographs) reported more confidence, less fear, and more enjoyment in their exploration of the natural environment than students not given any preparation. Additional research is needed to determine if there are effects on other portions of the proposed cycle as well.

Characteristics of the Physical Environment

There is no question that there are many and diverse differences across physical environments, but unfortunately there are few systems for categorizing relevant variables. The fact that there are relatively few standardized measures of the physical environment may be traced to two major factors. First, there is an incredible diversity in the environments and variables of potential interest. There are both "natural" and "built" environments, and each is divisible into major settings. For example, built environments include cities, shopping centers, factories, schools, homes, and living rooms. Each may be approached at various levels of analysis. Schools might be assessed with respect to locale; landscape setting; organization and number of classrooms; organization within individual classrooms, such as the number and arrangement of desks and chairs, placement of instructional materials, open space, and so on.

A concrete example of the highly specialized nature of measures developed for particular settings is the measure developed by Shafer and Thompson (1968) to assess variables affecting campsite use in the Adirondack State Park in New York. Sample items from that scale include average distance between campsites; average distance from campsites to nearest outlet for drinking water, to nearest sanitation unit, to nearest flush toilet, to edge of nearest lake; average slope of the campground; percentage of campsites where highway traffic sound can be heard; average density (percentage) of understory vegetation; average number of white birch stems per campsite; and similar items. Obviously, this scale would be of little use in any other setting.

The second factor that probably underlies environmental psychologists' reluctance to develop measures of the physical environment is that they are ultimately concerned with the environment as perceived or interpreted, rather than with the environment as it "is." As a result, so-called environmental measures tend to concentrate on assessment of individuals' interpretations of or reactions to the environment, rather than on physical qualities of the environment. The psychological focus of environmental measures may be illustrated by an examination of a review chapter by Craik (1971) on "The Assessment of Places." Only two paragraphs and one table are devoted to "physical and spatial properties of places," and four

paragraphs, one table, and one figure to the "organization of material artifacts in places." The remainder of the chapter is devoted to reviews of
measures concerning some aspect of the psychological meaning or value of
environments.

An additional illustration of this point is provided by a review of environmental research on schools. Some physical variables have been examined, most notably the presence or absence of partitions (as in the difference between "open" and "closed" classrooms, e.g., see Gump & Ross,
1977), and the availability of material and human resources per child (e.g.,
variations in density, see Fagot, 1977; or in equipment, see Stallings, 1975),
but far more attention has been devoted to social characteristics. The
"Classroom Environment Scale" (Moos & Trickett, 1974), for example, includes the following nine subscales: involvement, affiliation, teacher support,
task orientation, competition order/organization, rule clarity, teacher control, and innovation. In reviewing research on school environments, Gump
(1978) similarly concluded that the "variables most neglected are probably
those on the environmental side [p. 168]." If we are ever to investigate the
links between the environment and behavior without circularity, it is
necessary to develop measures of the environment (see also Craik, 1971
and Wohlwill, 1976).

Developmental psychologists have created some scales to measure particular environments, most commonly the home. Again, however, these
scales typically stress social, rather than physical qualities of the environment,
or how inanimate qualities are mediated by the social environment (e.g.,
Bayley & Schaefer, 1964; Clarke-Stewart, 1973; Elardo, Bradley, &
Caldwell, 1977; Yarrow, Rubenstein, Pedersen, & Jankowski, 1972). Those
physical dimensions that are assessed predominantly emphasize the presence
and qualities of objects found *within* the home environment (as in the variety, responsivity, and complexity of toys, see McCall, 1974; Yarrow *et al.*,
1972) rather than the organization and characteristics of the physical space
more broadly. Consistent with this observation, it is interesting to note that in
an excellent review of home environments, Parke (1978) includes only four
topics under "physical stimulation": specifically, toys, television, interior
noise, and exterior noise.

Probably the most "physical" home environment scale currently available
is the Purdue Home Stimulation Inventory developed by Wachs (e.g., see
Wachs, 1976, 1979; Wachs, Francis, & McQuiston, 1979). In addition to
items oriented to social variables and to contents of the environment, there
are also a few items concerning more stable, structural aspects of the environment and the child's access to it (e.g., the ratio of rooms to people in
the home; the amount of floor freedom; the frequency of visits to neighbors
and trips outside the neighborhood). Nevertheless, many other variables remain untapped.

Measures specifically concerned with constructed physical environments have been developed by architects (e.g., Flynn & Summers, 1978) to assess variables such as structure (e.g., massive-delicate); characteristics of furnishings (e.g., angular-curvilinear, fixed-moveable); textures; colors; light; and similar dimensions. Although scales of this type tend to be subjective and ignore many potentially relevant variables, they do hold considerable promise for further refinement and expansion because they begin with a clear focus on the physical aspects of the environment.

Without a generally-accepted taxonomy of important environmental variables, it is difficult to document how these variables affect spatial behavior and representation. The following discussion, then, simply samples the kinds of variables that might be of relevance.

One of the ways in which environments may be distinguished is the extent to which they are differentiated. Both the number and diversity of discriminable units in a given area may vary; for example, single-family dwellings may be spaced every quarter acre or every full acre, and may be highly individualized or identical (as in tract housing). The degree of differentiation has a direct bearing on the availability of landmarks, which can function as landmarks only in relation to the surrounding context. A ranch house serves as an excellent marker when found on a 100-acre farm, but is of little value in a suburban tract of identical houses. As discussed throughout this volume (see especially, Chapter 2 by Pick & Lockman; Chapter 3 by Acredolo; Chapter 7 by Siegel; Chapter 8 by Hart; Chapter 10 by Wapner et al.; Chapter 12 by Walsh et al.), landmarks are an important variable for spatial activity and representation. It should be recognized, however, that many seemingly stable features of environments are not static. For example, identical tract houses become differentiated over time as a consequence of the press for individuality (see Altman & Gauvain, Chapter 11 of this volume).

In addition to the sheer number and diversity of elements within environments (and their consequent effect on landmarks), there are also variations in the extent and manner in which these elements are organized. Two regions might, for example, contain an equal number of similar roads, but one might be organized into a neat grid of intersecting north-south, east-west streets whereas the other might have no apparent order (as in the difference between midtown Manhattan and Greenwich Village). The former might be expected to be much more conducive to learning the layout of the area (i.e., to better environmental cognition, as work by behavioral geographers and environmental psychologists on way finding and cognitive mapping suggests, e.g., see Appleyard, 1970; deJonge, 1962; Hart, Chapter 8 of this volume; Rand, 1969), and furthermore, might be more likely to enhance the use of Cartesian coordinates in conceptualizing space more generally (spatial abstraction).

Environments may differ in other more qualitative ways as well, as in the distinction between "carpentered" and "uncarpentered" environments. Whereas Western groups are typically exposed to angular shapes (contemporary architecture provides numerous examples), others, such as the traditional Zulu culture, emphasize roundness. These environmental distinctions have generally been studied in relation to individuals' susceptibility to visual illusions (e.g., see Cole & Scribner, 1974 for an excellent summary and critique), but they might in addition be related to the development of spatial concepts (e.g., a Cartesian coordinate system).

Although the preceding discussions have implied that highly differentiated, organized environments are likely to enhance spatial concepts, the opposite relationship is also possible. That is, environments with little differentiation or organization may force inhabitants to impose their own structure, hence fostering individuals' spatial abilities. Berry (1966, 1971) endorses the latter position. He finds that Canadian Eskimos are more field independent than the Temne of West Africa, and argues that this difference may be traced to the difference in ecologies. Eskimos must learn to pick out seemingly minor variations from a generally monotonous, barren environment, whereas the Temne need not develop comparable disembedding skills because they are surrounded by a highly differentiated jungle.

Recent research by Norman (1980) is also consistent with this interpretation: Rural Applachian children, who live in an underdeveloped terrain, performed better on mapping tasks than suburban (Branford, Connecticut) or urban (Boston) children, who live in a highly differentiated environment. As Cole and Scribner (1974) note, findings such as these must be interpreted cautiously in view of the difficulty in rating environments objectively, and in light of the many other potentially relevant distinctions among cultures. Nevertheless, cross-cultural research of this kind suggests some interesting environmental features for further study (see also Wohlwill, this volume).[8]

Existing cross-cultural research is also useful in suggesting the importance of the availability and form of spatial products. For example, not all cultures contain two-dimensional representations (line drawings, paintings) of objects in space. Cross-cultural data (e.g., Hudson, 1967; see review by Cole & Scribner, 1974) suggest that the interpretation and production of two-dimensional representations are dependent on prior experiences with such representations. Furthermore, even within cultures that *do* contain representations, the particular conventions used to represent space vary widely. Development consists, in part, of learning these conventions (e.g., see Goodnow, 1972). Conventions vary across historical eras as well as across cultures. Consider, for example, the map shown in Figure 1.3. It is as "accurate" from a cartographic standpoint as the Mercator projection with which

---

[8] A promising source for additional variables of relevance is the forthcoming volume, *Culture and Environments,* edited by Altman, Wohlwill, and Rapoport.

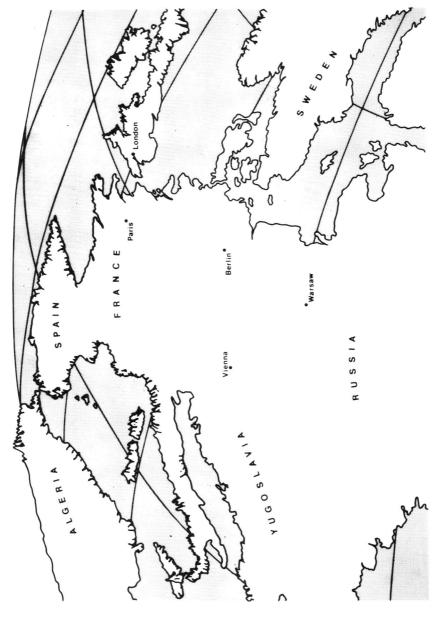

FIGURE 1.3. An unfamiliar projection of Europe. (Adapted from a map by Richard Edes Harrison, originally appearing in FORTUNE Magazine, 1944.)

most readers are familiar (see Downs, Chapter 6 of this volume). Never-theless, exposure to one rather than the other might well lead to different en-vironmental cognitions, for example, a distance estimate between Moscow and Paris. Researchers tend to be unduly adult-, culture-, and era-centered in their approach to spatial representations (see also, Downs; Hart; Downs & Siegel; Newcombe; Chapters 6, 8, 9, and 14 of this volume).

Various modes of spatial products may also have powerful effects (e.g., Olson, 1974). For example, television provides visual access to varied en-vironments, although it limits the time available (and, perhaps, motivation) for more active, manipulative interactions with the environment (see Parke, 1978). Particular presentations may have special impact, for example, satellite views of earth seen on television probably enhance individuals' con-cepts of the earth's roundness far more effectively than school lessons about Columbus.

In short, there are many aspects of the physical environment—its differen-tiation, its organization, its contents—that may affect spatial activity and representation. The development of reliable, detailed, comprehensive scales to record these characteristics would facilitate our study of the links between the physical environment and individuals' spatial activities and representa-tions.

Person-Environment Interactions

Although characteristics of individuals and environments have been separated for convenience in the preceding discussion, they do interact (see Figure 1.2). For example, although individuals alter their environments, the form of these alterations is determined, in part, by environmental condi-tions. Characteristics of homes, for example, vary with environmental features and constraints (Altman & Gauvain, Chapter 11 of this volume). Similarly, although in rare cases a particular environment may affect behavior relatively directly (e.g., a prison cell limits the individual's "free range"), it is far more common that the effects of the physical environment are mediated through individuals. For example, although a city environment may be said to present a highly differentiated and diverse space, this is func-tionally true only for individuals who have the capacities and motivation to explore that environment. An older person with low physical strength, fear of crime, and limited finances may avoid diverse environments, even though they are "available" (in this volume, see Chapter 12 by Walsh *et al.*; Chapter 13 by Patterson). Similarly, distinctive landmarks may be present, but the ability to use them is dependent upon the individual's cognitive capacities (see especially, Chapter 2 by Pick & Lockman; Chapter 3 by Acredolo; Chapter 7 by Siegel; Chapter 12 by Walsh *et al.*, this volume).

The impact of individuals' physical characteristics also varies across environments. For example, although it was suggested earlier that physical handicaps limit spatial activity, this need not be true: Ramps and other adjustments may make virtually the entire environment accessible. Furthermore, as discussed extensively by Wapner *et al.* (Chapter 10 of this volume), the individual's affective state has dramatic effects on the way in which a particular environment is used and represented. In short, we can only understand the impact of characteristics of individuals and of environments in the context of the transactions between them.

Biosocial Histories

The previous discussions have concerned how variations across individuals and environments may affect spatial activity and representation. The present discussion is concerned with how biological and social variables may account for these individual and environmental variations.

At the level of the individual, both genetic and experiential factors are pertinent, as, for example, in an individual's inherited intelligence or spatial abilities, or that individual's exposure to or reinforcement for work in geometry or drafting. These factors, in turn, may be traced to genetic and social variables at the cultural level such as the contents of the gene pool, mating practices of the culture, and socialization practices more generally. For example, different cultures vary with respect to the freedom infants are given to explore (e.g., Kagan & Klein, 1973) and in the degree to which children are encouraged to explore areas away from home (e.g., see Hollos, 1975; Hollos & Cowan, 1973). (Excellent reviews of the ways the social environment has a mediating affect on the experienced physical environment are found in Parke, 1978; and in Moore & Young, 1978. In addition, see Wohlwill, Chapter 5 of this volume.)

The various influences shown in Figure 1.2 may be illustrated by considering how the striking and consistent sex-related differences in spatial activity and representation might evolve. (See Harris, Chapter 4 of this volume, for a more extensive discussion of the evidence for sex-related differences and of biological and social explanations of these differences.) The culture has certain norms with respect to what are appropriate behaviors, values, and activities for males and females. These cultural values affect both the physical environment and social experiences. With respect to the former, for example, content analyses of boys' and girls' bedrooms reveal differences even from early infancy. Among other differences, boys' rooms contain more toys that are related to the development of spatial skills such as shape-sorting toys (Rheingold & Cook, 1975).

There are also differences with respect to the large-scale spaces encountered. In a study of children's use of the classroom and playground, Harper and Sanders (1975) found that boys used more space and entered a greater number of play areas than girls. From a review of several independent studies of children's use of indoor and outdoor environments, Moore and Young (1978) concluded that girls do not travel as far from their homes as boys; furthermore, they tend to make more routinized trips, apparently because of greater parental restrictions (Coates & Bussard, 1974; Hart, 1979; Moore's "Childhood Use of the Urban Landscape Project," see Moore & Young, 1978; Payne & Jones, 1977). Although the studies cited above included no direct observation of parental practices, some observational data do suggest that boys and girls are differentially reinforced in their use of space. Servin, O'Leary, Kent, and Tronick (1973), for example, found that teachers gave girls more attention when they were nearby, whereas they gave boys a fairly constant rate of attention regardless of their proximity.

Activities engaged in by boys and girls also differ. At the broadest level, Hoffman (1972) has suggested that boys and girls are reinforced for different problem-solving strategies. Specifically, when faced with a difficult problem (some of which are undoubtedly spatial in nature), males are more likely to be reinforced for mastering the task, whereas females are more likely to be reinforced for obtaining assistance. Boys also participate more in activities such as block play that have been shown to be linked to visual-spatial ability (e.g., Connor & Serbin, 1977; Shure, 1963). In later life, boys and girls are differentially encouraged to enroll in mathematics and science courses that may enhance spatial skills (see Fox, Tobin, & Brody, 1979). If girls receive less encouragement to explore space and less opportunity to acquire spatial knowledge and skills, they may in turn have reduced ability to assimilate spatial information in the future, because of avoidance, anxiety, and/or lack of prerequisite knowledge. Females who fail pretests on the horizontality of liquid, for example, seem relatively impervious to demonstration, practice, and explanations (e.g., Golbeck & Liben, 1979; Liben, 1978; Thomas, Jamison, & Hummel, 1973).

Spatial Activity and Representation

In view of the extensive discussion of spatial activity and representation given in the previous section of this chapter, no detailed discussion is needed here. It is, however, important to note that although in prior discussions spatial activity and representation have implicitly been treated as dependent variables, they function as independent variables as well. Thus, for example, the individual's activity in space at Time 1 becomes part of the individual's "history" at Time 2. Similarly, the very process of thinking about how to represent space (what might be called "meta-spatial cognition") may affect later spatial concepts and products. Hart (Chapter 8 of this volume) suggests that mapping activities are important for facilitating children's environmental cognition; Beck *et al.* (1973) found that subjects who had been asked to draw several maps over a 5-month period drew maps that were more complex than those produced by subjects who had no prior experience in mapping. As noted initially, then, it is necessary to remember that the constructs in Figure 1.2 must be understood as reciprocally influencing one another and thus, as continually undergoing change.

Summary

Although the discussion of influences on spatial representation and behavior given above is not exhaustive, it does illustrate the large number, complexity, and reciprocity of influences. Furthermore, it demonstrates the importance of attending not only to individuals, but to their immediate social and physical environments, and to the broader biological, social, and historical contexts in which these are embedded. This approach is, of course, consonant with several recent statements on the necessity for examining contextual influences in the study of individual development (e.g., Bronfenbrenner, 1979; Lerner & Busch-Rossnagel, 1981).

The review also highlights the need for greater attention to several areas. In particular, it reaffirms the need to examine environmental variables per se, and to examine individual differences as variables in their own right, rather than dismissing them as error variance.

Finally, the review also emphasizes the utility of using a developmental perspective to approach the study of spatial representation and behavior. The very obvious physical, cognitive, and socioemotional differences that exist across different portions of the life span suggest variables that are important to examine not only ontogenetically, but across settings as well. Furthermore, a developmental perspective, particularly a life-span developmental perspective (e.g., see Huston-Stein & Baltes, 1976), highlights the ubiquity and importance of change at all levels (e.g., in the physical environment, cultural norms) each contributing powerfully to individuals' spatial representations and behavior.

Conclusions

One theme that emerges consistently throughout this chapter is that there is a need to recognize and respect multiple definitions of space and spatial representation, and correlatively, a need to use diverse methods for studying these constructs. A second theme that is suggested both by the preceding discussions and by the collection of chapters found in this book is the importance of linking theory and application. Practical problems often suggest tasks that can be used to assess basic concepts. For example, an individual's ability to give directions to someone in a different location might be used to assess perspective-taking, or, an individual's ability to use an artificial horizon (attitude indicator) in a simulated airplane flight might be used to assess horizontality concepts. Implications from theory to practice are important as well. For example, the knowledge that young children's spatial concepts are largely topological suggests that hallways in elementary schools should be highly differentiated to enhance way-finding.

It is important to recognize, however, that the fact that one can find parallel tasks and links between theoretical and practical domains does not mean that the questions asked across domains are identical. Indeed, as noted earlier, work that appears to be similar may actually be motivated by very different questions. It is particularly important to remain cognizant of the underlying questions in an era in which researchers have been sensitized to the "ecological validity" of their tasks. As Bronfenbrenner (1977) has noted, there has been an unfortunate implication that an investigation is ecologically valid, and, therefore, legitimate, only "if it is carried out in a naturalistic setting and involves objects and activities from everyday life [p. 515]."

It is imperative, therefore, to specify what one is trying to measure (e.g., the type-content of representation). If for example, one is interested in what people know about the environments they have experienced, field studies in the natural environment are in order. If one is interested in how people can manipulate spatial representations, laboratory tasks (such as mental rotation tasks) may be best. In short, while theorists and practitioners have much to offer one another, the uncritical, wholesale import of methods from one domain to the other may ultimately be dysfunctional.

Viable links between theory and application and many of the other issues raised earlier in this chapter are discussed in more detail in the remaining chapters of the book. In closing this chapter, therefore, it is useful to highlight the contents that follow.

Part II focuses on "Developmental and Individual Differences." Within this part, Pick and Lockman discuss what body-object and object-object manipulations imply about spatial knowledge and frames of references, and how these change with development. In the next chapter, Acredolo discusses theoretical and empirical work on small- and large-scale spatial tasks, with particular emphasis on the distinctions between them. In Chapter 4, Harris documents the generalization that as a group, females typically do not perform as well as males in spatial tasks, and then considers possible factors—biological, social, and interactive—that might explain the etiology of these sex-related differences. In a commentary on these three chapters,

Wohlwill points out the need for integrating experimental and differential approaches, and the need to consider the diverse factors (e.g., attention, memory) that may underlie developmental differences in performance on spatial tasks. Wohlwill also discusses the need for moving beyond purely comparative research designs, and for future research directed toward the evaluation of the effects of specific experiential factors.

The topic of Part III, "Production and Comprehension of Spatial Representations," is approached from the perspectives of developmental psychology, environmental psychology, and geography. In Chapter 6, Downs discusses the importance and implications of recognizing that the map is a double metaphor, that is, a metaphor not only for the individual's knowledge, but for the world as well. Furthermore, Downs argues that some of the problems and limitations in current thinking about cognitive maps might be avoided by the notion of cognitive mapping as a process of spatial problem-solving. In Chapter 7, Siegel reviews theoretical and empirical work concerning individuals' developing landmark, route, and configurational knowledge, with a particular focus on the development of new methodologies to assess this knowledge. In Chapter 8, Hart describes the procedures and findings from an ecological field study in which children were asked to make models of their Vermont town. Particular attention is given to the ways in which children's models reflect their experiences in their environments. In a commentary on this part, Downs and Siegel stress the importance of recognizing that there is no single, universally acceptable criterion that can be used to assess graphic representations across cultures, eras, developmental levels, and purposes. Downs and Siegel also discuss the need to avoid unjustifiable attributions of investigators' models to subjects, and the need to study variations in individuals' spatial problem-solving strategies.

Part IV, entitled "Conceptualizing and Designing Spatial Environments," begins with a chapter by Wapner, Kaplan, and Ciottone in which it is argued that representation is only one of several uses of space, and thus, that representation and use should not be contrasted. The perspective of "genetic dramatism" is presented as a theoretical structure for conceptualizing the development of self-world relations. The expression of self in the use of space is a theme that also arises in the following chapter by Altman and Gauvain in their dialectic analysis of homes. Specifically, they suggest that the exteriors, interiors, and thresholds of homes across a wide array of cultures may be understood as the result of tensions between two dialectic processes: one individuality versus community; the other accessibility versus inaccessibility.

Chapter 12 by Walsh, Krauss, and Regnier represents the disciplines of psychology and architecture, and thus links theoretical and applied concerns. Described in this chapter are the procedures and results of a collaborative project concerning the relationships among older adults' spatial cognitive ability, knowledge of their neighborhoods, and their use of services in the environment. In commenting on Part IV, Patterson discusses the implications of this group of papers for the development of intervention programs, with particular emphasis on the importance of individuals' perceived control of their environments.

In the concluding chapter (Part V) of this volume, Newcombe discusses four major themes that arise repeatedly in the book: specifically, the relationships between behavior and representation; the validity of criteria used to determine "accuracy" of external representations; the interpretation of apparent décalages in development; and the utility of interdisciplinary perspectives. In addition to suggesting possible reconciliations across theories and data sets, Newcombe identifies several areas in need of further study.

Neither the present introductory chapter, nor the entire volume can hope to resolve the issues raised within it. The concluding sentence of *Concepts of Space*, written by Jammer in 1954, is as appropriate as ever:

—*Like all science, the science of space must still be classed as unfinished business.*

Acknowledgments

I would like to acknowledge gratefully the contributions of Roger Downs, Susan Golbeck, and Nora Newcombe. They have stimulated, expanded, and refined my thinking about the issues discussed in this chapter (although they do not, of course, bear responsibility for its final form). I thank them deeply for helping to make this a rewarding and manageable task. In addition, I would like to express my appreciation to Roger Downs, Richard Lerner, and Nora Newcombe for their helpful comments on earlier versions of this chapter, and to James Myer for preparation of the figures.

References

Altman, I., Wohlwill, J. F., & Rapoport, A. (Eds.), *Culture and environment*. New York: Plenum, in preparation.
Anderson, J. R. Arguments concerning representations for mental imagery. *Psychological Review*, 1978, *85*, 249-277.
Appleyard, D. A. Styles and methods of structuring a city. *Environment and Behavior*, 1970, *2*, 100-118.
Appleyard, D. A. *Planning a pluralistic city*. Cambridge, Massachusetts: MIT press, 1976.
Bayley, N., & Schaefer, E. Correlates of maternal and child behaviors with the development of mental abilities: Data from the Berkeley Growth Study. *Monographs of the Society for Research in Child Development*, 1964, *29*, No. 6.

Beck, R., Cohen, S. B., Craik, K. H., Dwyer, M., McCleary, G. F., Jr., & Wapner, S. Studying environmental moves and relocations: A research note. *Environment and Behavior*, 1973, 5, 335-349.

Berry, J. W. Temne and Eskimo perceptual skills. *International Journal of Psychology*, 1966, 1(3), 207-229.

Berry, J. W. Ecological and cultural factors in spatial perceptual development. *Canadian Journal of Behavioral Science*, 1971, 3(4), 324-336.

Bronfenbrenner, U. Toward an experimental ecology of human development. *American Psychologist*, 1977, 32, 513-531.

Bronfenbrenner, U. *The ecology of human development*. Cambridge, Massachusetts: Harvard University Press, 1979.

Bruner, J. The course of cognitive growth. *American Psychologist*, 1964, 19, 1-15.

Cassirer, E. *An essay on man*. New Haven: Yale University Press, 1944.

Cassirer, E. *The problem of knowledge*. New Haven: Yale University Press, 1950.

Cassirer, E. *The philosophy of symbolic forms. Volume 2: Mythical thought*. New Haven: Yale University Press, 1955.

Cassirer, E. *The philosophy of symbolic forms. Volume 3: The phenomenology of knowledge*. New Haven: Yale University Press, 1957.

Clark, H. H. Space, time, semantics, and the child. In T. E. Moore (Ed.), *Cognitive development and the acquisition of language*. New York: Academic Press, 1973.

Clarke-Stewart, K. A. Interactions between mothers and their young children: Characteristics and consequences. *Monographs of the Society for Research in Child Development*, 1973, 40, Serial No. 153.

Coates, G., & Bussard, E. Patterns of children's spatial behavior in a moderate-density housing development. In R. C. Moore (Ed.), *Childhood city, man-environment interactions*. Vol. 12 D. Carson (General Ed.), Milwaukee: EDRA, 1974.

Cole, M., & Scribner, S. *Culture and thought*. New York: Wiley, 1974.

Cooper, L. A., & Shepard, R. N. Chronometric studies of the rotation of mental images. In W. G. Chase (Ed.), *Visual information processing*. New York: Academic Press, 1973.

Connor, J. M., & Serbin, L. A. Behaviorally based masculine- and feminine- activity-preference scales for preschoolers: Correlates with other classroom behaviors and cognitive tests. *Child Development*, 1977, 48, 1411-1416.

Cox, M. V. Spatial depth relationships in young children's drawings. *Journal of Experimental Child Psychology*, 1978, 26, 551-554.

Craik, K. H. The assessment of places. In P. McReynolds (Ed.), *Advances in psychological assessment*. Vol. 2. Palo Alto, California: Science and Behavior Books, 1971.

deJonge, D. Images of urban areas: Their structure and psychological foundations. *Journal of the American Institute of Planners*, 1962, 28, 266-276.

Devlin, A. S. Some factors in enhancing knowledge of a natural area. In W. Preiser (Ed.), *Environmental design research*, Vol. 2, Stroudsburg, Pa.: Dowden, Hutchinson, & Ross, 1976.

Elardo, R., Bradley, R., & Caldwell, B. A longitudinal study of the relation of infants' home environments to language development at age three. *Child Development*, 1977, 48, 595-603.

Fagot, B. I. Variations in density: Effect on task and social behaviors of pre-school children. *Developmental Psychology*, 1977, 13, 166-167.

Flavell, J. H. The development of knowledge about visual perception. In C. B. Keasey (Ed.), *Nebraska Symposium on Motivation*. Lincoln, Nebraska: University of Nebraska Press, 1978.

Flynn, J. E., & Summers, L. H. Languages for building performance evaluation. In R. L. Brauer (Ed.), *Priorities for environmental design research*. Washington, D.C.: Environmental Design Research Association, 1978.

Fox, L. H., Tobin, D., & Brody, D. Sex-role socialization and achievement in mathematics. In M. A. Wittig & A. C. Petersen (Eds.), *Sex-related differences in cognitive functioning*. New York: Academic Press, 1979.

Freeman, N., Eiser, C., & Sayers, J. Children's strategies in producing three-dimensional relationships on a two-dimensional surface. *Journal of Experimental Child Psychology*, 1977, *23*, 305-314.

Freeman, N. H., & Janikoun, R. R. Intellectual realism in children's drawings of a familiar object with distinctive features. *Child Development*, 1972, *43*, 1116-1121.

Fruchter, B. Measurement of spatial abilities: History and background. *Educational and Psychological Measurement*, 1954, *14*, 387-395.

Golbeck, S. L., & Liben, L. S. Performance on Piagetian tasks and knowledge about the physical world. Paper presented at the biennial meeting of the Society for Research in Child Development, San Francisco, 1979.

Goodnow, J. Rules and repertoires, rituals and tricks of the trade: Social and informational aspects to cognitive and representational development. In S. Farnham-Diggory (Ed.), *Information processing in children*. New York: Academic Press, 1972.

Gump, P. V. School environments. In I. Altman & J. F. Wohlwill (Eds.), *Children and the environment*. New York: Plenum, 1978.

Gump, P. V., & Ross, R. The fit of milieu and programme in school environments. In H. McGurk (Ed.), *Ecological factors in human development*. New York: North-Holland Publishing Company, 1977.

Harper, L. V., & Sanders, K. M. Pre-school children's use of space: Sex differences in outdoor play. *Developmental Psychology*, 1975, *11*, 119.

Harrison, R. E. *Look at the World: The Fortune atlas for world strategy*. New York: Alfred A. Knopf, 1944.

Hart, R. A. *Children's experience of place*. New York: Irvington Publishers, 1979.

Hart, R. A., & Moore, G. T. The development of spatial cognition: A review. In R. M. Downs & D. Stea (Eds.), *Image and environment*. Chicago: Aldine, 1973.

Herman, J. F. Children's cognitive maps of large-scale spaces: Effects of exploration, direction, and repeated experience. *Journal of Experimental Child Psychology*, 1980, *29*, 126-143.

Hoffman, L. Early childhood experiences and women's achievement motives. *Journal of Social Issues*, 1972, *28*, 129-155.

Hollos, M. Logical operations and role-taking abilities in two cultures: Norway and Hungary. *Child Development*, 1975, *46*, 638-649.

Hollos, M., & Cowan, P. A. Social isolation and cognitive development: Logical operations and role-taking abilities in three Norwegian social settings. *Child Development*, 1973, *44*, 630-641.

Hubel, D. H., & Wiesel, T. N. Receptive fields of single neurones in the cat's striate cortex. *Journal of Physiology*, 1959, *148*, 574-591.

Hudson, W. The study of the problems of pictorial perception among un-acculturated groups. *International Journal of Psychology*, 1967, *2*, 89-107.

Huston-Stein, A., & Baltes, P. B. Theory and method in life-span developmental psychology: Implications for child development. In H. W. Reese & L. P. Lipsett (Eds.), *Advances in child development and behavior*, Vol. 11, New York: Academic Press, 1976.

Huttenlocher, J. Constructing spatial images: A strategy in reasoning, *Psychological Review*, 1968, *75*, 550-560.

Hyde, J., Geiringer, E., & Yen, W. On the empirical relation between spatial ability and sex differences in other aspects of cognitive performance. *Multivariate Behavioral Research*, 1975, *10*, 289-309.

Jammer, M. *Concepts of space*. Cambridge, Massachusetts: Harvard University Press, 1954.

Kagan, J., & Klein, R. Cross-cultural perspectives on early development. *American Psychologist*, 1973, *28*, 947-961.

Kaplan, R. Way-finding in the natural environment. In G. Moore & R. Gollege (Eds.), *Environmental knowing*. Stroudsburg, Pa.: Dowden, Hutchinson, & Ross, 1976.

Kosslyn, S. M. Imagery and cognitive development: A teleological approach. In R. S. Siegler (Ed.), *Children's thinking: What develops?* Hillsdale, New Jersey: Erlbaum, 1978.

Kosslyn, S. M., Pick, H. L. & Fariello, G. R. Cognitive maps in children and men. *Child Development*, 1974, *45*, 707-716.

Kosslyn, S. M., & Pomerantz, J. P. Imagery, propositions, and the form of internal representations. *Cognitive Psychology*, 1977, *9*, 52-76.

Lerner, R. M., & Busch-Rossnagel, N. A. Individuals as producers of their develoment: Conceptual and empirical bases. In R. M. Lerner and N. A. Bush-Rossnagel (Eds.), *Individuals as producers of their development: A life-span perspective*. New York: Academic Press, 1981.

Liben, L. S. Performance on Piagetian spatial tasks as a function of sex, field dependence, and training. *Merrill-Palmer Quarterly*, 1978, *24*, 97-110.

Liben, L. S. Contributions of individuals to their development during childhood: A Piagetian perspective. In R. M. Lerner & N. A. Busch-Rossnagel (Eds.), *Individuals as producers of their development: A life-span perspective*. New York: Academic Press, 1981.

Liben, L. S., & Golbeck, S. L. Sex differences in performance on Piagetian spatial tasks: Differences in competence or performance? *Child Development*, 1980, *51*, 594-597.

Marmor, G. S. Mental rotaton and number conservation: Are they related? *Developmental Psychology*, 1977, *13*, 320-325.

McCall, R. B. Exploratory manipulation and play in the human infant. *Monographs of the Society for Research in Child Development*, 1974, *39*(2).

Moore, G. T. The development of environmental knowing: An overview of an interactional-constructivist theory and some data on within-individual development variations. In D. Canter & T. Lee (Eds.), *Psychology and the built environment*. New York: Halstead Press, 1974.

Moore, R., & Young, D. Children outdoors: Toward a social ecology of the landscape. In I. Altman & J. F. Wohlwill (Eds.), *Children and the environment*. New York: Plenum, 1978.

Moos, R. H., & Trickett, E. J. *Classroom environmental scale manual*. Palo Alto: Consulting Psychologists Press, 1974.

Nagy, J. N., & Baird, J. C. Children as environmental planners. In I. Altman & J. F. Wohlwill (Eds.), *Children and the environment*. New York: Plenum, 1978.

Norman, D. K. A comparison of children's spatial reasoning: Rural Appalachia, suburban, and urban New England. *Child Development*, 1980, *51*, 288-291.

O'Keefe, J., & Nadel, L. *The hippocampus as a cognitive map*. Oxford: Oxford University Press (Clarendon Press), 1978.

Olson, D. (Ed.) *Media and symbols. The seventy-third yearbook of the National Society for the Study of Education*. Chicago: University of Chicago Press, 1974.

Olson, D. On the relations between spatial and linguistic processes. In J. Eliot & N. Salkind (Eds.), *Children spatial development*. Springfield, Illinois: Thomas, 1975.

Olton, D. S. Mazes, maps, and memory. *American Psychologist*, 1979, *34*, 583-596.

Overton, W. F., & Reese, H. W. Models of development: Methodological implications. In J. Nesselroade & H. Reese (Eds.), *Life-span developmental psychology: Methodological issues*. New York: Academic Press, 1973.

Parke, R. D. Children's home environments: Social and cognitive effects. In I. Altman & J. F. Wohlwill (Eds.), *Children and the environment*. New York: Plenum, 1978.

Pascual-Leone, J. The development of inferential behavior and field dependence. Unpublished manuscript, New York University, Toronto, 1967.

Payne, R. J., & Jones, D. R. W. Children's urban landscapes in Huntingdon Hills, Calgary. In P. Suedfeld & J. A. Russel (Eds.), *EDRA 7: The behavioral basis of design*, Book 2. Stroudsburg, Pennsylvania: Dowden, Hutchinson and Ross, 1977.

Piaget, J. *The construction of reality in the child.* New York: Basic Books, 1954.

Piaget, J. *Genetic epistemology.* New York: Norton, 1970. (a)

Piaget, J. Piaget's theory. In P. Mussen (Ed.), *Carmichael's manual of child psychology,* New York: Wiley, 1970. (b)

Piaget, J. *The grasp of consciousness.* Cambridge, Massachusetts: Harvard University Press, 1976.

Piaget, J., & Inhelder, B. *The child's conception of space.* London: Routledge & Kegan Paul, 1956.

Piaget, J., Inhelder, R., & Szeminska, A. *The child's conception of geometry.* New York: Basic Books, 1960.

Rand, G. Some Copernican views of the city. *Architectural Forum,* 1969, *132,* 77-81.

Rheingold, H. L., & Cook, K. V. The contents of boys' and girls' rooms as an index of parents' behavior. *Child Development,* 1975, *46,* 459-464.

Serbin, L. A., O'Leary, K. D., Kent, R. N., & Tronick, I. J. A comparison of teacher response to the preacademic and problem behavior of boys and girls. *Child Development,* 1973, *44,* 796-804.

Shafer, E. L., & Thompson, R. C. Models that describe use of Adirondack campgrounds. *Forest Science,* 1968, *14,* 383-391.

Shepard, R. N. The mental image. *American Psychologist,* 1978, *33,* 125-137.

Shepard, R. N., & Metzler, J. Mental rotation of three-dimensional objects. *Science,* 1971, *171,* 701-703.

Shure, M. B. Psychological ecology of a nursery school. *Child Development,* 1963, *34,* 979-992.

Siegel, A. W., & Schadler, M. Young children's cognitive maps of their classroom. *Child Development,* 1977, *48,* 388-394.

Siegel, A., & White, S. The development of spatial representations of large-scale environments. In H. W. Reese (Ed.), *Advances in child development and behavior,* Vol. 10. New York: Academic Press, 1975.

Stallings, J. Implementation and child effects of teaching practices in follow through classrooms. *Monographs of the Society for Research in Child Development,* 1975, *40,* Serial No. 163.

Thomas, H., Jamison, W., & Hummel, D. Observation is insufficient for discovering that the surface of still water is invariantly horizontal. *Science,* 1973, *181,* 173-174.

Trabasso, T., Riley, C. A., & Wilson, E. G. The representation of linear order and spatial strategies in reasoning: A developmental study. In R. Falmagne (Ed.), *Reasoning, representation and process.* Hillsdale, New Jersey: Erlbaum, 1975.

Wachs, T. D. Utilization of a Piagetian approach in the investigation of early experience effects: A research strategy and some illustrative data. *Merrill-Palmer Quarterly,* 1976, *22,* 11-30.

Wachs, T. D. Proximal experience and early cognitive-intellectual development; The physical environment. *Merrill-Palmer Quarterly,* 1979, *25,* 3-41.

Wachs, T. D., Francis, J., & McQuiston, S. Psychological dimensions of the infant's physical environment. *Infant Behavior and Development,* 1979, *2,* 155-161.

Willats, J. How children learn to represent three-dimensional space in drawings. In G. Butterworth (Ed.), *The child's representation of the world.* New York: Plenum, 1977.

Wohlwill, J. F. Searching for the environment in environmental cognition research: A commentary on research strategy. In G. T. Moore & R. C. Gollege (Eds.), *Environmental knowing.* Stroudsburg, Pennsylvania: Dowden, Hutchinson & Ross, 1976.

Yarrow, L. J., Rubenstein, J. L., Pedersen, F. A. & Jankowski, J. J. Dimensions of early stimulation and their differential effects on infant development. *Merrill-Palmer Quarterly,* 1972, *18,* 205-218.

Yates, F. A. *The art of memory.* London: Routledge & Kegan Paul, 1966.

II

Developmental and Individual Differences

2 From Frames of Reference to Spatial Representations[1]

HERBERT L. PICK, JR.
JEFFREY J. LOCKMAN

Introduction

The spatially coordinated behavior of children ranges from such actions as a young infant's getting its thumb into its mouth, to a preschool child's learning to throw a ball, to an adolescent's hand-sewing of intricate stitches in a homemade garment. The first of these behaviors may be regarded as involving body–body relations; the second of these behaviors involving body–object relations; and the third involving intricate object–object relations. The spatial adjustment of one body part with respect to another, such as getting the thumb into the mouth, is probably one of the earliest spatial behaviors to occur. Quite quickly after this, the child begins to perform a variety of tasks involving body–object relations as it begins to manipulate objects; these increase further as the child begins to locomote. Object–object relations are also implicated in the more complex tasks of object manipulation and locomotion.

It would be tempting to propose that there is a developmental trend in performance of spatial tasks involving these three types of spatial relations: from body–body, to body–object, to object–object relations. However, even a moment's reflection suggests that the sophistication in all three types of relations increases in the more complex spatial tasks of later childhood and adulthood. Consider, for example, the intricate body–body coordination of

[1] The preparation of this chapter was supported by a Program Project Grant HD 050207 from the National Institutes of Health to the Institute of Child Development of the University of Minnesota and by the Center for Research in Human Learning of the University of Minnesota. The work of the Center is supported by Research Grants from the National Science Foundation and from the National Institute of Child Health and Human Development.

39

the skilled gymnast and trampolinist, the incredible body-object skill of the juggler, or the locomotive skill of the orienteering sportsman.

Two concepts will be central to our discussion of spatial behaviors: frame of reference and spatial representation. A *frame of reference* will be used here to mean a locus or set of loci with respect to which spatial position is defined.[2] Egocentric frames of reference define spatial positions in relation to loci on the body. Thus, in body-object spatial relations the relevant frame of reference is almost by definition egocentric. Egocentric frames of reference are distinguished from allocentric or geocentric reference systems, which simply means that the positions defining loci are external to the person in question. When object-object relations are involved, the relevant reference systems are allocentric or a combination of egocentric and allocentric. For example, in positioning a shape into proper position for fitting into a form board, children presumably adjust the cut-out shape in relation to some of the salient properties of the form board. At the same time, they probably adjust their hands to fit some of the properties of the shape. Since both object manipulation and locomotive tasks involve body-object and object-object relations, egocentric and allocentric reference systems are typically implicated in their performance.

The *spatial representations* that people have or construct out of part of their environment can be defined by—or, perhaps even better, be characterized by—the kinds of operations that can be performed on their spatial information. First of all, there are the group properties (Piaget, Inhelder, & Szeminska, 1960; Yonas & Pick, 1975): (a) reversibility; knowing how to go from A to B implies knowing how to go from B to A; (b) transitivity; knowing how to go from A to B and B to C implies knowing how to get from A to C; and (c) detour ability; knowing how to go from A to B by some route implies being able to go from A to B by other routes. Secondly, spatial representations also imply performing other kinds of mental operations such as mental rotation, perspective taking, and scale changing (Hardwick, McIntyre, & Pick, 1976; Huttenlocher & Presson, 1979; Presson, 1980; Kosslyn, Ball, & Reiger, 1978).

To say that a particular task depends on an egocentric or allocentric frame of reference is only the crudest kind of initial classification. What is the particular locus or set of loci in the body that defines the egocentric frame? What are the particular loci that comprise the allocentric frame? This multiplicity of reference systems was recognized by Acredolo (1976) when she showed that children of different ages are differentially responsive to the reference

---

[2] Other definitions of "frame of reference" are possible. For example, Downs and Stea, 1973, use frames of reference to mean "methods of keying cognitive maps to environments . . . ." The present use is much more restrictive and by itself is not meant to imply function or process.

systems defined by the objects in a room and the shell of the room. Acredolo, in her contribution to this volume, also alludes to another facet of multiple reference systems—that is, that they may simultaneously influence behavior.

The relevance and simultaneous operation of multiple reference systems can also be illustrated by an unpublished experiment done in collaboration with W. H. Warren. Imagine simultaneously writing with both hands on a horizontal plane. The hand movements in one case are congruent; that is, the hands move left to right in synchrony. In a second case, the hand movements are symmetrical, that is, as the right hand moves left to right as it normally does, the left moves in synchrony from right to left. Now imagine that the horizontal plane is folded into a medial plane parallel to your line of sight while you continue to write simultaneously with your two hands on either side of this vertical plane now in a direction toward and away from your body. Corresponding to the previous second case of symmetrical hand movements is now a third case of the two hands moving in synchrony away from the body. And corresponding to the original first case of congruent left to right movements is a fourth case of the right hand moving away from the body and the left hand moving simultaneously toward the body.

What are the results of your thought experiment? Can you order the difficulty of these imagined conditions? If your intuitions are like ours, the third condition of the two hands simultaneously moving away from the body should be the easiest. The fourth condition—the right hand moving away from the body while the left hand moves toward the body—should be the most difficult. In our *thought* results, the symmetrical writing on the horizontal plane is next to easiest and the congruent writing in the horizontal plane is next to most difficult, although the difference between these latter two conditions is not great. We do have some nonimaginary results of this experiment and it appears that our intuitions were pretty sound. The third case is clearly the easiest and produces the best results. The fourth case is clearly the most difficult and the writing especially of the left hand is least legible. It is difficult to distinguish between the first and second cases.

These results can be interpreted by considering the egocentric frames of reference on which this activity might be based. One possible frame of reference takes the body as a whole; either side to side, or toward and away. The other considers the movements of each hand with respect to the limb or muscle structure: toward or away from the little finger or thumb. In this analysis the easiest third condition has both hands moving away from the body and both moving in the direction of the little finger. The movements of the two hands are congruent in both reference systems. In the most difficult fourth condition, one hand is moving away from the body in the direction of the little finger. The other is moving toward the body in the direction of the thumb. The movement is incongruent in both frames of reference. The first and second conditions of intermediate difficulty on the horizontal plane are congruent with respect to one frame of reference, but are incongruent with respect to the other. For example, the symmetrical movements have both hands moving in the direction of the little finger but one hand is moving right and the other left. The ease of performing these tasks is predicted by the degree of congruence of the movements in the *two egocentric* reference systems.

In this chapter we shall try to analyze especially the spatial aspects of the body-object and object-object relations in object manipulation and loco-motive behaviors. Initially we will try to point out that object manipulation involves a variety of spatially interesting behaviors that have been hitherto ignored. Attention will be on the characteristics of the frames of reference and spatial representations in this object manipulation behavior. Then a similar analysis will be done for locomotive behavior. One might indeed con-ceive of a 2 × 2 matrix of body-object and object-object relations appearing in both object manipulation and locomotive tasks. Recently one of us col-laborated in a discussion of how certain aspects of spatial perceptual development might be analyzed in terms of frames of reference (Pick, Yonas, & Rieser, 1979). This chapter attempts to continue that discussion moving from reference systems to mental representations of space.

Spatial Organization of Object Manipulation

Soon after the infant begins to reach, object manipulation becomes more common. The infant begins to explore objects systematically and establish relations between objects. We would like to suggest that the spatial organiza-tion of these perceptual-motor activities reflects important aspects of the in-fant's knowledge. What do we mean by spatial organization in this context? Consider this organization with respect to the concepts of spatial representa-tion and frames of reference.

In terms of the spatial representation of a manipulatory space, a refined knowledge of this space would mean that the infant could plan actions that reflect the kinds of operations mentioned previously. For example, the ability of an infant to rotate an object either way from end to end would imply an understanding of reversibility in this manipulative space. Or if a preferred route of rotation is blocked, the ability of the infant to rotate the object through an alternate route in space would imply an understanding of detours. In addition, the infant's ability to rotate an object consistently through the shortest route in space when the object's orientation is varied would imply an understanding of the metric properties of this space at some level.

When do these abilities develop? With the exception of Piaget (1952, 1954) such questions have not received much attention. In fact, there is little work on the development of visually guided *manipulation* of objects. Piaget's observations suggest that by 9 months the infant has at least a rudimentary understanding of reversibility in a manipulative space. Laurent could rotate a bottle to obtain the nipple even when the nipple was originally out of sight (Piaget 1954, p. 184). These observations should be replicated and additional questions about the infant's understanding of transitivity, detours, and the metric properties of this manipulative space should be investigated as well.

So far we have suggested that important aspects of the infant's spatial knowledge may be revealed in the organization of manipulative activities. In addition, the types of spatial relationships produced during these activities reflect advances in spatial development. We would like to make a further distinction between the spatial relationships that the infant establishes between itself and a single object and the relationships that the infant establishes between itself and several objects simultaneously. The former involves object–body knowledge and the latter also includes object–object knowledge. Important aspects of spatial development may go on in each of these domains. The relationship of these types of knowledge to the frames of reference in spatial development is discussed next.

Many investigators of sensorimotor development have noted that infants direct their actions towards single objects before establishing relations between objects (e.g. see Gesell & Thompson, 1934) although most have not been explicit in linking this general trend to the development of spatial knowledge. Research on the development of play has also revealed that infants under 10 months only establish relatively simple relations between two objects (Fenson, Kagan, Kearsley, & Zelazo, 1976; McCall, 1974). The relations that the 9-month-old produces, for example, often involve banging one object against another rather than more appropriate complex associations, such as putting a spoon in a cup (Fenson *et al.,* 1976).

What kinds of developments do we see in the spatial relationships that the infant produces between itself and a single object? There are two trends that we would like to emphasize in this domain: (*a*), the infant becoming more adept at localizing objects in space; and (*b*) motor acts becoming more precisely related to spatial properties like size, form and orientation of the object. The trend in infants' ability to locate an object precisely in space has been well documented in the research literature on reaching (Halverson, 1931; Piaget, 1952; White, Castle & Held, 1964). The role of experience in this development, however, has been a matter of controversy. Whereas some have argued that visual and motor spaces must be coordinated through experience (Piaget, 1952; White, Castle & Held, 1964), others have argued that this coordination is present soon after birth (Bower, 1974; Bruner & Kowlowski, 1972).

Nevertheless, there appears to be less disagreement on the need for relevant experience for the development of *finer motor behaviors* that are originally visually guided (Hein, 1972; Walk & Bond, 1971). Many of these types of behaviors correspond to the second trend we are emphasizing in this body–object domain; namely, motor acts becoming more precisely related to the spatial properties of the objects. For example, inspection of items on Bayley's (1969) scales of infant development indicates that by 7 months of age the infant is beginning to coordinate visual information specifying size and form with appropriate motor acts to exploit these relationships.

With respect to developments in the object–object domain, we can reiterate the following two related trends: (a) behavior of the child relevant to the interrelationships among objects becomes more precisely related to the spatial properties of the objects; and (b) these behavioral coordinations begin to reflect the representational capacities of the child.

The first trend may be examined in terms of the infant's understanding of the "in" and "on" relationships. Inspection of the Bayley (1969) scales indicate that the infant's initial understanding of "in" or "on" is rather imprecise. With respect to the "in" relationship, the infant at 9.4 months will place a cube in a cup though the cube may not be released. Soon afterward we can infer that the infant is beginning to understand the size constraints of this relationship. At 12.9 months the infant will put small beads through a hole. The understanding of form constraints, however, appears to develop later. It is not until 25.4 months that the child can correctly place three differently shaped objects in a form board when the objects are not directly below their appropriate forms. Similarly, for the "on" relationship, inspection of the Bayley exam reveals that it is not until some time after the second year that surfaces are correctly aligned one on another. For example, at 26.1 months, the child is able to place a doll's head correctly on the neck with the head facing forward in relation to the body.

After 1 year of age, these perceptual–motor activities also begin to reflect the child's representative capacity. As the infant becomes capable of planning actions that exploit potential spatial relationships between objects, the incidence of trial and error manipulations begins to decrease. Many of Bruner's (1970) observations on skill development illustrate these trends. Similarly, Piaget (1954) reports that by the end of Stage 5, the infant can foresee whether two objects will be balanced and will then adjust and correct the positions of the objects before releasing them. And many of the later items on the Bayley exam also reveal this systematic approach to establishing relationships between objects.

Until now, we have made a distinction between the spatial relationships that the infant establishes between itself and a single object and the spatial relationships that the infant is sensitive to among several objects simultaneously. What are the possible developmental relationships between these two domains? The first question to be answered is the following: Does spatial knowledge in the object-body domain develop before *analogous* knowledge in the object-object domain? Before this question can be answered in any meaningful way, systematic observations of visually guided object manipulation are needed and careful thought must be given to what constitutes analogous knowledge in the two domains. Despite these reservations, two of the preceding problems can be examined seeking analogous developments in the object-body and object-object domains: (a) the infant's global understanding of the "in" relationship; and (b) the infant's understanding of the motor implications of size and form. As noted above, these two problem areas suggested themselves after close inspection of items from Bayley's (1969) scales of infant development.

With respect to the "in" relationship, infants may understand that their fingers or hands may go inside an object before they understand that objects may go inside other objects. Inspection of the Bayley developmental scales reveals that at 8.9 months, the infant fingers holes in a pegboard (an object-body item) and at 9.4 months, the infant places a cube in or over a cup though it may not be released (an object-object item). Obviously, a difference of 2 weeks is hardly compelling, but these items suggest that before 9 months, infants' manipulation of a single object with an opening (e.g., a cup) should be contrasted with their simultaneous manipulation of a solid object and an object with an opening. By comparing the relationships the infant produces in these situations, one may be able to infer whether or not the infant understands the "in" relationship on an object-body level before understanding it on an object-object level.

With respect to the understanding of the motor implications of size and form, this knowledge may also develop first on an object-body level and then on an object-object level. This sequence is suggested by items that appear on the Bayley exam and in work done by other investigators. Halverson (1931) reported that the aim of the hand and type of grasp used become more related to the form of the object after 28 weeks of age. Similarly, inspection of the Bayley scales reveals that by 6.8 months of age, the infant appropriately adjusts its hand movements to the size of the perceived object. And recent work at the University of Minnesota indicates that by 9 months, infants will show appropriate anticipatory hand shaping as a function of the object's orientation (Ashmead, Bushnell, & Lockman, 1980).

It appears then that the understanding of the motor implications of size and form on an object-body level is well established by 1 year of age. With respect to the object-object domain, however, infants cannot consistently fit differently shaped objects into their appropriate forms until 21.2 months of age (Bayley, 1969). Thus, although infants correctly orient their hands as a function of the object's form before they are a year old, it is not until almost a year later that they correctly orient objects in relation to other objects. In this context, planning an appropriate act on the object-body level may develop before planning an analogous act on the object-object level.

Why might there be a lag between the development of analogous knowledge in the two domains? It is here that the notion of frames of reference might be useful. In the object-body tasks described above, the infant must only code spatial relationships between itself and a single object; these are basically egocentric. Indeed, egocentric coding of manipulatory acts extends into adulthood and is sufficient for most object-body tasks. Consider, for example, the actions involved in making a tie knot. When the tie is knotted on one's self, the actions are quite automatic. But when a person has to knot the tie on someone else (the person is now rotated 180° and the egocentric relationship is not preserved), most people experience some difficulty.

In terms of the frames of reference notion, we can say that these actions were coded egocentrically. In object-object tasks, however, the young child not only has to code relationships between itself and an object but also has to code relationships with respect to another object in the environment. The simultaneous use of both egocentric and geocentric reference systems in manipulatory tasks may pose problems for the young child. We will see this issue of simultaneous use of multiple reference systems arising again in connection with locomotor tasks.

Frames of Reference and Mental Representation in Spatial Layout

In the last few years the issue of place versus response learning in children has been thoroughly investigated by a number of developmental psychologists (e.g. Acredolo, 1978; Rieser, 1979; Smothergill, Hughes, Timmons, & Hutko, 1975). The term itself, *place versus response learning,* comes from the old animal learning literature and biases our conceptualization of spatial orientation. Remembering where (place) one has gone or where (place) some object was located implies sensitivity to landmarks; that is, orientation while in a space in terms of an allocentric frame of reference. This presumably implies a representation in memory of some landmark information. On this basis such orientation in current developmental literature has been referred to in terms of landmark coding, use of geocentric reference systems, use of allocentric reference systems, and so on.

Repeating the response one has made is a somewhat more ambiguous act. The term *response learning* may imply simple motor act learning or it may imply responding in terms of an egocentric reference system independent of any particular motor act. In current developmental literature, such responding has been referred to as "egocentric responding" rather than response learning. Such a distinction is experimentally researchable; Bremner and Bryant (1977) and Acredolo (1978) have demonstrated that infants do respond egocentrically rather than by repeating learned motor acts. Assuming that this distinction generally holds, Acredolo (1976, 1977, 1978) has demonstrated in a very systematic series of experiments that there is a progressive trend with age from egocentric responding to allocentric responding.

The age when this shift occurs depends a great deal on situational variables like nature of the task, the salience of the geocentric cues (landmarks), and the complexity of the change of position. Thus, Acredolo (1976) found in a task involving locomotion in a somewhat distinctively marked room the shift occurred between 3 and 7 years of age. On the other hand, in a situation where the room was not distinctively marked but where the response simply involved looking toward one of two windows (and when the change of position from training to test was passive), the shift occurred between 6 and 16 months.[3] Within this age range Acredolo has demonstrated that the age of shift from egocentric to allocentric can be pushed back toward the younger age by making the landmarks more salient. And, finally, Rieser (1979) has demonstrated that infants of 6 months of age reflect allocentric orientation in looking toward one of four windows when their change of position from training to test simply involves passive rotation around the line of sight rather than movement across an entire room plus rotation (see Figure 2.1).

If it is assumed that allocentric orientation is a more sophisticated level of behavior when dealing with problems of spatial layout, special problems are imposed when distinctive landmarks do not mark the significant places in the environment, that is, those places to be returned to by walk or by gaze. There are occasions when *where* one is going to is not distinctively marked in the environment but there are distinctive markings that indicate where one *is*. Under such conditions it is possible to maintain a place orientation on the

---

[3] The fact that the response was simpler—just looking—and the fact that the change of position was passive, perhaps freeing the child's attention to focus on the nature of the position change, might account for the shift from egocentric to geocentric that occurred so early here.

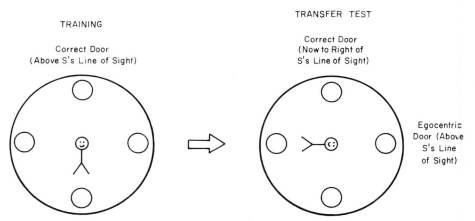

FIGURE 2.1. *Illustration of Reiser's (1978) training and transfer test (gravity irrelevant). Babies were supine looking up at four windows inset in the end of a large drum that surrounded the subjects.*

basis of using a combination of egocentric and allocentric frames of reference. Such a situation was created experimentally by Acredolo (1977) in a place versus response learning situation with 3- to 5-year-old children. The children learned to walk straight ahead from one end of a room and turn left or right to find a trinket hidden under a cup. Once they learned to do this without error, they were started from the opposite end of the room. In one condition, the loci of the hidden cups at the two sides of the room were distinctively and clearly marked; in another condition, the starting positions at either end of the room were distinctively marked. The "indirect" marking of the start positions brought performance of even the 3-year-olds above chance level. One might describe behavior in such a situation as reflecting a contingent use of different types of reference systems. Specifically, the child demonstrates this when starting by one landmark he should turn left (or right) whereas when starting by the other landmark he should turn right (or left).

One would expect that in general this contingent use of reference systems would be more difficult than use of a single reference system for maintaining orientation. In Acredolo's situation, this was not found. However, Goldsmith (1979) explored a number of more complex instances of such situations. Typical of her situations was the following: An otherwise uniform room consists of two opposite unmarked walls and two opposite distinctively colored walls, red and blue, as illustrated in Figure 2.2. A child observes a toy being hidden at the base of one of the uncolored walls. The child is then distracted and her position in the room is changed. She is then asked to retrieve the hidden toy. Presumably in order to perform this correctly, the child must reason something like this: When I face the red wall, the toy is by the un-

Red

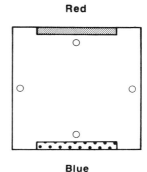

FIGURE 2.2. *Illustration of Goldsmith's (1979) room used in studying problems involving contingent use of frames of reference.*

Blue

colored wall on my right. Performance with respect to one reference system depends on orientation with respect to a second reference system.

Goldsmith presented such problems to children 3, 5, and 7 years of age. The 3-year-olds performed at chance level in both the tasks requiring use of a single allocentric frame of reference and tasks requiring the contingent use of allocentric and egocentric frames. The 5-year-olds performed at chance level on the contingent tasks but did better than chance in the single reference system tasks whereas the 7-year-olds performed above chance level in both.

It appears that the contingent use of reference systems poses some special difficulty for children above and beyond the use of single frames of reference since behavior on these problems only exceeded chance level when performance on the single reference system problems was perfectly accurate. This is reminiscent of the long lag between the development of appropriate spatial behavior in the object–body (anticipatory hand-orientation behavior) and object–object (anticipatory form-board behavior) problems.

The contingent use of reference systems for relocating a desired place requires that there be some distinctive landmarks in the environment even though that place itself may not be distinctively marked. However, it may be that in a particular space there are *no* clear landmarks. In such a situation, if one is to know where one is and how to get to desired places, it is necessary to keep track constantly of one's own position and movement, and relative positions of other things. Such might be the case when trying to move on a straight course through a rather uniform forest. The forest is indistinctive in the sense that without meticulous attention the trees and terrain all look pretty much alike. However, if one stays continuously oriented by focusing on a couple of arbitrary trees—one in the direction one wants to go and one near the starting position—it is possible to accomplish the goal of following a straight course. Experimentally this type of situation can be simulated in a uniform room where neither starting position nor desired end place is unambiguously marked.

Again, Acredolo (1977) has created such a situation in the context of place versus response learning experiments with infants. At one end of a uniform room, an infant is conditioned to look to left or right in anticipation of an experimenter appearing in a window with a friendly greeting. After learning, the infant is moved to the opposite end of the room and the conditioned signal is again presented. Acredolo found that 16-month-old infants apparently keep track of their movement even in the absence of landmarks; after the movement to the other end of the room, they will anticipate the appearance of the experimenter by looking to the very same window. Infants aged 6 and 11 months do not do this despite having their movement made as salient as possible.

Rieser (1979) obtained similar results in his study of 6-month-old infants rotated around the line of sight after learning to look at one of four windows. Notwithstanding the fact that the 6-month-olds rather precociously (as mentioned before) respond allocentrically in this situation in the presence of distinctive landmarks, they do not respond this way when the situation requires them to keep track or update their position while being moved. In this particular case, the infants were conditioned to look at a window above eye level or to the right of straight ahead and then they were rotated 90°. Besides the mechanical stimulation of the movement being available to the babies, there was the optical motion stimulation of a very coarsely textured visual field.

What actually is required when babies such as Acredolo's 16-month-olds do correctly anticipate? It is possible that they have maintained orientation toward the correct window while being moved across the room and turned around. In general, this implies keeping track of an important location while being moved. When a space is small and there is a single location, maintaining orientation in this way is not difficult. When the space is large and complex and where there is more than one location of interest and it is desired to stay generally oriented to the whole space, the task may be much more difficult; it requires some sort of a representation of the whole space.

An alternative way for babies to solve a problem like Acredolo's is to simply register their own movement; then when they are called on to return to (i.e., to look at) a particular location, they can calculate the direction to go. This would be the case, for example, if the baby noted it had been moved across the room and been turned around, and if it then reasoned that in order to get to that place on the right it should now look to the left. In this case, the strategy is not one of continuously updating the position of a particular window with respect to the self. Instead, one must note one's own movement, then at the end, calculate a change of direction. We don't know which of these ways of proceeding is used under what conditions.

One study by Lasky, Romano, and Winters (1980 ; Experiment V) illustrates a way of approaching this issue in a somewhat different situation. In their experiment, children aged 3 to 10 years were asked to observe a toy being hidden in one of two containers on the left and right sides of a small square table. The table was uniform except for one distinctive cue: a painted face positioned midway between the two sides and near one edge of the table. After the toy was hidden, the table was rotated 90°, 180°, 270°, or 360°; the child was then asked to retrieve the toy. Half the time the children would watch the table being rotated and half the time the rotation was accomplished with a screen occluding the view. In the latter case, it was of course impossible to stay oriented during the movement. Rather, the child had to use the orientation of the face afterward to infer the amount of movement of the table and then presumably calculate the new position of the toy container. As might be expected, errors across the whole age range were greater in the occluded condition than in the viewed condition in which the children were able to watch the spatial transformation take place. At the youngest ages, errors occurred especially when the incorrect container was nearer than the correct one or when the incorrect container ended up in an egocentrically similar position to the originally correct container.

The interesting feature of this experiment is that the occluded condition requires subjects to make the spatial inference at the end of the transformation. They obviously cannot update or track the relative spatial position of the container during the movement. Of course we do not know how much of the difficulty in children's performance in the occluded condition is due to the difficulty or error in registering the fact of, or amount of, rotation of the table and how much is due to error in making the inference itself. Presumably in situations that involve active movement through a space, subjects are aware of the fact of movement although they may make errors in registering the amount of movement. In active movement through a small space accessible from a single viewpoint with continuous information from the environment itself, it seems reasonable to keep continuously oriented toward all significant objects in the space.

However, the ability to remain oriented in spaces that are not accessible from one point of view requires some form of representation. How could a child keep track of its position in such a space? One way would be to update an egocentric response after movement. That is, a child would initially note and remember the relationship between herself and a location, register the change in position and then recompute the new relationship from this information. In more complicated series of movements, this would mean updating a series of egocentric responses for each relationship between the self and a location. If such a method was used, the necessity of inferring the interrelationships among locations, rather than the relationships between the self and a location, would add still more difficulty. It would require coordinating information about the relationship between the self and each location based on updated egocentric responses.

A second seemingly more efficient method of remaining oriented would involve updating one's position simultaneously with respect to all other objects in the space. This would require a representation of the interrelationships between objects in a space, not just a representation of the relationship between the self and individual loci in a space. A change in position therefore would involve updating one's position with respect to the representation as a whole. (This is analogous to Pinker and Kosslyn's, 1978, discussion of movement of an object through a spatial image.)

Is there any evidence about which of the two methods the children use in large-scale spaces that are not directly apprehendable? We would like to interpret some of our recent work with respect to this discussion (Hazen, Lockman, & Pick, 1978). In this study, 3–6-year-old children were taken through a series of rooms by a specified route. The younger children (3–5-year-olds) were taken through a four-room space; the older children (5- and 6-year-olds) were walked through a six-room space (see Figure 2.3). Once the route and landmarks along the route were learned, children were tested on their ability to travel the route in reverse (route-reversal knowledge) and to infer the relationship between parts of the environment through which they never traveled directly (reference knowledge). These points are marked INF in Figure 2.3.

Although 3-year-olds were almost perfect at being able to reverse a sequence of turns along a route, it was not until 6 years of age that children performed relatively well on the inference task. How can we account for the 3-year-olds' almost perfect performance on the route-reversal measure and their poor performance on the inference measure? Successful performance on the route-reversal task could be accomplished by updating a series of egocentric responses. For example, in the four-room U-route illustration Figure 2.3, the child could register the change in her position and update the necessary egocentric responses (a right and left turn) in order to get from the endpoint to the starting position.

Successful performance on the inference task, however, requires that the child update his position in this environment with respect to the representation of the space as a whole. The fact that 3-year-olds were able to reverse a route but not make inferences suggests that they are capable of updating egocentric responses but do not yet possess a general representation of a space that can be updated in response to a change in a position.

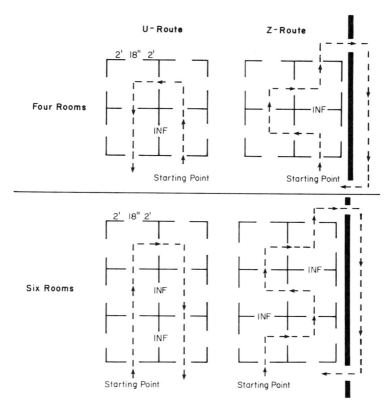

FIGURE 2.3. *Layout of four-room and six-room spaces. Children learned either a U-shaped path or a zig-zag path.*

What do these results imply for the general development of the representation of space? At the outset of this chapter, we described certain important properties in the representation of space—reversibility, detours, and transitivity. These properties apply to both manipulative and locomotive spaces. It may be that the ability to perform reversible operations in a space develops before the abilities to make systematic detours or inferences in a space. The reason for this earlier development would be that reversible operations only require the updating of a series of egocentric responses. Spatial inference operations, however, are most efficiently accomplished when the observer's position relative to a general representation of space can be updated.

This latter ability must be particularly valuable for blind people. That is, in the absence of visual landmark information, blind individuals must rely on a general representation of space that needs to be continually updated in order to remain oriented. In the absence of this ability, updating egocentric responses would be sufficient for planning familiar routes from one location to another. In instances, however, where new routes or detours would have to be constructed, only updating egocentric responses between the self and individual locations would make these tasks rather difficult. Is prior visual experience necessary to generate a general representation of a space? We have been investigating this question with John Rieser by comparing sighted, adventitiously blind and congenitally blind adults' spatial representation of a very familiar environment (Rieser, Lockman, & Pick, in press). In particular, we are interested in whether or not visual experience during a person's lifetime is necessary for the construction of a Euclidian, maplike representation of space. It is possible that lack of visual experience may result in a representation of space constructed along functional lines; understanding the relationship between landmarks in a space would only consist of knowing the route from one location to another. This could be accomplished as noted before by updating a series of egocentric responses.

To investigate this issue we asked sighted, adventitiously blind and congenitally blind adults to make relative distance judgments between pairs of locations in a very familiar space. This was done under two conditions. Subjects were instructed to think in terms of either the straight-line distance or the functional distance between points. These relative distance judgments were then subjected to a multidimensional scaling analysis and the resulting solutions were compared to the actual layout of the space. If visual experience is necessary for the construction of a Euclidian, maplike representation of a space, then the representations generated from the straight-line distance judgments of the sighted and adventitiously blind should be superior to the representations of the congenitally blind. Since all groups have extensive functional experience in the space, there should be little difference between them on the judgments of functional distance between locations.

What were the results? Indeed, the groups did not differ very much from each other on the judgments of functional distance between locations. Moreover, under the straight-line instructions, the scaling solutions of the sighted and adventitiously blind were quite similar and very accurate. Surprisingly, the scaling solutions of the congenitally blind, though not as accurate as either the sighted or adventitiously blind group, did resemble the actual space to a considerable degree. In examining the solutions more carefully, we did find differences under straight-line instructions that could be related to the hypothesized effect of lack of visual experience. For example, particular pairs of landmarks, though separated by a short straight line distance, are actually separated by a large functional distance. If we examine the positions of these landmarks in the representations generated from the sighted and blind groups, we find that the sighted group exaggerates such distances the least; the adventitiously blind group is intermediate; and the congenitally blind group exaggerates distances like these the most. Thus, the results provide some support to the hypothesis that prior visual experience facilitates the formation of accurate spatial representations.

Effect of Experience on Spatial Representation

How might experience affect the nature of mental representation of space? We conceive of two ways. The first is a general way. The life experience of individuals has an effect that makes them different from others without that experience in how they approach spatial situations, perhaps what spatial information they notice, and how that information is encoded. The differences between the spatial representations of the sighted and blind subjects just described may reflect this general effect of experience. The second way experience may affect the nature of one's spatial representations is much more specific. It has to do with how the nature of a particular spatial environment modulates a person's experience in that environment and how this experience affects the mental representation of that particular environment.

Thus, in a particular spatial environment the distance between one pair of points may be represented as greater than another, not because the real distance is greater but because traversing that distance requires greater expenditure of time and/or effort. Or, again, experience may affect one's spatial representation by virtue of how spatial information is acquired by a person. One may learn about a space in a variety of ways and these different experiences may result in different spatial representations. We would like to discuss a number of situations: Some for which there are data; some that seem interesting but that have not yet been investigated experimentally.

The first is the study by Kosslyn, Pick, and Fariello (1974) who taught preschool children and adults the layout of a small space consisting of 10 locations marked on the floor of a square area. The square was subdivided into four quadrants by an opaque barrier or fence, which divided the area in half laterally, and a transparent fence, which divided the square in half longitudinally. There was a small opening in each fence in the center of the space which permitted access to the four quadrants. Each quadrant contained 2 or 3 of the 10 locations. Subjects were trained to go on command directly to each of the 10 locations from a home base. Thus, they never had any specific experience going from one location to another.

After training, they were asked to make comparative judgments of the distances between all pairs of points. Both children and adults could do this, suggesting that they had induced spatial relations with which they had no specific experience. More relevant to the present discussion were the

judgments of equidistant pairs of points that fell within one quadrant or between two quadrants. Specifically, young children represented a distance between two locations as less when it was unobstructed than when there was a
barrier or fence between the two positions. It made no difference whether the
fence was opaque or transparent. Functional distance seemed to be important for these children.

Adults, on the other hand, represented the distance between two locations as less if that distance were unobstructed or only contained a
transparent barrier than when there was an opaque barrier between the locations. Optical distance was more important for the adults than for the
children. The difference between the adults and children may be attributable
to the difference in their life experience and, if so, exemplifies the general effect of experience. Perhaps the greater experience of the adults in dealing
with their spatial environment may help them overcome a biasing effect of
functional distance. Within the group of children or within the adults, the differences due to the nature of the barriers is the kind of effect of *specific* experience referred to before.

Another example of a *specific* biasing effect of functional distance on
spatial representation is a study by one of the present authors (Lockman, in
preparation). Subjects' mental representations of a three-dimensional space
(a two-story house) were investigated using a multidimensional scaling procedure. The subjects who were all familiar with the house ranked the
distance between all pairs of 20 locations, 10 from each floor. These proximity data were scaled for each subject. Although the scaling solutions for
each subject are unusually accurate, functional influences are apparent. In
particular, each subject consistently ranked distances between floors as
greater than comparable distances on the same floor. This effect is quite evident in the solution, presented in Figure 2.4, of one subject's projective view
of the house. Note how the height dimension is exaggerated relative to the
other dimensions, whereas the relationship of locations between the floors in
the other dimensions is preserved. The extra functional effort or distance in
traveling between floors appears to bias the representation of this distance,
although the overall representations are clearly organized in a Euclidian
manner.

This result is another example of a specific biasing effect of functional
distance on spatial representations. It leads one to speculate more generally
about the representation of distances in spaces where functional distance in
terms of time and /or effort conflicts with optical distance. Consider, for example, the representation of distances among sailboats: Sailboat A and B
both have to round the point of land to get to the dock (see Figure 2.5).
Sailboat A is clearly closer to point than B in Euclidian terms. But practically,

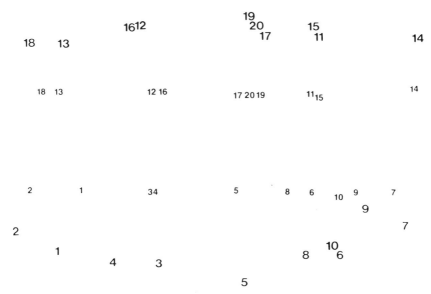

FIGURE 2.4. *One subject's scaling solution for a three-dimensional space (a two-story house). Small numbers represent the actual locations in the space. Large numbers represent the subject's judgment of these locations.*

the point is directly upwind from A and it must sail off on a tack away from the point. Meanwhile, B can round the point on the same course it is on. Moreover, that course is a reach—a particularly fast course relative to wind for most boats. The naïve viewer would presumably represent these distances as B having further to go than A in their cognitive maps. However, would the sophisticated sailor take into account the functional differences in distance between these boats in representing this distance?

Or, consider again spacecraft navigation. Space vehicle A is chasing vehicle B in the same orbit around the Earth. Vehicle A wants to overtake B. The naïve tendency would be simply to speed up. However, this would have the effect of taking A into a deeper orbit and slowing its angular velocity relative to the Earth. That is, the effect would be almost the opposite of that desired. One way for A to overtake B would be to use retrorockets to slow down, which would take A into a shallower faster orbit until it got ahead of B; then A should speed up into a deeper slower orbit at a rate that would permit B to catch up. How would all of this affect the representation of direction in the cognitive maps of astronauts?

Although there has been very little research on the topic, experience must be implicated in the nature of spatial representations by virtue of the way

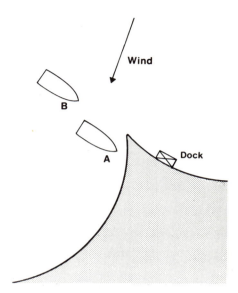

FIGURE 2.5. *Sailboat A is physically closer to the point of land than sailboat B but the point is directly upwind from A. Hence B can get around the point first.*

spatial information is obtained by a person. Most of our work has examined the nature of spatial representations resulting from information obtained through actual experience behaving in a space. The one study in which the nature of that experience was varied was that of Hazen, Lockman, and Pick in which different groups of children were given experience with two different paths through the set of rooms comprising the animal house. One was a U-shaped path and the other was a zig-zag path. Children who did not have very good configurational knowledge of the layout of the house reflected some sense of the different paths they had learned in models of the house that they were asked to build after completing the other probe tests mentioned previously in the description of that study. The models of those children who were exposed to the U-shaped path practically all had a single bend whereas the models of those exposed to the zig-zag path tended to be jagged or staggered.

This manipulation is, of course, a very minor way of varying the input of spatial information. One can conceive, for example, of providing spatial information sequentially-verbally at one extreme and of providing it simultaneously with an aerial view or a map of a space at the other extreme. In between, there are all sorts of variations such as a series of still pictures of a trip through a space (cf. Allen, Kirasec, Siegel, & Herman, 1979), a simulated tour through a space via closed circuit TV, and so on (cf. Walsh et al.). How do the spatial representations vary with the nature of such experience? How important is it that the simulated trip actually preserves a natural sequence?

Can the verbal description be structured especially to make some forms of representations preferable to others? Is this true of the more pictorial or analogous experiences as well?

Summary

The purpose of this chapter was to lead one by a hopefully nonrandom walk from an analysis of frames of reference in spatial orientation to a consideration of certain aspects of mental representations of space. It was suggested first of all that object manipulation is a potentially rich arena in which spatial knowledge and behavior is manifest at a very early age. By analyzing observations from Piaget and particularly the Bayley developmental scales, it was argued that in object-manipulation behaviors object-body relations are mastered by children earlier than object-object relations. If this developmental trend is confirmed, it would be analogous to the shift from egocentric to allocentric frames of reference noted by a number of investigators for locomotive behavior. A similar developmental trend was suggested with respect to spatial representation in object-manipulation tasks. Thus, the use of both these concepts of frame of reference and spatial representation can be generalized from the study of spatial layout to the study of object manipulation.

As the child becomes more and more mobile, not only are more remote frames of reference used but their use becomes progressively sophisticated as reflected in the contingent use of reference systems. In such use, responding to one frame of reference is contingent upon position with respect to another frame of reference. Such complex spatial problems appear to pose particular difficulties for young children.

As the child is confronted by more complex spatial problems, there is also greater need for more sophisticated formation and use of mental representation of space such as would be involved in updating one's position in a representation as one moves through the environment. While this could be done with respect to a motor-encoded or verbally encoded egocentric representation, such as a list of directions for turning, for more complex spaces an integrated simultaneous representation would be more desirable and efficient. Such a representation would more easily permit various kinds of operations in the space such as detour behavior.

It was suggested that the nature of such mental representations may depend on the experience of the person. Experience can be conceived to operate in a very general way as when one's life experience modulates the way spatial problems are confronted—the strategies one uses, or the general nature of the representations one constructs. And experience can be conceived to operate in a very specific way as when the nature of one's experience with a particular space affects the way that space is represented and subsequent behavior in it. There has been relatively little work done on how experience affects spatial representation, but we have good tools now for specifying the nature of representations—and they should be exploited in productive ways.

References

Acredolo, L. P. Frames of reference used by children for orientation in unfamiliar spaces. In G. Moore and R. Gollege (Eds.), *Environmental knowing.* Stroudsburg, Pennsylvania: Dowden, Hutchenson, & Ross, 1976.

Acredolo, L. P. Developmental changes in the ability to coordinate perspectives of a large-scale space. *Developmental Psychology* 1977, *13*, 1-8.

Acredolo, L. P. Development of spatial orientation in infancy. *Developmental Psychology*, 1978, *14*, 224-234.

Allen, G. L., Kirasec, K. C., Siegel, A. W., & Herman, J. F. Developmental issues in cognitive mapping: The selection and utilization of environmental landmarks. *Child development,* 1979, *50*, 1062-1070.

Ashmead, D. H., Lockman, J. J., & Bushnell, E. W. The development of anticipatory hand shaping during infancy. Paper presented at the International Convention on Infant Studies, New Haven, April 1980.

Bayley, N. *Bayley scales of infant development.* New York: Psychological Corporation, 1969.

Bower, T. G. R. *Development in infancy.* San Francisco: Freeman, 1974.

Bremner, J. G., & Bryant, P. E. Place versus response as the basis of spatial errors made by young infants. *Journal of Experimental Child Psychology,* 1977, *23*, 162-171.

Bruner, J. S. The growth and structure of skill. In K. Connolly (Ed.), *Mechanisms of motor skill development.* New York: Academic Press, 1970.

Bruner, J. S., & Koslowski, B. Visually preadapted constituents of manipulatory action. *Perception* 1972, 1, 3-14.

Downs, R. M., and Stea, D. (Eds.), *Image and environment.* Chicago: Aldine, 1973.

Fenson, L., Kagan, J., Kearsley, R. B., & Zelazo, P. The developmental progression of manipulative play in the first two years. *Child Development,*1976, *47*, 232-236.

Gesell, A., & Thompson, H. *Infant behavior.* New York: McGraw-Hill, 1934.

Goldsmith, L. T. The development of contingent coordination of spatial reference systems. Unpublished Ph.D. dissertation, University of Minnesota, 1979.

Halverson, H. M. An experimental study of prehension in infants by means of systematic cinema records. *Genetic Psychology Monographs* 1931, *10*, 107-287.

Hardwick, D. A., McIntyre, C. W., & Pick, H. L., Jr. The content and manipulation of cognitive maps in children and adults. *Monographs of the Society for Research in Child Development,* 1976, *41* (3, Serial No. 166).

Hazen, N. L., Lockman, J., & Pick, H. L., Jr. The development of children's representations of large-scale environments. *Child Development,* 1978, *49*, 623-636.

Hein, A. Acquiring components of visually guided behavior. In A. D. Pick (Ed.), *Minnesota Symposium on Child Psychology, Volume 6.* Minneapolis: University of Minnesota Press, 1972.

Huttenlocher, J., & Presson, C. C. The coding and transformation of spatial information. *Cognitive Psychology*, 1979, *11*, 375-394.

Kosslyn, S. M., Ball, T. M., & Reiser, B. J. Visual images preserve metric spatial information: evidence from studies of image scanning. *Journal of Experimental Psychology: Human Perception and Performance* 1978, *4*, 47-60.

Kosslyn, S. M., Pick, H. L. Jr., & Fariello, G. R. Cognitive maps in children and men. *Child Development*, 1974, *45*, 707-716.

Lasky, R. E., Romano, N., & Winters, J. Spatial localization in children after changes in position. *Journal of Experimental Child Psychology*, 1980, *29*, 225-248.

Lockman, J. J. Upstairs-downstairs: The mental representation of three dimensional space. Manuscript in preparation.

McCall, R. B. Exploratory manipulation and play in the human infant. *Monographs of the Society for Research in Child Development*, 1974, *39* (2, Serial No. 155).

Piaget, J. *The origins of intelligence in children*. New York: International Universities Press. 1952.

Piaget, J. *The construction of reality in the child*. New York: Basic Books, 1954.

Piaget, J., Inhelder, B., & Szeminska, A. *A child's conception of geometry*. New York: Basic Books, 1960.

Pick, H. L., Jr., Yonas, A., & Rieser, J. Spatial reference systems in perceptual development. In M. H. Bornstein and W. Kessen (Eds.), *Psychological development from infancy*. Hillsdale, New Jersey: Lawrence Erlbaum Associates, 1979.

Pinker, S., & Kosslyn, S. M. The representation and manipulation of three-dimensional space in mental images. *Journal of Mental Imagery*, 1978, *2*, 69-84.

Presson, C. C. Spatial egocentrism and the effect of an alternate frame of reference. *Journal of Experimental Child Psychology*, 1980, *29*, 391-402.

Rieser, J. J. Reference systems and the spatial orientation of six month old infants. *Child development*, 1979, *50*, 1078-1087.

Rieser, J. J., Lockman, J. J., & Pick, H. L., Jr. The role of visual experience in spatial representation. *Perception and Psychophysics*, in press.

Smothergill, D. W., Hughes, F. P., Timmons, S. A., & Hutko, P. Spatial visualizing in children. *Developmental psychology* 1975, *11*, 4-13.

Walk, R. D., & Bond, E. K. The development of visually guided reaching in monkeys reared without sight of the hands. *Psychomic science* 1971, *23*, 115-116.

Walsh, D. A., Krauss, I. K., & Regnier, V. A. Spatial ability, environmental knowledge, and environmental use: The elderly. Chapter 12, this volume.

White, B. L., Castle, P., & Held, R. Observations on the development of visually directed reaching. *Child development*, 1964, *35*, 349-364.

Yonas, A., & Pick, H. L., Jr. Infant space perception. In L. Cohen & P. Salapatek (Eds.), *Infant perception*. New York: Academic Press, 1975.

3 Small- and Large-Scale Spatial Concepts in Infancy and Childhood

LINDA P. ACREDOLO

Both environmental psychologists and developmental psychologists have been busy over the past decade acquiring information and advancing theories regarding the interaction between children and their environments. These two groups, however, differ somewhat in their overall goals. In general, Environmentalists are interested in understanding the effects of specific environmental factors on children's attitudes and behavior. For example, what factors facilitate exploration, promote social interaction, contribute to feelings of privacy, or determine whether a child will feel secure? In contrast, Developmentalists often view the child's attitudes and behavior in response to an environment as clues to the nature of the child's cognitive and perceptual development in general. In other words, the environmental interaction is seen as a tool to advance understanding of general developmental processes as much as it is a phenomenon to be understood in itself. It is largely this latter approach that will characterize this chapter.

Further limitation of the subject is still necessary, however. Indeed, if one were to detail all that developmental psychologists alone have learned about children's concepts of small- and large-scale spaces, an entire volume rather than a single chapter would be necessary. Besides, much of this information is already available in useful reviews of the literature (Hart & Moore, 1973; Siegel, Kirasic, & Kail, 1978; Siegel & White, 1975). Consequently, the focus of this chapter will be limited to a sub-issue that has yet to be addressed directly by others, that of small-scale *versus* large-scale space. Direct comparisons of the impact of each on the child will be made by addressing questions such as:

1. What concepts are important to both domains? Are there, in other words, any common denominators?

63

SPATIAL REPRESENTATION AND BEHAVIOR
ACROSS THE LIFE SPAN

2. What evidence do we have that performance differs in the two domains, and if it does, why does it do so?
3. How can the anwsers to these questions help us plan future research
   to answer the questions most effectively that we are interested in having answered?

Ideally, such an approach will not only result in highlighting important
concepts in the development of spatial cognition, but will also give direction
to future research in the field.

Definitions

The first thing needed, of course, are some definitions. Exactly how does
one differentiate between a large- and small-scale space? We know intuitively
that a room or a playground is large-scale and that a Monopoly board is
small-scale, but what are the true defining characteristics? A discussion by Ittelson (1973) is most helpful here. In describing large-scale space he suggests
"The quality of surrounding—the first, most obvious, and defining property—forces the observer to become a participant. One does not, indeed
cannot, observe the environment: one explores it [p. 13]." In other words,
one can be inside a large-scale space but not a small-scale space. Also included in Ittelson's statement is what Huttenlocher and Presson (1979)
refer to as single versus multiple vantage points. While many small-scale
spaces can be viewed from one perspective, a large-scale space, precisely
because it surrounds the individual, can not. This is why exploration or action is necessary, and this is why Ittelson contends that when one flies high
over Manhattan Island, one is no longer viewing an environment, but an object. Why bother distinguishing between "surroundingness" and number of
vantage points if they co-occur in large-scale spaces? Because a small-scale
stimulus can require multiple vantage points *without* surrounding the individual. In the Huttenlocher and Presson study, for example, subjects dealt
with either a large cube mounted on a table and viewed from outside or a
small four-sided room viewed from the inside. Both required multiple vantage points to be completely viewed, but only the room surrounded the subjects as well.

In summary, for the purpose of this chapter, a *large-scale space* will be
defined as one that both surrounds the individual and requires multiple vantage points to be totally apprehended. It will soon become apparent that this
definition is fairly appropriate for the developmental research to be discussed. What it does not do, however, is speak to the concerns of most environmental psychologists for whom a small-scale space is likely to be a

whole room and a large-scale space a neighborhood or city. The task of dealing with the distinction construed in that way I will leave to others.

Similarities

Until this point, differences between these two types of space have been emphasized. Yet, there are clear similarities as well. After all, they both involve spatial relationships among objects. Consequently, we should be able to discover some common denominator across the course of development. For example, one phenomenon they have in common is the phenomenon of "frames of reference" (Hart & Moore, 1973; Pick, 1972; Wapner, Cirillo, & Baker, 1971). In both types of space a child may rely on the relationship between objects themselves (objective or allocentric information) or on the relationship of objects to the child's own body (egocentric information). Thus, for example, Bremner and Bryant (1977) note egocentric responding among 9-month-old infants presented with a small-scale task clearly analogous to a large-scale task reported by Acredolo (1978; Acredolo & Evans, 1980) to also produce egocentric responding at that age. In other cases the specific ages at which particular reference systems predominate may differ, but not the importance of the notion of reference systems to each (e.g., Pufall & Shaw, 1973).

Piaget's assertion (Piaget & Inhelder, 1967; Piaget, Inhelder, & Szeminska, 1960) that development proceeds from topological spatial concepts to projective and Euclidean concepts is also applicable to both kinds of space. Although originally delineated by Piaget using small-scale materials (and reaffirmed by Laurendeau & Pinard, 1970), this course of development has increasingly appeared in descriptions of large-scale spatial performances. With some exceptions (e.g., Siegel & Schadler, 1977, in which knowledge of a large-scale space was tested using a small-scale model) the results of these latter experiments have generally supported Piaget's conclusions regarding the importance of topological concepts before age 7 and the perfection of Euclidean and metric concepts after age 7 (Acredolo, Pick, & Olsen, 1975; Hardwick, McIntyre, & Pick, 1976; Herman & Siegel, 1978). Additional studies with small-scale materials continue to do so as well (Day, 1977; Pufall & Shaw, 1973; Smothergill, 1973a).

However, the use of these terms as generally applied by psychologists to behavioral tasks has come under increasing criticism by mathematicians (Esty, 1979; Kapadia, 1974). In particular, Piaget's notion of "proximity" (Piaget et al., 1960) as a topological concept may need to be re-examined in light of the metric qualities that are automatically involved in deciding that one object is "near" or " not near" another. Within topological space items either touch or do not; there is no room, if you will, for "just a little room" between objects. Consequently, in a strict sense, references to the dependence of young children on nearness to landmarks as "topological" may be misleading. However, whatever mathematical label is used, there is no denying that proximity to landmarks appears to be a crucial component in the young child's ability to deal with both large- and small-scale spaces. It is to this issue that we next turn.

The question of exactly how sensitive children are to landmark information is one that has interested researchers dealing with both large- and small-scale spaces. Two theories highlighting the importance of landmarks have been advanced. According to Hart and Moore (1973) landmarks are important because they form the basis of the type of reference system that supersedes an egocentric system. Instead of relying primarily on the relationship between objects and one's body, the child comes to rely on a fixed frame of reference in which landmarks act as anchor points around which subsets of relationships are organized. These separate anchor points, however, are not yet perceived in correct relationship to each other. This knowledge awaits development of a coordinated reference system. The second theory is that advanced by Siegel and White (1975). They have suggested that knowledge of large-scale space begins with attention to landmarks and is then followed by attention to the routes leading from one landmark to another. Theoretically, then, landmarks are important to cognitive mapping. But what empirical evidence exists to support such a notion?

First let us deal with noninfants, that is, preschoolers and older children, since the research with them came first. Overall the evidence suggests that landmark information *is* important. Pufall and Shaw (1973), for example, used two small-scale identical boards filled with a variety of distinctive features. The child's job was to place a toy on one of them to match the position of an identical toy on the other. Sometimes the boards were aligned and sometimes one was rotated 180°. The finding relevant to the current topic is that the children, particularly by 6 years of age, were quite dependent on the distinctive features as anchor points to help them in both aligned and rotated conditions. Piaget's (Piaget & Inhelder, 1967; Piaget *et al.*, 1960); and Laurendeau and Pinard's (1970) findings with model landscapes also support this conclusion.

A similar picture is revealed by studies in large-scale space. In a study by Acredolo *et al.* (1975), an assessment was made of the ability of children to remember where in a hallway a set of keys had been dropped. When a landmark was present near this site, even preschoolers were remarkably accurate. However, in the absence of landmarks their performance deteriorated quite drastically in contrast to 8-year-olds who still did quite well. The facilitative effect of landmarks was also revealed in a large-scale spatial study (Acredolo, 1977) in which preschoolers were taught to find a trinket hidden either under a cup by the wall to their left or an identical cup by the wall to their right. They were then moved to the opposite side of the room and asked to find the trinket again. When no landmarks at all were present, both the 3-and 4-year-olds behaved quite egocentrically—that is, choosing the cup that was in the same direction relative to their bodies as during training. This tendency, however, practically disappeared when landmarks differentiating the positions of the cups or the starting positions of the children were added. In these conditions the children chose the correct cup from their new position even though it required a turn in the direction opposite to the one learned during training.

The final piece of evidence (Acredolo, 1976) indicates that sensitivity to landmark information is not an "all-or-none" affair. Children were taken into a small room containing walls with distinctive features but only one piece of furniture—a table along one wall. While standing at the table, the children were blindfolded and taken for a short walk in the room. The blindfold was then removed and they were simply asked to return to the place in the room where the walk had begun. Although this sounds simple enough, something was done to make it a little more challenging. While the child was blindfolded, the table was silently moved to the opposite side of the room. Consequently, choice of the table as the starting position was incorrect. In this situation 10-year-old children were not fooled at all, they were completely capable of using *all* of the landmark information in the space, including that contained on the walls themselves, and they immediately chose the correct spot. Many preschoolers, however, *were* fooled. They simply chose the table despite its new position, insisting all the time that it had not been moved.

Now, it can not be denied that these children were using landmark information—the table was a salient landmark—but they were not attending to the more important landmark information available on the walls themselves (including in one experiment a picture window and a door, and in the second experiment one striped wall and one brightly flowered). This issue of age differences in what features are perceived as landmarks has more recently been addressed by Alex Siegel and his associates (Siegel, Chapter 7 of this volume).

Having quickly reviewed some of the evidence indicating the importance of landmarks for preschool and older children, now let us turn to infancy. Are infants as reliant on landmark information as preschoolers appear to be, or do they, as Piaget contends, put higher priority on egocentric relations in which an object's location is based on that object's relation to other stable objects. Piaget's argument stems from his belief that the major task of infancy is the gradual differentiation of the infant's body from the rest of the environment and recognition that objects exist independent of one's actions upon them.

Although Piaget himself gathered casual data (Piaget, 1974) to support his theory, it is only quite recently that researchers have tried to more rigorously test Piaget's predictions about the primacy of egocentricity. Within the domain of small-scale spatial materials, for example, there is some information that the Stage IV (Bremner, 1978; Butterworth, 1975, 1979) and Stage VI (Bower, 1974) object-permanence problems are made easier when highly discriminable occluders are used. In addition, a study by Lucas and Uzgiriz (1977) has revealed that before about 9 months of age, infants are likely to search for an object in the vicinity of a "marker" screen adjacent (visually connected in true topological fashion) to which the object had stood before its invisible displacement to the side behind a moving "transport" screen.

Within the domain of large-scale space, the information about infants and landmarks to this point comes mainly from my own lab (Acredolo, 1978; Acredolo & Evans, 1980) and the work of Rieser (1979; Pick & Lockman, Chapter 2 of this volume). In the case of my own studies, the procedures are very simple (see Figure 3.1). An infant is seated at S_1 in a 10 × 10 ft (3.2 × 3.2 m) curtained enclosure and trained to expect the occurrence of an interesting event, an experimenter appearing and interacting verbally, at one of two identical windows every time a buzzer is heard. The question is what does the baby learn about the location of that event: that it is in a particular location objectively, or perhaps that it is always in the same direction relative to the child's body.

There is one easy way to find out: Simply move the baby to the opposite end of the room, S_2, sound the buzzer, and see which way he or she looks in anticipation of the experimenter's appearance. If the objective spatial relations are understood, then the infant should simply look back to the correct window. However, if egocentric relationships receive priority, then the infant will repeat a turn in the same direction as during training—a response that will result in a look to the wrong window. Finally, if the infant is unsure which is correct, this may even be indicated by looks to both windows. Once the baby is in S_2, five test trials take place in which the buzzer is sounded but no event occurs.

In the most recent study using this basic procedure, groups of infants aged 6, 9, and 11 months were tested in four landmark conditions (Acredolo & Evans, 1980). The subjects in the no landmark group had no information in the space to help them differentiate the windows. Those in the star landmark group had a yellow star around the target window. Those in the direct lights

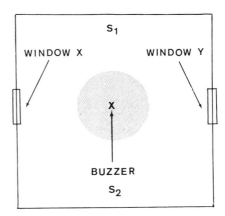

FIGURE 3.1. *Experimental space.*

and stripes group saw a panel of flashing lights around the target window and stripes on that wall. Finally, those in the indirect lights and stripes group saw the lights and stripes, but around the nontarget window, the one at which the event never occurred. In this last case the question was whether infants would use landmark information *relationally* (i.e., "She'll be at the nonlighted window," or "She'll be at the window opposite the lights"). Presented in Figure 3.2 are the results of an analysis based on categorization of each infant into one of three groups based on their behavior during the five test trials: *egocentric* (infant turns only to wrong window), *objective* (infant turns only to correct window), or *mixed* (infant turns toward both windows either on the same or across different trials). All infants fell into one of these categories.

Results

There were no age differences in the no landmark condition; subjects at all ages responded egocentrically. It appears, therefore, that when no information differentiates the two windows, infants in the first year do not keep track of their position relative to an interesting event even when their movement through the space is relatively simple.[1] In the star condition, however, egocentric responding did decrease some among the 11-month-olds, resulting in a significant difference between the 6-month-olds and the 11-month-olds, with the 9-month-olds falling in-between. However, it is readily apparent that the star's impact was not overwhelming. The results

---

[1] Additional data involving separating the child from the mother during the rotation to the opposite side leads us to believe that egocentric responding here is not simply due to the infant's being unaware that movement has taken place.

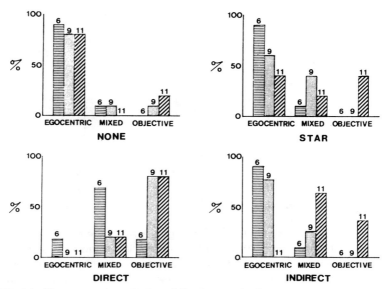

FIGURE 3.2. *The percentages of infants falling into each of three categories of responses in four conditions. (From Acredolo, L. P., & Evans, D. Some determinants of the infant's choice of spatial reference system. Paper presented at the biennial meeting of the Society for Research in Child Development, San Francisco, 1979.)*

from these two groups essentially replicate those from the earlier study in which these procedures were used (Acredolo, 1978).

What about the direct lights and stripes? Does a very salient landmark facilitate objective responding? The answer is a resounding "yes," the percentage of egocentric responders falling close to zero for all three ages. However, there was a significant and very interesting age difference in what replaced egocentric responding at each age. For 80% of the infants at the two older ages the presence of these landmarks enabled them to respond consistently objectively as though they were firmly convinced of the event's location. For the 6-month-olds, in contrast, 67% were mixed responders; this indicates that they were checking out *both* windows. What might account for this uncertainty at 6 months? Perhaps it is due to the competition of the two reference systems each specifying a different window, with the 6-month-olds simply finding it harder than the older subjects to ignore the egocentric information in favor of the landmark information. But could the infants have simply been looking at the lights during the test trials because they were pretty and not because of their landmark value? Four points make us think not:

1. If the lights were that captivating one would expect them to facilitate the original training; however, no training time differences were found.
2. The training trials averaged about 10 in number and could be expected to result in some habituation to the lights.
3. The recorded responses were only those immediately contingent on the buzzer.
4. And finally, if the lights are simply attractive and not informative, one would expect this to be especially true for the youngest age group. Yet it was this group that showed a high proportion of turns to the nonlighted window as well.

The only condition left to be discussed is the indirect landmark condition. The results showed that the 11-month-olds were the only group to use the landmark information relationally; the 6- and 9-month-olds still showed high proportions of egocentric responding. However, as with the 6-month-olds in the last condition, a large proportion (63%) of the 11-month-olds replaced egocentric responding with mixed responding—not with consistently objective responding—thus indicating some uncertainty about the landmark information. So, to review quickly, we found evidence that dependence upon past actions, what Piaget calls egocentricity, does hinder infants from keeping track of their position in space. However, objective responding is facilitated when particularly salient landmarks are present directly marking the target position. This facilitation, though, is greater at age 9 and 11 months than at 6 months. Finally, the ability to use landmark information relationally appears to be a fairly late achievement; our 11-month-olds even showed some uncertainty. However, in answer to the very general question being posed here, landmarks definitely do play a role in the ability of infants to act in large- and small-scale spaces. And, to the extent that a given task requires reliance upon memory, one can even say that the landmarks facilitate representation of important aspects of the space.

Differences

Having reviewed a few of the common denominators of small- and large-scale spatial behavior, particularly the impact of landmarks, let us now turn to the question of whether differences actually exist. Unfortunately, this question is not easy to answer because very few researchers have made actual direct comparisons between spaces. However, the results of those few that have made such comparisons are very suggestive. For example, Acredolo (1977) trained children to find a trinket hidden either to their right or left. The children were then moved to the opposite side of the space and allowed to search. Performance of this task in a specially constructed, landmark-free large-scale space resulted in significantly less "egocentric" responding among 5-year-olds than 3- and 4-year-olds. However, this age difference disappeared completely when the task was presented in a regular classroom using a small-scale model of the landmark-less room; there was practically no egocentrism exhibited at all.

A second example comes from the work of Piaget and Inhelder (1967) on the development of knowledge of horizontal and vertical axes. As one of their indices, they tested the ability of children to position trees correctly on the side of a hill. What they discovered, among many other things, was a discrepancy between performance of this task with a real sand hill and with a picture of a hill. At one particular stage of development, the children who were still drawing trees perpendicularly to the drawn hill were placing them vertically on the real hill.

Keogh (1971) presents us with a third example. The dependent variable here was the ability to copy a simple two-dimensional figure. Not very surprising, but in contrast to Piaget and Inhelder's results, Keogh found that when the copying was done by drawing the figures on paper, performance for girls was significantly superior to that resulting from walking out the patterns on the floor.

The final example is a recent study by Huttenlocher and Presson (1979). As part of an attempt to extend some of their earlier findings regarding differences between perspective-taking and rotation tasks (Huttenlocher & Presson, 1973), they compared use of a 2 ft-high cube mounted on a table and viewed from outside with use of a 5 ft-high room viewed from inside. Subjects in both cases were asked either to predict the outcome of their own rotation or rotation of the array. The finding relevant to the present issue is that the pattern of results depended in some important cases on which stimulus array was involved. When predictions of views different from 0° were involved, the room stimulus resulted in viewer-rotation being easier than array-rotation, whereas no difference was found with the cube. In addition, the proportion of egocentric responses (picking one's current view) in the viewer-rotation task exceeded that expected by chance for the cube ($p <$ .05) but not for the room ($p >$ .40). With this study then, we have two additional demonstrations that small- and large-scale spaces do not necessarily yield the same behaviors.

But why? What variables are responsible for the differences just outlined? Many possibilities exist, and quite probably the answer in the case of an individual study will involve different combinations of factors. One clear candidate is the mode of response involved in each. When, as in the Keogh (1971) study, performance in the two spaces requires very different motor abilities (e.g., drawing versus walking), we should not be very surprised to find different developmental patterns. These may stem in part from simple muscular differences, in that it takes different muscles to hold a pencil from those it does to walk. However, they may also stem from differences in higher order representational processes—for example, differences in the sensorimotor schema that have been acquired or the intermodal coordinations that have been achieved.

A second factor, which is undoubtedly involved, is the manner in which the different scaled spaces are viewed. As mentioned earlier, many small-scale models can be apprehended from a single vantage point, something that is not possible when one is located within a space. This factor, for example, probably contributed to the difference found by Acredolo (1977) between the landmark-less room and the small-scale model. When only a single vantage point is necessary, the memory load is reduced and the additional problem of coordinating different perspectives is eliminated. The problems that can arise for a child from moving around in complicated patterns within a space are exemplified by a finding in the Acredolo study: A large part of the problem for the 4-year-olds was a failure to realize that their position had changed during the test trials. When simply reminded that they had moved to the opposite side of the large-scale space, their performance became less egocentric.

Although these two variables, response mode and number of vantage points, may be important contributors, there is a third factor—yet to be recognized by most researchers—that I think is even more significant. Every small-scale space we have used in psychology has, by definition, been located within a large-scale space; that fact opens up the possibility that the large-scale space may provide useful information to subjects as they deal with the problem posed by the small-scale materials (Acredolo, 1973; 1974).[2]

The notion that the larger environment might have an impact on performance of a small-scale task has a long history in psychology. As far back as the early 1900s, psychologists such as Porter (1906) and Hunter (1911) were demonstrating that the performances of birds in mazes were disrupted by rotating the mazes relative to the external environment, thus indicating dependence on extramaze cues. Rats entered the picture with Watson in 1907 with similar results, and have continued to be the source of such data via Carr (1917) and through the 1940s with Tolman's rats ("buried in thought" but all the time gazing at a light in the lab), and up to 1976 with the work of Olton and Samuelson. These studies are consistent in indicating that the larger environment is a source of information for animals.

Can any less be true for humans? Some of the earliest data involving

---

[2] This same point has been more recently expressed by Huttenlocher and Presson (1979) as well.

humans performing a spatial task comes from the work of a Mr. Wilson as reported in a 1923 textbook by Smith and Guthrie. Subjects were required to learn to type a list of letters on a typewriter with keys arranged in a random order. Twenty-four hours later the same list was typed again and the amount of time to perfection was recorded. The crucial variable was whether or not the environment for this latter session was the same as during the original learning. And how was the environment changed? Was the subject's position relative to the typewriter altered? Was the typewriter moved in relation to the background? No. The environment was actually changed by infusing the room with the odor of peppermint; Mr. Wilson found that this environmental change affected performance. If you think psychology has progressed far beyond the use of peppermint since then, consider the study of rats in mazes done by Olton and Samuelson in 1976: They used Old Spice and Mennen's aftershave to alter a maze. However, in all fairness, it must be added that the theoretical justification here (dependence on olfactory cues) was a good deal stronger. Accuracy, by the way, was not affected.

The first real experimental evidence indicating reliance by children on large-scale spatial information while performing a small-scale task was provided by Lucille Emerson (1931) in an obscure study, which has escaped the notice of most reviewers. In this study, children aged 3–5 were each presented with an easel from which protruded six rows of seven pegs. The experimenter placed a ring on one of them and the subject's task was to place a ring on the corresponding peg of a second easel which varied in its position relative to the first. The placement most important to this issue is the one in which the easels were back-to-back so that the child had to walk around the first easel and end up facing the opposite direction while placing his own ring. An egocentric placement in this condition was considered correct. In other words, if the ring was on the left side of the experimenter's easel as the subject viewed it and the subject placed his ring on the appropriate peg of the left side of his easel, the response was considered correct.

When the easels were alongside one another, the subjects of the study made the most "correct" responses (534 our of 600, or 89%); however, when the easels were back-to-back the subjects made the fewest "correct" responses (48 out of 600, or 8%). The most interesting finding of the study was that many of the errors in the back-to-back condition were reversals of left and right, that is, placement of the ring on a peg on the right side of the subject's easel when the experimenter's ring was on a peg on the left side of his easel. Over 40% of the errors were pure left–right reversals of this type. The same pattern of errors was found for a similar condition in which the easels were facing each other and the child had to turn 180° from the experimenter's easel to see his own. How might one explain such a pattern of errors? To Emerson (1931), and to me, it seemed obvious that, "the children of this study used some external object as a point of reference rather than their own bodies [p. 140]." In other words, the children were coding the experimenter's peg as toward a certain part of the larger space. When they moved around to their own easel they had to reverse the left-right dimension in order to maintain the relationship they had observed with the external referents.

In what was expected to be a study simply showing increased ability over age to manipulate visual images, Smothergill and his associates (1973b, 1975) happened upon a similar pattern of results for 5-year-olds. The task materials consisted of two "Y" shapes, one of which had an upper arm marked with a yellow spot. The subject's task was to place a yellow spot of his own on the arm of the second Y that corresponded to the marked arm of the standard Y. As in the Emerson study, the easels upon which the Y's were mounted were alongside of each other on some trials and back-to-back on others. In addition, Smothergill varied the up-down orientation of the subject's Y whereas the standard Y was always in an upright position.

Once again a "correct" response was defined as an egocentric response when the comparison Y was upright; when the Y was upside-down, a "correct" response was an egocentric response rotated through 180°. As expected, performance improved with age, but according to Smothergill (1973b), the 5-year-olds "behaved curiously, at least to us if not them [p. 7]." Actually, these children were merely using the relation of the stimuli to the external environment as their frame of reference rather than the relation of the stimuli to their own bodies. As a result, in the alongside condition they performed better than average when their Y was upright, but worse than chance when it was upside-down. Likewise, in the back-to-back condition they performed below chance when their Y was upright and above chance when it was rotated 180°. After repeating the experiment and getting the same results, Smothergill concluded that:

> The young child is not egocentric. It might be said that he centrates on one feature of the environment, or that he does not possess the mental skills to deal with the Y as a unit within itself, but he seems anything but egocentric. Because rather than using himself as a referent for spatial judgments, he seems to be using something outside of himself as a referent [p. 10].

The obvious importance of the work of these two researchers is that it highlights the danger of using the label "egocentric" when the egocentric frame of reference is confounded with an objective frame of reference based on the larger environment. Such confounding occurs when the child remains in a constant position relative to the task materials and is, therefore, unfortunately common in traditional studies of perspective-taking and mental rotation.

What additional evidence do we have to support the claim that the larger space affects performance with small-scale spatial materials? First, let us refer back to Piaget and Inhelder's work on the development of knowledge of horizontal and vertical axes mentioned earlier in which they observed correct vertical placement of trees on a sand mountain by children who were still portraying these items perpendicularly in a drawing of a mountain. Piaget and Inhelder themselves conclude that the environment external to the sand mountain was responsible:

> This is probably because the sand mountain is an object standing in the room, with the vertical axis suggested by the walls, legs of tables and chairs, etc. The drawings, on the other hand, invariably give rise to perpendiculars because they contain only the slopes of the mountain on which the objects rest (and which all these objects are related to), and not the sheet of paper itself, which is perceived simply as a "ground [1967, p. 400]."

Second, consider the study by Acredolo (1977) mentioned previously in which preschool children were found to rely on egocentric information to find a trinket hidden in a real, landmark-less room, but on objective information in a small-scale model of the same room. While many variables may be contributing, it does seem reasonable to suggest that one helpful factor was the fact that the model was presented in a classroom with many potential landmarks available to help the child keep track of the trinket's location.

Evidence of a more direct nature comes from a recent and very interesting study by Herman and Siegel (1978) in which 5-, 7-, and 10-year-old children were required to replace toy buildings of a relatively large model village after various amounts of exposure to the village.[3] The first of the two reported experiments yielded results indicating that even the youngest children could accurately replace the buildings after repeated exposure—even when those buildings were isolated from other landmarks within the village. Moreover, the repeated exposure eliminated any age differences. These results seem, therefore, to indicate rather sophisticated knowledge of metric relations on the part of children supposedly restricted to dealing with topological properties.

A second experiment with the same village, however, produced a very different pattern of results. In this case, even after repeated exposure to the village, the 5-year-olds barely reached half the accuracy they had shown in Experiment 1 and half the accuracy shown by the two older age groups. In addition, accuracy with the isolated buildings was particularly low. Why the tremendous discrepancy? The answer lies in the only difference between the

---

[3] I realize that classifying a 4.9 × 6.1 m village through which a child can walk as a small-scale model is debatable. My main reason for doing so here stems from the fact that the village was viewable from a single vantage point since one could step out into the larger space.

two experiments: the nature of the environment external to the model. In Experiment 1 the village was set on the floor of a regular classroom with the furniture pushed to the perimeter, while in Experiment 2 it was set in the middle of the floor of a very large gymnasium. In the first case we have what Herman and Siegel refer to as a "bounded" space while in the second an "unbounded" space, and it is clear that the bounded space facilitated performance. How? By providing topological relations (landmarks) to augment those available in the village itself. Herman and Siegel (1978) conclude:

> These data, in the light of the difference in the experimental space, cast serious doubt on our earlier speculation that kindergarteners have a reasonable working knowledge of Euclidean spatial relations which is masked by various methodological artifacts. Clearly the level of accuracy attained by the kindergarteners might well be attributable entirely to the use of topological relations [p. 403].

The facilitating effect of a bounded as compared to an unbounded space was also demonstrated in the study by Keogh (1971). In addition to comparing the ability of children to draw and walk simple two-dimensional figures, Keogh compared walking accuracy when done on a 9 × 9 ft mat with accuracy when done without the mat simply in the middle of the floor of a large, empty school cafeteria. As in the Herman and Siegel study, the use of the unbounded space resulted in poorer performance on the part of the males; thus indicating once again the impact of the larger space on the specific task performed within.

All of studies cited so far as evidence have dealt with preschool children. What about infants? Does sensitivity to the environment external to task materials await the years beyond infancy? Some data we have just recently collected suggests quite strongly that the answer is "no." Infants can also be influenced by the larger space. Evidence in support of this conclusion comes from a recent study (Acredolo, 1979) in which a scaled down version of the large-scale procedure described previously (Acredolo, 1978; Acredolo & Evans, 1980) was used. Instead of an event occurring at one of two windows, a toy was hidden under one of two identical cloths placed on a small table, one to the right of the infant's midline, one to the left. In addition, instead of training the child to criterion to turn in one direction before rotation to the opposite side, in this case no training trials (except to a midline position in an initial phase) were used. The child simply was shown the object being hidden once to the right or left and then was immediately rotated to the opposite side of the table and allowed to search.

Why were the training trials eliminated? The reason, although tangential to the present issue, is really very important. The training trials were eliminated in order to determine whether the kind of egocentric responding observed in the large-scale task and in similar small-scale tasks (Bremner & Bryant, 1977) really is a function of reliance on an egocentric spatial framework or is instead simply a repetition of a learned motor habit. If the latter is true and we are simply seeing repetition of a learned behavior, then elimination of the training trials should eliminate what we have been calling "egocentricity" and should allow the child to choose objectively. However, if an egocentric frame of reference is actually involved, then elimination of the training trials should not result in a decrease in egocentric responding. Infants should continue choosing the wrong cloth from the 180° position.

What *is* relevant to this issue is the fact that the infant's performance depended strongly on the larger environment in which the task was presented. Quite simply, only 15% of the infants tested in their homes chose egocentrically, compared to 77% of those tested in a landmark-less laboratory enclosure and 77% of those tested in a landmark-filled office. This high proportion of egocentric responding in the laboratory and office environment in the absence of specific motor training is a clear indication that reliance on a body-centered or "egocentric" frame of reference does occur among infants, particularly in unfamiliar environments. In terms of the present issue, however, it is obviously the discrepancy between behavior in the home and the two unfamiliar environments that is most intriguing. Although it is possible that purely motivational factors account for this "home court advantage," it is also quite possible that the answer lies instead in the greater knowledge infants have of the spatial layout of their home—knowledge that facilitates their attempts to keep track of a toy's location.

Conclusions

In the preceding discussions I have tried to show (a) that both infants and children are sensitive to landmark information; (b) that this sensitivity may be resulting more often than we realize in the larger space affecting performance on small-scale spatial materials; and (c) that this situation probably helps account for many of the discrepancies noted in the literature between performances in large-scale environments and with small-scale models. If these arguments are correct, then the following points deserve some consideration as well.

First, it is absolutely imperative that researchers working with small-scale spatial materials in the future consider the potential information the larger environment is providing. At the very least, the nature of the larger environment should be routinely reported; at the other extreme, perhaps researchers might consider some ways of shielding subjects from such information as the small-scale tasks are performed. Until this is done there will continue to be occasions when egocentric and objective frames of reference will be confounded and when topological relations will masquerade as projective or Euclidean knowledge.

Second, actual investigation of the parameters involved in the impact of the larger environment on the small needs to be undertaken. Are there, for example, particular ages at which such influence most clearly plays a role? Piaget's notions of the importance of topological relations early in childhood may be suggestive here. In addition, are there particular spatial tasks or particular levels of task difficulty that are most likely to result in reliance by the child on extra-task information? And, finally, are there perhaps individual differences (such as field-dependence, field-independence) in the tendency for children to do so? These and many other questions remain.

Third, consideration should also be given to the reverse possibility —namely, that manipulation of small-scale materials may actually influence behavior in large-scale spaces. After all, that is exactly what map-reading is all about. Although not discussed in detail here, the role of maps in the development of spatial cognition is a potentially very interesting one (Bluestein & Acredolo, 1979). Quite closely related to this point is the observation made by Hart (Chapter 8 of this volume) that building extensive models of their town served in some instances to sensitize children to the real spatial environment so that their subsequent spatial experiences in the large space were enriched by their experiences with the small. Finally, there is the suggestion made by Downs and Stea (1977) that the hours young children spend gleefully manipulating toy farms and villages may be playing an instrumental role in helping them conceive of real-life, large-scale spatial relations. This possibility deserves careful consideration and some empirical investigation.

Finally, I think it almost goes without saying that we must exercise more caution now than we have in the past when we are tempted to extrapolate from research with small-scale tasks to problems involving large-scale environments. If we want to find out how children navigate through large-scale environments, that's exactly what we should study. It may be more difficult to come up with effective designs, and it certainly is more taxing to gather the data, but in the long run the price will be worth it because the answers discovered will more closely fit the actual questions asked.

References

Acredolo, L. P. The growth of where-am-I: The development of spatial orientation. Unpublished manuscript, University of Minnesota, 1973.

Acredolo, L. P. Frames of reference used by children for orientation in unfamiliar spaces. Doctoral thesis, University of Minnesota, 1974.

Acredolo, L. P. Frames of reference used by children for orientation in unfamiliar spaces. In G. Moore & R. Golledge (Eds.), *Environmental knowing*. Stroudsburg, Pennsylvania: Dowden, Hutchinson & Ross, 1976.

Acredolo, L. P. Developmental changes in the ability to coordinate perspectives of a large-scale space. *Developmental Psychology*, 1977, *13*, 1-8.

Acredolo, L. P. Development of spatial orientation in infancy. *Developmental Psychology*, 1978, *14*, 224-234.

Acredolo, L. P. Laboratory versus home: The effect of environment on the nine-month-old infant's choice of spatial reference system. *Developmental Psychology*, 1979, *15*, 666-667.

Acredolo, L. P., & Evans, D. Developmental changes in the effects of landmarks on infant spatial behavior. *Developmental Psychology*, 1980, *16*, 312-318.

Acredolo, L. P., Pick, H. L., & Olsen, M. G. Environmental differentiation and familiarity as determinants of children's memory for spatial location. *Developmental Psychology*, 1975, *11*, 495-501.

Bluestein, N., & Acredolo, L. P. Developmental changes in map-reading skills. *Child Development*, 1979, *50*, 691-697.

Bower, T. G. R. *Development in infancy*. San Francisco: Freeman, 1974.

Bremner, J. G. Egocentric versus allocentric spatial coding in nine-month-old infants: Factors influencing the choice of code. *Developmental Psychology*, 1978, *14*, 346-355.

Bremner, J. G., & Bryant, P. E. Place versus response as the basis of spatial errors made by young infants. *Journal of Experimental Child Psychology*, 1977, *23*, 162-171.

Butterworth, G. Mapping the self onto the world in infancy. Paper presented at the International Society for the Study of Behavioral Development, University of Surrey, England, July 1975.

Butterworth, G. Logical competence in infancy: Object percept or object concept? Paper presented to the Biennial Meeting of the Society for Research in Child Development, San Francisco, March 1979.

Carr, H. Maze studies with the white rat. *Journal of Animal Behavior*, 1917, *7*, 259-275.

Day, J. D. Veridical and inferential memory for the spatial layout of a small house. Unpublished Masters thesis, University of Illinois, Urbana, 1977.

Downs, R., & Stea, D. *Maps in minds*. New York: Harper & Row, 1977.

Emerson, L. L. The effect of bodily orientation upon the young child's memory for position of objects. *Child Development*, 1931, *2*, 125-142.

Esty, E. The development of children's conceptions of space: An analysis of the topological to Euclidean hypothesis. Paper presented at the Biennial Meeting of the Society for Research in Child Development, San Francisco, March 1979.

Fehr, L., & Fishbein, F. The effects of an explicit landmark on spatial judgments. In R. Suedfeld & J. Russell (Eds.), *The behavioral basis of design* (book 1). Stroudsburg, Pennsylvania: Dowden, Hutchinson, & Ross, 1976.

Hardwick, D. A., McIntyre, C. W., & Pick, H. L. The content and manipulation of cognitive maps in children and adults. *Monographs of the Society for Research in Child Development*, 1976, *41*, (3, Serial no. 166).

Hart, R. A., & Moore, G. The development of spatial cognition: A review. In R. M. Downs & D. Stea (Eds.), *Image and environment*. Chicago: Aldine, 1973.

Herman, J. F., & Siegel, A. W. The development of cognitive mapping of the large-scale environment. *Journal of Experimental Child Psychology*, 1978, *26*, 389-406.

Hunter, W. S. Some labyrinth habits of the domestic pigeon. *Journal of Animal Behavior*, 1911, *1*, 278-304.

Huttenlocher, J., & Presson, C. Mental rotation and the perspective problem. *Cognitive Psychology*, 1973, *4*, 279-299.

Huttenlocher, J. & Presson, C. The coding and transformation of spatial information. *Cognitive Psychology*, 1979, *11*, 375-394.

Ittelson, W. H. Environment perception and contemporary perceptual theory. In W. H. Ittelson (Ed.), *Environment and cognition*. New York: Seminar Press, 1973.

Kapadia, R. A critical examination of Piaget-Inhelder's view on topology. *Educational Studies in Mathematics*, 1974, *5*, 419-424.

Keogh, B. Pattern copying under three conditions of an extended spatial field. *Developmental Psychology*, 1971, *4*, 25-41.

Laurendeau, M., & Pinard, A. *The development of the concept of space in the child*. New York: International Universities Press, 1970.

Lucas, T. C., & Uzgiriz, I. C. Spatial factors in the development of the object concept. *Developmental Psychology*, 1977, *13*, 492-500.

Olton, D. S., & Samuelson, R. J. Remembrance of places passed: Spatial memory in rats. *Journal of Experimental Psychology: Animal Behavior Processes*, 1976, *2*, 97-116.

Piaget, J. *The construction of reality in the child*. New York: Ballantine Books, 1974.

Piaget, J., & Inhelder, B. *The child's conception of space*. New York: Norton, 1967.

Piaget, J., Inhelder, B., & Szeminska, A. *A child's conception of geometry*. New York: Basic Books, 1960.

Pick, H. L. Mapping children-mapping space. American Psychological Association, Honolulu, September 1972.

Porter, J. P. Further study of the English sparrow and other birds. *American Journal of Psychology*, 1906, *17*, 248-271.

Pufall, P. B., & Shaw, R. Analysis of the development of children's spatial reference systems. *Cognitive Psychology*, 1973, *5*, 151-175.

Rieser, J. Spatial Orientation of Six-Month-Old Infants. *Child Development*, 1979, *50*, 1078-1087.

Siegel, A. W., Kirasic, K. C., & Kail, R. V. Stalking the elusive cognitive map: The development of children's representations of geographic space. In J. F. Wohlwill & I. Altman (Eds.), *Human behavior and environment: Children and the environment* (Vol. 3). New York: Plenum, 1978.

Siegel, A. W., & White, S. H. The development of spatial representations of large-scale environments. In H. W. Reese (Ed.), *Advances in child development and behavior* (Vol. 10). New York: Academic Press, 1975.

Siegel, A. W., & Schadler, M. young children's cognitive maps of their classroom. *Child Development*, 1977, *48*, 388-394.

Smith, S., & Guthrie, E. R. *General psychology in terms of behavior*. New York: D. Appleton and Co., 1923.

Smothergill, D. W. Accuracy and variability in the localization of spatial targets at three age levels. *Developmental Psychology*, 1973, *8* 62-66. (a)

Smothergill, D. W. Spatial development in children: Mental manipulation of form images. Paper presented at the Biennial Meeting of the Society for Research in Child Development, Philadelphia, March 1973. (b)

Smothergill, D. W., Hughes, F. P., Timmons, S. A., & Hutko, P. Spatial visualizing in children. *Developmental Psychology*, 1975, *11*, 4-13.

Wapner, S., Cirillo, L., & Baker, A. H. Some aspects of the development of space perception. In J. P. Hill (Ed.), *Minnesota symposia on child psychology* (Vol. 5). Minneapolis: University of Minnesota Press, 1971.

Watson, J. B. Kinaesthetic and organic sensations: Their role in the reactions of the white rat to the maze. *Psychological Monographs*, 1907, *8* (no. 33).

Sex-Related Variations in Spatial Skill

LAUREN JULIUS HARRIS

Introduction

Friends of mine who know of my interest in spatial ability like to regale me with tales of route-finding gone awry, maps misread, and left and right confused. Mostly, my informants are men, and they are speaking, of course, not of themselves, but of the women with whom they have traveled. (All of them, one might suppose, are spiritual cousins to those recruits in the Czar's Army who marched to "hayfoot, strawfoot" rather than right, left.) The women do not usually disagree with the men's characterization, though more than one have noted that it was the man who got them lost on their last trip—usually because of his mulish refusal to admit he was lost and to stop and ask for directions. (Remember, too, that the Czar's soldiers were men.) Nevertheless, both the men and women agree that women have more difficulty.

These are only anecdotal accounts, but they are in accord with the results of formal surveys. For instance, we asked Michigan State University faculty members (294 men, 36 women) to reply to the statement: "As an adult, I have noted difficulty when I quickly have to identify right versus left." Only 16% of the men compared with 30% of the women reported being confused either "occasionally," "frequently," or "all the time," whereas 85% of the men and 70% of the women reported being confused "never" or "rarely" (Harris & Gitterman, 1978). We also asked college students the more general question: "How good is your sense of direction?" Men's self-ratings were significantly higher than women's (Thompson, Harris, & Mann, 1980).

People, of course, entertain all sorts of mistaken notions about themselves; in some cases, no doubt, they do this to insure consonance with

83

SPATIAL REPRESENTATION AND BEHAVIOR
ACROSS THE LIFE SPAN

their gender identity. Since sense of direction is probably a highly valued attribute for males, men simply might be less willing to admit to a deficiency. Still, the question is whether both men's and women's self-descriptions about spatial ability would conform reasonably well to their performance on objective tests. The evidence available so far suggests that self-ratings and performance *are* related (Kozlowski & Bryant, 1977), and other evidence shows, as we shall see in the review to follow, that the male's skills on spatial tasks are significantly greater.

As our questionnaire study had suggested, we did indeed find that women, when actually tested, were less accurate than men at telling the difference quickly between left and right. We briefly (3 sec) projected pictures of hands, feet, ears, and eyes shown in different orientations and asked college students to identify them as left or right. The women made significantly more errors than the men (Harris & Gitterman, 1977; see also Bakan & Putnam, 1974).

In identification tests like this one, some people say that before they can give the correct left-right name, they must mentally rotate or turn the drawing until it is congruent with (i.e., in the same orientation as) the same (left or right) part of their own body. Males also excel in "rotation" tasks when left-right labeling is not required. An example is a test in which the subject must decide whether pairs of drawings of geometric designs (usually asymmetrically stacked cubes) are of the same or different shapes. The degree of rotation between the pair varies on each trial from 20° to 180° by 20° intervals (Shepard & Metzler, 1971). In tests of fourth- and eighth-grade children (Kail & Carter, 1980), high-school students (Metzler & Shepard, 1974, p. 153), and college students (Tapley & Bryden, 1977), females took significantly longer than males to reach a decision, and made significantly more errors as well. In the case of the primary-school children, tests were modified to reveal processes underlying problem solution. Boys and girls proved to be very similar in most aspects of performance. The boys' superiority was linked to a single component of processing—the rate of mental rotation (Kail & Carter, 1980).

Still other tests, rather than calling only for "rotation" of a whole figure, also require the mental "folding" of a two-dimensional geometric pattern into a three-dimensional figure. An example is the Space Relations subtest of the Differential Aptitude Test (Bennett, Seashore, & Wesman, 1959). The subject must match the unfolded pattern to one of four completed figures, which vary from each other in shape, shading, or orientation. Again, males generally solve these tasks more accurately and quickly than females do.

"Mental rotation" (or "folding") tasks like those just described constitute one variety of spatial task. The so-called perceptual disembedding test represents another type. The best-known example is the embedded figures test, in which the subject must find, or disembed, a simple geometric form hidden in a complex geometric design. Males usually are faster and more frequently accurate than females (Witkin, Dyk, Faterson, Goodenough, & Karp, 1962).

There is another sense of the term "spatial ability" that neither mental rotation, pattern folding, nor perceptual disembedding tasks seem to capture, at least not in any very obvious way. That other sense is what we familiarly call "sense of direction," or way-finding ability.

When we asked college students to rate their "sense of direction," we left the interpretation of the term up to them. At perhaps its most basic level, "sense of direction" involves proprioception—knowledge of one's own orientation in space. The rod-and-frame test incorporates this feature, although it is conventionally classed with the embedded figures test as a perceptual disembedding test. The subject, usually seated in a darkened room, must adjust a tilted luminescent square frame; sometimes the subject's chair may be tilted as well. Particularly in the latter case, setting the rod to the gravitational upright would depend on the subject's knowing his own body orientation in space. Males usually are more accurate than females on this test (Witkin *et al.*, 1962).

On the rod-and-frame test, the subject, when tilted, must know whether he (as well as the frame) is tilted to the left or right in order to make the necessary correction in the rod. But the subject does not have to know whether the particular direction is left or right. That is, left–right discrimination, in the sense of being able to apply to a direction in space a label that itself contains no directional information, is not required. We presumably would be no more (or less) accurate on the rod-and-frame test if we only had the expressions "this way" and "that way." At another level, though, sense of direction could refer to our mastery of the conventional directional terms as descriptors of our movement through a spatial layout; in other words, knowing whether, when we turn "this way," it is to our left or our right.

I earlier cited reports that women are less accurate than men in quickly identifying a picture of a part of the body as a left or right part. Under speeded conditions, a similar difference appears in describing their own movements. An example is the "Road-Map Test of Direction Sense." The test consists of an outline map of city streets. The subject must imagine himself following a standard, marked route, and, without turning the map, must tell whether each turn is to his own left or right. Among 7– 18-year-olds, one study found that boys outscored girls at every age. Those turns requiring left–right reversal were especially difficult, particularly for girls (Money, Alexander, & Walker, 1965). Large differences also have been reported for college students, men's average times being nearly half and number of errors less than one-sixth those of women (Tapley & Bryden, 1977).

The route on the Road-Map test is, of course, already marked. Still another measure of direction sense is to find the route itself, for instance by tracing one's way through a printed maze or labyrinth. Here again, a sex difference favoring males appears, both in speed and accuracy (e.g., Porteus, 1965; Wilson, 1975). Perhaps a skill related to way-finding is involved in Keogh's (1971) "pattern-walking" task, which Acredolo (Chapter 3 of this volume) cites in her discussion of the difference between bounded and unbounded space. In this study, 8- and 9-year-olds were asked to make pencil copies of simple designs (e.g., circle, triangle) and designs consisting of combinations of the simple designs (e.g., a triangle within a circle), and then, to make the same patterns by walking—on the unmarked floor of a large room, on a 9 × 9 ft mat, and in a 9 × 9 ft sandbox, which left footprints. These conditions were designed—as Keogh conceived her study—to represent increasing levels of available reference points (or, in Acredolo's view, to represent different levels of boundaries of space). Acredolo noted only that performance was significantly better on the drawing than the walking tests. I was more interested to learn that there was a sex difference on the walking tests. The boys and girls were equally accurate in their drawing and in their walked patterns on the *unmarked* floor (unbounded space). But only the boys improved across the two remaining conditions as more visual cues became available (or as the boundaries became more limited), so that the boys were significantly more accurate than the girls in the mat and sandbox conditions.

For the most part, the studies mentioned so far only hint at the question alluded to in the anecdotes I recounted earlier—that is, whether the sex differences in spatial skills find expression in "practical" tasks or "real life" situations. Indications are that they do, though regretably this question has had little attention from psychologists.

With respect to "sense of direction," one practical kind of knowledge is knowledge of the direction one is facing—whether north, south, east, or west. In a test of about 1300 school children from kindergarten through sixth grade, boys were significantly more accurate than girls (Howe, 1931). Lord (1941) confirmed these differences in over 300 fifth- through eighth-graders. Fifty-five percent of the boys and 38% of the girls pointed correctly to all four cardinal as well as the four intermediate directions.

Another practical skill is to be able to remember and to reconstruct the route taken in going from one place to another. Lord gave his grade-school subjects such a test during an automobile trip in an unfamiliar part of town. Boys were more accurate than girls in reconstructing the route and in remembering stores and other buildings passed. More recently, Herman and Siegel (1978) had kindergarten, second-, and fifth-graders walk repeatedly through a large-scale model town consisting of roads, buildings, and railroad tracks. Afterward, the children had to reconstruct the layout of buildings from memory. Accuracy improved with age, and among the second- and fifth-graders, though not the kindergarteners, the boys were significantly more accurate than the girls.

The sex difference has been reported even when the child is questioned about a highly familiar place, and in this case, even in younger children. Siegel and Schadler (1977) asked 4½-6-year-olds to construct a three-dimensional scale model of their classroom by placing items such as tables and coat racks in their correct positions. The boys were far more accurate than the girls. Sex differences also have been reported in college freshmen's spatial knowledge of their campus. After 3 weeks in residency, men in comparison with women recalled and also recognized (from pictures) significantly more campus buildings. There were no sex differences, however, in knowledge of routes or of the configuration of the campus (Herman, Kail, & Siegel, 1979).

Given sex differences on the kinds of map-reading and way-finding tasks cited here, we might expect to find sex differences in academic disciplines that draw on similar cognitive skills. Geography is an obvious choice. For dissertation research in geography education, Bettis (1974) tested nearly 1700 fifth-grade school children representing 64 classrooms from 20 rural and urban school-districts throughout the state of Michigan. Nearly all questions required the reading of graphs or maps (e.g., interpretation of distances, direction of river flow, knowledge of place names on maps, and knowledge of geographic facts such as the nature of the land surface). Boys outperformed girls on 42 of the 49 questions, were equal on 3, and lower on only 4. For example, 47% of the boys and only 36% of the girls could identify Lake Huron on an unlabeled map of the Great Lakes.[1]

Females' poorer understanding of the direction of movement of water, as suggested by their performance on some of the questions in Bettis' (1974) geography study, may be exemplified also in Piaget and Inhelder's (1956) famous "water-level" test, or test of liquid horizontality. The subject's task is to draw, or otherwise construct, the waterline in a tilted container partly filled with colored water. By 12 years of age, significantly more boys than girls have mastered the principle that the waterline will remain horizontal, and this sex difference persists at least into young adulthood (e.g., Liben, 1974; Thomas, Jamison, & Hummel, 1973.) We have found comparable differences even when a simple recognition task is used. Over a series of experiments totaling over 1100 subjects, college men have answered 85% of the questions correctly, with more than half the men making perfect scores.

[1] Other academic disciplines in which boys excel and which, perhaps significantly, have visual-spatial components resembling those found in some of the standard visual-spatial tasks are mathematics, chemistry, and physics, and to a lesser extent, biology (Harris, 1979a; Kelly, 1978).

Women have answered 60% of the questions correctly, with less than 15% receiving perfect scores (Harris, Hanley, & Best, 1977). We repeated this test with first- through sixth-graders. Across grades, boys' scores improved from 25% to 52% correct; girls improved hardly at all, from 22% to only 28%, with the difference between the sexes becoming appreciable by fourth grade (Harris, Best, & Hanley, 1980; see also Thomas & Jamison, 1975).

Finally, females' more frequent failure to understand the behavior of liquid in a tilted container may be part of their poorer general understanding of mechanical or physical principles. On standardized tests of mechanical comprehension (e.g., anticipating the direction of movement of bevel gears or the course of an object dropped from a moving airplane, understanding the function of the rudder in steering, or understanding the relative efficiency of pulleys and tackles), males outperform females by a wide margin (Bennett, 1969).

There are still other spatial tasks that could be mentioned, but these examples will serve our purposes here. First, we can see that the sex difference appears in a broad spectrum of tasks or situations, and this, for me, enhances its theoretical and practical significance. Second, this variety at the same time underscores the difficulty we face in explaining the sex difference. Will an explanation for, say, mental rotation tasks necessarily apply to way-finding, to map-reading, or to the water-level test? A positive answer presupposes that all the tasks are alike in certain critical respects, that is, in sharing certain features or components, or in the extent to which they call on the same "basic" skills. A negative answer suggests that the tasks differ in these same respects.

On the basis of factor analytic studies, two factors have been proposed as major components of spatial tasks. The first, called "spatial orientation," has been defined by French, Ekstrom, and Price (1963) as the "perception of the position and configuration of objects in space . . . with the observer himself as a reference point"; the second—"spatial visualization"—has been defined as comprehension of imaginary movements of objects in three-dimensional space, wherein "the observer seems removed from the stimulus pattern in that he appears to manipulate and alter its image [French et al., 1963." Different tests very likely differ in the extent to which these factors are involved.

For instance, "mental paper-folding" tests like the Space Relations subtests of the DAT, as well as many items on tests of mechanical comprehension, seem to draw primarily on visualization skills. Perceptual disembedding likewise seems to call for visualization in the sense that the figure must be "lifted," or imagined separately, from its background. Way-finding tests, on the other hand, suggest an orientational component, particularly when left and right must be reversed as is required for certain turns on the Money Road-Map Test. The water-level test seems to be most different from the rest inasmuch as it is hard to see a particular "ability" that would be required for its solution other than simply to know the physical principle governing the behavior of a liquid in a tilted container. Even so, Geiringer and Hyde (1976) found high correlations between average number of errors on this task and performance on the Primary Mental Abilities (PMA) Spatial Relations test in twelfth-grade boys ($r = -.83$) and girls ($r = -.97$), so that with PMA performance as a covariate, no important sex differences remained on the water-level test. Geiringer and Hyde (1976) concluded that the water-level test is really a visual–spatial test "incognito."

The aforementioned functional characterizations seem reasonable. Nevertheless, our attempts to identify the critical components of various "spatial" tests are still part guesswork, particularly where we lack factor analyses involving both standard and nonstandard tasks. The factor structure also may be different for males and females (or for more- and less-skillful individuals). Unfortunately, analyses typically have combined the sexes. Furthermore, consensus is still lacking on the meaning of the two factors—orientation and visualization—most commonly identified as the major components of spatial tasks. At the outset, Guilford (e.g., 1947) provided somewhat different definitions from those offered by French et al. (1963), cited earlier; factor analysts continue to have difficulty in differentiating and interpreting these factors (see Carroll & Maxwell, 1979, pp. 618–621). Finally, in the case of the rod-and-frame and embedded figures tests, the very characterization of them as "spatial" tests has been challenged.[2] In light of all these problems, it is clearly risky to assume that there are certain discrete skills common to all the different tasks that have been called "spatial." Still, I am sufficiently impressed at least by superficial similarities among the various tasks that I am

---

[2] Witkin et al. (1962) argued that individual differences on these tasks are measures of cognitive "differentiation," meaning general cognitive or mentative style, and they distinguish two major types: the "field dependent," or "less differentiated," style, in which case the individual is sensitive to the stimulus background (in the sense that he cannot disregard it), and the "independent", more differentiated, style (showing less sensitivity to context or a greater ability to separate figure from context). Sherman (1967) argued, however, that because both the rod-and-frame and embedded figures tests are visual tasks, the male's superior performance is understandable and cannot be generalized into an all-encompassing statement about cognitive style. In other words, males look more cognitively "differentiated" than females only where a visual task is concerned. Witkin and Berry (1975) reject this analysis, calling it the "inappropriate lumping of 'perceptual disembedding' (field-dependence-independence) with 'spatial abilities' [1975, Note 9, p. 75]." They argue, instead, that perceptual disembedding and spatial abilities are "discrete dimensions" inasmuch as in factor-analytic studies, tests of these dimensions "have repeatedly been found to load different first-order factors. The existence and causes of sex differences must therefore be specifically and separately identified for each dimension [1975, Note 9, p. 75]."

going to make this assumption as a basis for framing explanations for the sex difference.

Before going further, some comment is needed about the nature of the evidence for sex differences in spatial ability. In this chapter, I have chosen not to provide extensive, much less exhaustive, documentation of the evidence. Where I have asserted an advantage for males on one test or another, I do not mean that the difference is consistently found in study after study, but only that where sex differences have been reported, the typical finding is better male performance. My citations are representative of those reports. The ratio of positive to negative reports will be larger for some tasks than for others. Furthermore, mean differences in any given positive report are usually smaller than the range of difference within a sex. The behavioral distinction between the sexes thus seems to be quantitative more than qualitative.

The size of the ratio of positive to no-difference reports, the minimum number of reports required before an inference of reliable sex differences should be made, and the significance of the numerically "atypical" reports of superior *female* performance, are still incompletely answered questions (see Block, 1976; Maccoby & Jacklin, 1974), and it is beyond the scope of this chapter to resolve these issues here. To serve the basically heuristic purposes of this chapter, the only assertion I would make is that the sex difference on tasks collectively called "spatial" is real, not illusory. This has been the conclusion of earlier, systematic reviews (e.g., Maccoby & Jacklin, 1974), and subsequent research, some of which has been cited in this chapter, continues to support this view. The recent suggestion that the differences are "trivially small" and that the search for explanatory mechanisms "may be an exercise in futility [Jacklin, 1979, p. 368]" therefore is a view with which I profoundly disagree [for further discussion see my review (1979b)]. I believe that the search is far from futile and ultimately will lead to important insights into the nature and origins of human cognition.

Socialization and Life Experiences

There have been a variety of attempts to account for sex differences in spatial ability. One long-prominent view is that they are a product of sociocultural influences, that is, that in the course of their upbringing, boys have received more opportunities, encouragement, and training than girls to acquire visual-spatial skills. In some traditional cultures, the differences in opportunity may be institutionalized into explicitly different work roles. Thus, among the Pulawat Islanders, whose remarkable navigational skills are noted elsewhere in this volume (see Pick & Lockman Chapter 2), only the young men are candidates for the rigorous and extended training needed to become a navigator.

Many less dramatic examples could be mentioned. For instance, recall Howe's (1931) test of children's knowledge of map direction. Though performance overall was miserable, the boys' advantage could mean that someone (a parent, a teacher) or something (a book, a radio show) had provided at least the bare beginnings of instruction, perhaps by pointing out how to use sun position. (In the out-of-door tests, children who had done well more frequently mentioned sun position as the basis for their choice.) Howe himself wondered whether the boys were more involved in activities, like scouting, that might have trained orientation skills.

Training Experiments

The socialization view also has been pressed through demonstrations that special training can bring females close to or at the male level of performance. Such demonstrations, as Maccoby and Jacklin have said, would be "strong evidence that sex differences in spatial ability are (in large degree) a product of differential training [1974, p. 129]." Various training experiments have been reported. For instance, eighth-graders who for 3 weeks did pattern-folding tasks and solid-object manipulation, later, when tested on the Space Relations Subtest of the Differential Aptitude Test, substantially outscored a control group matched in age and sex. There were no sex differences in the trained group, and the investigator concluded that "girls can at least hold their own when provided with the opportunity to learn something about a particular area in which they are often assumed to possess less ability [Brinkmann, 1966, p. 184]." A more direct approach is through practice on the test itself. By this means, Goldstein and Chance (1965) succeeded in eliminating the usual sex differences on the embedded-figures test with adults.[3]

---

[3] The means of improving spatial skills may be far less direct than simple practice. For instance, knowledge of map directions might be enhanced merely by orienting children's school desks to the north, and by placing maps on the north wall. In Lord's (1941) study, of the children with perfect scores on all map directions, 69.2% faced north in their classrooms compared with 50% and 59.5% for those facing east and west, and only 35.4% for those facing south. The children whose desks faced north also were twice as accurate as the others in pointing out locations (cities) on a map of the United States. The children whose desks faced south were described as being especially confused by the direction tasks, and tended to reverse directions 180°. These factors would not explain the sex differences (except in the unlikely case that classrooms with more boys in them tended to face north more often than classrooms having more girls), but they do suggest why the overall level of skill was so low in these early studies and, perhaps, in more recent reports, too (Bettis, 1974). In any case, these and other simple procedures could be put to wider use for the teaching of map and orientation skill.

Toys, Games, and Social Control

Needless to say, the origins of competence in any general sense lie in much earlier and more basic experiences than could be provided by scouting or other special training practices. Piaget's dictum about the role of action in spatial learning is relevant here and has been cited by other contributors to this volume. What Piaget proposed is that the mental image of a spatial form is originally the "interiorization" of the child's movements of exploration of the form. If so, then the developmentally critical early experiences for spatial competence probably would be object manipulation and visual-tactile exploration—experiences presumably better facilitated by the 'active' toys like blocks, cars, and construction sets given to boys than by the dolls and "domestic" objects associated with girls' play.

There is no question that such differences exist. For instance, a systematic count of the contents of the bedrooms of 1-6-year-old children of upper-middle-class parents disclosed that boys had significantly and substantially more vehicles, sports equipment, toy animals, depots, machines, and military toys, and even (surprisingly) more educational-art materials, whereas girls had dolls, doll houses, and domestic toys (Rheingold & Cook, 1975). Other research suggests that the differences go beyond the toys provided; they extend to parents' reactions to their children's manner or style of playing. Thus, Fagot (1978) found that parents (again from middle-class backgrounds) of 20-24-month-old children reacted more negatively to the child's manipulation of an object when the child was a girl than when the child was a boy. Fagot concluded that boys "are allowed to explore objects, to learn about the physical world with less chance of criticism than are girls [p. 465]." Girls, on the other hand, were reacted to more positively when they asked for the parent's help with a task. It is noteworthy that the parents did not seem to be acting from any deliberate plan to impose sex-appropriate behaviors in their child; although their reactions to these two classes of behaviors varied according to the sex of the child, they did not rate the behaviors as more or less appropriate for one sex than the other.

Differences in social control probably extend to the outside of the home as well. At least it is known that boys are more likely than girls to wander from the home, to use more space, to seek large areas for exploration and play, and to spend more time playing outdoors (e.g., Harper & Sanders, 1975). Among 5-7-year-olds, sex differences like these have been noted in children in playgrounds all over the world (Freedman, 1976). Roger Hart's field research (Chapter 8 of this volume) beautifully illustrates the relevance of such behaviors for the learning of spatial layouts.

If the extent of social control is important in the creation of sex differences in spatial (particularly way-finding) ability, it ought to be associated with individual differences *within* sexes as well. Some evidence bears this out. For example, Witkin *et al.* (1962) interviewed the mothers of middle-class 10-year-old boys living in New York City who excelled or did poorly on the embedded figures and rod-and-frame tests. The childrearing views of those mothers whose sons excelled (i.e., were field independent) are typified in the person of one mother who is described as wanting "to make her children independent, not to supervise them too closely, and to let them grow from within [p. 283]." Boys who excelled were described as having fewer restrictions imposed on them in their play areas and activities, as ranging farther from their homes, and as being less "watched over" by their parents.

Timing of Expression and Duration of Sex Differences in Spatial Skill

Another kind of evidence used in favor of a socialization explanation pertains to the timing of the sex diffference. In 1974, Maccoby and Jacklin summarized the results of numerous tests of spatial ability and concluded that "On the whole they show no sex differences until adolescence . . ." [p. 94]." Examples include the rod-and-frame and embedded figures tests, sex differences on which are far more reliable in 12–18-year-olds and in college-age adults than in preadolescent children. One inference that socialization theorists have drawn from this is that because society prescribes different experiences for males and females—experiences that differentially contribute to spatial competence—it takes time for these differences to become expressed in actual differences in skill. Understandably, so the reasoning goes, the differences typically first appear in adolescence, since sex-role prescriptions are most salient at this time (e.g., Nash, 1979, p. 288).

If sex-typed experiences play the critical role in these sex differences, then we also might expect the continuing enhancement of the differences *beyond* the time of their first appearance as more and more of the presumably critical experiences are amassed. Evidence supports this expectation. For example, on the DAT Mechanical Comprehension Test, the difference between the means of the sexes increases from eighth to twelfth grade from about .8 of a standard deviation to more than 1.2, so that by the time they are high school seniors, only about 10% of girls reach or exceed the mean of high school senior boys (Bennett, 1969).

Finally, it has been suggested that the sex differences will diminish beyond the adult years, or as Nash (1979) has written, "the exaggerated, cognitive sex-related differences, emergent during adolescence" are "age bound and ephemeral" rather than heralding "the beginning of lifelong, sex-defined differentiation [p. 290]." Nash makes this suggestion in light of reports that certain social behaviors, also presumably dictated by one's sex role, do not always persist beyond the adult years, or if they do, they are only situationally defined.

Some Counter-Instances

The evidence looks impressive for the view that sex differences in spatial ability are rooted in different childhood experiences, whether or not consciously or deliberately imposed as a part of a child's sex-role socialization. On several grounds, however, I think there is more to the story than this. For example, people do not invariably improve on spatial tests after practicing presumably relevant exercises. In one case, school teachers spent a month designing, constructing, and sketching models of three-dimensional shapes, but afterwards showed no improvement on various spatial tests (Mitchelmore, 1974). It also has been reported that college women who did not know that water remained level in a tilted container failed to achieve this understanding even after repeatedly watching a bottle of water being tilted (Thomas, Jamison, & Hummel, 1973). Similarly, twelfth-grade girls continued to make errors even after they were given demonstrations and were *told* that the liquid level would be horizontal (Golbeck & Liben, 1979; Liben, 1978). (For other examples, see Harris, 1978, 1979a.) But in any case, the lesson of both successes and failures is unclear. Bringing females up to the male level of skill through a training procedure *may* imply, as Maccoby and Jacklin have argued (1974), that a lack of training was responsible for the females' deficient expression of that skill in the first place, but it does not necessarily mean this. One could just as well declare that an agent that cures a disease must have been absent in the course of the disease's onset. (Please note that I am not likening poor spatial skill to a disease!) Of course, equal caution is demanded in interpreting instances in which "remedial" measures fail.

We should be cautious, too, in our interpretations of reports that children who do well on spatial tests range farther from home, are less "watched over," or, in general, are less controlled than children with lower scores. For one thing the empirical findings themselves have been questioned. In their study of the childrearing antecedents of field independence, Witkin *et al.* (1962) had relied on interviews with mothers. Hoppe, Kagan, and Zahn (1977) instead evaluated the actual interactions of mothers with their children (third-and fourth-graders). Contrary to Witkin's hypothesis, they found no consistent tendency for mothers of field-independent children to show a less assertive or less controlling style in comparison with mothers of field-dependent children. (See also Irving, 1970; Mebane & Johnson, 1970; Ramirez & Price-Williams, 1974).

Even where the relationship between parent and child behavior can be confirmed, it does not necessarily follow that degree of parental control is the underlying cause of the child's behavior. For example, observations of children ages 9 months–3 years in free-play settings indicate that boys wander from their mothers more often than girls do; that is, girls spend more time in close proximity (e.g., Goldberg & Lewis, 1969; Ley & Koepke, 1975). At least in the setting in which the behavior was observed, the mother herself did not obviously initiate or reinforce this behavior (Ley & Koepke, 1975). Boys also play outdoors more than girls do (Harper & Sanders, 1975). Again, the differences does not seem to be caused by others. The staff of the nursery school where the observations were made were described as women of egalitarian views, who did not pressure the children to conform to traditional roles. Indeed, they encouraged the girls to play outdoors, but without much success. Nor was there any sign that parents' attitudes or childrearing practices had contributed significantly to these sex differences.

Even granting all these points, what remains clear is that boys and girls receive different toys and games to play with. But even when other toys are available, boys more often than girls *choose* to play with "male" toys, such as blocks (e.g., Farrell, 1957; Harper & Sanders, 1975), and the choice simply does not look "compelled" by an outside agent. Surveys of 2–12-year-old children of well-educated parents have revealed that the mothers were, by and large, against sex-stereotyped toys, but the children's favorites were these very toys (Sutton-Smith, 1977). In another case, researchers made observations in the homes of families, each with a 1- or 2-year-old boy or girl. The boys showed more active play, more play with transportation toys, and more play generally forbidden by parents. Girls played more with soft toys and dolls. On a questionnaire, many parents rated these and other behaviors as sex-appropriate, but this time, in contrast to Fagot's (1978) results with 20–24-month-olds, actual sex differences in the parents' immediate response to the children were few or undetected. And there was no correlation with how stereotyped the parents' questionnaire responses were and the extent to which their children exhibited sex-typed behavior (Smith & Daglish, 1977).

Finally, certain relationships between spatial ability and personality factors conventionally associated with male- and female sex-typing do not come out as they presumably should according to the sex-role socialization hypothesis. From a large sample of fifth-graders, Ferguson and Maccoby (1966) identified children of each sex who were either high or low in spatial ability relative to verbal ability, but matched for total ability scores. After this, peer ratings were obtained for a variety of social behaviors. The authors predicted that spatial ability would be associated with masculine sex-role behavior for both sexes. For girls, the trend was in this direction, with high spatial girls being rated as higher than low spatial girls in aggression and masculinity, though the differences were nonsignificant. For boys, however, high spatial ability was significantly associated with low ratings on aggression, masculinity, and mastery, and high ratings on withdrawal. The authors therefore concluded that "high differential space ability seems to be associated with *inappropriate* sex typing in children of both sexes [1966, p. 565; emphasis in original]," and that the number and magnitude of significant differences between the differential-abilities groups "are not such as to suggest that a great deal of the variance in measures of ability is accounted for by interpersonal factors [p. 569]."

The question of the "late" appearance of sex differences in spatial tasks also deserves a closer look. The sex difference unquestionably is more common in later childhood, expecially after the onset of pubescence. But sex differences in younger children are by no means absent. We have already mentioned several instances—the Road-Map tests, model building of a spatial layout, and the water-level test. Another example is mazes. Even in the preschool years, ages 4-6, boys excel (Wilson, 1975; Fairweather & Butterworth, 1977). And on the Block Design subtest of the WISC, Roberts (1971) reported that in a test of over 7000 American 6-11-year-olds, boys showed a clear advantage over the *entire* age range. (This was a carefully chosen sample comprising 96% of a total probability sampling of Caucasian children.)

Lastly, changes in the magnitude of the sex diffference on standard tasks are not always tied to presumptive changes in the saliency of sex-role prescriptions with whatever different opportunities for training and practice as they might imply. Beyond the age when the sex difference first appears—whenever that is—the magnitude of the difference frequently remains unchanged. An example is Shepard and Metzler's mental-rotations test (1971). In a sample of nearly 2500 individuals, the male advantage was large and remarkably consistent over the entire age range from the teens (age 14) to middle age (53 years), both in the period of improvement of performance (ages 14 through the mid-twenties) and decline (late twenties and on) (Wilson *et al.*, 1975). Beyond the middle years through the eighties, overall performance continues to decline, but the male lead on standard visual-spatial tasks persists all the same (see review by Cohen & Wilkie, 1979; also Walsh, Krauss, & Regnier, Chapter 12 of this volume).

In summary, we certainly can accept the general proposition that certain experiences are necessary conditions for the development of spatial competence. We also probably can accept the further proposition that males have more of these experiences than females do. But if we accept the second proposition, I do not think that the evidence to date clearly shows that (*a*) these different experiences are *sufficient* to explain demonstrated sex differences in spatial competence; (*b*) the different experiences in *every* case are provided (or imposed) by others; or (*c*) where opportunities are equal, they are equally exploited or equally useful for the furthering of spatial ability. For these reasons, I think it reasonable that we broaden our inquiry into the

origins of sex differences in spatial ability to consider the possible roles of endogenous variables.

Neurological Models

The level at which endogenous factors ultimately must work in the creation of cognitive sex differences is, of course, that of the central nervous
system. For other mammals and certain birds, the concept of the sexual differentiation of brain function is well-established. This is true not only for sexual behavior itself (e.g., Gorski, 1974) but also for other functions not directly related to reproduction, including regulation of eating and body weight
(e.g., Nance, Gorski, & Panksepp, 1976), aggressive behavior (e.g.,
Quadagno, Briscoe, & Quadagno, 1977), and, in songbirds, singing (Nottebohm & Arnold, 1976). This concept, simply stated, is that those functions
recognized as either "masculine" or "feminine" in the adult animal are
assumed to be at least partly the result of the double action of sex hormones
on the central nervous system—first, during fetal or neonatal life to organize
the sexually undifferentiated brain into distinct "male" and "female" type
brains; then during a later "activation phase" (the increase of hormonal activity marking the onset of pubescence), to act on the central nervous system.
The question, then, is whether there is some comparable effect of sex hormone activity on nervous-system organization and functioning for cognitive
skills in man. This possibility is currently the subject of intense debate.[4]

[4] With respect to the animal literature, there is a difference of view as to the appropriateness
of the term "organization" to refer to the early phase. Goy (1968) used this term. Beach (1971),
however, noted that the term "organizational" was borrowed from embryologists studying the
organization of tissues in the developing fetus, and thus implies a structural change analogous to
the differentiation of the reproductive system by androgen and/or other "organizers." But as
there were no anatomical differences between the brains of males and females that might be correlated to the differences in behaviors between the sexes, the term "organizational" could not be
regarded as retaining its original morphological connotation with respect to the nervous system.
Beach (1971) therefore proposed that early testicular hormones merely influence, rather than
organize, the nervous system, thus sensitizing it for later activation during puberty.

Since Beach's (1971) review, there have been very convincing demonstrations of morphological sex differences in the brains of several mammals and songbirds of the sort that seem
to meet Beach's criterion. For example, in zebra finches and canaries, only the male normally
sings, and Nottebohm & Arnold (1976) found that the overall volume of neural vocal control
areas was significantly larger in males in both species (See also Gorski et al., 1978; Greenough et
al., 1977; Kolata, 1979; Nottebohm & Arnold, 1979). Though there is as yet no such evidence
for human beings, I nevertheless have chosen to retain the use of the term "organization" when
applying the hypothesis of sex-hormone induced neurological differentiation to human beings.
This may be unwise. For one thing (needless to say), in the case of human cognitive skill, we are
hardly dealing with the kind of gross behavioral-sexual dimorphism that is found in other
animals.

Historically, the major evidence for this hypothesized role of sex hormones in the expression of spatial ability has come from clinical research on individuals with various forms of hypogonadism. One is the female with Turner's syndrome (karyotype = 45 + XO). The Turner's individual is sterile (gonadal agenesis) and remains sexually infantile in appearance until treated with female sex hormones. Turner's individuals once were believed to be globally retarded, but more recent work shows that the retardation is largely confined to certain nonverbal skills. This selective retardation shows up not only in standard tasks, such as the performance (nonverbal) subtests on the WAIS and the Money Road-Map test, but in "real life" settings as well (e.g., losing one's way in familiar environments). A similar selective retardation also appears among genetic males with "testicular feminizing syndrome," a specific end-organ or tissue insensitivity to androgen (e.g., Masica, Money, & Ehrhardt, 1971). A less familiar example is the male with ideopathic hypogonadotrophic hypogonadism. These individuals have a normal 46 X,Y male karyotype but have low circulating levels of LH (luteinizing hormone) ascribed to deficient hypothalmic peptide LRD (luteinizing hormone releasing factor) and low testosterone. In contrast with the Turner's female and the androgen-insensitive male, these individuals are normally masculinized at birth because of intrauterine production of testosterone under control of maternal chorionic gonadotrophin, but they fail to virilize at puberty in the absence of the usual rise in LH and testosterone levels. Daniel Hier (1979, personal communication) has examined eight such individuals (mean age 34 years plus or minus 10 years) at Massachusetts General Hospital and found above-average performance on two tests of verbal ability (vocabulary and information subtests of WAIS) but significantly impaired performance on three visuospatial tests (block design subtest from WAIS, space relations test, and embedded figures test).

From such clinical evidence, it has been suggested that expression of spatial skill in hormonally normal individuals also depends on the production of sex hormones above some threshold level, so that spatial ability might be related to the degree of androgenization within the normal range. There is some evidence for this, but the relationship is complex. In 13-18-year-old girls, spatial scores do tend to be lower (relative to "fluent production" scores) in less androgenized, more "feminine" girls, and higher in more androgenized, more "masculine" girls (as rated from nude-body photographs using conventional staging criteria). But in normal boys of the same age range, spatial scores are *inversely* related to androgenization, being higher in the *less* androgenized, *less* "masculine" boys, and lower in the more androgenized, more masculine boys (Petersen, 1976; see also Broverman & Klaiber, 1969). Note the similarity between these findings, based on physical indexes of masculinity, and those of Ferguson and Maccoby (1966), dis cussed earlier in this chapter, which used psychological (interpersonal) measures.

These results thus suggest that the relationship between androgenization and spatial ability is not linear but curvilinear, meaning that within the normal range of androgen dosage, there is some middle range within which spatial ability is maximized and beyond which—either at the pathologically low extreme, or at the normal upper bounds—spatial ability is depressed. Within the normal range, though males' and females' distributions largely overlap, more males than females nevertheless fall within the middle part of the range most favorable to spatial ability. This implies that it is the physically androgynous, or less sexually differentiated, individual of either sex, who is more likely to be high in spatial ability.[5]

Arousal or Sensitivity

Sex-differentiated effects of hormonal action might be realilzed at different levels of nervous-system functioning. At one level, the major effect might be on arousal or sensitivity to stimulation. This possibility is compatible with the views of McGuinness (1976a,b), who proposes that the male's superior visual-spatial skills could be seen as growing out of the greater tendency among males than among females to be aroused by visual stimuli. In support of this idea, McGuinness (1976a) cites Watson's (1969) well-known finding that in 10- and 14-week-old infants, visual stimulation is a more effective reinforcer for boys than for girls.[6] The underlying difference, McGuinness goes on to say, may lie in physiological sensitivity to light, and here she cites reports that men are more light-sensitive, have superior foveal vision, and generally have greater photopic persistence, when compared with women.

McGuinness (1976a, 1974) goes on to propose comparable sex differences, this time favoring females, in sensitivity for the auditory modality. Infant girls thus are reportedly more responsive than boys to the "emotional

___

[5] Bock (1973) has suggested that the degree of sexual differentiation within each sex is influenced by an X-linked gene and that this differentiation in turn influences spatial ability. For a review of genetic models of spatial ability, see Vandenberg & Kuse (1979). Also see discussion in Harris (1979a).

[6] These results, however, were not confirmed by Watson himself (Ramey & Watson, 1972). but as Maccoby and Jacklin have suggested, the method used in these infant studies—experimental presentation of stimuli one at a time, isolated from their usual context—may have been "too reductionist; perhaps differences, if they exist, involve the sequential and organizational properties of perception, so that (the usual method) may have been a self-defeating strategy [1974, p. 381]." (See also Cohen & Gelber, 1975, pp. 381–383.) This sounds like a critical qualification; that is, it suggests that it is in *how* males and females organize and process complex visual stimuli in natural conditions that is the key to understanding sex differences in spatial skill.

and meaningful properties" of sounds (1976a, p. 133), human sounds being especially salient for girls.[7] Likewise, in young school-age children, girls show greater sensitivity to sound intensity as indexed by their relative intolerance of loud sounds and their greater accuracy in distinguishing changes in auditory intensity. These sex differences, McGuinness suggests, thus provide the underpinnings for female superiority in language production. These differences have long been reported (see examples in Harris, 1977), although all the qualifications mentioned earlier about sex differences in spatial ability apply here as well.

The measures on which differences have been reported include (a) frequency of vocalization during the preschool years; (b) time of occurrence of first words; (c) early growth of vacabulary; and (d) grammatical complexity during preschool and early school-age period. The sex difference also seems to be clearer in the more sheerly mechanical aspects of speech such as articulation, intelligibility, and speed. Language also seems to be a more pervasive aspect of girls' games and play, especially in the form of verse and rhyme. As Sutton-Smith (1979) has remarked, it is no accident that a recent authoritative work on *Speech Play* (Kirschenblatt-Gimblett, 1976) is largely about the games of girls. Like certain visual-spatial skills, sex differences in some of the linguistic skills and sensitivities listed here have been found throughout the life span (Cohen & Wilkie, 1979).

Cortical Organizational Models

Noting that too little is known about how coding occurs in the relevant neuro-anatomical pathways, McGuinness (1974, 1976b) does not speculate about the actual nervous-system structures that might underlie sex differences in modality sensitivities. She instead confines herself to the suggestion that both the auditory and visual sensitivity data might be explainable in terms of general mechanisms of sensory inhibition, so that in the case of audition, the female's heightened perception of loudness, as well as her greater attention to auditory stimuli, could be a result of finer tuning in this sensory mechanism.

---

[7] McGuinness cites a single report by Simner (1971), who, over four separate experiments with 2-3-day-old infants, found that girls cried more than boys in response to the cry of another infant. The differences, however, were not statistically reliable. Subsequently, Sagi and Hoffman (1976) reported similar, marginally significant ($p < .06$) differences in 1-day-old infants, and noted that the consistent pattern of sex differences over the total of five experiments (theirs in addition to Simner's four) was unlikely to have occurred by chance ($p < .03$). Perhaps the sex difference depends as much on what is heard—or seen—as on the modality itself. That is, human sights as well as sounds may be more salient for females. Hittelman and Dickes (1979) have reported finding that among neonates, girls spent significantly more time than boys in eye-to-eye contact with an adult.

Speculation about relevant nervous-system structures has been rife, however, among other neuropsychologists who have been interested in sex differences in cognitive functioning but who, in contrast to McGuinness, have been directly concerned with more complex cognitive skills. The almost exclusive focus of their attention has been on the two hemispheres of the cerebral cortex. The reason is understandable: In light of male superiority in visual–spatial skills, and in view of clinical and experimental evidence pointing to a prominent role for the right hemisphere in the detection and processing of visual–spatial information, the possibility has been raised that this functional specialization has proceeded further, or has reached a higher level, in the male than in the female brain.

Taking into account the known *left*-hemisphere specialization for linguistic skills, the corollary proposal is that in the female brain in contrast to the male, there is further, or a higher level of, specialization of the left hemisphere. Beyond these generalities, several more specific and related forms of this neurological hypothesis have been advanced. We shall consider the three most prominent.

RATE OF FUNCTIONAL MATURATION OF CEREBRAL HEMISPHERES

One hypothesis is that the fetal sex hormones determine the *relative* rates of functional maturation of each hemisphere, with faster maturation on the left in females (thus favoring earlier language development), and faster on the right in males (thus favoring earlier development of spatial functions). I have already mentioned the supporting evidence for language development. The question is whether these behavioral data are consistent with evidence from neuropsychological tests where behavioral (e.g., perceptual or motor) lateral asymmetries, such as the direction of ear advantage on a dichotic listening test [8] or of visual field advantage for tachistoscopically projected stimuli,[9] are used to index the separate and different specializations of the

[8] In dichotic listening, the subjects wear earphones that permit a different signal to be played to each ear at the same time. For instance, a tape recorded sequence of spoken words or digits might be played to one ear, and different words or digits to the other. Or the two sets of signals might be nonlanguage sounds such as coughing, mechanical noises, or even musical chords. Asked to report what they have heard, subjects usually report those language sounds more accurately that were played to the right ear, and show a left ear advantage for nonlanguage sounds. Keeping in mind the contralateral design of the ear–brain system, the "right-ear advantage" and "left-ear advantage" are believed to reflect the different specialization of the two hemispheres (see Kimura, 1973).

[9] The stimuli are projected very rapidly either to the left or right visual half-field of the eyes. Stimuli in the left half-field fall on the right hemiretinae, which project to the right occipital lobe; stimuli in the right half-field fall on the left hemiretinae, which project to the left occipital lobe. Generally, language stimuli (e.g., nonsense syllables and words) are recognized more easily in the right visual half-field. Spatial stimuli (e.g., obliquely oriented lines) are recognized more easily in the left visual half-field.

two cerebral hemispheres. (The distinction between these *behavioral* asymmetries and the underlying lateral specialization is important, as we shall see later.)

At best the neuropsychological evidence is mixed. For infants, the clearest demonstration of a sex difference comes from a study of auditory evoked potentials of 3-month-old infants while verbal and musical passages were played. Regardless of the stimulus condition, seven of eight girls, but only one of eight boys, showed a higher amplitude of left than right responses (Shucard, Shucard, Cummins, & Campos, 1979). In 2-5-month-old infants responsiveness to phoneme boundaries, as measured by auditory evoked responses, has been reported for girls but not for boys (Molfese & Molfese, 1979). Dichotic listening tests with infants, however, have failed to reveal sex differences in the strength or time of appearance of a right-ear advantage for linguistic stimuli (e.g., Glanville, Best, & Levinson, 1977).

For children in the early school years, the evidence is also inconclusive. For instance, sex differences, by and large, have not been found on dichotic listening tests (e.g., Hiscock & Kinsbourne, 1977), although they have been reported for motor-output, mechanical production, or motor-sequencing. For instance, in finger tapping a steady beat or rhythm, and in following the beat of a metronome (presumably a left-hemisphere task), 6-10-year-old girls, compared with boys of the same age, were found to be more accurate and superior with their right hand relative to their left to a significantly greater degree (Wolff & Hurwitz, 1976).

The evidence that right-hemisphere functional maturation proceeds earlier in males than in females is also mixed. In the auditory evoked potential experiment cited earlier (Shucard *et al.,* 1979), the seven infant boys who failed to show the "female" pattern instead showed precisely the reverse pattern from the girls—that is, higher amplitude responses of the right than the left hemisphere. But as before, in older children, no presumably comparable differences for auditory discrimination (namely, earlier or larger left-ear [right-hemisphere] advantage for nonlinguistic sounds) have been found. Where sex differences have been reported for older children, they instead have been in studies of somesthetic, or tactual, perception.

Witelson (1976) had 6-13-year-old children feel pairs of different nonsense shapes, one shape with each hand, and then try to identify the pair felt from a visual display containing the pair along with other shapes. The object was to see whether making recognition depend on a gestalt, or wholistic, perception of the whole shape would create an advantage for the *left* hand because it projects more directly to the right hemisphere. The left hand indeed proved to be superior in even the youngest boys but not until age 13 in girls, and Witelson suggested that the right hemisphere therefore becomes specialized for spatial perception earlier in boys than in girls. Rudel *et al.* (1974) reported similar results on a Braille-letter discrimination task in sighted children. In the most convincing demonstration to date, Dawson, Farrow, and Dawson (1980) tested first- and sixth-graders and college students and found a significant left-hand advantage at every age for the males only. The males' overall scores also were significantly higher than the females'. In other investigations, however, no sex-related differences have been found (Flanery & Balling, 1979; Harris, 1980; Hatta, 1978; Pomerantz, 1980; Wagner & Harris, 1979), so the precise circumstances under which the sex difference will appear remain to be determined. Variations in task difficulty, type of response required, and the linguistic codeability of the stimuli are among the potentially critical variables (Cioffi & Kandel, 1979).

It may be that on tests of lateralized responding, we have concentrated too much on measures of overall performance and not enough on those subtler features that usually escape notice. Studies of drawing disability in brain-injured adults provide an interesting illustration of this point. These studies show that the drawings are defective whether the patient's injury is on the left or the right side of the brain, but the defects differ according to the side of injury. Patients with left-sided injuries tend to produce drawings that are deficient in internal features and in organization of planning but adequate in overall spatial configuration. Drawings by patients with right-sided injuries tend to be strong and weak in just the reverse way (see Kaplan, 1976; Warrington *et al.*, 1966). Perhaps, then, if there are sex differences in cortical organization in childhood, they will appear on a test of drawing skill in these particular, evidently lateralized, stylistic features. Acting on this premise, Waber and Holmes have reported some fascinating results in normal 5-13-year-olds' copies of the Rey-Osterreith Complex Figure. At the youngest age, girls drew more internal details and more of the discrete parts, whereas boys concentrated more on the external configuration. At 11 years, boys drew their designs in "long, sweeping, continuous lines," whereas girls "drew theirs part by part [Waber, 1979, p. 173]." In other words, where stylistic differences appeared, the boys' style tended to be characteristic of right-hemisphere processing, the girls' of left-hemisphere processing. Perhaps the same kind of finer-grain analysis of performance could be applied to other tasks.

EXTENT OF LATERALIZATION OF FUNCTIONS IN ADULTHOOD

So the first cortical organization model supposes that sex differences in cognitive abilities are rooted in sex differences in the rate of functional maturation of each cerebral hemisphere. In light of the persistence of sex differences in cognitive skills and sensory sensitivities beyond adolescence and in many instances throughout life, a straightforward extension of this model to adulthood might be that these sex-differentiated growth trends in childhood culminate, in adulthood, in superior (because further-developed) left-hemisphere specialization in women, and superior right-hemisphere specialization in men. At least as applied to right-hemisphere functioning, however, the reasoning has taken a new turn. It goes as follows: We know that lateral separation of functions is not complete in any individual. The left hemisphere has primary, perhaps exclusive, control of articulate speech (cf. Zaidel, 1976), but auditory language comprehension seems to be more nearly bilaterally organized, especially for syntactically simpler constructions (see Searleman, 1977, for review). The idea, then, is that whatever may have been the nature or course of the sex-differentiated growth trends in childhood, the result in adulthood is a greater measure of bilateral language commitment in women than in men.

Support for this idea has come from several different quarters. The evidence for these broad generalizations about lateral cortical specialization came largely from early clinical studies of males only—an understandable limitation, since the patients typically were either young men who suffered unilateral head injuries in war or they were predominantly male, middle-aged or elderly stroke victims. Recent studies, however, indicate that the usual pattern of intellectual deficits following unilateral brain injury is different in female patients.

The best of these studies is by McGlone (1977, 1978). In a sample of right-handed adults with strictly unilateral brain lesions (vascular or neoplastic), she found the incidence of aphasia (as measured by performance on an aphasia test battery) to be at least three times more frequent in men than in women after left-hemisphere lesions. Sex differences persisted when only nonaphasic patients were considered. On the Wechsler Adult Intelligence Scales (Verbal and Performance) and on several visuospatial tasks, men clearly showed the usual pattern of deficits: depressed verbal ability in men with left-sided lesions, and imparied spatial ability in men with right-sided lesions. In women with left-sided lesions, however, language deficits were significantly less severe, and impaired spatial ability was just as likely to follow lesions on *either* side. Finally, in women with left-sided injuries, spatial test scores correlated highly ($r = .80$) with aphasia scores. These sex differences were not explicable on the basis of age, education, etiology, length of illness, neurological signs (hemiparesis and/or visual field defects), locus or severity of lesion, familial sinistrality, or generalized intellectual deterioration. The same results also were found in a replication study.

This clinical evidence is consistent with the results of tests of lateralized functioning in neurologically normal adults, where sex differences have been found. For example, electroencephalographic recordings of cortical activity while men and women performed selected cognitive tasks disclosed that only men as a group showed the expected differences, that is, relatively greater right-hemisphere dysynchrony during visualization tasks, relatively greater left-hemisphere dysynchrony during verbal and simple arithmetic tasks requiring verbal answers (Ray, Morell, & Frediani, 1976). In comparison with women, men also show a stronger right-ear advantage for verbal stimuli in dichotic listening (e.g., Lake & Bryden, 1976), a stronger right-field advantage for recognition of language stimuli on tachistoscopic visual recognition tests (e.g., Day, 1977), and a stronger, more consistent left-field superiority for spatial targets (e.g., Berlucchi, Marzi, Rizzolatti, & Umilta, 1976).

Finer-grain analyses have begun to suggest more precisely where the sex differences lie. Especially promising is the technique used by Bradshaw and Gates (1978). They studied adults' performance in a tachistoscopic recognition task with different linguistic materials (e.g., words varying in concreteness and imageability; nonword letter-strings some of which were homophonic with nonpresented real words) and in two kinds of tasks—when overt naming was required, or when a lexical decision had to be made with discriminatory manual responses. Both latency and error measures showed that right visual-field superiority was more consistent when naming was required, and was more consistent with men than with women. The difference was clearest for task type: When only a lexical decision was called for, the women often showed superior left visual-field (right hemisphere) performance, especially early in the experimental sequence. But on the overt naming task, women showed field asymmetries similar to males. The authors suggest that in females, right-hemisphere space normally reserved for visuospatial processing has been "invaded by secondary speech mechanisms" that "appear to operate at an essentially lexical level and may act in a supportive or auxiliary capacity for difficult or unfamiliar material; they seem to be equally concerned with both phonological and graphological processing . . . [p. 166]."

The question is what any of these reports have to do with sex differences in spatial ability. If the female's right hemisphere tends to be committed, secondarily, to language to a relatively greater degree than is the male's, then, as McGlone's (1977, 1978) work suggests, this will work to her advantage in some situations, for example, following left-hemisphere injury, her aphasic symptoms will be fewer and less severe, perhaps because of greater right-hemisphere involvement in language even prior to injury. But the implication for her overall spatial skills will be negative: To the extent that the female's right hemisphere is relatively more committed for language than the male's, it becomes less efficient as a processor of spatial information.

We are assuming, then, that this negative outcome for the female's spatial ability follows necessarily. There is a hidden premise in the chain of reasoning that now must be made explicit. It has to do with the presumptive capacity of each hemisphere, or each kind of hemispheric information-detecting and processing "system," to do the other's work. The two hemispheres are believed to function in different ways, each appropriate for the tasks it does best. The "logical," "analytical" left hemisphere analyzes stimulus information sequentially or serially, abstracting out the relevant details to which it attaches verbal labels, and programming the precise sequencing of events in time, not just including speech production but also various nonlinguistic motor skills. The right hemisphere is primarily a synthesist—more concerned with the overall stimulus configuration, simultaneously analyzing parallel sources of information, and organizing and processing information in terms of wholes. It is especially good in dealing with stimuli that cannot be named. (We earlier saw how these different specializations are reflected in the kinds of drawing defects made by patients with unilateral lesions.)

In light of these characterizations, it has been suggested (Levy-Agresti & Sperry, 1968, p. 1151) that the left hemisphere therefore is "inadequate for the rapid complex syntheses achieved by the right hemisphere"—in other words, that spatial problems are difficult, sometimes impossible, to solve through logical, analytical modes, including language. Geometry is a good example. Although the left hemisphere seems to be as competent as the right in identifying the Euclidean (and nameable) properties of objects (i.e., points, lines, and planes), it is much less capable than the right in identifying the less nameable topological properties such as transformations involving changes in lengths, angles, and shapes (Franco & Sperry, 1977).

If the characterizations of lateral cortical specialization in males and females are correct, it ought to follow that in neurologically intact individuals, overall performance on a spatial test will be positively related to the extent to which there is lateral separation of functions in any given individual, and this relationship should hold within a sex as much as between the sexes. In other words, "well-lateralized" individuals should be superior in spatial ability to "less-well-lateralized" individuals, whether they are male or female. Recent experiments support this prediction. Zoccolotti and Oltman (1978) found that among 18–30-year-old men, those who did well on the rod-and-frame and embedded figures tests showed the expected significant right-visual-field advantage in reaction time to tachistoscopically projected letters, whereas men who did poorly showed no hemifield difference. A second study confirmed this finding and revealed a similar difference for a right-hemisphere task. Men with high perceptual disembedding scores showed a significant left-visual-field superiority in tachistoscopic face discrimination, whereas men with low scores showed no significant hemifield difference. The authors concluded that perceptual disembedding ability (which, as suggested earlier, draws heavily on visual–spatial ability) is related to the degree of segregation, or separation, of functioning between the hemispheres, as indexed by the degree of perceptual asymmetry on the tachistoscopic test.[10]

RATE OF PHYSICAL MATURATION

So far we have discussed two hypotheses that, respectively, link cognitive sex differences to sex differences in the relative rates of functional maturation of each hemisphere and (in adulthood) to extent of lateralization. The third hypothesis, proposed by Waber (1979), builds on the first two but proposes a specific feature of growth whereby the sex differences in extent of lateralization in adulthood are created. The key ingredient in this model lies in an as yet unmentioned, and in this instance, abundantly documented difference between males and females: namely, in their overall rate of physical maturation. On the average, boys mature (reach pubescence) at 14 years and girls at 12 years, as measured by the attainment of "peak height velocity," the point of fastest acceleration in growth of height. (The actual ages vary according to several factors, especially diet and body weight, but the sex difference is fairly constant. The ages cited here are for "moderately well-off British or Northern American children [Tanner, 1971, p. 909].")

Waber's general proposition is that the organization of brain functions should be conceptualized as a growth process that is continuous with physical

[10] The hypothesis linking degree of lateralization to spatial ability was first proposed by Levy (1974). However, as her test of the hypothesis, Levy deliberately chose to make the comparison not between males and females but between left- and right-handers, since there was abundant independent evidence that left-handers as a group are less well-lateralized than right-handers. It would seem, then, as though the hypothesis, as it subsequently has been applied to the question of sex differences in spatial ability, should stand or fall on the evidence for left- versus right-handers, the groups to which the hypothesis was, with good reason, originally applied. If so, the fairest judgment must be, I think, that the status of the hypothesis is still very much unclear. One problem is that new studies suggest complex interactions between cognitive performance scores and family history of sinistrality, the kind of left-handedness under consideration (sinistrals being a very heterogenous group even within the familial and nonfamilial categories), and even the sex of the individual. Another problem is that tests of the hypothesis typically are based on the expectation that left-handers will be deficient in spatial ability in some absolute, and therefore clinically relevant, sense, and therefore necessarily inferior in ability to right-handers. Levy, however, was concerned with *within*-subject contrasts, predicting only a greater verbal-spatial difference in skill in left-handers than in right-handers. It therefore is not clear how the model, as developed for application to the two handedness groups, should be "translated" so as to address the question of sex differences in cognitive abilities, where we clearly are concerned with explaining differences in the absolute level of skill. Another reason to question the direct "translatability" of the hypothesis to the question of sex differences is that the etiological variables underlying the hypothesized sex differences in cortical organization must be different from those underlying the differences between handedness groups.

growth itself. Consequently, overall maturation rate and lateral, functional cortical organization will be related such that late maturing individuals ultimately will be more lateralized than early maturers. Inasmuch as males are over-represented in the former group, males therefore also will be over-represented in the group of individuals who are well-lateralized. The model therefore posits that the greater reliability of cognitive sex differences after adolescence is related to the "further reorganization of brain functions [that] occurs as part of the maturational spurt in the CNS" at this time—a spurt perhaps "analogous to the spurt in physical growth and, like that spurt, characterized by a proces of sexual differentiation [Waber, 1979, p. 181]." The model does not thereby reject the potential sex-differentiating role of fetal hormones described earlier; it proposes, instead, that an important aspect of these early effects will be reflected later in differences between early- and late-maturing adolescents. (Waber, 1977a, notes the establishment of such a link over time in animals; cf. Reinisch, 1974.[11]

We have already cited some of the evidence for a maturation-rate hypothesis in the reports of stronger lateralization effects in men than women. But more telling would be evidence for a relation between rate of physical maturation and the pattern of cognitive abilities *within* each sex. Here, there have been several reports. Broverman *et al.* (1964) found that boys who were strong in certain spatial tasks relative to verbal tasks tended to be later maturers than boys with the reverse pattern of cognitive skills. Kohen-Raz (1977) reports similar trends. Waber (1977a) corroborated this

[11] Waber's model thus fits with the concept, outlined earlier, that posits two stages of hormonal action on the nervous system—first during fetal or neonatal life, then during pubescence—though the distinctions between "organizational" and "activational" (or "sensitization" and "activational") do not clearly apply.

The description of Waber's model, as presented here (from Waber, 1979), represents an important change from its initial formulation (Waber, 1977a). In that formulation (at least as I have interpreted it; Harris, 1979a), a basic assumption of the model seemed to be that lateral specialization of the cerebral hemispheres *increases* with age, with the extent of the increase presumably depending on the timing of pubescence. Thus, just as puberty is seen as inhibiting linear growth by initiating the onset of bone ossification, so it was seen as inhibiting the maturational process of cerebral lateralization "in the same way [Waber, 1977a, p. 35]." Males, therefore, are ultimately more lateralized than females because the process of lateralization goes on for a longer time in males than in females. This formulation, however, was inconsistent with a growing body of new reports that failed to find significant increases with age in the extent of lateralized responding on standard neuropsychological tasks (see review in Kinsbourne & Hiscock, 1977). Waber has taken specific account of these reports in her current (1979) version of her model, though her substituted concept, as exemplified in the phrase, "further reorganization of brain function [that] occurs as part of the maturational spurt in the CNS," needs much explication. Even in its unexplicated state, however, the concept at least underscores the important idea of CNS functioning as a dynamic, growth-related process, though, as we have just noted, not the simple "increasing lateralization" process that had been proposed earlier.

finding in both boys and girls, and took the critical (for her model) additional step of showing that the later maturers of either sex also showed stronger lateralized responding, as indexed by the strength of right-ear advantage for dichotic recognition of phonemes. Rovet (1979) extended the test to endocrinological patients who had either pathologically precocious or delayed development (in contrast to the subjects in prior studies whose timing of maturation was in the normal range). This time, the results were mixed. Among females the predicted relation between verbal–spatial contrast and strength of lateralized responding held, but for males, *contra* hypothesis, *both* precocious and delayed developers had higher spatial than verbal scores and showed strongly lateralized performance on a dichotic listening task. Finally, in the study of normal 13-18-year-olds mentioned earlier, Petersen (1976) found *no* relationship between spatial or verbal ability and the timing of maturation in either sex; however, recall that she did find a relationship between androgenization and spatial ability. Many more comparisons of early- and late-maturing children are needed before these conflicting reports can be resolved.

ANATOMICAL AND PHYSIOLOGICAL DIFFERENCES

If there are sex differences in functional organization of the cortex, it stands to reason that there will be underlying sex differences at either the anatomical or physiological level. As already noted, such differences recently have been clearly established for other mammals and for songbirds (see footnote 4). A further critical difference however has not yet been found: that, accompanying lateral functional dominance for a certain behavior (e.g., left hypoglossal vocal control in songbirds), there are lateral structural differences consistent either with the lateral functional differences or with the sex differences in performance of the behavior in question.

At the human level, where much research also has been carried out, the situation is somewhat different. Here, both functional and structural lateral asymmetries are known to exist in cortical regions of distinct cellular architecture and with distinct physiological characteristics. In particular, portions of the language-related frontal and temporal regions tend to be larger in the left hemisphere than in the right, whereas the parietal and occipital regions, critical for visual perception, tend to be larger on the right (Galapurda, LeMay, Kemper, & Geschwind, 1978). Understandably, the search for neuroanatomical and neurophysiological differences underlying presumptive sex differences in cognitive functioning has concentrated on these areas. The results so far are disappointing: The only evidence yet of a sex difference is a reported trend showing that the asymmetry in the region of the left temporal plane—an extension of the temporal speech cortex (Wernicke's area)—is slightly more evident in female than in male brains (Wada, Clark, & Hamm, 1975.)[12]

As with other animals, the search for lateral physical differences probably must be sought in still finer structure, as well as in other parts of the nervous system. McGuinness's (1974, 1976) view that sex differences in cognitive functioning originate as sex differences in arousal or sensitivity to stimuli in different modalities suggests sex differences at the level of brain stem. Of possible significance here is a report of "significantly faster auditory brain-stem responses from female than male subjects [Seitz, Weber, Jacobson, & Morehouse, 1980].

Specific subcortical forebrain structures also deserve attention. These include the hippocampus, in light of the claimed specialization of the right hippocampus for way-finding and orientation in space (O'Keefe & Nadel, 1978), and the thalamus. I would emphasize the thalamus because of its predominantly direct, ipsilateral cortical connections in man (Van Buren & Borke, 1972), its functionally asymmetric organization along lines similar to the cortex (Ojemann, 1976), and specifically its role as an area of integration preparing information for distribution to the cortex. That there are sex-related differences at this level is suggested in Lansdell's (1973) report of the same sex-dependent asymmetries on a word-association test after left thalamotomies as are found in the clinical literature on patients with cortical injuries.

There also may be specific neurochemical factors at work. This notion, of course, is implicit in the view that fetal hormones organize the nervous system along sex-differentiated lines. Broverman, Klaiber, Kobayashi, & Vogel (1968) have emphasized the increase in hormone secretions that initiate pubescence as constituting what, in this context, we would call the "activational" stage of the double-action model. They specifically have proposed that male and female sex hormones differentially affect nervous-system functioning (in particular the balance among neurotransmitter substances) so as to facilitate male performance on spatial tasks as well as female performance on certain linguistic (e.g., fluent production) tasks (see review in Petersen, 1979).

If sex hormones have different effects on nervous-system function-

[12] The meaning of sex differences in size of temporal plane or other structures (whether size refers to volume, density, or weight) also will remain unknown until we understand the functional significance of the size difference in the first place, quite apart from the question of sex differences. The answer to this more basic question is still largely unknown and, as McGlone (1980) has remarked, will probably remain unknown "until it is clear that surface linear measurements of the brain accurately predict the total number of neurons in a functional region. . . . Thus it is still an open question whether asymmetrical morphology forms the basis of subsequent functional specialization or whether it merely reflects balanced accommodation for an irregularly expanding cortical mantle [p. 223] " (see also Galapurda et al., 1978).

ing, the effects may have specific foci. For instance, the thalamus has been found to be strongly asymmetric for distribution of norepinephrine (Oke, Keller, Mefford, & Adams, 1978), concentrations being higher on the left side in the pulvinar region, higher on the right side in the somatosensory region. It has been suggested that the pulvinar region plays a major mediating role between anterior and posterior speech zones (Penfield & Roberts, 1959; see review in Brown, 1975). Ojemann (1976) has suggested that there may be greater somatosensory representation in the right thalamus than in the left. Perhaps, then, the Oke *et al.* (1978) report implies a connection between functional and chemical neuroanatomical differences, and perhaps individual, including sex-related, differences in functional lateralization of the thalamus, suggested by Lansdell's (1973) report, are related to the asymmetric distribution of a neurotransmitter substance.

Summary and Conclusions

A neurological "program" for creating a male advantage for visual–spatial ability might go as follows: Fetal testicular hormones act on an initially sexually undifferentiated nervous system so as to bring about sensitization to visual input (presumably through brain stem influence), earlier right-cerebral-hemisphere development, and ultimately greater lateral separation of function with consequent enhancement of right-hemisphere functional efficiency. Thalamic and hippocampal differences also may be involved. The enhancement of sex differences in spatial ability during pubescence can be seen as related to the increase in sex hormones that initiate this developmental period, either as a consequence of further, major cortical organizational changes or as a result of other, more direct effects on nervous-system functioning. Presumably, these various outcomes are more likely in the middle range of androgen dosage where more males than females fall, which would account for the linear relation between androgenization and spatial ability in girls, and the curvilinear relation in boys.

This hard-wiring analysis is appealingly neat. Still, if we could not accept the view that diffferent life experiences are sufficient to explain sex differences in spatial ability, there are also good reasons to question any proposition asserting the sufficiency of hormonal or neurological factors, however convincingly they might someday be established. As we consider these reasons, perhaps we shall begin to see how the two major categories of explanation might be brought together.

Let us begin with the clinical and experimental neuropsychological studies. The distinction between behavioral lateral asymmetries and "lateral specialization" becomes critical here. We can see that sex differences in "lateral specialization" have always been inferred from behavioral asymmetries rather than measured directly by neuroanatomical or neurophysiological indicators. The problem is that some investigators, perhaps unwittingly, have assumed that sex differences in behavioral asymmetries correspond directly to the hypothesized sex differences in lateral specialization. This not only takes, say, the male's stronger right-ear advantage for recognition of language stimuli as direct evidence for greater lateral specialization but also equates the degree of ear advantage to the degree of language lateralization. Any such equation is flawed for several reasons, as several critics have pointed out (e.g., Harris & Witelson, 1977; Kinsbourne & Hiscock, 1978).

First, perceptual tests underestimate the population incidence of left lateralization of language as estimated by clinical (aphasia) studies and by invasive techniques (e.g., Wada sodium amytal test). Satz has shown that the investigator who infers anomalous lateralization from a *left*-ear advantage could be wrong 90% of the time with a sample of adult right-handers (cited in Kinsbourne & Hiscock, 1978, p.1). The second reason follows logically—and empirically: Ear differences in dichotic listening, visual asymmetries on tachistoscopic tasks, and hand differences on tactual tasks are less reliable on retesting than measures of a presumably *fixed, structural* property should be. This implies the third reason—that lateralized responding on such tests is easily modified, which it should not be if it were measuring fixed, structural properties of nervous systems (see Kinsbourne & Hiscock, 1978, esp. p.192 ff.). For example, a concurrent verbal task will introduce a rightward bias in visual perception (Kinsbourne, 1970); vowel sounds may yield either a right-ear advantage or no ear asymmetry according to whether the context in which the sounds were heard is linguistic or nonlinguistic (Spellacy & Blumstein, 1970). Thus, it seems as though a variety of sex-related individual differences in the deployment of attention, problem-solving "set," and specific strategy used can influence or even radically change the results of a behavioral test designed to measure cerebral function. Bryden (1978) has pointed out that, to date, most behavioral measures of cerebral function fail to control properly for these individual differences. It is noteworthy that in his own work on dichotic listening, Bryden (1978) has failed to find sex-related differences in strength of ear advantage when attentional biases are reduced to a minimum.

What might be the nature of the individual, sex-related differences that, in uncontrolled situations, could bring about the sex differences in lateralized responding? In light of the evidence suggesting female superiority in certain language skills, it has been widely suggested that the critical factor is the female's greater reliance, across a broad spectrum of cognitive tasks, on verbal mediation. This would not only reduce her left-visual field advantage for recognition of tachistoscopically projected spatial stimuli but would tend to reduce her overall score to the extent that verbal mediation is a less efficient mode of processing spatial information.

The origins of such a presumed difference in the disposition to use language probably would go back to earliest childhood, given McGuinness' proposal that infant boys and girls are differentially sensitive to visual and auditory stimulation. These physiological and behavioral differences then would find natural expression in what males and females *attend to*. This means that "types of stimulus information are more salient to one sex than to the other [McGuinness, 1976a, p. 132]," and this is "related to the way in which the developing child seems to control and interpret his environment [p. 132]," and in his "choice of stimuli in natural conditions [p. 133]."

Such differences may find expression as well even in general intellectual development. Longitudinal studies of intellectual development support this possibility. Intelligence-test scores in infancy and scores in later childhood are, for the most part, uncorrelated. But when scores for language-related items on infant tests are considered independently (e.g., in the 5-13-month age range, the items "vocalizes eagerness," "vocalizes displeasure," "uses expressive jargon"), the predictive power of the infant test improves. The improvement, however, appears only for girls. In one investigation, females with high "language" scores during infancy had high intelligence test scores at 6-26 years, whereas females with low infant scores had low scores during the same later period. For males, no relationship was found (Cameron, Livson, & Bayley, 1967; see also Moore, 1967). According to McCall *et al.* (1972), these findings "indicate that vocalization in infancy may have a special salience for females that it does not connote for males with respect to predicting later mental performance [p. 735]." They go on to note that it is unlikely that the sex difference merely reflects precocious verbal behavior by females relative to males; for if this were true, then the age-of-first-passing scores (in Cameron *et al.*, 1967) "would merely be a few months younger for girls than for boys, and such a difference in the means of these distributions should not influence the correlation. Thus, there may be some special qualitative sense in which early vocalization behavior has special meaning for girls [p. 736]."

These considerations suggest that if there are sex differences in style or strategy of spatial analysis, their roots lie in early infancy and childhood. Whereas the girl's early lead in language development would dispose her to one intellectual path, perhaps the boy's different sensitivities would take him in a different direction. While girls are becoming increasingly skillful in expressive language skills, boys are still focused on things and on spatial-perceptual activities. Having spent more time in early childhood in the analysis of the spatial features of their environments (encouraged by the toys and other objects more often provided them), perhaps boys continue along the "spatial" course, even though they eventually equal females in most if not all aspects of language skill.[13]

This line of reasoning suggests some different ways of thinking about the effects of socialization from those conventionally advanced. For example, the girl's earlier language development may lay the groundwork for early differences in social-emotional interactions with parents and, later, with other children that would redound to her advantage for certain skills but to her disadvantage for others. Young girls, therefore, may learn less than boys about the spatial layouts of their environments not only because girls may be inherently less interested in these visual-environmental features but also because they are more attentive to the social-affective and linguistic-communicative dimensions of the same environment.

Sagi and Hoffman (1976) see the roots of this orientation in earliest infancy (see footnote 7, this chapter). Among preschoolers, it also has been reported that girls show greater interest in children who are newcomers (McGrew, 1972) and have a superior knowledge of the names of other children in class (Feldstein, 1976). Over a broad age range, females also tend to show greater interest in infants and young children (Berman, Monda, & Myerscough, 1977; Blakemore, 1979). The diffference in this "thing" versus "person" orientation even seems to be reflected in the content of conversation. In adulthood, as in childhood, males talk more about objects or things; females more about people and social relationships (Haas, 1979; Harris, 1977). Finally, the sex difference seems to extend to the realm of nonverbal communication, females being superior in the decoding of nonverbal cues (Hall, 1978).

From all these considerations, it is tempting to suppose that sex differences on neuropsychological tests of lateralized functioning (and, by implication, on spatial-ability tests) are *purely* a matter of strategy differences and that therefore there is no convincing evidence of sex differences in the extent of lateral cerebral specialization. I do not think this strong conclusion is warranted. The remarkable clinical data reported by McGlone (1977), in particular the sex differences in incidence and severity of aphasia after left-hemisphere injury, are difficult to explain by this reasoning. Even the normative data resist this kind of explanation. As Harshman, Remington, and Krashen (1974) have noted, to explain why men show stronger lateralized responding, one would have to postulate the improbable situation in which women prefer to verbalize spatial analyses but they prefer nonverbal processing for linguistic analyses. The point is well-taken, and I agree with McGlone (1980) that "A more parsimonious explanation . . . would be that functional brain asymmetry is less marked in females than in males [p. 221]."

[13] Moore (1967) and Sherman (1967), among others, have proposed an analysis along similar lines.

This hardly means that "strategy" is irrelevant. It does mean that if we want to understand the *proximate* causes of individual differences in cognitive skill, we now must ask, what are the different mechanisms of attention, memory, information-processing style, and the like, that might be engendered by different kinds of brain organization? And, given these probable differences in the "bias" of the neurological substratum, what has been the contribution of the social and intellectual milieu from earliest childhood? These are the questions on which psychologists, using their traditional tools of experimental analysis, should concentrate their attention.

Like the neuropsychological findings, the hormone data also should be considered in broader perspective. At several points, they certainly are not incompatible with sociocultural explanations. For instance, males with testicular feminization syndrome, although born with testes, are feminized in appearance (including external genitalia), are nearly always reared as females, and are exclusively feminine in their gender role and gender identity. Their lowered spatial scores thus could be related as much to their social upbringing as to their nervous systems. The same may be true of the spatial–language contrast scores for normal females. More androgenized, "masculine" girls may be superior on spatial tasks not as a direct expression of the influence of sex hormone level but because these girls are more likely to enjoy and even to be rewarded for engaging in the kinds of "masculine" activities that build spatial skill.

Certainly there is more to it than this. At least the same possibilities do not so obviously apply in the case of the male with ideopathic hypogonadotrophic hypogonadism, since these individuals, being normally masculinized at birth, presumably would have had more nearly normal (for their sex) upbringings. Likewise, the curvilinear relation between androgenization and performance on spatial—relative to language—tasks found for normal males seems inconsistent with a socialization account, as Petersen herself has noted (1979, p. 205). Even so, the important point is that we still know virtually nothing of the real-life behavioral correlates of androgenization, whether at clinically subnormal levels or within the normal range. For example, if we accept the reasonable possibility that certain ways of interacting in an environment help in building spatial skills (and even if we also accept the further and, to me, equally reasonable possibility that in comparison to females, males are inherently more disposed toward such interactions), then we should like to know whether and how the sex hormone ratio or balance affects these particular behaviors.

With respect to males, we have a clue in research that suggests that high fetal androgenization (as indexed, imperfectly, by androgen level sampled from umbilical blood) is associated with rough-and-tumble play when the child is in the preschool years (Maccoby & Jacklin, 1979). In light of the aforementioned inverse relation in males between androgenization and spatial ability, the question arises whether high androgenization predisposes the kind of high-energy, big muscle motor output that actually may be inimical to the achievement of excellent spatial-visualization ability. Moving through one's environment is important for learning about it, but too fast a pace may preclude taking much notice of where one has been and where one will be next. This means that quieter, more visually contemplative activities, like block play or sandbox construction, would be superior to more stereotypically masculine pursuits like high-energy sports as a builder of spatial skill.[14] In short, "androgen level" explains nothing about cognition until we understand not only the neurophysiological effects of androgenization but also the kinds of social and behavioral milieus associated with various androgen levels for both boys and girls.

The preceding points could be extended to our consideration of other findings, in particular, to the more frequent appearance of sex differences after rather than before adolescence, and to the interpretation of within-sex cognitive differences between early- and late-maturers. The social environments of early- and late-maturers are clearly different (see discussion in Jones, 1965; Waber, 1977b). Are they also different in ways that specifically contribute to the development of different cognitive skills, and might these differences be foreshadowed even in early childhood? This is a virtually uncharted and extremely promising region for new research.

In conclusion, both hard-wiring neurological and socioexperiential models of complex cognitive abilities are misleading if we interpret them to mean that there is some simple input-output relationship between the neurological structure or the life experience and a certain cognitive ability—as though one gives rise to the other without any intervening steps. It is in the specification of all the intervening steps where the real psychological work must be done. Finally, no single method of identification and analysis of these "steps" is likely to suffice. If we are ever to grasp the origins of individual differences in cognitive abilities, we must begin to heed Wohlwill's call (Chapter 5 of this volume) for a more balanced attack—a synthesis of differential, experimental, and developmental approaches, informed by a clearer realization of the mutuality of physiological and sociocultural influences.

Does it matter?

McGlone (1980) closed her critical survey of sex differences in human brain asymmetry with the unanswered question: "Does it matter?" It is a hard

---

[14] In this connection, it is interesting to note that preschool boys who are *more* disposed to make-believe, or fantasy, play—play perhaps likely to include a strong element of visualization—are reportedly less physically active than, and less agressive in play than, low-fantasy boys (Pulaski, 1973).

question. One reason is that the study of sex differences in human cognition has become value-laden, both inside and outside the scientific community. Among other unfortunate effects of this development has been the making of many uninformed social pronouncements about sex differences in society. For instance, consider the question of the relevance of high spatial ability for certain disciplines and professions. According to estimates of trait requirements prepared by the U.S. Employment Service, most technical-scientific occupations require spatial ability in the top 10% of the U.S. population. These fields run the gamut from draftsman, airplane designer, and architect to chemist, engineer, mathematician, and physicist—including all subspecialities in all fields. Some *statistical* justification thus has been claimed for the grossly disproportionate representation of men and women in these fields of work. (The proximate educational reason for the disproportions, however, is probably the lack of *mathematical* training among women rather than their poorer spatial ability per se [see Ernest, 1976], although spatial-visualization as I noted earlier, may be a critical element in mathematical ability.)

On the one hand, there are those who, noting the current neuro-psychological evidence, will see the differences in sex representation in these technical-scientific fields as biologically fitting and therefore both fundamentally immutable and socially justified. Biology is fate, they would say. Their counterparts on the other side, rejecting the same evidence, will see the same differences as purely and wholly an accident of our social history, and therefore unjust and changeable—complete parity of the sexes in every field of human endeavor being the ostensible goal. Surely, neither position is defensible. A Victorian physician once said, "the tendency to symmetry in the two halves of the cerebrum is stronger in women than in men [Crighton-Brown, 1880, p. 65]." If current research seems to have shown this early view to be correct in some sense, so, I think, has another Victorian put the question of such differences in proper perspective. A Mrs. Fawcett, a leader of the women's movement of that day, is quoted as having said, "No one of those who care most for the women's movement cares one jot to prove or to maintain that men's brains and women's brains are exactly alike or exactly equal. All we ask is that the social and legal status of women should be such as to foster, not to suppress, any gift for art, literature, learning, or goodness with which women may be endowed [Romanes, 1887, p. 672]."

References

Bakan, P., & Putnam, W. Right-left discrimination and brain lateralization: Sex differences. *Archives of Neurology*, 1974, *30*, 334-335.
Beach, F. A. Hormonal factors controlling the differentiation, development, and display of cop-

ulatory behavior in the ramstergig and related species. In E. Tobach, L. R. Aronson, & E. Shaw (Eds.), *The biopsychology of development.* New York: Academic Press, 1971.

Bennett, G. K. *Bennett Mechanical Comprehension Test.* New York: The Psychological Corporation, 1969 (Manual, Forms S and T).

Bennett, G. K., Seashore, H. G., & Wesman, A. G. *Differential aptitude tests, 3rd Ed.* New York: Psychological Corporation, 1959.

Berlucchi, C., Marzi, C. A., Rizzolatti, G., & Umilta, C. Functional hemispheric asymmetries in normals: Influence of sex and practice. Paper presented at 21st International Congress on Psychology, Paris, France, July, 1976.

Berman, P. W., Monda, L. C., & Myerscough, R. P. Sex differences in young children's responses to an infant: An observation within a day-care setting. *Child Development*, 1977, *48*, 711-715.

Bettis, N. C. *An assessment of the geographic knowledge and understanding of fifth-grade students in Michigan.* Unpublished doctoral dissertation, Michigan State University, 1974.

Blakemore, J. E. O. Age and sex differences in interaction with a human infant. Paper presented at Biennial Meeting of the Society for Research in Child Development, San Francisco, 18 March, 1979.

Block, J. H. Issues, problems, and pitfalls in assessing sex diffferences: A critical review of *The psychology of sex differences. Merrill-Palmer Quarterly*, 1976, *22*, 284-308.

Bock, R. D. Word and image: Sources of the verbal and spatial factors in mental test scores. *Psychometrika*, 1973, *38*, 437-457.

Bradshaw, J. L., & Gates, E. A. Visual field differences in verbal tasks: Effects of task familiarity and sex of subject. *Brain and Language*, 1978, *5*, 166-187.

Brinkman, E. H. Programmed instruction as a technique for improving spatial visualization. *Journal of Applied Psychology*, 1966, *50*, 179-184.

Broverman, D. M., Broverman, I. K., Vogel, W., & Palmer, R. D. The automatization cognitive style and physical development. *Child Development*, 1964, *35*, 1343-1359.

Broverman, D. M., & Klaiber, E. L. Negative relationships between abilities. *Psychometrika*, 1969, *34*, 5-20.

Broverman, D. M., Klaiber, E. L., Kobayashi, Y., & Vogel, W. Roles of activation and inhibition in sex differences in cognitive abilities. *Psychological Review*, 1968, *75*, 23-50.

Brown, J. W. On the neural organization of language: Thalamic and cortical relationships. *Brain and Language*, 1975, *2*, 18-30.

Bryden, M. P. Strategy effects in the assessment of hemispheric asymmetry. In G. Underwood (Ed.), *Strategies of information processing.* New York: Academic Press, 1978.

Cameron, J., Livson, N., & Bayley, N. Infant vocalizations and their relationship to mature intelligence. *Science*, 1967, *157*, 331-333.

Carroll, J. B., & Maxwell, S. E. Individual differences in cognitive abilities. In M. R. Rosenzweig & L. W. Porter (Eds.), *Annual Review of Psychology, Vol. 30.* Palo Alto, California: Annual Reviews, Inc., 1979. Pp. 603-640.

Cioffi, J., & Kandel, G. Laterality of stereognostic accuracy of children for words, shapes, and bigrams: A sex difference for bigrams. *Science*, 1979, *204*, 1432-1434.

Cohen, D., & Wilkie, F. Sex-related differences in cognition among the elderly. In M. A. Wittig & A. C. Petersen (Eds.), *Sex-related differences in cognitive functioning: Developmental issues.* New York: Academic Press, 1979. Pp. 145-159.

Cohen, L. B., & Gelber, E. R. Infant visual memory. In L. B. Cohen & P. Salapatek (Eds.), *Infant perception: From sensation to cognition.* New York: Academic Press, 1975. Pp. 347-403.

Crighton-Browne, J. On the weight of the brain and its component parts in the insane. *Brain*, 1880, *2*, 42-67.

Dawson, G. D., Farrow, B. J., & Dawson, W. E. Sex diffferences and haptic cerebral asymmetry. Paper presented at Annual Meeting of the Midwest Psychological Association, St. Louis, Missouri, 2 May, 1980.

Day, J. Right-hemisphere language processing in normal right-handers. *Journal of Experimental Psychology: Human Perception and Performance*, 1977, *3*, 518-528.

Ernest, J. Mathematics and sex. Santa Barbara: Department of Mathematics, University of California, 1976.

Fagot, B. The influence of sex of child on parental reactions to toddler children. *Child Development*, 1978, *49*, 459-465.

Fairweather, H., & Butterworth, G. The WPPSI at four years: A sex difference in verbal-performance discrepancies. *British Journal of Psychology*, 1977, *47*, 85-90.

Farrell, M. Sex differences in block play in early childhood education. *Journal of Educational Research*, 1957, *51*, 279-284.

Feldstein, J. H. Sex differences in social memory among preschool children. *Sex Roles*, 1976, *2*, 75-79.

Ferguson, L. R., & Maccoby, E. E. Interpersonal correlates of differential abilities. *Child Development*, 1966, *37*, 549-571.

Flanery, R. C., & Balling, J. D. Developmental changes in hemispheric specialization for tactile spatial ability. *Developmental Psychology*, 1979, *15*, 364-372.

Franco, L., & Sperry, R. W. Hemisphere lateralization for cognitive processing of geometry. *Neuropsychologia*, 1977, *15*, 107-114.

Freedman, D. G. Infancy, biology, and culture. In L. P. Lipsitt (Ed.), *Developmental psychobiology: The significance of infancy*. New York: Wiley, 1976. Pp. 35-54.

French, J. W., Ekstrom, R. B., & Price, L. A. *Manual for Kit of Reference Tests for Cognitive Factors*. Princeton: Educational Testing Service, 1963.

Galapurda, A. M., LeMay, M., Kemper, T. L., & Geschwind, N. Right-left asymmetries in the brain. *Science*, 1978, *199*, 852-856.

Geiringer, E. R., & Hyde, J. S. Sex differences on Piaget's water-level task: spatial ability incognito. *Perceptual & Motor Skills*, 1976, *42*, 1323-1328.

Glanville, B., Best, C., & Levinson, R. A cardiac measure of cerebral asymmetries in infant auditory perception. *Developmental Psychology*, 1977, *13*, 54-59.

Golbeck, S. L., & Liben, L. S. Performance on Piagetian spatial tasks and knowledge about the physical world. Paper presented at Biennial Meetings of the Society for Research in Child Development, San Francisco, 17 March, 1979.

Goldberg, S., & Lewis, M. Play behavior in the year-old infant: Early sex differences. *Child Development*, 1969, *40*, 21-32.

Goldstein, A. G., & Chance, J. E. Effects of practice on sex-related differences in performance on embedded figures. *Psychonomic Science*, 1965, 3, 361-362.

Gorski, R. A. The neuroendocrine regulation of sexual behavior. In G. Newton & A. H. Riesen (Eds.), *Advances in Psychobiology, Vol. II*, New York: Wiley, 1974. Pp. 1-58.

Gorski, R. A., Gordon, J. H., Shryne, J. E., & Southam, A. M. Evidence for a morphological sex difference within the medial preoptic area of the rat brain. *Brain Research*, 1978, *148*, 333-346.

Goy, R. W. Organizing effects of androgen on the behavior of rhesus monkeys. In R. P. Michael (Ed.), *Endocrinology and human behavior*. New York: Oxford University Press, 1968.

Greenough, W. T., Carter, S. C., Steerman, C., & DeVoogd, T. J. Sex differences in dendritic patterns in hamster preoptic areas. *Brain Research*, 1977, *126*, 63-72.

Guilford, J. P. Printed classification tests, AAF Report No. 5. Washington, D.C.: U. S. Government Printing Office, 1947.

Haas, A. Male and female spoken language differences: Stereotypes and evidence. *Psychological Bulletin*, 1979, *86*, 616-626.

Hall, J. A. Gender effects in decoding nonverbal cues. *Psychological Bulletin,* 1978, *85,* 845-847.

Harper, L., & Sanders, K. Preschool children's use of space: Sex differences in outdoor play. Extended report (mimeo) of a paper by the same title published as a "Brief Report" in *Developmental Psychology,* 1975, *11,* 119.

Harris, L. J. Sex differences in the growth and use of language. In E. Donelson & J. Gullahorn (Eds.), *Women: A psychological perspective.* New York: Wiley, 1977. Pp. 79-94.

Harris, L. J. Sex differences in spatial ability: Possible environmental, genetic, and neurological factors. In M. Kinsbourne (Ed.), *Asymmetrical function of the brain.* Cambridge, England: Cambridge University Press, 1978. Pp. 405-522.

Harris, L. J. Sex-related differences in spatial ability: A developmental psychological view. In C. Kopp (Ed.), *Becoming female: Perspectives on development.* New York: Plenum, 1979. Pp. 133-181. (a)

Harris, L. J. Variances and anomalies. Review of M. A. Wittig & A. C. Petersen (Eds.), *Sex-related differences in cognitive functioning. Science,* 1979, *206,* 50-52. (b)

Harris, L. J. Which hand is the 'eye' of the blind?—A new look at an old question. In J. Herron (Ed.), *Neuropsychology of left-handedness.* New York: Academic Press, 1980. Pp. 303-329.

Harris, L. J., Best, C. T., & Hanley, C. Sex and age differences in representation of liquid horizontality: The role of inferred motion. Submitted for publication, 1980.

Harris, L. J., & Gitterman, S. R. Sex and handedness differences in well-educated adults' self-descriptions of left-right confusability. *Archives of Neurology,* 1978, *35,* 773.

Harris, L. J., & Gitterman, S. R. Sex differences in college students on the Culver Laterality Discrimination Test. Unpublished data, Michigan State University, 1977.

Harris, L. J., Hanley, C., & Best, C. Conservation of horizontality: Sex differences in sixth-graders and college students. In R. C. Smart and M. S. Smart (Eds.), *Readings in child development and relationships,* 2nd Ed. New York: Macmillan, 1977, 375-387.

Harris, L. J., & Witelson, S. F. The analysis of cognitive processes in children through the study of hemisphere specialization in different perceptual systems. Paper presented at a symposium, "Towards a developmental neuropsychology," Biennial Meetings of the Society for Research in Child Development, New Orleans, Louisiana, March, 1977.

Harshman, R., Remington, R., & Krashen, D. Sex, language, and the brain, Part II. Evidence from dichotic listening for adult sex differences in verbal lateralization. Paper presented at the UCLA conference on human brain function, Los Angeles, 1974.

Hatta, T. The functional asymmetry of tactile pattern learning in normal subjects. *Psychologia,* 1978, *21,* 83-89.

Herman, J. F., Kail, R. V., & Siegel, A. W. Cognitive maps of a college campus: A new look at freshman orientation. *Bulletin of the Psychonomic Society,* 1979, *13,* 183-186.

Herman, J. F., & Siegel, A. W. The development of cognitive mapping of the large-scale environment. *Journal of Experimental Child Psychology,* 1978, *26,* 389-406.

Hiscock, M., & Kinsbourne, M. Selective listening asymmetry in preschool children. *Developmental Psychology,* 1977, *13,* 217-224.

Hittelman, J. H. & Dickes, R. Sex differences in neonatal eye contact time. *Merrill-Palmer Quarterly,* 1979, *24,* 171-184.

Hoppe, C. M., Kagan, S. M. & Zahn, G. L. Conflict resolution among field-independent and field-dependent Anglo-American and Mexican-American children and their mothers. *Developmental Psychology,* 1977, *13,* 591-598.

Howe, G. F. The teaching of directions in space. *Journal of Geography,* 1931, *30,* 298-304.

Irving, D. The field-dependence hypothesis in cross-cultural perspective. Unpublished Ph.D. dissertation, Rice University, 1970. *Dissertations Abstracts International,* 1970, *31,* 3691-B.

Jacklin, C. N. Epilogue. In M. A. Wittig & A. C. Petersen (Eds.), *Sex-related differences in cognitive functioning*. New York: Academic Press, 1979, Pp. 357-371.

Jones, M. C. Psychological correlates of somatic development. *Child Development*, 1965, *36*, 899-911.

Kail, R. & Carter, P. Cognitive bases of sex differences in spatial ability. Paper presented at Annual Meetings of the Midwestern Psychological Association, St. Louis, Missouri, 3 May 1980.

Kaplan, E. F. Noncompromised hemisphere in patients with local brain disease. In H. L. Teuber (Chairman), *Alternations in brain functioning and changes in cognition*. Symposium presented at the Annual Meeting of the American Psychological Association, Washington, D. C., 6 September 1976.

Kelly, A. *Girls and science. An international study of sex differences in school science achievement*. International Association for the Evaluation of Educational Achievement Monograph Studies, No. 9. Stockholm: Almqvist and Wiksell, 1978.

Keogh, B. K. Pattern copying under three conditions of an expanded spatial field. *Developmental Psychology*, 1971, *4*, 25-31.

Kimura, D. The asymmetry of the human brain. *Scientific American*, 1973, *228*, 70-78.

Kinsbourne, M. The cerebral basis of lateral asymmetries in attention. *Acta Psychologica*, 1970, *33*, 193-201.

Kinsbourne, M., & Hiscock, M. Does cerebral dominance develop? In S. J. Segalowitz & F. A. Gruber (Ed.), *Language development and neurological theory*. New York: Academic Press, 1977. Pp. 169-191.

Kinsbourne, M., & Hiscock, M. Cerebral lateralization and cognitive development. In J. S. Chall and A. F. Mirsky (Eds.), *Education and the brain*. 77th Yearbook of the National Society for Studies in Education. Chicago: University of Chicago Press, 1978, 169-222.

Kirschenblatt-Gimblett, B. *Speech play*. Philadelphia: University of Pennsylvania Press, 1976.

Kohen-Raz, R. *Psychobiological aspects of cognitive growth*. New York: Academic Press, 1977.

Kolata, G. B. Sex hormones and brain development. *Science*, 1979, *205*, 985-987.

Kozlowski, L. T., & Bryant, K. J. Sense of direction, spatial orientation, and cognitive maps. *Journal of Experimental Psychology: Human Perception and Performance, 1977, 3,* 590-598.

Lake, D. A., & Bryden, M. P. Handedness and sex differences in hemispheric asymmetry. *Brain and Language*, 1976, *3*, 266-282.

Lansdell, H. Effect of neurosurgery on the ability to identify popular work associations. *Journal of Abnormal Psychology*, 1973, *81*, 255-258.

Levy, J. Psychobiological implications of bilateral asymmetry. In S. Dimond & J. C. Beaumont (Eds.), *Hemispheric function in the human brain*. London: Paul Elek, 1974.

Levy-Agresti (Levy), J., & Sperry, R. W. Differential perceptual capacities in major and minor hemispheres. *Proceedings of the National Academy of Science*, 1968, *61*, 1151.

Ley, R., & Koepke, J. Sex and age differences in the departures of young children from their mothers. Paper presented at Biennial Meetings of the Society for Research in Child Development, Denver, Colorado, April, 1975.

Liben, L. S. Operative understanding of horizontality and its relation to longterm memory. *Child Development*, 1974, *45*, 416-424.

Liben, L. S. Performance on Piagetian spatial tasks as a function of sex, field dependence, and training. *Merrill-Palmer Quarterly*, 1978, *24*, 97-110.

Lord, F. E. A. A study of spatial orientation of children. *Journal of Educational Research*, 1941, *34*, 481-505.

McCall, R. B., Hogarty, P. S., & Hurlburt, N. Transitions in infant sensorimotor development and the prediction of childhood I.Q. *American Psychologist*, 1972, *27*, 728-748.

Maccoby, E. E., & Jacklin, C. N. *The psychology of sex differences.* Stanford, California: Stanford University Press, 1974.

Maccoby, E. J., & Jacklin, C. N. Sex hormones in umbilical cord blood: Their relationship to sex, birth order, and behavioral development. Paper presented at Biennial Meetings of the Society for Research in Child Development. San Francisco, 17 March 1979.

McGlone, J. Sex differences in the cerebral organization of verbal functions in patients with unilateral brain lesions. *Brain,* 1977, *100,* 775-793.

McGlone, J. Sex differences in functional brain asymmetry. *Cortex,* 1978, *14,* 122-128.

McGlone, J. Sex differences in human brain asymmetry: A critical survey. *The behavioral and brain sciences,* 1980, *3,* 215-227.

McGrew, W. C. Aspects of social development in school children with emphasis on introduction to the group. In N. Blurton-Jones (Ed.). *Ethological studies of child behavior.* London and New York: Cambridge University Press, 1972. Pp. 129-156.

McGuinness, D. Hearing: Individual differences in perceiving. *Perception,* 1974, *1,* 465-473.

McGuinness, D. Sex differences in the organization of perception and cognition. In B. Lloyd & J. Archer (Eds.), *Exploring sex differences.* New York: Academic Press, 1976. Pp. 123-156. (a)

McGuinness, D. Away from a unisex psychology: Individual differences in visual sensory and perceptual processes. *Perception,* 1976, *5,* 279-294. (b)

Masica, D. N., Money, J., & Ehrhardt, A. A. Fetal Feminization and female gender identity in the testicular feminizing syndrome of androgen insensitivity. *Archives of Sexual Behavior,* 1971, *1,* 131-142.

Mebane, D., & Johnson, D. L. A comparison of the performance of Mexican boys and girls on Witkin's cognitive tasks. *Interamerican Journal of Psychology,* 1970, *4,* 227-239.

Metzler, J., & Shepard, R. N. Rotation of tri-dimensional objects. In R. L. Solso (Ed.), *Theories in cognitive psychology: The Loyola Symposium.* New York: Wiley, 1974. Pp. 147-201.

Mitchelmore, M. C. The perceptual development of Jamaican students, with special reference to visualization and drawing of three-dimensional geometrical figures and the effects of spatial training. Unpublished doctoral dissertation, Ohio State University, 1974.

Molfese, D. L., & Molfese, V. J. VOT distinctions in infants: Learned or innate? In H. Whitaker & H. A. Whitaker (Eds.), *Studies in neurolinguistics, Vol. 4.* New York: Academic Press, 1979. Pp. 225-240.

Money, J., Alexander, D., & Walker, H. T., Jr. *A Standardized Road-Map Test of Direction Sense* (manual). Baltimore: Johns Hopkins Press, 1965.

Moore, T. Language and intelligence: A longitudinal study of the first eight years. Part I: Patterns of development in boys and girls. *Human Development,* 1967, *10,* 88-106.

Nance, D. M., Gorski, R. A., & Panksepp, J. Neural and hormonal determinants of sex differences in food intake and body weight. In D. Novin, W. Wyricka, & G. Bray (Eds.), *Hunger: Brain mechanisms and clinical implications.* New York: Raven Press, 1976. Pp. 257-271.

Nash, S. C. Sex role as a mediator of intellectual functioning. In M. A. Wittig & A. C. Petersen (Eds), *Sex-related differences in intellectual functioning: Developmental issues.* New York: Academic Press, 1979. Pp. 263-302.

Nottebohm, F., & Arnold, A. P. Sexual dimorphism in vocal control areas of the songbird brain. *Science,* 1976, *194,* 211-213.

Nottebohm, F., & Arnold, A. P. Songbirds' brains: Sexual dimorphism. *Science* (Letter), 1979, *206,* 769.

Ojemann, G. A. Asymmetric function of the thalamus in man. Paper presented at Conference on *Evolution and Lateralization of the Brain.* New York Academy of Science, 15 October, 1976.

Oke, A., Keller, R., Mefford, I., & Adams, R. N. Lateralization of norepinephrine in human thalamus. *Science,* 1978, *200,* 1411-1413.

O'Keefe, J., & Nadel, L. *The hippocampus as a cognitive map.* New York and London: Oxford University Press, 1978.

Penfield, W., & Roberts, L. Speech and brain mechanisms. Princeton: Princeton University Press, 1959.

Petersen, A. C. Physical androgyny and cognitive functioning in adolescence. *Developmental Psychology,* 1976, *12,* 524-533.

Petersen, A. C. Hormones and cognitive functioning in normal development. In M. A. Wittig & A. C. Petersen (Eds.), *Sex-related differences in cognitive functioning: Developmental Issues.* New York: Academic Press, 1979. Pp. 189-214.

Piaget, J., & Inhelder, B. *The child's conception of space.* New York: Humanities Press, 1956.

Pomerantz, A. A developmental study of hand specialization using a dichaptic perception task. Unpublished M.A. thesis, Michigan State University, 1980.

Porteus, S. D. *Porteus maze test: Fifty years' application.* Palo Alto, California: Pacific Books, 1965.

Pulaski, M. A. Toys and imaginative play. In J. L. Singer (Ed.), *The child's world of make-believe.* New York: Academic Press, 1973. Pp. 74-103.

Quadagno, D. M., Briscoe, R., & Quadagno, J. S. The effect of perinatal gonadal hormones on selected nonsexual behavior patterns: A critical assessment of the nonhuman and human literature. *Psychological Bulletin,* 1977, *84,* 62-80.

Ramey, C. T., & Watson, J. S. Nonsocial reinforcement of infants' vocalizations. *Developmental Psychology,* 1972, *6,* 538.

Ramirez, M., & Price-Williams, D. Cognitive styles in children: Two Mexican communities. *Interamerican Journal of Psychology,* 1974, *8,* 1-2.

Ray, W. J., Morell, M., and Frediani, A. W. Sex differences and lateral specialization of hemispheric functioning. *Neuropsychologia,* 1976, *14,* 391-394.

Reinisch, J. Fetal hormones, the brain, and human sex differences: A heuristic, integrative review of the recent literature. *Archives of Sexual Behavior,* 1974, *3,* 51-90.

Rheingold, H. L., & Cook, K. V. The content of boys' and girls' rooms as an index of parents' behavior. *Child Development,* 1975, *46,* 459-463.

Roberts, J. Intellectual development of children by demographic and socioeconomic factors (DHEW Publ. No. HSM 72-1012, Series 11, No. 110, Washington, D.C.: U.S. Government Printing Office, 1971.

Romanes, G. J. Mental differences between men and women. *The nineteenth century,* 1887, *21,* 654-672.

Rovet, J. Individual differences and rate of development. Paper presented at Biennial Meetings of the Society for Research in Child Development, San Francisco, March, 1979.

Rudel, R., Denckla, M., & Spalten, E. The functional asymmetry of Braille letter learning in normal, sighted children. *Neurology, 1974, 24,* 733-738.

Sagi, A., & Hoffman, M. L. Empathic distress in the newborn. *Developmental Psychology,* 1976, *12,* 175-176.

Searleman, A. A review of right hemispheric linguistic capabilities. *Psychological Bulletin,* 1977, *84,* 503-528.

Seitz, M., Weber, B., Jacobson, J., & Morehouse, R. Sex differences in auditory brainstem responses. Paper presented at Eighth Annual Meeting of International Neuropsychology Society, San Francisco, 1980.

Shepard, R. N., & Metzler, J. Mental rotation of three-dimensional objects. *Science,* 1971, *171,* 701-703.

Sherman, J. A. Problem of sex differences in space perception and aspects of individual functioning. *Psychological Review*, 1967, *74*, 290-299.

Shucard, J. L., Shucard, D. W., Cummins, K. R., & Campos, J. J. Auditory evoked potentials and sex-related differences in brain development. Paper presented at Biennial Meetings of the Society for Research in Child Development, San Francisco, 1979.

Siegel, A. W., & Schadler, M. The development of young chldren's spatial representations of their classrooms. *Child Development*, 1977, *48*, 388-394.

Simner, M. L. Newborn's response to the cry of another infant. *Developmental Psychology*, 1971, *5*, 136-150.

Smith, P. K., & Daglish, L. Sex differences in parent and infant behavior in the home. *Child Development*, 1977, *48*, 1250-1254.

Spellacy, F., & Blumstein, S. The influence of language set on ear preference in phoneme recognition. *Cortex*, 1970, *6*, 430-439.

Sutton-Smith, B. The play of girls. In C. B. Kopp (Ed.), *Becoming female: Perspectives on development*. New York: Plenum, 1979. Pp. 229-257.

Sutton-Smith, B. Quoted in Lansing (Michigan) *State Journal*, 21 February, 1977.

Tanner, J. M. Sequence, tempo, and individual variation in the growth and development of boys and girls aged twelve to sixteen. *Daedalus* (Proceedings of the American Academy of Arts and Sciences), 1971, *100*, 907-930.

Tapley, S. M., & Bryden, M. P. An investigation of sex differences in spatial ability: Mental rotation of three-dimensional objects. *Canadian Journal of Psychology*, 1977, *31*, 122-130.

Thomas, H. & Jamison, W. On the acquisition of understanding that still water is horizontal. *Merrill-Palmer Quarterly*, 1975, *21*, 31-44.

Thomas, H., Jamison, W., & Hummel, D. D. Observation is insufficient for discovering that the surface of still water is invariantly horizontal. *Science*, 1973, *181*, 173-174.

Thompson, E. G., Harris, L. J., & Mann, I. Relationships among sex, measures of cognitive complexity, and performance on spatial tasks in college students. *British Journal of Psychology*, *1980*, in press.

Van Buren, J., & Borke, R. *Variations and connections of the human thalamus, Vol. 2, Variations of the human diencephalon*. Berlin and New York: Springer-Verlag, 1972.

Vandenberg, S. G., & Kuse, A. R. Spatial ability: A critical review of the sex-linked major gene hypothesis. In M. A. Wittig & A. C. Petersen, (Eds.) *Sex-related differences in cognitive functioning*. New York: Academic Press, 1979, Pp. 67-95.

Waber, D. P. Sex differences in mental abilities, hemispheric lateralization, and rate of physical growth at adolescence. *Developmental Psychology*, 1977, *13*, 29-38. (a)

Waber, D. P. Biological substrates of field dependence: Implications of the sex difference. *Psychological Bulletin*, 1977, *84*, 1076-1087. (b)

Waber, D. P. Cognitive abilities and sex-related variations in the maturation of cortical functions. In M. A. Wittig & A. C. Petersen (Eds.), *Sex-related differences in cognitive functioning*. New York: Academic Press, 1979. Pp. 161-186.

Wada, J. A., Clark, R., & Hamm, A. Cerebral hemispheric asymmetry in humans: Cortical speech zones in 100 adult and 100 infant brains. *Archives of Neurology*, 1975, *32*, 239-246.

Wagner, N. M., & Harris, L. J. Hand asymmetries in braille letter learning in sighted nine- and eleven-year-olds: A cautionary note on sex differences. Paper presented at meetings of the International Neuropsychology Society, New York, 3 February, 1979.

Warrington, E. K., James, M., & Kinsbourne, M. Drawing disability in relation to laterality of cerebral lesion. *Brain*, 1966, *89*, 53-82.

Watson, J. Operant conditioning of visual fixation in infants under visual and auditory reinforcement. *Developmental Psychology*, 1969, *1*, 508-516.

Wilson, J. R., DeFries, J. C., McClearn, G. E., Vandenberg, S. G., Johnson, R. C., & Rashed, M. N. Cognitive abilities: Use of family data as a control to assess sex and age differences in two ethnic groups. *International Journal of Aging and Human Development*, 1975, *6*, 261-276.

Wilson, R. S. Twins: Patterns of cognitive development as measured on the Weschler Preschool and Primary Scale of Intelligence. *Developmental Psychology*, 1975, *11*, 126-134.

Witelson, S. F. Sex and the single hemisphere: Right hemisphere specialization for spatial processing. *Science*, 1976, 425-427.

Witkin, H. A., & Berry, J. W. Psychological differentiation in cross-cultural perspective. *Journal of Cross Cultural Psychology*, 1975, *6*, 4-87.

Witkin, H. A., Dyk, R. B., Faterson, G. E., Goodenough, D. R., & Karp, S. A. *Psychological Differentiation*. New York: Wiley, 1962.

Wolff, P. H., & Hurwitz, I. Sex differences in finger tapping: A developmental study. *Neuropsychologia*, 1976, *14*, 35-41.

Zaidel, E. Auditory vocabulary of the right hemisphere following brain bisection or hemidecortication. *Cortex*, 1976, *12*, 191-211.

Zoccolotti, P., & Oltman, P. K. Field dependence and lateralization of verbal and configurational processing, *Cortex*, 1978, *14*, 155-163.

Commentary on Part II

5 Experimental, Developmental, Differential: Which Way the Royal Road to Knowledge about Spatial Cognition?

JOACHIM F. WOHLWILL

Introduction

In his 1957 Presidential Address to the American Psychological Association, Cronbach (1958) argued persuasively that experimental and differential approaches to the study of behavior represent two different worlds, whether considered in terms of methodology, treatment of data, role of theorizing, or even professional identity of the practitioners of each approach. Cronbach concluded with a plea for a rapprochement between these two opposing sides, and for attempts to arrive at a synthesis between them, a plea given more concrete expression in a subsequent paper on the same subject (Cronbach, 1975).

The chapters discussed in this commentary appear to align themselves distinctly on the one side or the other of this still largely unbridged chasm, and probably as a result, convey a very different view of the field. On the one hand we have those by Pick and Lockman (Chapter 2), and Acredolo (Chapter 3), who represent a very similar experimental-developmental approach to the field. They emphasize the strong dependence of responses in spatial cognition tasks on particular situational and task variables, in interaction with age, that is, developmental level. On the other we find Harris (Chapter 4), himself a former representative of this experimental-developmental approach, moving unabashedly into the differential camp to examine differences between the sexes in response to spatial cognition tasks. His chapter leaves one with a sense of the pervasiveness of these differences regardless of the specific nature of the task, and by implication with an impression of this aspect of cognition as representing a single, unitary entity.

The contrast between the two paradigms of research emerges muted,

129

however, because of the incorporation in the work of Acredolo, Pick, and their colleagues of the age variable; this is treated much like Harris does the variable of sex—that is, as a dimension of individual differences, only superimposed on the effects of experimentally manipulated variables. Their work represents, in effect, a replication of an experimental study at different age levels, analyzed comparatively, rather than in terms of a direct concern with change with age (cf. Wohlwill, 1973b). As a result, we have here not so much a synthesis between the experimental and differential paradigms, as much as a hybrid form of research involving elements of both.

Before we turn to the question of how one might shift from such a differential conception of age to a more truly developmental focus, let us point to a more positive achievement of the experimental approach followed by Acredolo, and by Pick and Lockman: Their work points clearly to the operation of a number of differentiable processes that govern children's performance in spatial-cognition tasks. Thus, notwithstanding the seeming generality of the sex differences encountered in this realm, to which Harris' review points, it would clearly be a mistake to treat these differences as reflecting the operation of a unitary process. Rather, what seems to be called for is an attempt to analyze "spatial abilities" and "spatial cognition tasks" into their component skills or processes. This will not only provide a taxonomy of such tasks that will help us recognize the dimensions of the developmental changes encountered in this area, but should be equally valuable in sorting out the diverse factors that may be implicated in the reported differences between the sexes.

Without any claim to exhaustiveness, and at the risk of making some seemingly arbitrary distinctions among "perception," "learning," "memory," and "cognition," I propose that we differentiate among the following aspects of the tasks encountered in the chapters under discussion. This list should not be read as a typology of tasks cast in concrete, or of processes operating in complete independence of one another, but rather as a heuristically useful differentiation among diverse processes that enter into tasks of spatial cognition, which may be of some relevance for a more comprehensive formulation of the developmental changes found in this area.

An Inventory of Spatial Skills and Processes

*Attention to and Selecting Out of Relevant Information
in the Stimulus Field*

This aspect of the situation is taken for granted in most of this research, which does not typically make great demands on the subject's attentional power, or ability to sort out relevant from irrelevant information. Nevertheless, Acredolo's findings with regard to the role of landmarks illustrate the potential relevance of this factor, and the importance of considering the salience of such stimuli and their potential influence on the individual. As Acredolo shows, young children are apt to be particularly susceptible to that influence—both for better and for worse, depending on the ecological validity of the landmark in the situation as a cue to orientation.

Cue-Learning

The preceding reference to the ecological validity of landmarks brings up another aspect of the situation that is not typically the focus of the experimenter's attention but may well play a major role in the subject's response. Consider our sense of "up" and "down." Typically, we rely on gravitational cues to permit us to differentiate these two directions; the ubiquity of this information for terrestrial beings means that it is rarely a source of difficulty for us. It probably accounts for the relative ease with which young children can discriminate up–down reversals, for example, for letter-like shapes, as compared to left–right or mirror-image reversals. Yet we need only consider what happens to our sense of up-and-down in a gravity-free environment such as that of the orbital Space Lab, and the complex and at times ingenious ways that the Space-Lab crews devised to invent their own set of cues for "up" and "down" (Cooper, 1977) to realize the importance of such associational cue learning in spatial orientation. The same process undoubtedly operates in our learning of left–right discrimination. How many of us rely on the side on which we wear our watch to mediate our sense of left and right? It seems even possible that this differentiating cue may be implicated in sex differences in this area, if we assume that boys tend to be given watches at an earlier age than girls, and that the latter lack other similar cues directly tied to their body that could play a similar function. (Bodily symmetry around the vertical axis precludes the use of the body itself for this purpose—as expressed in the old saw that "right is where the thumb is on the left.")

Memory

A further factor that some may regard as infracognitive, but that plays a major role in many tasks of spatial cognition is that of memory for spatial relations among stimuli. It might be argued that this factor presupposes the formation of a spatial-reference system, and should thus be treated as part of a larger process relating to the establishment of such a system. Yet it is clear, particularly in regard to spatial orientation in the large-scale environment, that the learning and remembering of the sequential order of stimuli, or of their locations relative to some landmark or prominent axis of organization, plays an important role in the formation of spatial-reference systems, while remaining separable from the establishment of such a system per se. For instance, in going over a certain route, a particular corner may be learned as "the place two blocks from the one where I have to make a left turn"; similarly, two salient buildings may be remembered as being on the same side, or on opposite sides, of a river.

A number of the studies reviewed by both Acredolo and by Pick and Lockman, such as Goldsmith's (1979), clearly place a considerable burden on the encoding of such information about spatial relations in memory. Part of the problem here, and the part that may be implicated in the age changes observed in many of these tasks, concerns the integration of temporally experienced stimuli over time into some cohesive whole, much as is entailed in the mastery of auditory or tactual patterns by young children.

Formation of Stable Spatial Reference Systems

A signal achievement of Acredolo and Pick, and Lockman is their careful and insightful delineation of the function of different kinds of reference systems in spatial orientation, and of the intricacies of the supposed development from an egocentric to an allocentric system. By definition, the cognition of spatial relations involves the establishment of some system of relations among stimuli in space that have some degree of stability over displacement and locomotion of the individual through space. Such a developmental shift would be in accord with diverse theories such as Piaget's (Piaget & Inhelder, 1956) and Schachtel's (1959) among others. Yet it is apparent that the kind of reference system utilized by the individual is a function of situational factors, such as the presence or absence of landmarks, the demands of a particular task, and possibly the individual's experiential history, as suggested by certain findings from animal research to be cited presently. These considerations lead to the suggestion that what is characteristic of individuals at a given level of development may not be their use of a particular frame of reference as such, but rather the ability to utilize multiple frames of reference, and to switch from one to another in accordance with the demands of a task and the information available in a given situation.

Spatial Representation and Cognitive Mapping

This may be considered to be the most elaborate expression of spatial cognition, and to incorporate most if not all of the preceding. For that very reason the results of a cognitive mapping task or one of navigation through the environment assumed to depend on the internalized representation of that environment may be difficult to interpret, precisely because performance on it is so multidetermined. This may account in part for the neglect of this type of task in the chapters under discussion. The experimentalists among us seem to avoid them because of the difficulty of subjecting these processes to systematic study and of demonstrating the role of particular variables on mapping performance, though the program of research of Siegel and his colleagues described and discussed in Chapter 7 of this volume represents a notable exception in this regard. At the same time the sex-difference literature has also failed to make extensive use of this type of task—perhaps because of the preference of the differential psychologist for tasks yielding reliably measurable and quantifiable responses.

Developmental and Experimental Aspects of Spatial Reference Systems

As noted at the outset, this review of differentiable skills that may be involved in spatial cognition tasks is not to be taken as a taxonomy of discrete processes operating one independent of the other. Rather, they should be thought of as representing a quasi-hierarchy, each dependent to some degree on the preceding ones, though the particular requirements of a given task will determine the extent to which each is in fact called into play. It seems likely, furthermore, that to this structural-hierarchical order corresponds a developmentally ordered sequence of abilities, in the sense that a set of tasks could be devised that call into play each of the skills of the hierarchy in turn, and success on such tasks would probably constitute a scalable and developmentally orderable set. Yet this purely structural approach has its limitations for the student of developmental process, and even more for the investigator of sex differences and other differential aspects of the development of spatial cognition.

Here we come up against a signal limitation of both the experimental-developmental research undertaken and reviewed by Acredolo and by Pick and Lockman, and the sex-difference research analyzed by Harris. This body of research, both in its approach to developmental change and to sex differences, remains purely comparative; that is, it relies exclusively on comparison among groups, whether differentiated by age or by sex. This leaves the meaning of the observed differences in doubt. What is ultimately needed is an approach that will allow us to chart the developmental course that the component aspects of the individual's cognition of space goes through, as well as to unravel the semingly divergent paths taken by the two sexes in this respect. This aim can only be realized through an investigation focused on the role of the individual's experience, difficult as this may be to realize.

The results of two closely parallel studies undertaken in Hebb's laboratories in the early 1950s to verify the Hebb's views of the importance of sensory stimulation in early life may be cited to concretize this point. Both Hymovitch (1952) and Forgays and Forgays (1952) devised several different conditions of early experience, varying from "enriched" (relative to the norm of the standard laboratory environment) to "impoverished." The effects of raising the animals (rats) in these different environments were then examined by testing them in the Hebb-Williams "closed field" test, which involves learning a route to a goal based on the spatial location of the goal relative to the starting point, in the face of changing barriers placed in the animal's path. Following the learning of this problem, the mazes were rotated 180° in the laboratory room, and the speed with which the animals were able to relearn the maze under these conditions of disorientation was determined.

As Table 5.1 indicates, the efficiency with which the animals learned the problem originally was directly related to the amount of stimulation present during rearing, although the two studies differed in regard to the importance of sensory-motor as opposed to purely visual experience: In Hymovitch's study, mesh cages that restricted the animals' movement were as effective as the free-environment cages, whereas this was not true under Forgays' and Forgays' somewhat different conditions. In any event, both sets of results indicate overall that visual experience is important for the ability to learn tasks depending on orientation in space—hardly a startling finding, but certainly important to demonstrate empirically. But the meaning of these results is seen in a different light, once we look at the second column of the table, showing the performance on the transfer task under spatial rotation of the maze.

Here it turns out that the animals that had originally learned fastest were

TABLE 5.1

Performance of Rats on the Hebb-Williams Closed Field Test[a]

Condition of rearing	Mean errors to learn	Mean errors following rotation of maze
	Hymovitch	
Free environment (FE)	137	53
Mesh cages (in a visually complex environment)	140	57
Stovepipes	233	30
Activity wheels	235	
	Forgays and Forgays	
Free environment with playthings	126	25
Free environment without playthings	162	21
Mesh-caged with FE animals and playthings	190	17
Mesh-caged without FE animals or playthings	192	19
Mesh-caged without FE animals but with playthings	192	16
Mesh-caged with FE animals but without playthings	227	9
Restricted animals	241	9

[a] Based on data by Hymovitch (1952) and Forgays and Forgays (1952).

slowest to relearn the maze once it had been rotated—indeed, there is a virtually perfect inverse relationship between the sets of means for original learning and transfer, within each experiment. What appears to have happened is that the supposedly "enriching" sensory experience had served to increase the animal's reliance on extramaze cues in the outside environment, as opposed to kinesthetic or within-cage cues. Once the maze was rotated, such reliance on extramaze cues would of course hinder the relearning of the problem. The relatively deprived animals, on the other hand, had been thrown back on cues based on their own pattern of movement, along with possible subtle visual and olfactory cues within the maze itself, to learn the problem. This added considerably to the difficulty of the task (as shown in the first column in Table 5.1), but resulted in highly efficient transfer under rotation: The most deprived animals in Forgays and Forgays' study hardly seemed to have "noticed" the change at all.

Here, then, we have a clear demonstration of the manner in which particular conditions of early experience may determine the type of reference system utilized by the individual. There may in fact be a general shift from a predominant egocentric to an allocentric frame of reference with development; however, it is apparent that this shift has to be understood in the context of the cues available to the individual in a given situation, and the role of experience in predisposing the child to make use of information of a particular kind. Thus, it seems more profitable to look for the ability to shift from one frame of reference to another as the situation demands as the ultimately more significant developmental change occurring in this realm of cognitive functioning.

What, then, is the moral of this tale for us? As investigators of cognitive functioning at the human level, we are clearly in no position to emulate the Hebbian approach via experimental manipulation of experience. Nevertheless, there is much that can be done to provide clearer information about the role of such experience, which is alluded to repeatedly in the chapters under discussion, but almost never attacked directly.

At one level, an observational-ecological approach to the determination of the quality and dimensions of the child's experience relative to the development of spatial cognition has much to offer. Wachs's work (cf. Wachs, 1979) may be cited as one variant of this approach, via the use of a scale for inventorying the amount and kind of environmental stimulation that the child receives in its home environment. Wachs's work is limited to the period of infancy, and concerned with cognitive development in a broad sense, but the approach may be adapted to chart development in the spatial domain, and at later stages of development, at least through early childhood. At the same time, one would want to modify it by including aspects of the child's own spontaneous behavior that may be relevant to developmental changes in this realm to supplement measures of the environment. For instance, certain kinds of play behavior such as block play and similar constructive manipulations of materials to create complex three-dimensional structures may plausibly be assumed to have a bearing on the child's spatial cognition. Connor and Serbin (1977) do in fact report a correlation between scores on a block-design test and preference for masculine versus feminine activities among preschool-aged boys, though not among girls.

At a different level, one might monitor the child's traversal through space, at all levels from the indoors environment to that of the large-scale geographic environment such as a city, with particular reference to evidence on navigating and orienting behavior. The work on children's territorial range, recently reviewed by Moore and Young (1978), offers some suggestive leads in this regard, although it is confined for the most part to charting the distribution of children's occupancy over different types of settings at a single point in time, rather than their patterns of movement through the environment.

Unfocused and pretheoretical as such an approach may seem, it could be expected to yield information of direct relevance to the role of differing reference systems, of the learning of spatial cues, and the like, and could readily be developed into a more systematic effort, along the lines of Wachs's work, correlating measures of environmental stimulation with level of development attained. But there are other ways in which the role of experience can be studied nonexperimentally.

One method compares groups of children subjected to contrasting environmental circumstances. Here again we have a convenient model in the work of Hollos (Hollos, 1975; Hollos & Cowen, 1973) on the effects of isolation on cognitive development, comparing children growing up in isolated farms in Norway and Hungary with those living in villages and towns. For our purposes, this approach might be adapted to provide comparisons between preschool children living in urban apartment complexes, and those residing in a typical suburban single-family home. Consider the former: They are confined for a large portion of their everyday lives in indoor environments (with only limited access to a larger environmental surround) and may have difficulty relating those aspects of the surrounding environment visible to them from their apartments with those they encounter when they move out into the street. Should this not favor a reliance on egocentric frames of reference, in comparison to suburban children? The latter should find it easier to piece together their surrounding environment from what they can see from different places in their own home; furthermore, they have more opportunity for exploring that outside environment around their home (e.g., in the yard), and thus to relate it to the home. All this may be expected to favor a more precocious use of an allocentric frame of reference, at least in early childhood. (Hart's discussion, in Chapter 8 of this volume, of the role of the child's experience in and around its home is directly pertinent to this notion.)

The possibility should be recognized that the seeming advantage of the suburbanite child in its single-family home over a child living in an urban high-rise apartment may in fact be reversed in subsequent years, as the child's "territorial range" (cf. Moore & Young, 1978) expands and opportunities for exploration of the area beyond the home increase. Now, if we assume that the urban setting provides a more differentiated and perhaps more complex environment than that of a typical suburban development, the urban child would be at an advantage, because such differentiation, and the possible availability of a greater variety of landmarks, should favor the development of a more effective allocentrically based spatial frame of reference. The intriguing question in this respect is whether this potential advantage of the city environment in later childhood can overcome the possible negative impact of the apartment-home environment in early childhood. More generally, we need to investigate how earlier and later experiences interact to determine the course of the development of spatial cognition.

There are, furthermore, changes in the environmental experience encountered by children whose impact on the child's development of spatial cognition should bear examination. One such change that children experience universally, but which has received scant attention, takes places upon their assumption of erect posture. Consider the visual world of the 8-month-old infant, moving through diverse rooms in its home most efficiently on all fours, but without the opportunity, through turns of the head, to scan the visual surroundings to obtain an integrated image of its surroundings. Compare that to the 15-month-old toddler, who, standing erect, is able to survey the scene from a given point in all directions. One would guess that this shift will have an impact on the infant's cognition of space, perhaps causing it to change from response learning to place learning, to make more effective use of landmarks, and to adopt an allocentric frame of reference where that may be indicated. Some of the results reported by Acredolo in her study with Evans (Acredolo & Evans, 1979), showing a decrease between 6 and 11 months in egocentric responding in the presence of landmarks, might well be interpreted in this fashion.

There are other changes in children's lives occuring less consistently, but still with some regularity, that could have a bearing on children's functioning in the spatial cognition area. For instance, if the preceding analysis of possible differences between apartment-dwellings and suburban homes as environmental settings for the development of spatial frames of reference is valid, it follows that a change in environment from one to the other will itself have an impact on the child, at least during the early-childhood period. A child's entrance into nursery school could likewise be studied as a problem in adaptation to spatial relations in a new environment, possibly as a function of characteristics of the child's home environment.

This analysis is of relevance also to the issue of sex differences and their possible meaning and origin. It is not necessary to decide the issue of the contribution of possible genetic factors to these sex differences in order to proceed with a search for early-experience factors as major contributors to such differences. The reason is that experience, and environmental stimulation, are to a considerable extent the products of the child's own behavior (cf. Sameroff, 1975; Wohlwill, 1973a). Thus, any incipient differences between the sexes that result in differential responsivity, and modes of response to environmental stimulation—such as the differences in sensitivity to auditory as opposed to visual stimuli suggested by McGuinness (1976), which Harris discusses at some length—would themselves bring about differences in the quality of the early experience of the individual that may lead to different patterns of cognitive development, and of spatial cognition in particular. The realm of exploratory behavior, which itself has been found to be subject to important sex differences (Hutt, 1972), comes to mind as one important behavioral dimension of this kind.

In conclusion, the analysis presented here suggests the desirability in future research of this type of closer collaboration among those following the three paradigms referred to in the title of this chapter. Age changes, individual differences, and situational and task-related factors are clearly interdependent, and in a real sense alternative sides of the same coin (perhaps a pyramid would represent a better metaphor). A combined focus from these differing perspectives on the role of experience, both self-instigated and externally induced, in shaping the several facets of the development of spatial-cognition delineated in this chapter will surely yield dividends in the form of a more effectively integrated view of this aspect of cognitive development, and its relationship to other aspects of the intellectual and behavioral functioning of the individual.

References

Acredolo, L., & Evans, D. Some determinants of the infant's choice of spatial reference system. Paper presented at the meetings of the Society for Research in Child Development, San Francisco, March 1979.

Connor, J. M., & Serbin, L. A. Behaviorally based masculine- and feminine-activity-preference scales for preschoolers: Correlates with other classroom behaviors and cognitive tests. *Child Development*, 1977, *48*, 1411–1416.

Cooper, H. S. F. *House in space*. New York: Holt, Rinehart & Winston, 1976.

Cronbach, L. J. The two disciplines of scientific psychology. *The American Psychologist*, 1957, *12*, 671–684.

Cronbach, L. J. Beyond the two disciplines of scientific psychology. *American Psychologist*, 1975, *30*, 116-127.

Forgays, D. G., & Forgays, J. W. The nature of the effect of free environmental experience in the rat. *Journal of Comparative and Physiological Psychology*, 1952, *45*, 322-328.

Goldsmith, L. T. The development of contingent coordination of spatial reference systems. Unpublished Ph.D. dissertation, University of Minnesota, 1979.

Hollos, M. C. Logical operations and role taking ability in two cultures: Norway and Hungary. *Child Development*, 1975, *46*, 638-649.

Hollos, M. C., & Cowen, F. A. Social isolation and cognitive development: Logical operations and role-taking abilities in three Norwegian social settings. *Child Development*, 1973, *44*, 630-641.

Hutt, C. Sex differences in human development. *Human Development*, 1972, *15*, 153-170.

Hymovitch, B. The effects of experimental variations on problem solving in the rat. *Journal of Comparative and Physiological Psychology*, 1952, *45*, 313-321.

McGuinness, D. Sex differences in the organization of perception and cognition. In B. Lloyd & J. Archer (Eds.), *Exploring sex differences*. New York: Academic Press, 1976.

Moore, R., & Young, D. Childhood outdoors: Toward a social ecology of the landscape. In I. Altman & J. F. Wohlwill (Eds.), *Children and the environment (Human Behavior and the Environment*, Vol. III). New York: Plenum, 1978, 83-130.

Piaget, J., & Inhelder, B. *The child's conception of space*. London: Routledge & K. Paul, 1956.

Sameroff, A. J. Early influences on development: Fact or fancy? *Merrill-Palmer Quarterly*, 1975, *21*, 267-294.

Schachtel, E. G. *Metamorphosis: On the development of affect, perception, attention, and memory*. New York: Basic Books, 1959.

Wachs, T. Proximal experience and early cognitive-intellectual development: The physical environment. *Merrill-Palmer Quarterly*, 1979, *25*, 3-41.

Wohlwill, J. F. The concept of experience: S or R? *Human Development*, 1973, *16*, 90-107. (a)

Wohlwill, J. F. *The study of behavioral development*. New York: Academic Press, 1973. (b)

III

Production and Comprehension of Spatial Representations

6 Maps and Mappings as Metaphors for Spatial Representation

ROGER M. DOWNS

> *The chief practical use of history is to deliver us from plausible historical analogies.*
> — JAMES BRYCE

In current discussions of spatial representation, one of the most frequently encountered concepts is the map. It is usually preceded by the modifier, "cognitive," although some recalcitrants, notably in geography and architecture, still cling to an obsolete modifier with considerably less cachet, "mental." In both instances, the referent map is taken to be a seemingly "natural" expression, one which is intuitively obvious, self-evident, and similarly interpreted by everyone. Moreover, and perhaps most importantly, map is such a simple concept that people think it needs little or no elaboration.

The map is a ready-made shorthand symbol. But for what? This naive question can be readily dismissed. The map is a metaphor for an internal spatial representation, for the world in the head. But this is a misleading oversimplification; the map is considerably more than this. If we pay careful attention to the contexts within which map appears, we find that it serves two distinct functions: It is a double metaphor.

The first, and overt use of map is as a metaphor for knowledge itself. The second, and covert use is as a metaphor for the "real world." In this sense, any map is a surrogate expression of, or a substitute for, part of the real world. It is a representation, which is like the real world. In all too many instances, however, this metaphorical character of the map is obscured and overlooked; for many people, the map is taken to *be* the real world. Thus, the map is thought to mirror the world, to miniaturize it. It would be *more* appropriate to say that if the map is a mirror, it is an anamorphic mirror; if the map is a miniature, then it is a model.

If we continue to pursue the uses and contexts of map, there are three further points that are significant. First, the general understanding of the idea of

143

SPATIAL REPRESENTATION AND BEHAVIOR
ACROSS THE LIFE SPAN

a map is conditioned, if not determined, by exposure to cartographic maps, particularly that restricted class of map forms found in school atlases, the *National Geographic,* and *Time* or *Newsweek*. In fact, in nearly every instance of a reference to a map, we can take the modifier cartographic as implicitly assumed. The limitations of such a position are potentially dangerous. Not only is thinking restricted to one particular class of map forms but there is the concomitant failure to recognize that cartographic maps in general are highly stylized representations whose form and function are determined by a complex mixture of mathematical theory, technological possibility, semiarticulated principles of graphic design, and the peculiarities of established convention.

Second, the importance of maintaining the distinction between the dual functions of the map metaphor is not widely appreciated. In effect, current usage transforms the map into a bridging concept that conveniently links some of our most fundamental, persistent, and awkward dichotomies: knowledge and the real world; the internal and the external environment; even the subjective and the objective.

Third, there are some hidden consequences, which follow directly from this bridging role. These consequences give shape to and constrain attempts to understand cognitive maps. Thus, for example, by acting as a metaphor for internal knowledge, the idea of a (cartographic) map guides thinking about the necessary form, structure, and functions of internal spatial representations. Ideally, it serves as a base for expectations and it helps to generate hypotheses. It suggests appropriate methodologies for externalizing spatial representations. From the other end of the bridge, the map stands for the real world. It becomes a baseline or a yardstick, against which the form, structure, and functions of internal spatial representations can be measured. From this position, it is a very easy transition to the belief that the cartographic map is *the* only yardstick for such comparisons. Thus, it controls the process of analysis and it gives rise to judgments about the accuracy and distortion of internal spatial representations.

By now, it should be clear that the term *cartographic map* plays a vital and pervasive role in thinking and research. While we have devoted the bulk of attention to understanding the implications of the "cognitive" part of the expression, the map part has gone unquestioned. In this chapter, I want to explore the dual function of the map in accounts of the world in the head and the real world. If it is a bridging concept, then how strong are the foundations on either side? What does it mean to argue that the map is a metaphor? Have we tried, consciously or otherwise, to overextend the metaphor, to convert it into an analogy?

In effect, I want to question the power, effectiveness, and validity of the double metaphor. Using some perspectives taken from geography and cartography, I want to consider the nature of maps and mappings, and suggest that the concept of a mapping is more appropriate for the purpose at hand. In passing, I will question the use of judgments about accuracy and distortion, suggesting that we can mislead ourselves if we do not appreciate the meaning of maps and mappings. The purpose of this exploration is to point to some of the problems and limitations in current thinking about cognitive maps. In its place, I want to develop the idea of cognitive mapping as a process of spatial problem-solving. In this way, we can see that cartography is but one possible "language" system for mapping, albeit a highly specialized, constantly changing one.

The Map: Metaphor or Analogy?

To a geographer, there is a basic paradox, a delightful irony in the use by philosophers and psychologists of the map as a metaphor for the internal representation of knowledge. It is extremely flattering when philosophers of the stature of Suzanne Langer (1951), Michael Polanyi (1964), and Stephen Toulmin (1960) make such profound use of one of "our" basic concepts. We are a discipline which is all-too-often denied respect; that the map is basic to our self-esteem as members of a discipline is revealed by suggestions such as "the map is the language of geography" and "that is not geography which could not be mapped." We have literally wrapped ourselves in and around the map.

The irony comes from the basic requirements of a metaphor or an analogy: That is, its usefulness depends upon likening some lesser-known concept to some better-known concept. From the perspective of geographers and cartographers, it is clear that we still have trouble understanding what is meant by a cartographic map. Two titles are sufficient to make the point. Two eminent cartographers, Robinson and Petchenik (the former reputed to be the dean of American cartographers), produced a book, *The Nature of Maps* (1976), whose subtitle is: "Essays toward Understanding Maps and Mapping." In like fashion, an equally eminent colleague of mine wrote a paper entitled: "The first and last frontier of communication: The map as mystery" [Zelinsky, 1973]." His introduction is worth quoting in detail:

The map as mystery? The question sounds frivolous or even mischievous. Surely we geographers and map librarians, who are so helplessly smitten with map-love, know and understand the objects we cherish, those beautiful, fascinating things that are so much a part of our working lives and inmost thoughts. After all, a map is a map, isn't it—something even the dullest school child can recognize and describe.

Unfortunately, as is the case with many another simple-seeming phenomenon, the real nature of the geographic map is still far beyond our grasp. (If you find this disconcerting, so do I; but the history of science is one long series of embarrassing revelations [p. 2].)

The irony of others using map as a metaphor is accentuated by the unending search in cartography for metaphors and analogies for the map itself. We have considered, borrowed, and eventually discarded ideas from linguistics (Petchenik, 1974), information theory (Jolliffe, 1974), psychophysics (McCleary, 1970), and musical notation.

My point should not be misunderstood: I am not suggesting that we cannot use the map as a metaphor or analogy for spatial representation. Neither am I trying to belittle my own discipline. The point is that *if* part of the grounding for both sides of the double map metaphor is believed to rest on a secure footing in geography and cartography, *then* that grounding is highly suspect. However, as I hope to suggest in the next section of this chapter, there are some important things that we can learn about maps from geographers and cartographers.

Perhaps we should return to the origins of the map metaphor and ask this: Why was a metaphor necessary and why was this particular metaphor chosen? Without question, the tradition of metaphorical thinking is well established in psychology (see, for example, Chapanis, 1961). Both Blakemore (1977) and Miller (1978) have provided essays on the natural history of metaphors, Blakemore for metaphors for memory and Miller for metaphors for the body as a whole. The record of these metaphors is clear.

Blakemore describes how, in seeking an understanding of the mind and the body, we have turned to technology and machines for metaphors. Telephone switchboards, computer programs, holograms, or more primitively, wax tablets (the famous tabula rasa) have all served at one time or another as metaphors for the functioning *and* form of the mind and the memory. They were derived from the dominant, most exciting technology and offered a comfortable (in the sense of familiar) way of describing, of talking about something that lacked tangible substance.

The record is equally clear that none of the metaphors endured for too long. Although, as Blakemore argues, each had a particular attraction because it mirrored some selected feature(s) of the mind or memory, in the end technological metaphors seemed woefully inadequate. None of the technologies could provide even a good metaphoric description of the mind although they did capture the imagination for a while. In fact, having argued that mechanistic analogies for the brain have been misleading, Wall (1979), in his review of Miller's book, suggests that: "I think we will learn more about how to build interesting machines from studying the brain than the other way around [p. 22]." Although we need not replace technological optimism with its biochemical counterpart, the short half-life of metaphors for mind should give us pause in considering the map metaphor. I use "half-life" deliberately to point to the residual effects of a metaphor. These effects are pervasive: they inhabit our thinking (and teaching) long after the reasons and enthusiasm for the original metaphor have been lost. Metaphors are more easily generated than they are put to rest; for example, information theory continues to be a favorite source for metaphor despite its notable lack of success in illuminating other phenomena. Green and Courtis (1966) attempt to make the case that information theory failed as a metaphor for figure perception, while Robinson and Petchenik (1976) claim that "the fundamental concepts upon which information theory rests makes its direct application in cartographic communication impossible [p. 37]."

It is in this context that McKellar's (1957) comment bears repeating:

> As we have already seen in the case of a supposed 'explanation' of the superiority of verbal recollection, confusion arises if we treat abstract ideas as though they were concrete 'things.' It is, for example, important to remind ourselves that the Freudian 'unconscious' is a way of talking about certain aspects of human behaviour; and a philosopher with acute insight once remarked to the writer about the psychoanalytic unconscious: 'There is no such *place!*' Such insight is perhaps even more valuable in psychology than in other sciences, because of the tendency for many of its ideas to find expression in spatial metaphors [p. 179].

And as spatial metaphors go, the map is a classic precisely because it is a metaphor and is doubly dangerous. Not only is there the danger that McKellar is pointing to—the danger of objectifying the map into a "thing" that we "have" somewhere—there is the danger that stems from the apparently perfect match between experience, language, and thought. The use of spatial expressions is fundamental to natural language and thinking; hence the intuitive "obviousness" of the map metaphor. The dangers inherent in a metaphor are most vividly shown by the idea of a mental image as a picture, a metaphor with an equally "obvious" basis and an even more contentious history.

Putting the map as real-world-metaphor aside for a moment, what is it that we are using map as a metaphor for? This is simply an inelegant way of asking one of the most fundamental of questions: What is the form of knowledge in the mind? This is scarcely the place, nor am I the person to try to answer such a question but it is worth considering the answer of Michael Polanyi (1964), especially because it is an answer that is finding its way into cartography (see Robinson & Petchenik, 1976). From this perspective—and in one sense—the question has no meaning because knowledge does not *exist as* imagery or verbal encoding or even as some combination of the two. Knowledge has no form at all; it is pure relation. Polanyi makes the vital distinction between tacit and explicit knowledge. Knowledge becomes explicit and takes on a particular form for the purposes of expression and communication. It can take on a variety of forms: words, images, maps, and so on. Since we are limited by the range of ways in which we can make knowledge explicit, we always know more than we can tell (or draw or build or whatever). If we include spatial behavior, that is movement patterns, as a form of explicit knowledge, then we can begin to see why the map metaphor has become so popular. We can also begin to see hints that our exclusive, unthinking focus on (cartographic) maps may be misplaced and misleading. Yet another part of the footing for the map as a bridge may be insecure.

With these ideas, we can return to the question: why a metaphor and why the map metaphor in particular? It would be pointless, if not impossible to say who first introduced the map metaphor into the context of internal spatial representations. It is sufficient to point to Edward Tolman's (1948) paper simply because so many people (and rightly so) pay homage to it (see O'Keefe & Nadel, 1978; Olton, 1979 for recent reinterpretations). What was Tolman trying to convey (and trying *not* to convey) in the original cognitive map paper? Forgive me if I put ideas into Tolman's head when I reconstruct his thought patterns; this is a revisionist and cognitive interpretation.

First, the facts, the patterns of rat spatial behavior, were agreed to: It was the theory and mode of explanation that were subject to question. Second, Tolman and the field theorists were faced by the stimulus-response school who were not only entrenched but had their own powerful metaphor—the telephone switchboard. To understand Tolman's parry in this duel by metaphor, I can do no better than to turn to an article by Jerison (1975). In supporting one of his own basic concepts, Jerison refers to: "Craik's (1943) concept of thought and explanation as the construction (by the mind) of a model system (usually mechanical for those brought up in Western culture) in which cause and effect are related in the same way that they appear to be in the thought-system or in whatever we seek to understand and explain [p. 415]." In view of my earlier point about the "naturalness" of spatial expressions in language, the map metaphor is an obvious way of relating spatial behavior to the brain. It allows us to match behavioral response (effect), in this case spatial, with the workings of the map control room, the thought-system (cause). Moreover—and this is a crucial issue that we will return to—not only do we have a mechanical model system, (the cognitive map and its control room) but that model system, the map, is itself a model. We are inevitably caught in a circular, self-reflexive system of thoughts: The model by which we understand the mind is itself a model created by the mind. Shainberg (1979) captures the disturbing nature of such a position.

During brain surgery, the thalamus was likened to spaghetti in aspic. In looking at the thalamus, Shainberg became disoriented because: "this was one of the times when metaphor displaced reality in the operating room: the thalamus, after all, is the region of the brain in which all sensory experience is processed before being transmitted to the cortex. It was no small piece of ambiguity to confront it with one's own sensory apparatus [p. 104]."

It is also worth remembering that Tolman (1935) had set the stage for the use of intervening variables or hypothetical constructs in the linking of stimulus and response, cause and effect. That he intended the cognitive map as both metaphor and intervening variable is clear from these excerpts:

> We believe that in the course of learning something *like* a field map of the environment gets established in the rat's brain. . . .

> Secondly, we assert that the central office is far more *like* a map control room than it is like an old-fashioned telephone exchange . . . the incoming impulses are usually worked over and elaborated in the central control room into a tentative, cognitive-*like* map of the environment [Tolman, 1948, p. 192, emphasis added].

Tolman's new metaphor was to replace the "old fashioned" telephone exchange.

It is the subsequent use and interpretation/ misinterpretation of Tolman's ideas that is causing problems. First, Tolman was trying to describe a process, not a product. In confronting the classic problem of the process–product dilemma, Tolman was forced to speak about maps as products. But these maps were only products in the sense of transitory stages in an ongoing process. The constraints of language should not mislead us. Thus, the rat's brain was working *as if* it were a map control room through which information and decisions were flowing in some continuous stream. Admittedly, Guthrie's famous comment about Tolman's rats being "left buried in thought" is still valid. The question might be this: "Who" is running the map control room and making the decisions? If we are not careful, we are in mortal danger of resurrecting the homunculus, this time in the guise of the cartographic map reader. (O'Keefe and Nadel, 1978 show us how to avoid this danger.) In subsequent usages of Tolman's paper, we have focused on cognitive map, on the product rather than the process. It is this unfortunate narrowing of focus that has led us toward McKellar's danger of objectifying an abstract idea into a concrete "thing." We have done an injustice to Tolman. On the other hand, it is clear that Tolman intended the reader to think of the cognitive map as a cartographic map. There can be no other interpretation given the image that is created by expressions such as "map control room" and "field map."

A second problem in the use of the cognitive map–mapping concept is even more serious. How are we to regard the concept: Is it a metaphor or an analogy? The distinctions between these two modes of expression are crucial. In its most simple form, a metaphor is a statement of strict identity between two sets of phenomena. Thus, A *is* B; whatever is true of A (the known set) is also taken to be true of B (the semiknown set). In contrast, an analogy is a more selective, controlled statement. Thus, A *is like* B; whatever is true of some of the specified properties of A is also true of some of the specified properties of B.

So, is the cognitive map a metaphor or an analogy? The question depends upon the distinctions between expression and explanation, between implicit and explicit understanding, and most significantly, between image and model. The danger lies in mistaking a metaphor for an analogy, in allowing a powerful means of expression to become thought of as a pseudo-explanation. Tolman clearly intended cognitive map as a metaphor: In fact, on one occasion, he placed map in single inverted commas (Tolman, 1948, p. 195). At no point did he specify what particular properties of the mind were equivalent to a (cartographic) map. The workings of the map control room were left to the reader's imagination. It is unfortunate that he chose to refer to "something like a field map of the environment" because this statement is easily misconstrued. It does not indicate an analogy; it is better read in the characteristic form of a metaphor as, the mind *is* a map. Moreover, to use Gordon's (1961) terms, it was probably a decorative rather than a generative metaphor. The former appears after-the-fact; it does not discover but it describes and makes vivid the already discovered. The generative metaphor is an inductive leap, before-the-fact, that provides an initial impetus to the process of discovery.

It is the post-Tolmanian users of cognitive map who have made the more spectacular leap. The map has shifted from metaphor to analogy, from expression to functional and formal explanation. In the general case, such shifts are possible and productive. Miller (1978) shows how analogies progress to hypothesis and to experiment: The success of the analogy is then subject to empirical test. Bruner (1966) makes a similar point with his idea of "the left to right hand" shift. Bruner views creative thinking as being based on a metaphoric search for hunches: these hunches are "the combinatorial products of his metaphoric activity."

Metaphors must be "tamed" by shifting them from the left to the right hand, from the intuitive, emotional side to the objective, rational side. (McKellar's observation about spatial metaphors in psychology is borne out again.) In this way, we can progress from metaphoric hunch to testable hypothesis. But if the cognitive map has shifted from metaphor to analogy, it has not done so by the formal, empirical route, subject to the scrutiny of testing. (The work of O'Keefe and Nadel (1978) is an exception to this statement.) Waldo Tobler (1976), perhaps the most provocative of theoretical cartographers, makes the point well:

> We assume that the subjects being studied have a representation of their environ-ment and that this is somehow maplike and can be observed by some type of measurement procedure. I am not convinced that the basic assumption is mean-ingful, but I have been unable to devise an experiment that would force me to give it up. Clearly, some representation of the environment is required, but whether this is hierarchical or maplike is not known. [p. 70].

If not on secure empirical grounds, then on what grounds are we justified in using the cognitive map concept? Now we can return to the ideas of Polanyi and the question of the form of knowledge. The map is a convenient *metaphor* for the form of knowledge for several interlocking reasons. The process of mapping is a process of relating. Maps are particular expressions of pure relation. Relations are the sine qua non of a map, and structure is derived by the reader from the map of relations. (The derivation may be the result of a painstaking, lengthy scrutiny, or the structure [the pattern] may leap off the page and hit you between the eyes.) By drawing upon natural language and everyday expressions, by borrowing from the technology of cartography and navigation, by mirroring many of our everyday experiences (such as drawing a sketch map to show a friend how to get to your house), by the confirmation of the contents of random introspections, the map does indeed let us describe and give form to knowledge. It is, above all else, a plausible image in which, to paraphrase Craik, cause and effect are related in the same way that they *are*, not just appear to be in the thought system.

We can use explicit knowledge (in Polanyi's sense) to give a sense of, a feel for, tacit knowledge. But perhaps the most powerful support for the map as metaphor comes from the fact that cartographic maps are models; internal representations are models. The latter is readily acknowledged in the spatial representation literature; the former is forgotten. Cartographic maps are only models of the real world: They are not the real world itself. The "world ac-cording to Rand McNally," to use Wohlwill's phrase, is precisely that—the world *according* to Rand McNally. Obviously, Rand McNally is some mysterious collective, like Ellery Queen, but we are speaking about the world as modeled by Rand McNally. It is no different in principle than the world ac-cording to Roger Downs. Maps are models; internal representations are models. Taking the term model in a very broad sense, metaphors and analogies are models. That we should find the map a useful, almost over-poweringly obvious device should therefore come as no surprise.

But this is only part of the point that I am trying to make. The second part comes down to this: We are in danger of using *one* of the particular products of the "thing" (the process of mapping) that we are trying to understand to explain that self-same thing. If, as I believe, we cannot avoid this circular reasoning and must share Shainberg's feeling of ambiguity, then I am in favor of choosing the circular argument with the widest diameter to encompass the most ground. To me, this is the concept of mapping, not map. It is broader than cartographic mapping since the latter is but a special case of mapping. But whatever the choice, map or mapping, cartographic map or cartographic mapping, neither constitutes an analogy, at least in their present guise.

Having excavated and shaken the foundations of the double map metaphor, I do not want to destroy and abandon it. Instead, in the next section, I want to explore cartography to try to understand some of the limitations and potentials of continuing to use maps and mapping as metaphors. Assuming that you agree with these explorations, the last section of this chapter will provide one possible interpretation of the cognitive mapping metaphor, one which I hope can begin to lead us to an answer to Tobler's question.

Maps, Mappings, and Spatial Representations

In trying to understand the validity of the original double map metaphor, we need to establish a general framework. One useful way to begin is to treat the idea of mapping as a transformation process. This is particularly appropriate given the interest in spatial representations since a mapping is one of the three basic ways in which the properties of a geometry can be formally specified: The other two specifications, in terms of axioms and geodesics, are less useful to our purpose.

A mapping is the transformation of an object set into an image set via a function (see Figure 6.1): Of vital concern are the set definitions and the nature of the mapping function. The set definition establishes certain properties or relations between objects: In our concern, these properties are usually spatial relations (measures of distance, shape, direction, etc.). The mapping function determines which of these relations will be "maintained" in the image set: The maintained relations are said to be invariant or preserved. (For a more elaborate and cartographic interpretation of these ideas, see Bunge [1966, 213-229].)

Even from this simplistic sketch, we can begin to see some interesting parallels to the attempt to understand the form of knowledge. There are classes or groups of mappings that preserve specific properties: area, shape, distance, and so on. One key group of mappings is called homomorphic. These many-to-one mappings are the reason why I earlier referred to cartographic maps as models. Many objects and their relations in the object set

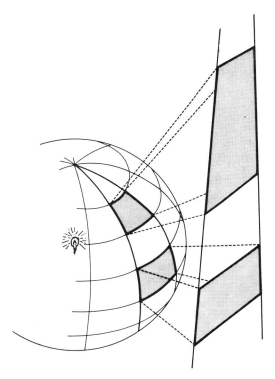

FIGURE 6.1. *Projecting from*
three dimensions to the plane.

are mapped onto (or into) one object in the image set. This is logically equivalent to the process of generalization, simplification, filtering, and consolidation of information: There are many synonyms expressing this most basic of operations. Some information is preserved, some lost, and lost irretrievably: The mapping function determines which is which.

With this information in hand, we can return to the idea of a cartographic map. A cartographic map is invariably the result of a homomorphic mapping, and as such it is a model. It is not the "real world" since it stands for only part of the real world. The parts (or properties) of the real world that are preserved depend upon the nature of the mapping function. Two additional points are crucial: (a) there are an infinite number of possible mapping functions available to the cartographer; and (b) there are fundamental inference problems in going from the cartographic map as an image set back to the real world as an object set. It is only possible if you know the nature of the mapping function. Even then, you cannot reconstruct all of the relational properties of the object set. The cursory interpretation of cartography that follows will show why I consider the cartographic map to be of limited value in the attempts to understand internal spatial representations.

Let me demonstrate the *metaphorical* character of a cartographic map in two ways: geometrically and graphically. From a geometrical standpoint, the modeling problem is clear. All small-scale cartographic maps are inevitably distorted. We can control the nature of the distortion, choose, for example, to minimize the distortion of shape by employing conformal or orthomorphic projections, but we cannot generate distortion-free maps. (Distortion is to be distinguished from error, although neither can we produce error-free maps.) The problem of distortion is inherent in the relationship between the two surfaces that we are considering: The earth's surface is finite and unbounded; the cartographic map is finite but bounded. The earth is three-dimensional, the cartographic map (generally) two-dimensional. We can state this relationship in another mathematically more elegant way.

The earth and the cartographic map are both two-dimensional surfaces; the former has positive (though slightly irregular) curvature and the latter has zero curvature. The earth's surface is not a developable surface, which means that distortion is inevitable; therefore we can only build models (maps) that accept this state of affairs. The transformation (map projection) from the earth's surface (the object set) to the plane of the map (the image set) comprises a complex series of steps:

> The first step is to project the highly irregular surface of the earth onto a more regular imaginary surface known as the *geoid*. This is the surface that would result if the average level of the world's oceans were extended under the continents. The second step is to project the undulating geoid onto a still more regular oblate *ellipsoid*. This new surface serves as the basis for geodetic and astronomic coordinates used by surveyors. The third step is to project the oblate ellipsoid onto a still more regular *spheroid*. This produces the standard globe, which serves as the model for the common spherical coordinates of latitude and longitude. The fourth transformation . . . involves the mapping of the spheroid onto a *plane* surface [Muehrcke, 1978, pp. 421-422].

We can also cheat: In large scale maps of relatively small areas, we can ignore the earth's positive curvature and treat both map and earth as having zero curvature. Thus, we can speak of the earth as being locally Euclidean. But even this flat earth model cannot obscure the fundamental issue of transformations and distortions. All relational properties of the earth's surface cannot be preserved in the cartographic map.

Although all map projections lead to cartographic maps, which are homomorphic with respect to the earth's surface, there are two important qualifications to this statement. First, many object relations in the object-and-image set are in one-to-one correspondence. Second, some object relations are in one-to-many correspondence. Because the map is finite and bounded, the earth's surface is "interrupted" on the cartographic surface. In a Mercator projection, the world is split, by convention, at the International Date Line and thus the line of surface locations along 180° west is identical to the line along 180° east, although the latter numerical designation is never included and therefore does not "exist." Likewise, the two poles (points) become stretched into lines as long as the Equator. Both mapping operations violate fundamental continuity and proximity relations, relations that are at the heart of the concept of a space.

From a graphical standpoint, we can paint a similar picture of the cartographic map as a model or metaphor. A basic question is, should cartographic maps be perceptually or representationally correct? Usually, the cartographer opts for the latter and thus employs a whole bag of tricks to defeat the eye. What one might call cartographic license leads to (a) charts relating apparent to absolute magnitude scalings for area and volume symbols (see Figure 6.2); (b) charts relating apparent to absolute magnitude scalings for texture, color value, and color intensity (see Figure 6.3); and (c) rules of thumb that say, simplify coastlines because form complications draw undue visual attention to the coastline, use dot and not line patterns with irregular borders, delete the grid under land masses to "lift" the land out of the water, avoid parallel lines because they "hurt" the eyes, and avoid "wiggly" lines because they are indecisive.

There is a science, a technology of cartography; there is also an art of cartography. Instead of viewing cartographic maps as miniatures in a mirror, we would do better to view them as cartoons, as the work of a skilled caricaturist. What price now for the world according to Rand McNally? The import of the phrase "according to" should be clear. It is a variant of naïve cartographic realism to believe that not only is there a real world out there but that this same world is faithfully captured by the cartographic map. Perhaps the most ironic reason for rejecting this position is the realization that it denies the fundamental constructivist assumption of the whole cognitive approach. There are innumerable projections available to the cartographer, each of which preserves distinct properties; the vantage point for the projection can be infinitely varied (see Figure 6.4); the graphic and compositional tools are equally varied. The choices are ways of constructing a spatial representation (cartographic map) with specified properties suited to a particular purpose. The choices are not ways of mirroring and miniaturizing.

The cartographic map is not a good basis for an analogy although it does work as a metaphor. Analogies demand a well-known situation with clearly specified concepts and laws of relationship that can be translated into the terms of the lesser-known situation. The cartographic map is not that well understood. From a geometrical perspective, we have a reasonably good

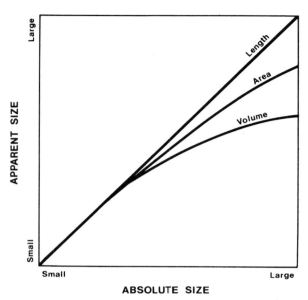

FIGURE 6.2. *Relation between apparent and absolute size for graphical symbols of increasing dimensionality. (Adapted from Figure 2.15A in Muehrcke,* Map Use, *1978.)*

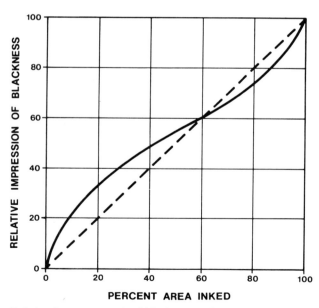

FIGURE 6.3. *Relation between perceived blackness and actual area inked. (Adapted from Figure 2.15B in Muehrcke,* Map Use, *1978.)*

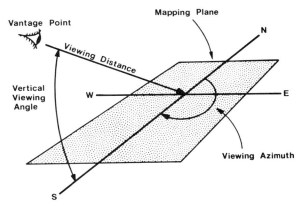

FIGURE 6.4. *The elements of the vantage point: viewing angle, viewing azimuth, and viewing distance. (Adapted from Figure 1.4 in Muehrcke,* Map Use, *1978.)*

sense of the nature of mapping functions. It is the translation of this theory into graphical construction that poses problems. Much of cartography remains an art: Map design is notoriously subjective. Cartographers know virtually nothing about the cognitive process of map reading and interpretation. As the long, and sad history of attempts to produce a legible subway map for New York City attests, cartographers cannot predict what effect a map will have. To make matters worse, much of the public conception of cartography is either the result of a misunderstanding or it is in error. How else can we account for the famous "Greenland" effect on a Mercator projection? Greenland "looks" the same size as Africa on the map, although we "know" that Africa is 14 times larger and that Greenland is really the same size as Saudi Arabia! Try some other questions: Flying due south from Detroit, what foreign country do you reach first? Which is nearer Miami: California or Brazil? Does a geodesic from Tokyo to the Panama Canal pass east or west of San Francisco? (See Gardner [1975] for more of these questions.)

As an alternative basis for analogy, therefore, let us return to the idea of a mapping. The map is the product of a mapping process, and the cartographic map simply the product of one particular class of mappings. The cartographic map is no different in principle from an architectural model, an aerial photograph, a remotely sensed image, and so on. All of these forms are spatial models in which specified relational properties are preserved by the mapping function. As important as the question of form is that of function. Why are mappings of use in the attempt to understand the form of knowledge?

We are interested in mappings as a means of spatializing information. Thus, we are not concerned with any class of objects (phenomena) per se but with the idea of a space acting as a medium for relating pieces of information.

The objects and the relations defined on them form the object set; the mapping function produces the spatial model wherein we can "see" the image set of objects as forming a structure or pattern. Viewed in this perspective, mapping functions are ways in which tacit knowledge can be rendered explicit for the purposes of expression and communication. Communication can be to the self or to others. Mappings are rule systems for expressing and communicating knowledge via spatial models.

It is important to realize that spatial models should not be viewed simply as convenient repositories for existing information. Cartographic maps, for example, have a dual function. On the one hand, they are powerful instruments for preserving and recording old truths: They are data stores par excellence. On the other hand, maps are a device for the invention or discovery of new truths. As Toulmin argues, not all of the retrievable information is deliberately "put" into the map in the first place. We can "read off" new information. Maps can help us to discover ("see") previously unsuspected patterns of relationship (structures). The key property of a spatial model is simultaneity; it is this which makes discovery of pattern possible. The graphical output of a multidimensional scaling program functions in precisely this way. Maps are creative devices for discovery and, in the case of cartographic maps, not mirror images of the real world. In the cartographic map, the two functions of storage and discovery must be traded-off against each other. There is a fundamental incompatibility between an inventory that demands detail, completeness, and accuracy, and the expression of structure. To the extent that the inventory function is achieved, the map becomes "cluttered" and the structure is likely to be buried by "visual static." (The use of visual static and seeing should not limit concern to visual spatial models: Spatial models can exist in other sensory modes.)

The word "see" directs attention back to the starting point of the map metaphor, to visual spatial models, to maps and graphics, to mapping functions that allow us to comprehend a pattern or structure. However, we have returned with a different understanding of the map-mapping concepts. It is an understanding that emphasizes the need to consider:

1. The definition of the object set
2. The nature of the relations between the objects in the set
3. The nature of the mapping function (i.e., the nature of the space itself, of the properties that will be preserved)
4. The recognition and interpretation of pattern and structure in the image set

We can replace the double map metaphor with the double mapping metaphor. The value of such an exchange is twofold. First, it allows us to isolate some basic questions and remove some misconceptions that have grown around the idea of the cognitive map as cartographic map. Second, it gives us an alternative means for answering the basic question about the form of knowledge. The acid test of the mapping metaphor is, in the end: Does it provide an understanding of what we already know and can it generate testable hypotheses? The final section of this chapter is one translation of the mapping idea into the cognitive context. I want to use mapping to account for and reinterpret some existing empirical findings, to consider the limitations of current research design practices, and to draw attention to some questions that we have, to this point, chosen to ignore.

Cognitive Mapping Again

Although I had earlier accepted Tolman's (1948) claim that "all students agree as to the facts . . . [p. 189]," I now want to reconsider the so-called facts. Part of the problem in seeking satisfying explanations is confusion over what is to be explained. What are the facts that constitute the dependent variable? What shall we call it?

In both rats and people, we are concerned with competence in problem solving. Competence is manifested by successful (i.e. adaptive) behavior: finding the water or food box, getting to the airport on time, and so on. The problem is to account for this *spatial competence*. We run into two difficulties immediately. First, it is ironic that we seem to have a better sense of what people cannot do, with spatial *incompetence*, than we do with successful problem solving. For example, the education literature offers many statements about the ages before which children are presumed unable to read cartographic maps: There have been few attempts to understand the processes of map reading. Second, given that one adopts the constructivist assumption and subscribes to Tolman's (1935) thesis about the status and role of hypothetical constructs, we are confronted with some awkward "facts" that we must account for or circumvent. For example, competent behavior appears to precede representation, particularly in children. We know that people can do things in the spatial environment that they cannot represent. Thus, David Stea (1976) differentiates between knowing the spatial environment, in the sense of recognizing and being able to use, and knowing, in the sense of constructing and representing that same environment. One way to cope with the behavior competence/representation incompetence problem is to claim that representational incompetence is simply a methodological problem, the artefactious result of a confounding variable. In like fashion, the first difficulty, the spatial incompetence finding, is a consequence of the research designs that we choose.

For the moment, let us ignore these two difficulties and return to the idea of spatial competence. In considering the wide range of behaviors that fall under this term, a twofold classification is useful. The classification was introduced by Piaget and subsequently elaborated by Hart and Moore (1973).

The first class of behaviors are derived from the idea of *fundamental spatial relations:* the capacity to think spatially, to understand the concept of space in the abstract, and to use a space as a vehicle for structuring knowledge and for solving problems. Space is not taken in the sense of the particular environment or geographic space, but as a model framework for expressing simultaneity and degrees of interrelationship. Command over fundamental spatial relations is intimately (although not necessarily) associated with the process of visualization as in, for example, the formation, manipulation, and rotation of spatial images. The second class of behaviors are dependent upon *environmental cognition:* the comprehension and understanding of the arrangement and properties of phenomena that are distributed on the earth's surface. This permits us to form cognitive representations of the large-scale environment: This is the classic "world in the head."

If we can agree that these two classes of behavior constitute the facts of spatial competence, let me offer an explanation that draws on three key ideas from earlier sections of this chapter: (a) the question of the form of knowledge; (b) the distinction between tacit and explicit knowledge; and (c) the idea of a mapping as a transformation process (or rule system for communicating knowledge via a spatial model).

In explaining the roles of fundamental spatial relations and environmental cognition in spatial competence, it is convenient to distinguish between structural and process-oriented models. For two reasons, I prefer a process-oriented model. First, it gets away from the concentration on the product, on the idea of a cognitive map. Second, a process-oriented model matches everyday language accounts of what is happening in spatial competence. Siegel and White (1975) prefer a structural model and, at present, the choice between the two is very much a matter of personal taste.

A simple version of the process-oriented, mapping-based model has the following characteristics. It views spatial competence as the outcome of problem solving. Thus it asks, how do we respond to problems that either demand or that can make use of spatial models in arriving at a solution? It does not define a class of spatial problems per se. In developing the model in detail, we must consider the nature of the problem itself: (a) what are the demands that it poses?; (b) what do we mean by the process?; and (c) what are the strategies whereby these demands are or can be met?

Given space limitations, I want to concentrate on the latter issue, the process of problem solving. It appears to have three characteristics: (a) there are multiple strategies available; (b) there is flexibility via some "switching" mechanism; and (c) the problem-solving system has built-in redundancy.

These characteristics are clearly illustrated in Tolman's (1948) discussion of Krech's (1932) work:

> The individual rat went through a succession of systematic choices. That is, the individual animal might perhaps begin by choosing practically all right-hand doors, then he might give this up for choosing practically all left-hand doors, and then, for choosing all dark doors, and so on. These relatively persistent, and well-above-chance systematic types of choice Krech called "hypotheses." In using this term he obviously did not mean to imply verbal processes in the rat but merely referred to what I have been calling cognitive maps which, it appears from his experiments, get set up in a tentative fashion to be tried out first one and then another until, if possible, one is found which works [p. 202].

In this passage, it is clear that Tolman was not using map in the sense of a static repository of information. A map is a creative device for solving a particular problem, more akin to a plan of action than an inventory of what is known.

There are several additional, and equally powerful reasons for suggesting the three characteristics of problem solving. On purely logical grounds, they make plain good sense. Arguments of intuitive plausibility underlie the selection of metaphors and are acceptable *if* they are supported by other evidence. In this case, we can find evidence from two distinct sources. There are extensive parallels with the existence of physiological mechanisms in birds. The mechanisms for homing and migrating rely on several perceptual capacities and strategies for calculating position and heading. These mechanisms are redundant in perfect environmental conditions but are designed to operate in a hierarchical sequence in less than perfect conditions. The same is true for human way-finding processes. The anthropological accounts of Gladwin (1970) and Lewis (1972), the instruction manual of Gatty (1958), and the orienteering literature (Disley, 1967) confirm the idea of multiple strategies, flexibility, and built-in redundancy.

This model is not purely a statement of spatial competency defined as environmental cognition. It also can encompass the use of space and spatial models as vehicles for solving problems other than way-finding. Thus, for example, it relates to Huttenlocher's (1968) study of strategies for solving three-term syllogisms, to Luria's (1968) discussion of spatial mnemonics, to Bower's (1970) argument that the method of loci is not the necessary form of a mnemonic but it is sufficient for the problem at hand, and to the literature on the cognitive processes of chess (De Groot (1965), Chase and Simon (1973), and Steiner (1974).

Additional supportive evidence for this position comes from the two chapters by Siegel and Hart (Chapters 7 and 8 of this volume). Both point to the existence of significant individual differences in the ways in which their respondents solved the tasks that were demanded of them. In Siegel's perspective convergence technique, there were marked individual differences. Accuracy of judgments under both mental rotation and perspective-taking tasks was equal for some individuals, the former greater than the latter for others, and vice versa. In Hart's landscape modeling task, some children cartographically mapped only elements that they could relate to their home; others mapped clusters of elements that were internally organized but which "floated" in relation to the other clusters. These, and many other instances of individual differences could be viewed as a function of maturational differences in children or as the result of confounding, methodological variables. They could equally well be interpreted as variations in competence in any given problem-solving strategy, or as examples of preference for a particular strategy.

Lest the point become obscured, I argue that we are looking at the individual's capacity to engage in mapping in order to solve a particular problem. A mapping permits the person to generate a spatial model that is useful in the given context. It can be useful because the resultant map already contains the needed solutions (the map as repository idea) or because the solutions can be discovered within the map patterns (the map as a creative tool for generating hypotheses). If this omnibus view of spatial competence *as* problem solving *as* cognitive mapping is accepted, some very significant consequences follow. Of the three that I want to discuss, the first is by way of an addendum to the discussion of what is it that we "have." The latter two are direct responses to the demand that we go from analogy to hypothesis to experiment.

One answer to the "what is it that we have" question must be simple. People have a body of tacit knowledge about whose properties we (as researchers) know very little and can expect to know very little. People do have available to them a range of mappings, which can convert tacit into explicit knowledge. These mapping functions exist as rules for transforming objects and relations into spatial models. I realize that this is little different from the current answer to the "have" question.

It is interesting, however, to look at what has happened to the cognitive map concept. Tolman began with the cognitive map as a hypothetical construct. To the extent that the cognitive map became objectified as a thing, it had to have an existence. Whereas some people insist on purging the cognitive map as a "metaphysical conceit," which quite literally intervened in explanations, others such as O'Keefe and Nadel (1978) and Olton (1979) have begun to make a convincing case for an anatomical-physiological basis for cognitive maps in rats. Perhaps we should not be too harsh on the semantic confusion surrounding the metaphor; the cognitive map is less suspect than many believe it to be.

The second consequence relates to the research strategies that are used to investigate spatial competence. Siegel argues (Chapter 7 of this volume) that the behavior competence/representation incompetence paradox may center on a competence/load trade-off where load is a measure of the task demands. In general, therefore, researchers try to look at developmental differences in competency by manipulating the load demands. In effect, this research strategy leads to: pushing the problem-solving system to its limits, constraining it, and/or disaggregating it. Each of these efforts may have awkward consequences. The first leads to apparent incompetence, especially if the problem-solving system is disaggregated, constrained, *and* pushed to its limits. This is a description of the "classic," "clean" experimental design. The second and third combine to deny the problem solver flexibility and therefore prevent switching to alternative mapping strategies. It is analogous to the classic problem of rats "cheating" in mazes, an amusing thought because it was these "cheaters," reported by Lashley in 1929, which gave rise to Tolman's development of the cognitive map concept in the first place (see Tolman, 1948, p. 202). Taken together, all three research strategies cause us to lose sight of the relative ordering of mapping strategies in problem solving.

In a sense, we are in danger of looking at impoverished forms of spatial competence. This is not my major point. As a matter of self-defense, I should hasten to add that my point is *not* an attack on the general use of experimental designs and manipulations. Instead, I believe that we should bear in mind the distinction between what one can do versus what one would normally do in problem solving. In some ways, the concern with fundamental spatial relations emphasizes what one can do whereas the concern with environmental cognition emphasizes what one would normally do. It is not the research design itself that is at fault but the interpretations that we place on the results and the conclusions that we allow ourselves to draw.

The third major consequence is the most important one for the future of research in this area. We should treat modes of mapping, that is the mapping functions or rule systems for producing a spatial model, as topics to be studied in and of their own right. This is not done at present for two reasons. First, and at best, modes of mapping are viewed as convenient vehicles for getting at something else. The something else is usually thought to be the internal form of knowledge. Given my arguments about what it is that we have and what inferences we can usefully draw, it is obvious that I have serious objections to such a research strategy. Second, and at worst, modes of mapping are seen as confounding variables that generate all manner of unpleasant artifacts. Thus, we get the argument that the maps (data) are unreliable, low in validity, and so on. This is most frequently seen with respect to freehand sketch maps.

As an alternative to both of these views, I would propose that we cease to view modes of mapping either as artifacts or as vehicles of convenience.

They are mappings, the means of generating spatial models, of converting tacit knowledge into explicit knowledge. In short, they are the whole point of studying spatial competence.

As a quick sketch of where such an alternative approach might lead us, consider the history of cartography. Cartographic maps have been found in nearly every culture; they exist early in the development of most civilizations—and they show few dramatic innovations of technique or theory. In short, maps are early, everywhere, and "sophisticated." Now consider the "evolution" of graphic techniques. Ferguson (1977) has outlined a sequence of innovations: pictorial perspective, exploded views, orthographic projections, isometric views, and graphs. And finally, what about graphics and cartographics in children? We could repeat the statement that cartographic maps are early, everywhere, and sophisticated. Instead of dismissing or ignoring them, how are we to try to understand these modes of mapping? Can we speak about the genesis (onto- and phylo-genesis) of cartographic languages? Are we justified in seeking parallels between cultures and cultures, between individuals and cultures? Can we talk about the "microgenesis" of a new graphic technique such as the use of the "fish-eye" lens technique to give an egocentric spatial model with a sense of the foreshortening of distance?

To all of these questions, I would answer "yes." Modes of mapping are languages for problem solving. An understanding of spatial competence necessitates an understanding of the processes whereby object sets are converted into image sets by mapping functions. An individual has available several different types of mapping function: Any given mapping function can generate a series of possible solutions to the problem or one can switch to an alternative form of mapping function. Individual differences are thus variations in the command of a given type of mapping function and/or variations in the preference for choosing which mapping function to use in order to solve a given problem.

This reinterpretation of cognitive mapping does not do violence to any of our existing empirical findings, and moreover, it avoids some of the confusion that I believe has been self-inflicted. We should try to look at the idea of cognitive mapping as an answer to the question, what is the form of knowledge that permits spatial competence. To paraphrase and twist Bryce's epigram, the chief practical use of cartography is to deliver us yet another plausible source of analogy.

Acknowledgments

I would like to acknowledge the assistance of Lynn Liben, Nora Newcombe, and Karen Schmelzkopf, all of whom commented on a draft of this chapter. I am especially grateful to James Meyer who drew the figures and acted as a sounding board for many of the ideas.

References

Blakemore, C. *Mechanics of the mind*. London: Cambridge University Press, 1977.

Bower, G. The analysis of a mnemonic device. *American Scientist*, 1970, *58*, 496-510.

Bruner, J. *On knowing: Essays for the left hand*. Cambridge: Harvard University Press, 1966.

Bunge, W. *Theoretical Geography*. 2nd edition. Lund: C. W. K. Gleerup, 1966.

Chapanis, C. Men, machines, and models. *American Psychologist*, 1961, *16*, 113-131.

Chase, W. and Simon, H. Perception in chess. *Cognitive Psychology*, 1973, *4*, 55-81.

Craik, K. *The nature of explanation*. London: Cambridge University Press, 1943.

De Groot, A. *Thought and choice in chess*. The Hague: Mouton, 1965.

Disley, J. *Orienteering*. Harrisburg, Pennsylvania: Stackpole Books, 1967.

Ferguson, E. The mind's eye: Nonverbal thought in technology. *Science*, 1977, *197*, 827-836.

Gardner, M. On map projections (with special reference to some inspired ones). *Scientific American*, November, 1975, 120-125.

Gatty, H. *Nature is your guide*. New York: Dutton, 1958.

Gladwin, T. *East is a big bird*. Cambridge: Harvard University Press, 1970.

Gordon, W. *Synectics*. New York: Harper & Row, 1961.

Green, R., & Courtis, M. Information theory and figure perception: The metaphor that failed. *Acta Psychologica* (Amsterdam), 1966, *25*, 12-36.

Hart, R., & Moore, G. The development of spatial cognition: A review. In R. Downs and D. Stea (Eds.), *Image and environment*. Chicago: Aldine. 1973. Pp. 246-288.

Huttenlocher, J. Constructing spatial images: A strategy in reasoning. *Psychological Review*, 1968, *75*, 550-560.

Jerison, H. Evolution of the brain and intelligence. *Current Anthropology*, 1975, *16*, 403-426.

Jolliffe, R. An information theory approach to cartography. *Cartography*, 1974, *8*, 175-181.

Krech, D. (formerly Krechevsky, I) The genesis of "hypotheses" in rats. *University of California Publications in Psychology*, 1932, *6*, No. 4.

Langer, S. *Philosophy in a new key*. New York: New American Library, 1951.

Lewis, D. *We, the navigators*. Hawaii: University Press of Hawaii, 1972.

Luria, A. *The mind of a mnemonist*. New York: Basic Books, 1968.

McCleary, G. Beyond simple psychophysics: Approaches to the understanding of map perception. *Proceedings of the American Congress on Surveying and Mapping*, 30th Annual Meeting, Washington, D. C., 1970, 189-209.

McKellar, P. *Imagination and thinking*. London: Routledge & Kegan Paul Ltd. (Cohen & West), 1957.

Miller, J. *The body in question*. New York: Random House, 1978.

Muehrcke, P. *Map use: Reading, analysis, and interpretation*. Madison, Wisconsin: J. P. Publications, 1978.

O'Keefe, J., & Nadel, L. *The hippocampus as a cognitive map*. New York: Oxford University Press, 1978.

Olton, D. Mazes, maps, and memory. *American Psychologist*, 1979, *34*, 583-596.

Petchenik, B. A verbal approach to characterizing the look of maps. *American Cartographer*, 1974, *1*, 63-71.

Polanyi, M. *Personal knowledge*. New York: Harper & Row, 1964.

Robinson, A., & Petchenik, B. *The nature of maps: Essays toward understanding maps and mapping*. Chicago: University of Chicago Press, 1976.

Shainberg, L. *Brain surgeon: An intimate view of his world*. Philadelphia: J. B. Lippincott, 1979.

Siegel, A., & White, S. The development of spatial representations of large-scale environments. In H. W. Reese (Ed.), *Advances in child development and behavior* (Vol. 10). New York: Academic Press, 1975.

Stea, D. *Environmental mapping*. Milton Keynes, England: The Open University Press, 1976.

Steiner, G. *Fields of force*. New York: Viking Press, 1974.

Tobler, W. The geometry of mental maps. In R. Golledge & G. Rushton (Eds.), *Spatial choice and spatial behavior*. Columbus: Ohio State University Press, 1976. Pp. 69-81.

Tolman, E. Psychology versus immediate experience. *Philosophy of Science*, 1935, *2*, 356-380.

Tolman, E. Cognitive maps in rats and men. *Psychological Review*, 1948, *55*, 189-208.

Toulmin, S. *The philosophy of science: An introduction.* New York: Harper & Row, 1960.

Wall, P. House call (A review of *The Body in Question* by Jonathan Miller). *The New York Review of Books*. 1979, April 5, 20-22.

Zelinsky, W. The first and last frontier of communications: The map as mystery. *Bulletin of the Geography and Map Division Special Libraries Association*, 1973, No. 94, 2-29.

7

The Externalization of Cognitive Maps by Children and Adults: In Search of Ways to Ask Better Questions[1]

ALEXANDER W. SIEGEL

Introduction

Problems, Purposes, and Assumptions

Imagine that you live east of the city of Pittsburgh and usually go to work via Interstate 376. You hear on the radio that traffic is backed up to Philadelphia. What do you do? You do not abandon your car—rather, you figure out your current position and consider alternative routes to work. How do you do this? What is the nature of the knowledge system that permits you to solve the problem? One day last summer, I was driving my children to the community swimming pool, and I missed my turn. My 9-year-old son soon said, "Daddy—we've never been [this far] on this road. I think we're lost." How did he know?

These are problems in cognitive mapping. In this chapter I will first present briefly the theoretical framework that has guided our research in the development of the processes underlying the solution to such problems in environmental navigation. A major point of this chapter is that the problems of externalizing spatial knowledge—cognitive maps—are pervasive, and are major stumbling blocks to our understanding of cognitive mapping and its development. To document this, I will focus on the procedures that we, and others, have used to externalize cognitive maps and try to indicate their strengths and limitations. I will briefly describe some of our research, which I view as progressive attempts to overcome some of the problems inherent in externalizing the cognitive maps of children and adults.

My approach to the development of cognitive mapping entails a number

[1] Preparation of this chapter was made possible, in part, by NICHHD Grant #09694.

SPATIAL REPRESENTATION AND BEHAVIOR
ACROSS THE LIFE SPAN

of assumptions that need to be made explicit at the outset. (Although the heuristic utility of these assumptions may be debated, they are statements about a model—not a theory—of development, and, as such, their adequacy is not subject to the criterion of empirical verification or falsification, only that of heuristic utility [Reese & Overton, 1970]):

1. Since neither children nor adults typically consult road maps or use compasses and typically do not get lost in way-finding, I assume that environmental navigation is guided by some internal representation of (some piece of) the environment. Although these representations are often distorted, fragmented, and probably not "maplike" (Appleyard, 1970; Siegel & White, 1975), the term "cognitive map" is nonetheless a useful descriptor and has been used for some time (Tolman, 1948; Trowbridge, 1913). Furthermore, I assume that humans are neurologically canalized to create such maps (Fishbein, 1976; Harris, Chapter 4 of this volume; Webster, 1977).

2. The process of cognitive mapping is constructive and develops both in children and adults. As the products of cognitive mapping, cognitive maps will reflect these developmental changes. The maps do not change simply by accretion, but rather by progressive transformation both over ontogenesis, and over repeated experience in adults and children. The acquisition of maps, like any learning, is not a process of "getting full", but rather a process of becoming unconfused (White & Siegel, 1976).

3. The study of the development of cognitive mapping need not be confined to a particular time span (e.g., years) nor to particular organisms (e.g., children). The process of development can be studied profitably in children over months and years and in adults and children over shorter periods of time (e.g., over repeated encounters with environments (Kaplan, 1967; Wapner, Kaplan, & Ciottone, Chapter 10 of this volume).

4. The extent of cognitive mapping and the nature of the resultant representation are, to a large degree, a function of the agenda (purposes) of the individual doing the mapping. For example, a casual visitor to a city and a prospective home-buyer will probably differ in the extent to which they actively map the environment, and thus the nature and detail of their respective cognitive maps will differ (Wapner, Kaplan, & Cohen, 1973; Wapner et al., Chapter 10 of this volume).

5. The fundamental problem in understanding the acquisition and development of cognitive mapping is the externalization of cognitive maps—getting the spatial knowledge out in some public medium, unconfounded by (theoretically) "nonspatial" task load. These externalized products are, in essence, "re-representations" (Jackson, 1884; Spencer, 1855) of spatial experience.

6. The nature and development of cognitive maps, in particular, and en-

vironmental cognition, in general, can be investigated productively within the context of an experimental approach. Furthermore, it is possible and necessary to design experimental procedures that are "representative in design [Brunswik, 1956]."

Large- and Small-Scale Spaces

I am concerned primarily with cognitive mapping of *large-scale* environments. Scale and size of environments (or space) are not synonomous. The scale of space is defined not by size, but rather by the perceptual (and motor) mechanisms with which it is explored (and constructed). Specifically, the structure of large-scale space is deduced from a number of observations over time, rather than being perceivable simultaneously from a single vantage point (Kuipers, 1977). Furthermore, one acts *in* (or explores) large-scale space, while one acts *on* (or observes) small-scale space (Ittelson, 1973). For example, most of the City of Pittsburgh is simultaneously perceivable from the top of the US Steel Building, and thus in this case, is small-scale—albeit large-size—space. Similarly, the partition in my office separating my desk from my secretary's precludes the structure of the office from being perceivable simultaneously from a single vantage point; thus, my office is large-scale—albeit a smaller-sized—space.

Small- and large-scale spaces both involve spatial relationships among objects and "frames of reference" (Hart & Moore, 1973; Wapner, Cirillo, & Baker, 1971). However, the cognitive processes involved in operating on a spatial extent that can be viewed simultaneously from a single vantage point may well be somewhat different from those processes involved in operating in a real space that includes the observer as one of its objects. Both Acredolo (1977) and Siegel, Kirasic, and Kail (1978) have argued that caution must be used in generalizing from children's performance in small-scale space, which has been the concern of the vast majority of the developmental literature, to their competence in cognitively mapping large-scale space. (Acredolo, Chapter 3 of this volume, addresses these issues more explicitly).

Theories of Cognitive Mapping of Large-Scale Environments

Not surprisingly, most theoretical accounts of the development of cognitive mapping emphasize the roles of objects (landmarks), relationships between objects (routes), and frames of reference. Piaget's theory on the development of spatial concepts is derived essentially from research on small-scale spatial displays. According to Piaget (Piaget & Inhelder, 1967;

Piaget, Inhelder, & Szeminska, 1960), the young child encodes the spatial location of landmarks in relation to self (an egocentric system) rather than in terms of its relation to other objects in the array (an "objective" frame of reference). The most convincing evidence favoring Piaget's developmental sequence comes from the work of Linda Acredolo and her colleagues (Acredolo, 1976; Acredolo, Pick & Olsen, 1975; Feldman & Acredolo, 1978). Acredolo has shown convincingly, for example, that the development of accurate cognitive maps of large-scale space is highly dependent on the differentiatedness of landmarks.

The sequence of development of frames of reference is specified in somewhat different terms within a Wernerian framework. Wapner et al. (1971) describe a progression from a coding system based on the relationship of landmarks to the child's body and perspective to a system in which landmarks become central features for a fixed frame of reference (topological in nature), and finally to a coding system based on abstract axes (i.e., a coordinate frame of reference that is Euclidean in nature). Hart and Moore (1973; Moore, 1976) describe the development of cognitive mapping in terms of a series of stages of successively more integrated frames of reference from (a) undifferentiated egocentric to (b) differentiated and partially coordinated into fixed subgroups to (c) abstractly coordinated and integrated systems.

These descriptions of the development of cognitive mapping in both Piagetian and Wernerian terms are essentially consonant with the model that I proposed with Sheldon White (1975) for the development of cognitive maps of large-scale space. In this model, landmarks and routes are the predominant elements of cognitive maps. Landmarks are first noticed and remembered. While acting in the context of these landmarks, routes linking them are formed. Finally, routes are integrated within an overall framework as configurations or survey maps (Shemyakin, 1962). The maps of adults and children probably differ in detail, but the underlying developmental sequence is the same: landmarks to route maps to configurations.

Within the model, the three elements are hierarchically related, that is, routes or linear maps are superordinate to landmarks, and subordinate to configurations. In children, one should find that landmarks are salient, and that route maps should be organized around them. Additional experience should permit children and adults to scale and metricize the distances between landmarks, resulting in more accurate route maps. Finally, with the development of coordinated frames of reference (possibly involving the functional maturity of parietal neocortex) in children (and additional experience in adults), routes should become integrated into configurational or survey maps.

Procedures for Externalizing Cognitive Maps: Some Initial Steps

For the most part, research with both children and adults has focused on route knowledge (i.e., the sequence of landmarks along a path) and configurational knowledge. From diverse theoretical orientations, inferences about individuals' cognitive maps have been derived from research using a variety of procedures, whose central aim is to "externalize" the maps (or selected aspects of them). The issue of externalization of cognitive maps is thus a core issue for the field of environmental cognition: How do you get internal representations out in public so that they can be analyzed qualitatively and quantitatively? A number of procedures have been used with differing degrees of success. I will examine some of them in detail, and indicate some of their strengths and weaknesses.

Techniques of the Pioneers: Verbal Protocols and Sketch Maps

Subjects' verbal recall (protocols) of their spatial experiences and of the resultant representations has a long history of use both in the literatures of the cognition of urban environments (e.g., Carr & Schissler, 1969; Lynch, 1960) and in developmental psychology (Piaget, *et al.*, 1960; Piaget & Inhelder, 1967). There are a number of problems with this technique, however. Although less of a problem with adults than with children, the technique confounds linguistic ability (or propensity) and spatial knowledge. "Where did you go? Out! What did you do or see? Nothing!" That is, spatial knowledge must be distinguished from the communication of such knowledge via verbal description, in which developmental differences are already well documented (Brown, 1976; Shatz, 1977). Furthermore, for both children and adults, there is a problem in taking input that is *simultaneous* and transforming it into *successive* output. (This could prove to be a pragmatic concern for the investigator as well.) For example, look about the room carefully. Now close your eyes and tell me *everything* you just saw. We could be here for some time!

Another technique widely used by investigators in environmental cognition (e.g., Appleyard, 1970; Lynch, 1960) and in cognitive development (e.g., Moore, 1976: Piaget *et al.*, 1960) is that of having subjects draw freehand sketch maps of familiar spatial environments. Having the young child draw a sketch map confounds cognitive mapping ability and "externalizing" ability (i.e., understanding and producing conventions and symbolizations). It is surely the case that young children's cognitive maps of environments are more accurate than the products they draw that "represent" those environments (Goodnow, 1977; Kosslyn, Heldmeyer, & Locklear, 1977). A further problem is that sketch mapping requires "translation" from the large-scale space of the world to the small-scale space of a piece of paper. Although Bluestein and Acredolo (1979) and Blaut, McCleary, and Blaut (1970) have shown that 5-year-olds are capable of this translation, the settings used have been very simple, and the response demands made on the child minimal (e.g., recognition).

Microspatial Models of Macrospace

The confounding of cognitive mapping and linguistic or praxic ability can be alleviated to some extent by having children construct small-scale maps or models of environments. For example, in one of our earliest studies (Siegel & Schadler, 1977), we had kindergarteners reconstruct from memory a tabletop model of their classroom. Children who had 8 months of experience in the classroom or who were given several landmarks to guide their performance constructed more accurate models than children with only 1 month of experience or who were given no landmarks. However, within-group performance was highly variable. Some children constructed extremely accurate models; the performance of one child who obtained perfect scores on all measures of locational accuracy is presented in Figure 7.1. Some children constructed extremely inaccurate models; the performance of one such child is present in Figure 7.2. Perhaps no quantitative scoring system could reflect adequately the quality of Buffy's performance. How does one account for such variability? Neither of these two children were ever seen bumping into walls in their classroom (kindergarteners generally know their way around pretty well). Thus, the source of Buffy's poor performmance is not in her internal representation of the classroom, but rather in the technique used to externalize the children's spatial knowledge (i.e., their cognitive maps).

Having children construct small-scale models of large-scale spaces eliminates the confounding of verbal and praxic ability with spatial knowledge. However, the problems of "representation" (i.e., knowing that a model "stands for" some piece of the real world) and translation of scale remain. Recently, we demonstrated that accuracy of construction of a spatial layout from memory was greater for both 5- and 7-year olds when they constructed their models in the same scale environment as that in which they had initially encountered it, than when they had to translate their cognitive map to a model of a different scale (Siegel, Herman, Allen, & Kirasic, 1979).

In summary, verbal protocols, sketch maps, and tabletop models make young children look spatially incompetent. Yet these are the very techniques

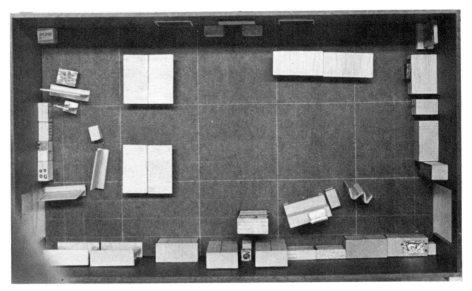

FIGURE 7.1. *An accurate model: David. (Siegel & Schadler, 1977.)*

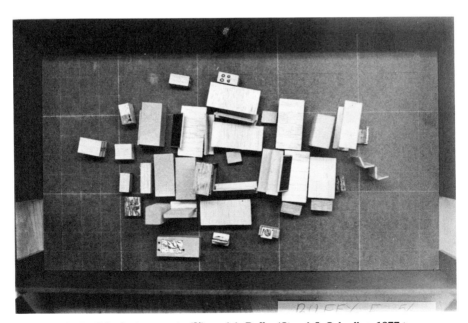

FIGURE 7.2. *An inaccurate (?!) model: Buffy. (Siegel & Schadler, 1977.)*

used by some of the major developmental theorists. It should come as no surprise then that developmental theorists have repeatedly argued that young children are spatially incompetent: for example, that they lack Euclidean concepts; that they're "egocentric." However, little children can readily get around in the neighborhood by age 4, and from home to school and back by age 6. In short, they have elaborate and rather accurate spatial knowledge. This paradox seems to center on what I call a competence-load tradeoff (White & Siegel, 1976). Performance, within this context, is considered to be a joint function of *competence* and *load*—a major component of which is task demands. Developmental differences in competence can be inferred only when task load is reduced to a minimim or varied systematically. Our own subsequent research has taken both tacks.

Reconstruction of Large-Scale Spatial Layouts: A Small Step Forward

In a series of studies (Herman, 1980; Herman & Siegel, 1978; Siegel *et al.*, 1979), we had children encounter large-scale layouts and then reconstruct the arrangements of objects in these layouts from memory. At the very least, this technique eliminates (a) the confounding of verbal and praxic competence with cognitive mapping competence; (b) the problem of "representation" (i.e., that a model "stands for" some piece of the real world); and (c) the problem of translation-of-scale. In these studies, kindergarten, second; and fifth-graders were walked through a 16 × 20 ft model town, which contained roads, railroad tracks, and eight buildings. Children's attention was directed to the buildings and their positions, and they were told that they would have to rebuild the town from memory. Following exposure to the layout, the buildings were removed, and the children were instructed to put the buildings back in their original positions. This procedure was followed three times for each child.

We believed that much of the demonstrated spatial "incompetence" of young children and their inability to use Euclidean relations was an artifact of yet another methodological problem: providing children with only limited experience with the experimental procedures and environment. In the real world, children develop their cognitive maps over repeated encounters with the environment. However, in most research a child is asked to construct a model or recall a location of a target only once or after only one exposure. For example, Acredolo *et al.* (1975) gave their young children but a single opportunity to relocate the site of an event (the experimenter dropping her keys), and found that placement accuracy was unaffected by whether the environment was familiar or unfamiliar. We felt that the lack of repeated experience (in the task) might well explain this counterintuitive finding. Thus, in our studies children were given repeated opportunities to encounter and reconstruct the layout of objects.

The accuracy of children's performance as a function of grade level and successive constructions is presented in the left-hand portion of Figure 7.3. Children became increasingly accurate in their placement of the buildings in the layout, and by the third construction the accuracy of the kindergartners was essentially equivalent to that of the fifth-graders. Absolute placement scores (reflecting whether a building was placed within 1 ft of where it belonged) reflect at least a rudimentary level of Euclidean accuracy, and by the third construction these scores were quite high. So, it seemed that even kindergarteners were capable of using metric distance relations between buildings and other features of the layout to improve the accuracy of their cognitive maps.

There is also a strong indication that all children were relying on topological cues; buildings isolated from the paths and/or endpoints were placed less accurately than buildings with clear topological positions. Thus, it appears that when young children are given repeated encounters with, and

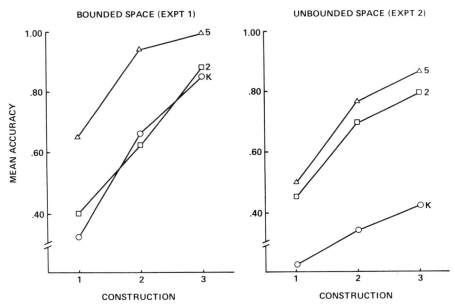

FIGURE 7.3. *Mean placement accuracy at each grade level after each construction in bounded and unbounded space. (Herman & Siegel, 1978.)*

opportunities to perform in, a large-scale environment (as they typically are in the real world), their performance improves dramatically and their inferred spatial "incompetence" seems to diminish markedly.

Things are never that simple, however. A major flaw in this argument was discovered during the course of a second study with children of the same ages. In the study just described, the town had been laid out on the floor of a classroom—the classroom walls were only a few feet away from the edge of the layout. There was a "frame," and the frame cues could have served to guide the performance of any or all of the children. In a second study, the town was laid out in the middle of a gymnasium, with the closest wall or frame cue some 15–20 ft away. One can consider this as "unbounded" space, as opposed to the bounded space of the first study. Performance of children in the unbounded space of the second study is presented in the right-hand portion of Figure 7.3. Note that, as in the first study, the kindergarteners did poorly initially. More importantly, in this study their performance improved little as a function of repeated construction experience. It appears, then, that in the bounded space of the first study, all buildings (including the "isolated" buildings) have topological relations to the surrounding room and that kindergarten children were able to use these relations to guide their performance. When these "frame" cues were absent, task load was increased, children had to rely exclusively on "intralayout" relations (many of which were Euclidean), and accuracy diminished markedly. Note further that the performance of the second- and fifth-graders was little affected by the nature of the experimental space. (See Acredolo, Chapter 3 of this volume, for an explicit discussion of frames of reference.)

Although this technique has great promise both for externalizing cognitive maps and for manipulating load factors, it has some serious weaknesses and constraints. The space was large-size, but not truly large-scale, that is, the space was perceivable simultaneously from a single vantage point. Given the probable noncomparability of processes used to explore and construct large- and small-scale space, and given that one is interested in cognitive mapping of large-scale space, the technique seems somewhat limited in representativeness (Brunswik, 1956). There are also pragmatic limitations: It is simply a pain in the neck (and often impossible) to obtain exclusive rights from a school to their gymnasium for several hours a day, several days a week, for several weeks.

Perhaps most importantly, although the procedure does tap memory for locational information, it does not tap directly either route or configurational knowledge. Thus, the technique seems to have little theoretical relevance for our proposed model of the development of cognitive maps (Siegel & White, 1975; Siegel et al., 1978). The remainder of this chapter will focus on new procedures that can yield data of more direct theoretical relevance to our model.

Procedures for Investigating the Development
of Route and Configurational Knowledge

Some Advances in the Externalization of
Adults' Route Knowledge: Photographic Simulation of
Environmental Routes and the Use of
Multidimensional Scaling Procedures

The general hypothesis is that a route is a linear representation of some piece of the large-scale environment; it is temporally and spatially integrated and constructed and organized around landmarks. Route learning is core to Siegel and White's (1975) structural model of cognitive mapping. In their hierarchical model, routes are both superordinate to landmarks and supraordinate to configurations. That is, routes are the structures which become elements in higher-order configurations (Mandler, 1962). Furthermore, route learning is also central to the more process-oriented model of cognitive mapping proposed by Gladwin (1970) and elaborated by Downs and Stea (1977): orientation, route choice, route monitoring, and recognition of when you have arrived at your destination. Thus, from both a structural and process model of cognitive mapping, route mapping is a logical focus for empirical investigation.

In a series of studies (Allen, Siegel, & Rosinski, 1978), we assessed the route knowledge of adults by presenting to them a simulated walk through the environment and subsequently testing their knowledge about the distance relationships among various landmarks (scenes) along the walk. Initially, a series of 215 color slides were taken at points 3 m apart through a commercial/residential neighborhood in Pittsburgh (unfamiliar to all of our subjects). From this series, a presentation set of 50 slides was constructed, taken at points separated by gaps from 3-42 m. Slides were presented at a rate of one per 4 seconds from two projectors alternatively (with dissolve between slides to eliminate dark intervals). Such a pictorial protrayal of movement through large-scale space is both an economical alternative to field research (and/or supplement to it), while having the advantage of permitting significant experimental control (Garling, 1972; Jenkins, Wald, & Pittenger, 1978).

In the first two studies, following their viewing the walk, subjects made magnitude estimates of distances between a reference scene and each of 25 target scenes. The high correlation between log-estimate to log-actual distances (.96) and the rather steep slope of the power function representing the best fit (.74) provided clear evidence that the slide presentation gave subjects spatial information that they apparently organized and stored as a route map of the walk.

A more critical theoretical question is the extent to which people organized routes around distinctive landmarks. In our initial study we had selected certain landmarks (scenes) and had asked subjects to make distance estimates about them. What happens if we let the subjects tell us what good landmarks are? To what extent will their estimates of distances among these "good landmarks" be more accurate? If subjects do use distinctive landmarks to organize their map of the walk, then estimates of distances among good landmarks should be much more accurate than estimates of distances among poor landmarks.

A rather promising set of procedures to assess route knowledge (i.e., knowledge of sequence and interlandmark distances along a route) involves multidimensional scaling (MDS) of ordinal distance judgments among environmental targets. Multidimensional scaling involves a set of procedures that take proximities (similarities or distances) among a set of objects as input, and attempts to reduce the complex matrix of such proximities to a simple picture that portrays spatially the interrelationships among objects. Nonmetric MDS (Shepard, 1974; Subkoviak, 1975) is a statistically powerful technique that takes ordinal data (e.g., ranked distances) as input and yields a maplike array of points that accurately portrays the metric relations among those objects in the subject's psychological space (Kruskal & Wish, 1978).

Initially, eight undergraduates were shown the same "walk" as in the first experiment (the 50-slide presentation), and were then instructed to select the nine pictures with the highest landmark potential and the nine with the lowest (e.g., "which pictures would [most or least] help you find your way or help you to know where you are?") from a display containing prints of all 50 presentation slides. A schematic diagram of the walk is presented in Figure 7.4, with the location of the scenes judged as having high- and low-landmark potential marked. Note that high-landmark potential scenes include intersections and changes in heading; low-landmark potential scenes portray poorly differentiated areas in the middle of blocks.

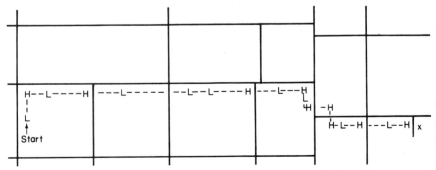

FIGURE 7.4. *Diagram of the walk showing locations of scenes with high (H) and low (L) landmark potential. (Allen, Siegel, & Rosinski, 1978.)*

Following this selection procedure, a different group of 32 undergraduates viewed the presentation set. To assess the effects of repeated perceptual experience on the accuracy of the route map, half the subjects viewed the presentation set twice, then judged distances; the other half viewed it twice, but made distance judgments after each viewing. Within each of these subgroups, eight subjects judged distances among only high-landmark potential scenes, eight judged distances among low-landmark potential scenes. During the test phase, ordinal distance rankings were obtained using the method of multidimensional rank order (Subkoviak, 1975). One scene was presented as a standard; subjects ranked the other eight scenes in order of increasing distance from the standard; this was repeated until each of the nine scenes had served as a standard. This procedure yielded a total of 72 judgments.[2] In addition to making the ordinal distance judgments, subjects also gave magnitude estimates of distances from each scene to the remaining eight.

Analysis of the ordinal distance judgments is computationally difficult and time consuming (requiring a computer), but conceptually simple. Initially, the 72 distance rankings for each subject are entered into KYST with instructions to provide the best one-dimensional solution.[3] KYST thus provides "map" coordinates for the location of each scene in each subject's psychological route-map. Next, the 72 actual or veridical distance rankings among scenes in each category are also entered into KYST, yielding "correct" maps. Then, subject's maps are compared individually against the appropriate correct map via CONGRU—a specialized MDS program yielding an error score ranging from 0 to 1.[4] Finally, more traditional analyses can be performed on these error scores.

[2] Interval scale proximities can be obtained from these rank orders (Torgerson, 1958), and given such data, MDS permits the determination of the projection or coordinates of each object on each dimension (in this case, 1) from which a spatial representation of the n objects can be constructed.

[3] The KYST (Kruskal-Young-Shepard-Torgerson) program is a two-way scaling program which combines the best features of TORSCA and MD-SCAL. Despite the fact that the walk contained changes in heading, the distance relations among test scenes could only be described as linear. Thus, as indicated by Shepard (1974) and Kruskal and Wish (1978), a two-dimensional solution was unwarranted on conceptual grounds. The "best" solution is defined in terms of minimal stress—a kind of spatial "badness of fit" (the lower the stress, the better). More precisely, stress is a normalized sum of squared deviations about a monotonic curve fit to the scatter plot of corresponding distance and proximity values.

[4] CONGRU is a specialized MDS program which compares the coordinates of points between different n-dimensional arrays without regard to array shrinkage, expansion, or rotation. This analysis provides an error index that ranges from 0 (indicating total congruence between estimated and correct map coordinates) to 1 (indicating total incongruence between the two sets of coordinates). The CONGRU computer program was developed by D. Oliver at Harvard University, and was made available to us through the cooperation of B. Green, Johns Hopkins University.

The "maps" comparing the actual and judged locations of scenes with high-and low-landmark potential are presented in Figure 7.5. As expected, distances among scenes with high-landmark potential (Figure 7.5a) were judged more accurately than distances among scenes with low-landmark potential (Figure 7.5b). Furthermore, this superiority held after both one and two views of the walk. Not surprisingly, the maps of subjects who viewed the walk twice were more accurate than those of subjects who had viewed the walk only once. (Since there were no differences in accuracy between subjects' judgments after two views and one test and after two views and two tests, the increase with repeated viewing is attributable to perceptual experience alone, rather than to repeated testing.)

Regression analyses were performed on subjects' magnitude estimates of interlandmark distances. Log-estimate and log-actual distance correlations increased from .78 after one view to .96 after the second view, indicating increasing linearity. More remarkably, the exponent of the power function that best fit the data (i.e., the slope) increased from .63 to .98 after a second viewing—a nearly perfect relationship between actual and estimated distance among landmarks.

Developmental Differences in Route Knowledge

Taken together, results from these studies indicate clearly that adults use landmarks as organizing features within the context of spatial events, and that repeated perceptual experience increases the accuracy of route maps of large-scale environments. With additional experience, adults calibrate and scale the distance relations among distinctive landmarks quite accurately. What about the *development* of route mapping? Are there developmental differences in what makes a good landmark? How do children use landmarks to construct accurate route maps? We conducted two developmental studies to address these issues.

In an initial study (Allen, Kirasic, Siegel, & Herman, 1979), second-and fifth-graders and adults first viewed the same 50-slide presentation and then selected scenes with high landmark potential from a display containing prints of all 50 presentation items. All subjects were originally instructed to view the presentation so that they would be able to retrace the steps of the person who took the photographs. After viewing the walk, subjects were asked to select from the display the nine scenes that would most help them remember where they were along the walk.

The nine critical areas (i.e., changes or potential changes in heading) within the walk were visible in 26 of the 50 presentation slides. The number of scenes selected as having high-landmark potential that were within these critical areas increased significantly with grade level: Adults chose more

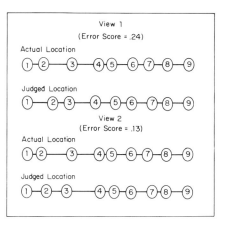 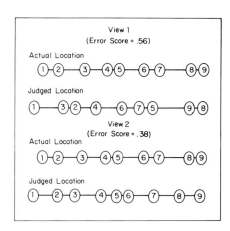

FIGURE

FIGURE

FIGURE 7.5. *"Maps" comparing actual and judged locations of scenes with high (5a) and low (5b) landmark potential. (Allen, Siegel, & Rosinski, 1978.)*

scenes from these critical areas (8.5/9) than did fifth-graders (6.9) than did second-graders (5.6). However, the second-graders' selections within the critical areas was significantly greater than chance. The nine scenes selected most frequently as having high-landmark potential by the subjects at each grade level were used as sets of test items in Experiment 2.[5]

Different children were tested using the set of scenes selected by their grade-peers and the set of scenes selected by adults. If children produce more accurate distance rankings with adult-selected than with peer-selected scenes, then it could be argued that the ability to *utilize* landmark potential in making distance comparisons precedes developmentally the ability to *assess* that potential. This argument would be further bolstered if improvement were found only for fifth-graders—the grade level at which there was appreciable overlap with adults' judgments of high-landmark potential in the initial study (four out of nine scenes).

We tested 32 second-graders, 32 fifth-graders, and 16 adults. Subjects were told that they would see a walk through a neighborhood (unfamiliar to all), and that afterward they would be asked questions about what they had seen along the walk. The 50 slide presentation from Allen *et al.* (1978) was used. Within each grade level, half the subjects viewed the walk once and

[5] The term "landmark" is used here to refer to spatially defined environmental reference points, and thus has perceptual, cognitive, and environmental implications (see Kaplan, 1976, for a discriminate taxonomy of uses). "High landmark potential" simply refers to the relative value of various environmental features as reference points—nothing is expected or assumed as to why these features make better landmarks.

half viewed it twice prior to being tested in the distance ranking task (the method of multidimensional rank order as described previously). Initially, a one-dimensional scaling solution was obtained for each subject's matrix of distance rankings using KYST.[6] A KYST solution was also obtained for the veridical distance rankings, and the fit of the subject's maps to the correct maps was determined by CONGRU. Analyses were performed on congruence scores (1-CONGRU error), with higher scores indicating more accurate maps. The critical interaction of grade level and scene-type is presented in Figure 7.6. While second- and fifth-graders were equally accurate (or inaccurate) in judging distances among peer-selected scenes (.46 and .43, respectively), fifth-graders were much more accurate than second graders in judging distances among adult-selected test scenes (.70 and .45). In short, second-graders' performance seemed little affected by whether peer- or adult-selected scenes were used. In contrast, fifth-graders were as accurate as adults when they had to judge distances among adult-selected scenes, and as inaccurate as second-graders when they had to judge distances among peer-related scenes. This suggests that the ability to make use of the potential landmark value of features in environmental scenes precedes developmentally the ability to discriminate among scenes on the basis of potential landmark value.

In summary, research employing photographic simulations of environmental routes and using the technique of ordinal distance ranking followed by MDS analyses has contributed significantly to our understanding of the process of route learning. Clearly, young children, older children, and adults construct route representations from perceptual experience with large-scale environments. These routes are temporally and spatially integrated and are organized around distinctive landmarks. Furthermore, learning a sequence of landmarks along a route is followed by calibrating distance relations among landmarks; this latter process improves developmentally and over repeated experience.

*The Externalization of Configurational Knowledge:
Multidimensional Scaling and Triangulation*

According to our theory (Siegel & White, 1975), once learned, routes themselves become elements to be integrated into a configuration or survey map. These survey properties of cognitive maps seem to be acquired last in adults' mapping of the environment (Appleyard, 1970; Shemyakin, 1962), are the first to be subject to dissolution (Critchley, 1971; Luria, 1966), and

---

[6] As in the earlier study, KYST yielded a linear configuration of the nine test scenes and a stress measure. At all grade levels and in all conditions, stress values were significantly less than those expected through chance performance for nine points in a one-dimensional solution as approximated through Klahr's (1969) tables.

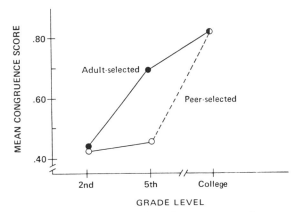

FIGURE 7.6. *Effects of adult- versus peer-selected test scenes on the accuracy of cognitive maps. (Allen, Kirasic, Siegel, & Herman, 1979.)*

do not seem to develop until later childhood when children are purportedly capable of constructing objective and coordinated frames of reference (Piaget & Inhelder, 1967). The strong possibility that this ability rests on a neurological substrate is further argued by Carey & Diamond (1977). It appears that age 10 marks an inflection point in the development of right hemisphere specialization, and thus, possibly, in the development of configurational spatial knowledge.

All of the techniques previously described—verbal protocols, sketch maps, constructions of mini- and quasi-large-scale models—have also been used to assess configurational knowledge. The drawbacks that were discussed apply equally to their use in the externalization of configurational as well as route knowledge. Similarly, ordinal distance ranking and the concomitant use of MDS techniques represents a significant advance over a number of the previously discussed techniques for assessing configurational knowledge. That is, it is directly applicable to studying knowledge of large-scale environments, and is unconfounded by verbal and praxic abilities or representational competencies. Furthermore, the technique is clearly appropriate for use with young (Kosslyn, Pick, & Fariello, 1974) and older children.

We have used the procedure (Herman, Kail, & Siegel, 1979) as one of several measures of college students' spatial knowledge of their campus. We had freshmen and upperclassmen make ordinal distance rankings among familiar campus landmarks in an attempt to assess the development of their configurational knowledge over the school year. Interestingly, we found that measures of landmark and route knowledge increased dramatically over the first three months of the freshman year, but increased little after that. Configurational knowledge (defined in terms of CONGRU accuracy, as in Allen *et al.,* 1978), however, increased little over the first 3 months; the more dramatic increase came between 3-6 months.

MDS procedures are not, however, without their problems. MDS derives or recovers metric relationships from ordinal judgments—it is a statistically powerful technique. But, subjects never have to make judgments of absolute distance. Although there are no empirical data to back me up, I am just a little uneasy about the fact that subjects never have to make judgments of absolute distance. It seems possible that the technique might tend to underestimate subjects' precise metric configurational knowledge. The practical problem is that the procedure is time-consuming. For example, Kruskal, Young, and Seery (1973) recommend nine as the absolute minimum number of objects that should be used in attempting nonmetric multidimensional scaling in two dimensions. Since directionality of judgments may be critical (Siegel *et al.,* 1979), each subject needs to make a minimum of 72 ordinal distance judgments. This number of judgments is manageable down to around early elementary school age—but may be more than children younger than that can handle. In other words, whereas MDS procedures have a number of advantages, there are some developmental constraints to their use.

Hardwick, McIntyre, and Pick (1976) have developed an excellent technique for externalizing children's configurational knowledge. Their procedure involves triangulation, conceptually much like that used in nautical navigation; it appears to be usable with children of preschool age. In their study, first- and fifth-graders and adults were initially familiarized with the positions of four target objects, one on each wall of a school library. Then a screen was interposed and subjects were asked to point a sighting tube in the direction of each of the four unseen objects. These sightings were taken from each of three different locations within the library. Angular settings were recorded for each sighting, and the three sighting lines for each target were plotted and continued out (in a forward direction only). The essence of Hardwick *et al.*'s procedure is presented graphically in Figure 7.7. The location of each target in the subject's cognitive map was inferred from the midpoint of the triangle formed by the intersection of the three lines—when this intersection occurred (as in Target 1). Additionally, Hardwick *et al.* (1976) asked their subjects to make sighting of the four targets under imaginal conditions—either mental rotation or perspective-taking. Generally, consistency and accuracy improved with increasing grade level, and children did more poorly in the imaginal conditions. Interpretation of the data is made difficult because "triangles" (i.e., intersection of the three sighting lines for each target object) were obtained for only 50% of the targets (e.g., Target 2, Figure 7.7) of the 10-year-olds and less frequently for the younger children. It should also be noted that although the space was large-*size,* under unscreened conditions, it

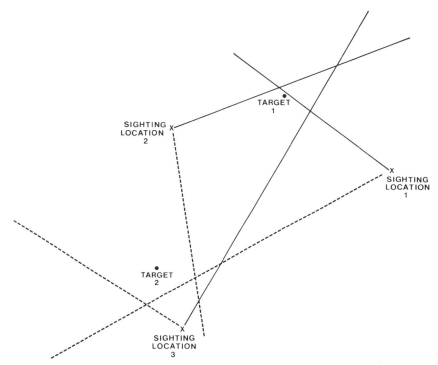

FIGURE 7.7. *Diagram illustrating the procedure of triangulation (using only angular bearing estimates) used by Hardwick* et al., *1976.*

was not large-scale (i.e., the entire library was perceivable from a single vantage point.)

Projective Convergence: A New Procedure for
Externalizing Configurational Knowledge

We have developed a technique that, we believe, represents a significant improvement over many of the techniques discussed. The procedure seems to meet the objections raised by the other methodologies, and is developmentally appropriate and economical for a wide age range of children. In essence, the technique—which we call "projective convergence"—combines triangulation and magnitude distance estimates. We simply obtain from subjects both bearing and distance estimates to a number of landmarks from three different locations in a large-scale environment. The essence of the procedure and resultant data are presented in Figure 7.8. Obtaining distance estimates from each sighting location guarantees getting the

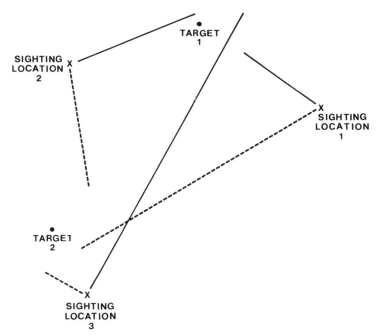

FIGURE 7.8. *Diagram illustrating the procedure of projective convergence (using bearing plus distance estimates). (This and the following figure are from Kirasic, Siegel, Allen, Curtis, & Furlong, 1980, submitted for publication.)*

"triangle" every time that Hardwick *et al.* could get only some of the time.

The combination of bearing and distance estimates to targets from different locations permits the derivation of several dependent measures:

1. Mean angle error/setting (in degrees) is a measure of bearing or directional accuracy.
2. The sum of the distances from the vertices of the triangle to the actual location of the object (in cm) is a measure of locational accuracy.
3. The length of the perimeter of each triangle (in cm) is a measure of locational consistency, that is, the extent to which the target is consistently located from all three sighting locations.
4. An overall spatial "goodness-of-fit" can be obtained for each map by comparing the coordinates of the midpoints of the triangles to actual object locations via CONGRU.

Since Hardwick *et al.* (1976) obtained only bearing estimates from their subjects, they could derive the first measure for all targets for all subjects, but could derive the locational accuracy and locational consistency measures *only* when the intersection of the sighting lines resulted in triangles. The projective convergence procedure (in which bearing and distance estimates are used) assures that all three measures will be derivable for each target for each subject and thus permits us to derive an overall measure of "fit" for each map.

We have completed an initial study using the projective convergence technique (Kirasic, Siegel, Allen, Curtis, & Furlong, 1980). This was a feasibility study conducted with adults. We were interested in the effects of experience on the accuracy of configurational knowledge, and the flexibility with which adults could use this knowledge.

The subjects were 24 freshmen and 24 upperclassmen at the University of Pittsburgh. Testing was done in September and October, so that freshmen had had less than one month of on-campus residential experience. In an initial session, subjects were walked to each of three locations on campus. These locations were inside buildings so that the to-be-sighted landmarks were not visible. From each sighting location, subjects made angular bearing and distance estimates to each of nine familiar campus buildings. They were told to draw on a piece of paper (with a stylus) a line that represented the direction and distance of each target from a designated starting point (with the edge of the paper serving as the campus boundaries). All nine estimates were scorable on the same piece of paper (the bottom piece of a "paper-carbon-paper" sandwich), while the paper the subject saw remained blank. (This was done so that a subject's estimate of Building n was not visually affected by his previous estimate of $n-1$.)

Mental rotation and perspective-taking were chosen as manipulations to assess the flexibility of configurational knowledge. In perspective-taking, subjects are instructed to imagine themselves at a different location and judge where some target is from that location. In mental rotation, subjects are instructed to imagine the array rotating until it is in front of them, and then judge the location of the target. Huttenlocher and Presson (1973) have found that young children cannot do either operation very well; for somewhat older children mental rotation is easier (i.e., performance in the condition is more accurate) than perspective-taking. Hardwick *et al.* (1976) found the same pattern of results. Furthermore, their adult data show no difference in mean accuracy between the two conditions. Interestingly, all adults and most children predicted that perspective-taking would be the easier operation. Both Hardwick *et al.* and Huttenlocher and Presson argue that mental rotation is the less complex operation and thus should develop prior to perspective-taking: In perspective-taking you need to keep in mind where you are, where you should be, then hold both in memory, and judge location. In mental rotation, knowing where you should be is eliminated. We had an initial hunch, however, that when the array to-be-rotated is a whole lot larger than the person, it might be easier for subjects to mentally move themselves than to mentally rotate their map of the campus.

To test this, all subjects participated in a second session about a week later. Bearing and distance estimates to the same nine targets were made under both mental rotation and perspective-taking instructions. Thus, each subject made an additional 27 bearing–distance estimates under each of two imaginal conditions (the order of which was counterbalanced). To compare the cognitive maps derived from the projective convergence technique with that derived from MDS scaling of ordinal distance judgments, all subjects made 72 ordinal distance judgments among the nine targets using the method of multidimensional rank order.

Four maps were derived for each subject—three from projective convergence (actual walking, mental rotation, and perspective-taking) and one from the MDS procedure (the best two-dimensional solution from KYST). To give you a flavor of the projective convergence maps, a typical performance in the walking condition is presented in Figure 7.9.

Each subject's three maps derived from the projective convergence procedure and the one map derived from the ordinal ranking procedure (i.e., the KYST solution) were compared to the actual positions of the targets via CONGRU. Analyses of the mean congruence scores (1-CONGRU error) indicated that accuracy was greater in the walking (i.e., nonimaginal condition (.73) than in either the mental-rotation (.66) or perspective-taking conditions (.66). Furthermore, the map derived from ordinal distance judgments was significantly less accurate (.60) than any of the maps derived using the projective convergence procedure. That is, the ordinal distance ranking procedure did, indeed, lead to a relative underestimate of the accuracy of subject's cognitive maps. Surprisingly, accuracy was unaffected by experience: The maps of upperclassmen were no more accurate than those of freshmen for any of the conditions. (Identical patterns of results were obtained in analyses on the measures of directional accuracy, locational accuracy, and locational consistency.)

Although *mean* accuracy was equivalent in mental-rotation and perspective-taking, there were marked individual differences. For some subjects, accuracy under mental rotation and perspective-taking was equivalent; for others, accuracy was greater under mental rotation; for still others, accuracy was greater under perspective-taking. Interestingly, the correlation between CONGRU scores under mental rotation and perspective-taking for the sample as a whole was positive, but not impressively so. This would seem to corroborate previous arguments (e.g., Huttenlocher & Presson, 1973) that mental rotation and perspective-taking may involve somewhat different processes or operations.

Of greatest importance is the demonstration that the method of projective

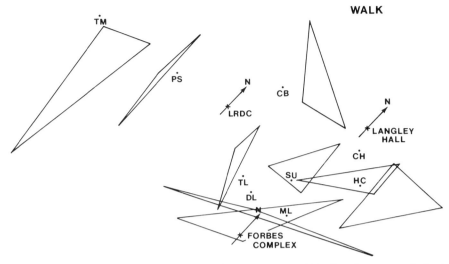

FIGURE 7.9. *An individual subject's map of the University of Pittsburgh campus, derived from the projective convergence procedure.*

convergence is a feasible procedure for externalizing, in rather differentiated ways, configurational knowledge of large-scale environments. Furthermore, the procedure seems quite workable with children. Hardwick *et al.* (1976) have shown that young children can readily make bearing estimates; pilot data and previous research in magnitude estimation (Siegel & McBurney, 1970) indicate that we can get reliable distance estimates from children as young as 6 years.

The Development of Configurational Knowledge in Children: Explorations in Outer Space

Let me describe briefly a developmental study using projective convergence that is currently in progress (Siegel, Curtis, & Furlong 1979). First-, second-, fifth-, and eighth-graders attending the same school are being tested. Initially, we have the child walk us to each of six familiar target locations inside the school and on the adjacent grounds (e.g., cafeteria, principal's office), placing a small yellow marker on the focal point or center of each (e.g., the entrance door). Then the child is returned to the first sighting location and a screen is interposed so that none of the six targets is visible. The child is told that he or she is to show the experimenter the direction and distance to the various locations that had just been visited. After pretraining in pointing and in magnitude estimation, the child is told to aim a pointer (with a swivel base mounted on a compass with the scale invisible to the child) to a specified landmark (i.e., the yellow star on the principal's door) and to push a joystick (in a slot along which are mounted a series of 20 miniature lights) to indicate the distance from the sighting point to the target. This procedure is followed for each of the six targets from each of three sighting locations. Inquiries are also made as to what the child would see as he or she proceeds from one sighting location to another (i.e., an attempt is being made to assess route knowledge as well as configurational knowledge in the same children). The results should give us an initial, but detailed, glimpse of developmental differences in configurational knowledge of large-scale environments.

Summary and Conclusions

My interest is in the development of cognitive maps of large-scale environments—environments not simultaneously perceivable from a single vantage point. In this chapter I have focused on what I consider to be the key issue in this enterprise: externalizing the map. A variety of techniques has been used to externalize the spatial knowledge of children and adults. The use of sketch-maps, verbal protocols of spatial experiences, and the construction from memory of small-scale models have characterized most research (until quite recently), and allowed Lynch, Piaget, and others to get our "foot in the door." Unfortunately, these techniques tend to lead to underestimates of children's spatial competence because they confound spatial knowledge with externalizing ability and other theoretically nonrelevant task loads (e.g., translation of scale, etc.). Although large-scale mapping and reconstruction tasks eliminate these problems, for the most part their representativeness in design and relevance to particular theories of cognitive mapping are limited (see Hart, Chapter 8 of this volume, for a refreshing exception). Finally, recently developed techniques such as photographic simulation of environmental routes, multidimensional scaling procedures, triangulation, and projective convergence seem to focus more directly on aspects of spatial knowledge central to contemporary conceptualizations of cognitive mapping and its development. That is, they enable us to externalize the landmark, route, and configurational knowledge of a wide developmental range of subjects.

Although the Piagetian and Wernerian frameworks for the development of spatial concepts are comprehensive, and have, in general, been supported by converging empirical evidence, their formal statements are insufficiently specific. Comtemporary theories of the cognitive mapping of large-scale space (e.g., Hart, Chapter 8 of this volume; Siegel et al., 1978) and the concomitant use of contemporary techniques should permit a more detailed specification of the developmental sequence of cognitive maps in children and adults.

I have used the term "cognitive map" extensively throughout this chapter, and this may have inadvertently "reified" the concept. It needs to be remembered that "cognitive map" is an inferred construct. "Cognitive map" is a state description, and like other state descriptions (as in the labels for various cognitive-developmental stages) can be misleading. "Maps" are not static realities, forever fixed in form residing somewhere in the right parietal lobe. Like cognitive stages, cognitive maps are "hypostatizations"-abstractions that we use in understanding the order, sequence, and development of the continual activity of cognitive mapping (Downs & Stea, 1977; Kaplan, 1967; Siegel & White, 1975; see also Downs, Chapter 6 of this volume). In this sense, "cognitive maps" are useful fictions.

These cognitive maps are argued to be the products of cognitive mapping. I have stressed throughout the paper that we need to be cautious in interpreting the externalized cognitive maps—the "public" products of cognitive mapping activity. If spatial environments are experienced or "presented" to the organism, then cognitive maps are "representations" of these experiences. Thus, the externalizations are "re-representations" and two levels removed from spatial activity. Clearly, further refinements in the techniques used to obtain *and interpret* these "re-representations" will be necessary.

Finally, children and adults are not monolithically motivated mappers; they have different purposes, agenda, and instrumentalities to accomplish these. The problem of the agenda of the mapper has to be considered seriously in future research as it has critical importance not only for the domain of cognitive mapping, but also for the broader domains of environmental cognition and cognitive development.

Although we are far from having any clearcut answers, I think we have made considerable progress in asking better questions and in devising procedures to address these questions concerning the development of cognitive mapping of the real world.

References

Acredolo, L. P. Frames of reference used by children for orientation in unfamiliar spaces. In G. Moore and R. Golledge (Eds.), *Environmental knowing.* Stroudsburg, Pennsylvania: Dowden, Hutchinson & Ross, 1976.

Acredolo, L. P. Developmental changes in the ability to coordinate perspectives of a large-scale space. *Developmental Psychology,* 1977, *13,* 1-8.

Acredolo, L. P., Pick, H. L., & Olsen, M. C. Environmental differentiation and familiarity as determinants of children's memory for spatial location. *Developmental Psychology*, 1975, *11*, 495-501.

Allen, G. L., Kirasic, K. C., Siegel, A. W., & Herman, J. F. Developmental issues in cognitive mapping: The selection and utilization of environmental landmarks. *Child Development*, 1979, *50*, 1062-1070.

Allen, G. L., Siegel, A. W., & Rosinski, R. R. The role of perceptual context in structuring spatial knowledge. *Journal of Experimental Psychology: Human Learning and Memory*, 1978, *4*, 617-630.

Appleyard, D. Styles and methods of structuring a city. *Environment and Behavior*, 1970, *2*, 100-118.

Blaut, J. M., McCleary, G. S., & Blaut, A. S. Environmental mapping in young children. *Environment and Behavior*, 1970, *2*, 335-349.

Bluestein, N., & Acredolo, L. P. Developmental changes in map-reading skills. *Child Development*, 1979, *50*, 691-697.

Brown, A. L. The construction of temporal succession by preoperational children. In A. D. Pick (Ed.), *Minnesota symposia on child psychology*, (Vol. 10). Minneapolis: University of Minnesota Press, 1976.

Brunswik, E. *Perception and the representative design of psychological experiments*, Berkeley: University of California Press, 1956.

Carey, S., & Diamond, R. From piecemeal to configurational representation of faces. *Science*, 1977, *195*, 312-314.

Carr, S., & Schissler, D. The city as a trip: Perceptual selection and memory in the view from the road. Environment and Behavior, 1969, *1*, 7-36.

Critchley, M. *The parietal lobes.* New York: Hafner, 1971.

Downs, R. M. & Stea, D. *Maps in minds.* New York: Harper & Row, 1977.

Downs, R. M., & Stea, D. Cognitive maps and spatial behavior: Process and products. In R. M. Downs & D. Stea (Eds.), *Image and Environment: Cognitive mapping and spatial behavior.* Chicago: Aldine, 1973.

Feldman, A., & Acredolo, L. P. The effect of active versus passive exploration on memory for spatial location in children. *Child Development*, 1979, *50*, 698-704.

Fishbein, H. D. *Evolution, development, and children's learning.* Pacific Palisades, California: Goodyear, 1976.

Flavell, J. H. Stage related properties of cognitive development. *Cognitive Psychology*, 1971, *2*, 421-453.

Garling, T. Studies in visual perception of architectural spaces and rooms. In *Reports from the psychological laboratories*. University of Stockholm, Supplement 15, November, 1972.

Gladwin, T. *East is a big bird.* Cambridge, Massachusetts: Harvard University Press, 1970.

Goodnow, J. *Children drawing.* Cambridge, Massachusetts: Harvard University Press, 1977.

Hardwick, D. A., McIntyre, C. W., & Pick, H. L. The content and manipulation of cognitive maps in children and adults. *Monographs of the Society for Research in Child Development*, 1976, *41*, (3, Serial No. 166).

Harris, L. J. Neurophysiological factors in the development of spatial skills. In J. Eliot & N. J. Salkind (Eds.), *Children's spatial development*. Springfield, Illinois: Charles C. Thomas, 1975.

Hart, R. A., & Moore, G. T. The development of spatial cognition: A review. In R. M. Downs & D. Stea (Eds.), *Image and environment: Cognitive mapping and spatial behavior.* Chicago: Aldine, 1973.

Hazen, N. L., Lockman, J. J., & Pick, H. L. The development of children's representations of large-scale environments. *Child Development*, 1978, *49*, 623-636.

Herman, J. F. Children's cognitive maps of large-scale spaces: Effects of exploration, direction, and repeated experience. *Journal of Experimental Child Psychology*, 1980, *29*, 126-143.

Herman, J. F., Kail, R. V., & Siegel, A. W. Cognitive maps of a college campus: A new look at freshman orientation. *Bulletin of the Psychonomic Society*, 1979, *13*, 183-186.

Herman, J. F., & Siegel, A. W. The development of cognitive mapping of the large-scale environment. *Journal of Experimental Child Psychology*, 1978, *26*, 389-401.

Huttenlocher, J., & Presson, C. C. Mental rotation and the perspective problem. *Cognitive Psychology*, 1973, *4*, 277-299.

Huttenlocher, J., & Presson, C. C. The coding and transformation of spatial information. *Cognitive Psychology*, 1979, *11*, 375-394.

Ittelson, W. H. Environment perception and contemporary perceptual theory. In W. H. Ittelson (Ed.), *Environment and cognition*. New York: Seminary Press, 1973.

Jackson, J. H. Evolution and dissolution of the nervous system. (Croonian Lectures.) Published in parts in the *British Medical Journal, Lancet*, and *Medical Times and Gazette*, 1884. Reprinted in J. Taylor (Ed.), *The selected writings of John Hughlings Jackson* (Vol. 2). New York: Basic Books, 1958. Pp. 45-75.

Jenkins, J. J., Wald, J., & Pittenger, J. B. Apprehending pictorial events: An instance of psychological cohesion. In C. W. Savage (Ed.), *Minnesota studies in the philosophy of science* (Vol. 9). Minneapolis: University of Minnesota Press, 1978.

Kaplan, B. Meditations on genesis. *Human Development*, 1967, *10*, 65-87.

Kaplan, S. Adaptation, structure, and knowledge. In G. T. Moore & R. G. Golledge (Eds.), *Environmental knowing: Theories, research, and methods*. Stroudsburg, Pennsylvania: Dowden, Hutchinson, & Ross, 1976.

Kirasic, K. C., Siegel, A. W., Allen, G. L., Curtis, L. E., & Furlong, N. A comparison of methods of externalizing college students' cognitive maps of their campus. Submitted to the *Journal of Experimental Psychology: Human Learning and Memory*, 1980.

Klahr, D. A Monte Carlo investigation of the statistical significance of Kruskal's non-metric scaling procedure. *Psychometrika*, 1969, *34*, 319-330.

Kosslyn, S. M., Heldmeyer, K. H., & Locklear, E. P. Children's drawings as data about internal representations. *Journal of Experimental Child Psychology*, 1977, *23*, 191-211.

Kosslyn, S. M., Pick, H. L., & Fariello, G. R. Cognitive maps in children and men. *Child Development*, 1974, *45*, 707-716.

Kruskal, J. B., & Wish, M. *Multidimensional scaling*. Beverly Hills: Sage Publications, 1978.

Kruskal, J. B., Young, F. W., & Seery, J. B. *How to use KYST, a very flexible program to do multidimensional scaling and unfolding*. Murray Hill, New Jersey: Bell Telephone Laboratories, 1973.

Kuipers, B. *Spatial knowledge*. Massachusetts Institute of Technology Artificial Intelligence Laboratory, Memo 359, June, 1977.

Luria, A. R. *Higher cortical functions in man*. New York: Basic Books, 1966.

Lynch, K. *The image of the city*. Cambridge, Massachusetts: M.I.T. Press, 1960.

Maier, N. R. F. Reasoning in children. *Journal of Comparative Psychology*, 1936, *21*, 357-366.

Mandler, G. From association to structure. *Psychological Review*, 1962, *69*, 415-427.

Milgram, S. Introduction. In W. H. Ittelson (Ed.), *Environment and cognition*. New York: Seminar Press, 1973.

Moore, G. T. Theory and research on the development of environmental knowing. In G. T. Moore & R. G. Golledge (Eds.), *Environmental knowing*. Stroudsburg, Pennsylvania: Dowden, Hutchinson, & Ross, 1976.

Piaget, J., & Inhelder, B. *The child's conception of space*. New York: Norton, 1967.

Piaget, J., Inhelder, B., & Szeminska, A. *The child's conception of geometry*. New York: Basic Books, 1960.

Presson, C. C. Spatial egocentrism and the effect of an alternate frame of reference. *Journal of Experimental Child Psychology*, 1980, *29*, 391-402.

Reese, H. W., & Overton, W. F. Models of development and theories of development. In L. R. Goulet & P. B. Baltes (Eds.), *Life-span developmental psychology: Research and theory.* New York: Academic Press, 1970.

Shatz, M. Relationship betwen cognitive processes and the development of communication skills. *Nebraska Symposium on Motivation,* 1977, 1-42.

Shemyakin, F. N. Orientation in space. In B. G. Ananyev *et al.* (Eds.), *Psychological Science in the USSR* (Vol. 1, Pt. 1). U.S. Office of Technical Reports (#11466), 1962.

Shepard, R. N. Representations of structure in similarity data: Problems and prospects. *Psychometrika,* 1974, *39,* 373-421.

Siegel, A. W., Allen, G. L., & Kirasic, K. C. Children's ability to make bi-directional distance comparisons: The advantage of thinking ahead. *Developmental Psychology,* 1979, *15,* 656-657.

Siegel, A. W., Curtis, L. E., & Furlong, N. A developmental study of the accuracy and flexibility of children's cognitive maps of familiar large-scale environments. Manuscript in preparation.

Siegel, A. W., Herman, J. F., Allen, G. L., & Kirasic, K. C. The development of cognitive maps of large- and small-scale space. *Child Development,* 1979, *50,* 582-585.

Siegel, A. W., Kirasic, K. C., & Kail, R. V. Stalking the elusive cognitive map: The development of children's representations of geographic space. In J. F. Wohlwill & I. Altman (Eds.), *Human behavior and environment* (Vol. 3). New York: Plenum, 1978.

Siegel, A. W., & McBurney, D. H. Estimation of line length and number: A developmental study. *Journal of Experimental Child Psychology,* 1970, *10,* 170-180.

Siegel, A. W., & Schadler, M. Young children's cognitive maps of their classroom. *Child Development,* 1977, *48,* 388-394.

Siegel, A. W., & White, S. H. The development of spatial representations of large-scale environments. In H. W. Reese (Ed.), *Advances in Child Development and Behavior* (Vol. 10). New York: Academic Press, 1975.

Spencer, H. *The principles of psychology.* (3rd ed.) Vol. 1. New York: Appleton, 1894. (First edition, 1855).

Subkoviak, M. J. The use of multidimensional scaling in educational research. *Review of Educational Research,* 1975, *45,* 387-423.

Tolman, E. C. Cognitive maps in rats and men. *Psychological Review,* 1948, *55,* 189-208.

Torgerson, W. S. *Theory and methods of scaling.* New York: Wiley, 1958.

Trowbridge, C. C. Fundamental methods of orientation and imaginary maps. *Science,* 1913, *38,* 888-897.

Wapner, S., Cirillo, L., & Baker, A. H. Some aspects of the development of space perception. In J. P. Hill (Ed.), *Minnesota symposia on child psychology* (Vol. 5). Minneapolis: University of Minnesota Press, 1971.

Wapner, S., Kaplan, B., & Cohen, S. B. An organismic developmental perspective for understanding transactions of men and environments. *Environment and Behavior,* 1973, *5,* 255-289.

Webster, W. G. Territorality and the evolution of brain asymmetry. *Annals of the New York Academy of Sciences,* 1977, *299,* 213-221.

White, S. H., & Siegel, A. W. Cognitive development: The new inquiry. *Young Children,* 1976, *31,* 425-435.

Children's Spatial Representation

of the Landscape: Lessons

and Questions from a Field Study

ROGER A. HART

Introduction

The research reported here arises out of theoretical foundations developed during my years as a student at Clark University. My colleague, Gary Moore, and I developed some hypotheses concerning the development of children's cognition of the spatial properties of the geographic-scale environment after reviewing the large, but at that time, disparate and largely atheoretical literature on the subject (Hart & Moore, 1971).

One of the most outstanding aspects of the literature was that children's ability to represent the spatial properties of the environment had always been investigated in the abstract. Such an arbitrary separation of cognition from other dimensions of experience is not valid, particularly when one is interested in the development of children's knowledge of their everyday surrounding environment with which they have a highly selective engagement. I hypothesized that children's ability to represent the spatial properties of the geographic environment must be related not only to intellectual ability, but also to such factors as their degree of access to the landscape and their freedom to manipulate it. For these reasons, I decided to investigate children's experience of the geographic environment more wholistically by looking at their cognition of the environment, and simultaneously examining their exploration, use, and feelings for places. Much of what follows is extracted directly from this larger investigation of children's place experience in a New England town (Hart, 1979).

195

SPATIAL REPRESENTATION AND BEHAVIOR
ACROSS THE LIFE SPAN

The Initial Theoretical Formulation

In attempting to integrate the dispersed and largely atheoretical literature on geographical orientation, Moore and I identified three reference systems which develop sequentially in a child (Hart & Moore, 1971). A reference system is essential to any workable topographic representation. It spatially orients an individual in some systematic manner to the environment. We used the terms egocentric, fixed, and coordinated for these three systems of orientation. Our thinking was strongly influenced by Piaget and his colleagues, who we thought offered the only comprehensive account of the development of children's spatial knowledge, and a remarkably insightful paper by Freeman (1916) that specifically outlined the three reference systems, which we discovered in the Clark University Library's dustiest section. The relationship of these systems of reference to Piaget's developmental scheme is illustrated in Figure 8.1. They are graphically summarized in Figure 8.2. In order to illustrate Piaget's developmental scheme, reference will be made only to one of his many experiments. I have chosen the sandbox modeling of the school and neighborhood experiment because it is the one that is the most specifically geographical in the task required and the most similar to my own method. Piaget, Inhelder, and Szeminska (1960) described their experiment in this way:

> The subject comes into the experimental room attached to the school and is taken to the window where he is asked to point out various buildings and well-known places. This is merely to ascertain the extent of his local knowledge and sense of direction. Next, he is made to sit at a table with his back to the window and given a sand tray with wet sand, carefully leveled off. He is also given a number of little wooden houses of various sizes, representing greens, recreation grounds, public squares and bridges, and a ribbon to represent the Arve. (The experiment was carried out at a school quite close to the river.) The experimenter takes the biggest house and puts it in the middle of the sand tray, saying: "Now this is the big school (meaning the primary school as against school as against the kindergarten). There are plenty more houses, little ones and big ones. These little bits of wood are to make bridges with and this blue ribbon is the Arve. Now I want to know everything near the school. You put the things in the right places." (Children who are too nervous to use the models can be asked to draw it all on the sand for a start.) At the end of the first part of the experiment the subject is asked to draw a plan in the sand or on a piece of paper, showing how he would go home from school or to a place which they all know. The drawing is a free drawing but the child is asked to show how it fits in with his general plan. Next the child is asked to make a drawing of the sand-model on a large sheet of paper. When he has done this, the experimenter turns the "school building" through 180° and asks: "Now if I turn the school round like this, must we move everything else about as well or can we leave it just as it is?" The child is asked to make the necessary changes himself. With older children the entire experiment can be carried out with pencil and paper [p. 5].

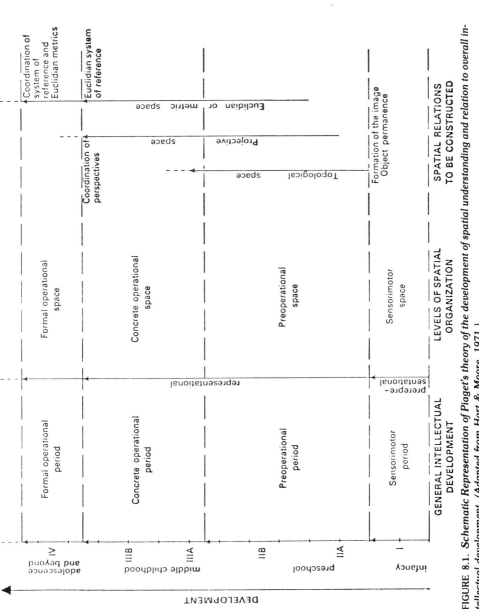

FIGURE 8.1. *Schematic Representation of Piaget's theory of the development of spatial understanding and relation to overall intellectual development. (Adapted from Hart & Moore, 1971.)*

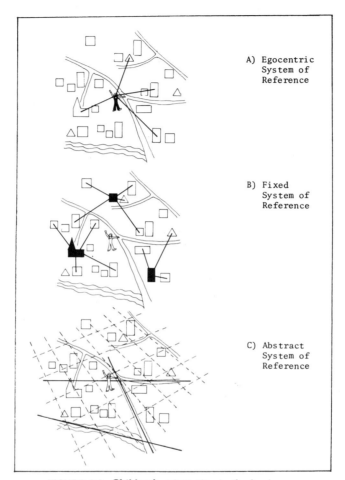

A) Egocentric
   System of
   Reference

B) Fixed
   System of
   Reference

C) Abstract
   System of
   Reference

FIGURE 8.2. *Children's orientation in the landscape.*

The three systems of reference, which Moore and I hypothesized from the work of Piaget *et al.* and many others, are described next in the sequence they are believed to follow in a developing child.

Egocentric System of Reference

During the preoperational period (approximately 2-7 years) children develop the ability to represent spatial relationships. At first, a child's representations of space are linked to sensorimotor activity and merely evoke successive states that have already been carried out on manipulated or perceived objects. As with preoperational thought in general, a preoperational child cannot reverse thought and hence can only return to a point of origin in thought by tracing a cyclical route. The topographic representations during this period are egocentric, that is, the child's conception of space is still tied to his or her own point of view, although these are some beginning trends toward decentering.

In the "sandbox experiment," an action-centered, egocentric, reference system was utilized by the children of preoperational level. Representation occurred only when they thought out a route. Landmarks were mentioned by these children, but were simply "tacked on" to recollections of their own actions, that is, the routes they had traversed. Children of this level could anticipate the spatial relations between one landmark and the next when they were walking and when reproducing this route on paper, but they could not mentally reverse their knowledge of this route. Consequently, children of this preoperational period could represent pairs of neighboring objects topologically, but they could not organize three or more objects successfully into a coordinate system. This ability, it was claimed, could not be achieved until a child entered the concrete operational period, which will be described next.

Based on a review of empirical findings, the Soviet psychologist, Shemyakin (1962), described a similar developmental sequence. He distinguished two fundamentally different types of topographical representations: route-maps and survey-maps. A route-map was described as a representation constructed by mentally "tracing the route" of locomotion through an area (Shemyakin, 1962). This agreed with Piaget's account in the "sandbox experiment" of how children represented their school environment in the form of the internalized actions of known routines. A "survey-map" was described by Shemyakin (1962) as a representation of "the general configuration or schema of the mutual disposition of local objects [p. 218]." We considered this equivalent to what Piaget described as representation utilizing a coordinate reference system.

Shemyakin suggested from his own empirical work and that of others, that route-map representations were necessary prior development to the formation of survey-map representations. He argued that after a child learns to walk, a new stage in the understanding of space relations is opened up. A child is not only able to orient in space among familiar objects immediately around the house, but is also able to retain a reasonably accurate representation of the position of individual familiar objects in space. However, it was suggested that the task of *externally* representing spatial knowledge was much more difficult than spatial orientation within a setting. Shemyakin found, for example, that even children of 6-8 years, when asked to draw a plan of some locality familiar to them, did so mainly by drawing the route.

Fixed System of Reference

For orientation in large-scale environments, Freeman (1916) noted the importance of a child's ability to free the self from the limitations of the early egocentric orientation system. After a child has used the egocentric process of localizing places when occupying various positions among places, he hypothesized that they build up a notion of their directions and distances with reference to the position of some fixed object, or of some fixed direction, instead of with reference to the self (Freeman, 1916, p. 170). Piaget has also shown that a child begins to orient in terms of fixed elements in the environment, rather than relying entirely upon orientation to the self. We therefore chose to name this the fixed system of reference.

Piaget found that around the age of 7 or 8, a child enters the concrete operational period. Thought is no longer limited to representing previously perceived images in sequences. Spatial information may now be manipulated through logical operations which are, however, still concrete (that is, dependent on the presence of real or represented objects). For early concrete operational children (substage IIIA: 7–8 years) the representation of the model school environment could be partially coordinated with the use of landmarks. These children were, however, unable to coordinate the system as a whole, either in demonstrating the topographical relations between landmarks with wooden models, or in describing a route. They could relate objects to each other in discrete local areas, but they could not appreciate the totality of relations between landmarks which occur in the environment because the landmarks were fixed in partially coordinated subgroups, each based on an independent vantage point or on a particular journey.

In summary, it seemed that during the preschool and early school years to about 7 or 8 years, a child graduates from an entirely egocentric system of reference to a fixed one centered on a small number of uncoordinated routes and landmarks. These differentiated, but uncoordinated, representations of the environment begin to be coordinated with the development of logical thinking.

Coordinated System of Reference

In accord with Piaget's theory, Shemyakin (1962) explained that "the crux of the general development of the understanding of space is the transition from a (fixed) point of reading to a system with a 'freely transferable' point of reading [p. 190]." Children need a coordinated system of reference. This is achieved during Piaget's substage IIIB (8–9 to 11–12 years). We noted that the coordinated system of reference need not be one we are most familiar with in the use of published maps and compasses, that is, cardinal directions.

For example, none of the children in the Piaget sandbox model experiment was reported to have utilized the cardinal directions in constructing their models yet some (substage IIIB) did utilize a two-dimensional coordinate system (Piaget *et al.*, 1960). The coordinates were based upon physical features in the experienced environment, but they nevertheless served the purpose of enabling the children to produce models that were coordinated wholes.

In drawing a plan of the school area, children of this advanced level used two complementary methods: Either they grouped together the elements of the plan in terms of relations between local areas, or they selected one or more commons starting points and reconstructed routes that radiated from them. They were then able to relate them all to each other through the advanced logical abilities found at this level of development. Through "associativity," each point could be reached mentally by any one of a variety of routes, and through "reversibility," each route could be represented in the reverse direction to that experienced. A child was finally able to produce a fully coordinated typographical representation when he or she could decenter from each of the partially coordinated fixed systems of reference. A child's individual route-type topographical representations could then be coordinated into a comprehensive survey-type representation. This represents the close of Piaget's substage IIIB, the achievement of fully equilibrated concrete operations.

The final development in a child's conception of spatial relations in Piaget's scheme comes with the formal operational period (stage IV: from 11-12 years). Children at this level of development were able to build the sandbox experiment taking into account the projective and euclidian relations of proportional reduction to scale, accuracy of distance, and metric coordinates. Such sophisticated metric mapping falls within the realm of science and technology. It is not necessary for peoples' everyday knowledge of the spatial properties of their environments. There are, however, practical advantages to operating at this level. Once a child becomes capable of operating on spatial relations completely removed from any actions upon phenomena in space, he or she can enter into a space of ideas with a multitude of spatial possibilities. He or she can, for instance, presumably form generalized models of types of environments such as towns or cities.

The New England Field Study

A variety of techniques have been used for the study of place cognition as part of an investigation of children's place exploration, knowledge, and feelings in a New England town (Hart, 1979). The following account is drawn from this larger study.

Method

One of the primary methods of the research was similar to the general approach used by Piaget in exploring the specific development of children's fundamental conceptions of space. The materials used were similar to his sandbox model neighborhood experiment (Piaget et al., 1960, p. 326). A critical summary of this and other previously used techniques for studying "cognitive maps," or "topographical representations," led me to the use of models over drawing (Hart, 1979; Mark, 1972). In his investigation of the reference systems used by children to facilitate their representation of changes of their position in the larger environment, Piaget used model elements (ribbon rivers, wooden houses, etc.) in a sandbox and asked them to map their home area. This is very similar to the method finally adopted in this research but with one very important difference: My interest was not to determine the level of children's intellectual development with regard to space in general, but was specifically to discover: (a) how they represented the spatial arrangement of places in their everyday home environment; and (b) what places they knew of. It was therefore important that there be more standardization in the interviewer's questions to the child than there is in Piaget's clinical method.

If the children had chosen to model only those places in their backyard, or on the way to school, for instance, I would not have as clear a picture as possible of the extent of children's knowledge of places and the relationship of those places to one another. I was not able to pursue in depth the level of logical operations children were bringing to the task, but this was not the primary interest of my research endeavor. A second difference was that rather than have the children build their places in a sandbox, the children laid out their places on very large sheets of paper, enabling us to record the location of each place and to write alongside them the names of the places as given to my by the child. Because I anticipated that each child would have some unique needs, I decided to provide as diverse a set of elements as possible and encouraged them to speak out if they needed anything else or any more of the original set of materials. In addition to model elements, the children had clay and crayons, and frequently used these to supplement their model/maps with details. The children shared with me the task of laying out the paper, and care was taken to make sure they understood and were interested in the task. This helped the children see the task in a more personal and meaningful way than is common in experimental designs. It also enabled them to realize that later it would be no problem for them to add further pieces of paper. By the time the children had cut the paper off the roll and

FIGURE 8.3. *An oblique photograph of a child's landscape model.*

stuck it down on the floor, they were ready to respond eagerly to the following instructions:

> Choose something that we can pretend is your house and put it on the paper. Now, put on the paper all of the places that you know, including this school. Show me where as many places are as you can. This will help us to build a giant model of Inavale later to show other children what Inavale looks like and how to get to places. If you don't have the right kind of toys to show me these places, you can also use crayons to draw on the paper, or modeling clay to build places with. If you need any more things or anything else, tell me and I will get them for you. Each time you put something on the paper, tell me what it is and I will write it down so that we won't forget what to call it. [Hart, 1979, p. 95].

When the child moved away from building around the house to some other part of the landscape, he or she was lightly reminded not to forget to put the elementary school on the paper. The elementary school had been included in the instructions in order to introduce some communality of scale between the children's model landscapes. It was the only feature situated a considerable distance from the town center (2 miles) which I could be sure all of the children were familiar with.

When children said they had completed the model they were asked:

1. Do you need anything else to add to the model that you don't have now?
2. Would you make any changes to your model if you had the chance to do it again?

Once assured of the child's satisfaction with the model, an imaginary driving tour of the landscape was taken by the child and myself in one of the model cars: (a) to ascertain if the child's previous naming of places had been arbitrary; and (b) because it was difficult for me to recall which names applied to which model elements in all cases. Together we drew lines around each model and wrote the name alongside. Finally, we removed all of the models and toys, and the child was congratulated on having made a map, usually to his or her great surprise and satisfaction, for this was the first time the word "map" had been used.

Throughout the modeling procedure, I sat on a chair in the corner of the room, encouraging the child without supporting or rejecting any of the modeling activity. If a child became absorbed for an extended period of time with play in the landscape he or she had created, I would encourage them to complete the model first and explained that later we would have time to play in it. Full tape recordings were made alongside a thorough record of the child's actions in relation to key words on the tapes.

Data Analysis

Two types of qualitative analysis were performed on the map versions of the children's model landscapes. One, made by three independent judges (including myself), was a general sorting of the maps into three categories following the three developmental levels of map representation formulated by Gary Moore (1973), primarily from the theoretical perspective of Piaget. This first analysis is designed to provide an independent measure of the level of organization that the schematic maps exhibit. I felt that by using the same system as the one carefully devised by Moore for analyzing the high school students of Worcester, Massachusetts, an additional replicative value might ensue. The second analysis, scored by myself, was a detailed breakdown of the structure of each map, designed so that a reader can literally "see" how the children's landscape models differ and how I have analyzed them. This more detailed analysis is the focus of this report because it offers valuable insights concerning the influence of experience.

The spatial structure of each child's model map is analyzed by first breaking it down into clusters or groupings of elements. These clusters are determined by the spatial relationships of elements. Any grouping of at least three elements (includes roads as well as places) that exhibit a higher degree of spatial organization within the group than with other elements outside of the group, is identified as a "cluster." There are five levels of spatial organizations:

1. No spatial organization even though the elements may be logically classified
2. Linked (i.e., elements are joined by a known route or path)
3. Spatial proximity (i.e., elements juxtaposed according to their relative proximity to or separateness from each other)
4. Spatial order (i.e. elements correctly related along a linear sequence)
5. Positional (i.e., relative locations are accurate, front/behind and left/right)

It is important to note that these are not conceived of as "stages," "levels," or "thresholds" in any developmental manner; they are simply points along a continuum that has been designed by me to describe the type and extent of spatial organization expressed in the model maps themselves. Having identified these clusters on a child's map, each cluster is numbered, using Roman numerals. Cluster I is the cluster surrounding the child's home, and so on, moving farther away from the home until all of the clusters are numbered. The level of spatial organization of elements *within* each of these clusters is expressed as a Roman number from 1 through 5.

Having identified all of the clusters, the level of spatial organization *be-*

tween clusters is determined using the same five levels that are used for describing the level of spatial organization *within* clusters. An "integrated map score" was arrived at by determining the average level of spatial organization within the clusters and multiplying it by the level of spatial organization between these clusters. Because the modeling instructions for each child were "show me where as many places are as you can," it was necessary for me to make some independent measure of the extent of area mapped. Some children's maps may be extremely well organized but only cover a very samll area, whereas other children may choose to map a large area even though they do not know it well. What might therefore be scored as a qualitative difference in the maps of two children may in fact be largely an expression of different personality traits: one child being more careful than another. An overall "composite map score" was obtained for each map by multiplying the "integrated score" by an "extent of area" score.

Although great care was taken to design a scoring system, the most valuable insights into understanding the factors influencing the representations comes not from comparing groups of children's representations with one another. They come instead from looking at individual children's representations in relation to data on their everyday environmental experiences. For this reason, the following discussion focuses on individual children's maps. (For an aggregate comparison of the data, see Hart, 1979.)

The Importance of Environmental Experience in Children's Ability to Represent the Environment

In describing the results of his "school and neighborhood modeling" experiment, Piaget noted that the development of children's knowledge might suggest that such knowledge is not the result of logical manipulation by a child but the accumulative result of direct experiences:

> At four years of age, a little boy is brought to school by his mother; he is aware only of the school, of his own home, of "the house with the surprises" (i.e., the grocer's store on the corner), and of the "theatre" (i.e., the traveling circus on the Plaine de Plain palais); he makes up a plan of the area with the few reference points which he is required to show, and he indicates the journeys he makes on the plan. At seven a child knows several roads; those which take him to school where he now goes himself and those which he walks along with his family when they go their customary walks; he can therefore describe several fragmentary routes, and he can draw a plan showing a number of discrete areas. At nine or ten, a child is free as a man and can roam at will all over the town; he therefore answers all the questions satisfactorily [Piaget *et al.*, 1960, pp. 23-24].

But, Piaget went on to argue that spatial representation cannot be explained simply in terms of a child's expanding ranges of spatial activity:

In short, the growth of knowledge is not a matter of mere accumulation, and while it is true that between the ages of four and ten, children collect a good deal of information about their district, they also coordinate the picture which they have of it, which is an infinitely more complex process of development [p. 24].

I agree that the growth of knowledge is not a matter of "mere accumulation." However, Piaget's lighthearted account of the development of a child's spatial knowledge through exploration is ironically a more accurate account of the factors that influence children's ability to represent the large-scale environment than are purely cognitive accounts such as the one hypothesized by Moore and myself, and which continue to be the total emphasis of research on children's cognition of large-scale environments.

My research suggests that the development of children's spatial activity in their everyday geographic environment, and variations in the freedom of this spatial activity, are the most important forces influencing the quality, as well as the extent, of children's ability to represent the spatial relations of places in the large-scale environment. Children's earliest maps, produced at the preschool and kindergarten ages, are not necessarily limited to routes as the literature states. Instead, I found that most of these young children are able to coordinate places in the immediate environs of their home into a "survey" type representation. Furthermore, the ability to coordinate larger, more distant areas was so markedly influenced by the degree and nature of a child's transactions with the landscape that the influence of the child's general intellectual level does not seem to be the most important factor. Piaget *et al.* (1960) are undoubtedly correct in stating that "the growth of knowledge is not a matter of mere accumulation" and intellectual coordination must also be achieved, but because the opportunity for children to explore places freely varies so greatly, the extent of a child's spatial range and such factors as the mode of locomotion through the environment become overwhelmingly important. A close look at children's model maps in the light of their spatial activity best illustrates the point and its implications.

Spatial Range and Spatial Representation

The landscape models of the following two children illustrate the relationships between children's ranges of spatial activity and their ability to represent the landscape.

MARGARET (5:0)[1]

Margaret was able to locate precisely the important places around her home (Figure 8.4a, Cluster I). Most of these places lie within her "free

---

[1] Throughout this paper, the child's age is expressed in years and months in parentheses after his or her name, for example 4 years, 6 months is (4:6).

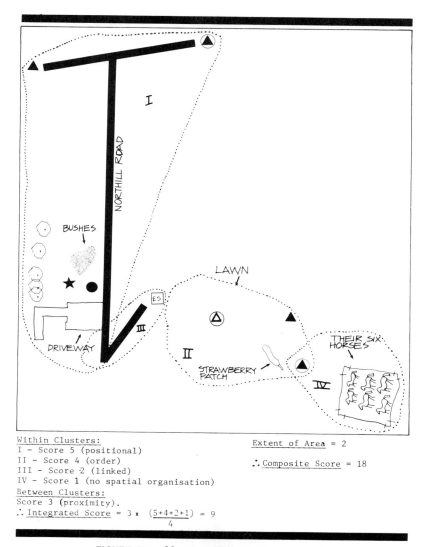

Within Clusters:
I - Score 5 (positional)
II - Score 4 (order)
III - Score 2 (linked)
IV - Score 1 (no spatial organisation)

Between Clusters:
Score 3 (proximity).

$$\therefore \underline{\text{Integrated Score}} = 3 \times \frac{(5+4+2+1)}{4} = 9$$

Extent of Area = 2

$$\therefore \underline{\text{Composite Score}} = 18$$

FIGURE 8.4a. *Margaret (5:0): Landscape model.*

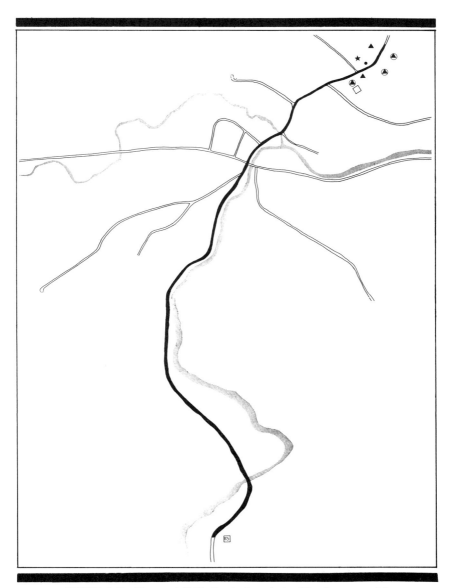

FIGURE 8.4b. *Margaret (5:0): Content analysis of landscape model.*

range." (Free range refers to the area a child may visit without asking permission or telling an adult each time; it describes the primary area of play.) As is common for children of this age, Margaret's free range is limited to the visually accessible environs of her home. Margaret was also able to locate correctly the houses of two neighbors living over the brow of the hill, which lie within her "range-with-permission." Together, these places form the positionally accurate cluster number one.

There are a number of families living across the street whom Margaret is also allowed to visit with her brother with permission—her mother knowing full well that the adults in those three homes will watch out for her daughter. Internally, this cluster (number II) shows the three homes in the correct spatial order, but in relation to the home, it is simply located across the road and hence cannot be considered positional in organization. There is, of course, no practical reason why Margaret would need to represent these homes positionally, for Margaret can see her home from any of them and would have no difficulty returning to it any time.

As with all children of this age, the journey to school (Cluster III) is simply expressed as a short strip of road heading off in an arbitrary direction away from the place where the small "school bus" (car) picks her up each day. The paddock (Cluster IV), shows no spatial relationship whatsoever to the remainder of her map. It is located next to the Watson's house, no doubt because they own the horses; the paddock is actually located on Wood Lane beyond Margaret's "free range." If she had been allowed to visit this paddock by herself she may have learned its location. Instead she locates it near its owners: an organizing principle that Piaget calls "conceptual proximity."

ENID (5:11)

Enid's map reflects directly the extent of her contact with the world (Figure 8.5a). Cluster I was built first. It is a detailed spatial expression of her neighbors' homes and some of the other important physical features lying around her home. The extent of this "home cluster" is precisely coincident with the shape and extent of her walking range without her mother. The features within this cluster are positionally located.

Enid went on to draw the hill down to the town center (Cluster II). She had, it seems, made one or two walking trips "down street" with her mother but clearly she had not learned much about the location of places from these trips; no doubt the responsibility for making ones own decisions about orientation and navigation is very important in the formation of topographic representations. She remembers the house at the end of her road where her school bus turns to go down the hill, for each morning the bus stops there to pick up some children, but the direction of the turn itself is completely wrong.

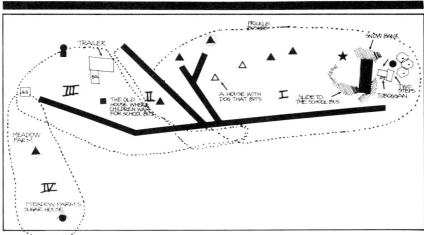

Within Clusters:
I   = 5 (positional)
II = 3 (spatial proximity)
III = 3 (spatial proximity)
IV = 4 (spatial order)

Between Clusters: 4 (spatial order)

$\therefore$ Integrated Score $= 4 \ (\dfrac{5+3+3+4}{4}) = 15.2$

Extent of Area $= 2$

$\therefore$ Composite Score $= 30.4$

FIGURE 8.5a. *Enid (5:11): Landscape model.*

This mistake is most likely a reflection of the problem children of this age had when wishing to express a slope on the two-dimensional surface.[2]

Having drawn the hill, Enid remembered the elementary school and so looked for buildings to represent it as well as the associated farm buildings where one of her classmates lives. These three buildings are rather carefully placed, beginning with the school, followed by the farm house and, in the distance, the "sugar house" which she had recently visited to see maple syrup being made (Figure 8.5a, Cluster IV). The principle of beginning with places that can be seen from some well-known starting point (in this case the

---

[2] At the time of building this model, Enid was sitting facing south and so drew the hill going "down," that is, she reverted to using the bottom of the paper from her perspective as a baseline. This problem was rare because it usually occurred only when children chose to use a crayon. Such examples confirmed the value of using modeling rather than drawing as a means of maximizing representational ability and reducing the skill component of external representation.

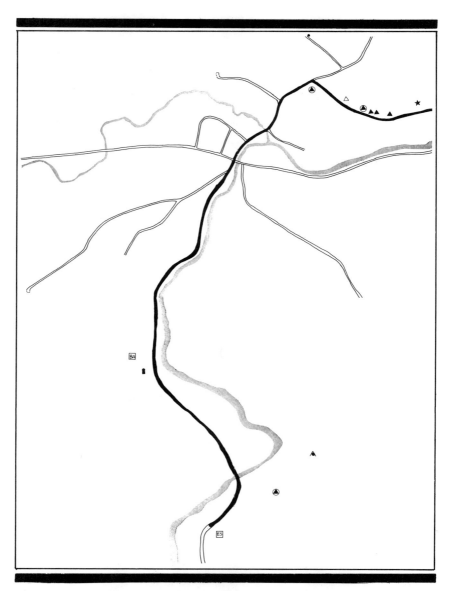

FIGURE 8.5b. *Enid (5:11): Content analysis of landscape model.*

school), and expanding outwards to places visually accessible and then on to places less accessible seems to be a most common system, producing a useful, ordinally organized map or map cluster.

Finally, Enid joins this school cluster to her home cluster by mentally returning home and retracing her daily school bus journey (Cluster III). It is notable that she, and all other children of similar age chose to proceed from home to school in this task rather than from school to home, even though the return journey has, of course, been made precisely the same number of times!

DISCUSSION

In each of these models, the highest level of spatial organization was within Cluster I, the "home cluster." The average score for all 63 models produced by the town's 4–9-year-old children was significantly higher for this home cluster. Forty-five out of the 63 children produced "home clusters" which were positionally organized. Eight of the 12 preschool and kindergarten children (i.e., under 7 years of age) produced home clusters that were organized at this high level. I suspect that even this is an understatement of their representational ability because of a weakness in my method. A high proportion of the modeling elements were buildings in shape. This led most children to emphasize the mapping of buildings rather than some of the more intimate details of their home setting such as "the slippery steps," the "washing line," the "sled," and so on. Those younger children who, for whatever reason, found the means to model these home elements with my loose parts model elements (clay and sticks), were able to show me positionally organized maps around their homes. Other children probably failed to produce such well organized home clusters because, as with Piaget's experiment, they were largely limited to buildings that cannot be seen from one another in the landscape. A most important problem in mapping is undoubtedly the representing of places that cannot ever be perceived from a single location.[3]

In our review of the subject, Moore and I emphasized the importance of body locomotion in being able to build up internal representations of the geographic-scale environment. It was not possible for me to discover whether or not the children were mentally retracing routes back and forth from their home to the important places nearby—their swing, shed, tree, and so on. It may be that head and eye movements from a house window are all that is required in the development of a representation of the immediate environment

---

[3] I do not wish to go as far as calling this a defining attribute of mapping. For example, a classroom can be perceived from a single location but it still remains a challenge for a child to represent the desks, tables and cupboards, and so on in their spatial relatedness to one another from an orthogonal perspective.

around the home. That so many of the modeled "home clusters" are limited in extent to a few hundred yards around the home is probably related to what would be approximately the field of vision from the house. That this kind of perceptual activity is important in children's earliest representations was suggested by Freeman (1916). Freeman suggested that the direction to a place (present or imagined) is "represented in the mind" in terms of movement of the body through turning the head or pointing, both of which brings us into alignment with the place. Freeman believed that through this method a preschool child of 4–5 years of age builds up a "fairly definite notion of the direction of buildings or streets in the immediate vicinity of his home [Freeman, 1916, p. 164]."

The System of Reference in Spatial Representation

Very young children studied in this research were able to use a "fixed" system; that is they were able to think of places and of themselves in relationship to some independent fixed object or well-known route. Even the youngest children, 4-year-olds, were able to use their home as the base from which to recall the relative location of important objects and places. This method of using the home as a sole organizing pole for spatially representing the environment was common in children throughout the kindergarten and first-grade level (i.e., up to 7 years of age).

In spite of the methodological weakness with modeling noted earlier, a large proportion of children of kindergarten age and younger (i.e., below 7 years) did produce "survey" type clusters. As reviewed above, Moore and I had anticipated that children of these ages would represent the environment as a series of unconnected journeys they had made, each beginning with the home. As we shall see, this is true of much of the remainder of their maps (i.e., beyond the "home cluster"). Why then is it not true of this home cluster? Why should they be able to represent places around the home in t!.e correct relative positions to the home.

I propose that the ability for a child to decenter and to take another perspective will vary according to the nature of the object/place/person to which the child is decentering.[4] If it is a doll that a child has never seen before, standing at the side of a mountain, the child is less likely to be able to

---

[4] Recent experimental research on egocentricity in the development of children's thinking suggests that Piaget and his colleagues may have overemphasized children's difficulty in decentering through experiments that are not particularly meaningful to children. In a redesign of the famous "Three Mountains" experiment, for example, Hughes found that children found it much easier to understand others' perspectives in a game where a model boy was trying to hide from a model policeman than they had found it to understand a doll's perspectives of three mountains (Hughes, 1975, reported in Donaldson, 1978).

decenter to it than if it were a model of their own home, from which they have looked out many times. While building the model landscapes, the children probably imagine themselves somewhere around the doorstoop of their home, looking out. In this way, they figuratively recreate this familiar view in a positional manner from a fixed location, rather than in the sequential manner that results from an egocentric moving (route-like) perspective. It seems that the egocentric system of reference, which is characteristic of children at this age, can more easily give way to a "fixed" system when children use their home as the locus for their imagination. We might call it a "domocentric" (house-centered) system of reference. Thereafter, it was common for children to use a number of well-known points to base or "fix" the relative locations of other places and routes. More common among older children, particularly those of fourth-grade level (9-10 years of age), was the use of some system of reference abstracted from the environment, commonly the structure of the road network. Abstract, coordinated systems, however, were also found to degrees in children as young as first-grade level (6-7 years), demonstrating that these are overlapping, rather than discretely sequential categories. An older child may presumably use any one, or all three systems of reference depending upon the task, the extent of the child's familiarity with the environment, and, as will later be argued, its potential "imageability."

The Influence of the Mode of Travel

It has been hypothesized that given that the representation of space begins with the internalization of action in space, we might anticipate that walking or cycling would be most important to the child's formation of topographical representations and that more passive modes of travel would not serve the same purpose. This point has been suggested by Lee (1963) as a result of his fascinating study of the effects of busing on children in an area of Devon, England where all children had previously walked to school. He found that young children (6-7 years) who were bused to school suffered serious problems of social and emotional adjustment in comparison to their peers who walked to school each day. He hypothesized that the bus journey took them beyond their known (representable) world, into a space through which they had had no opportunity to articulate their own body locomotion through the environment. Because of this, he claimed, children felt separated from their mother, home, and the physical expressions of security. He believed this resulted in anxiety during difficult periods in school, leading to relatively poor academic performances, and relatively low ratings of social and emotional adjustment to school. I did not investigate academic or other teacher ratings of school performance in Inavale, but the landscape models most dramat-

ically confirm Lee's hypothesis that children younger than 8 years of age cannot (with rare exceptions) incorporate the school bus journey into their
topographical representations. The school is usually quite arbitrarily placed at
the end of a short section of road that begins wherever the child catches the
bus; some children from their home, others from the high school.

For most children under 8 years of age their positional or "survey" type
clusters lie within their "free range" or "range-with-permission" rather than
within their much larger, but less "active" in terms of learning, "ranges-with-
other (older)-children." Again, two example models serve best to illustrate
these points.

MARGARET (6:3)

The second map produced by Margaret, 15 months later, is similar to the
one described in the previous section in the quality of its spatial organization
but it is a little more elaborate and markedly more extensive in scale (cf.
Figures 8.4 & 8.6). This is an expression of at least three important changes
in her life: moving home from the top of North Hill Road to Factory Lane,
much closer to the center of town; walking to the high school to catch the
large yellow school bus, instead of waiting for a car beside her home; and
those changes in intellectual ability which this investigation can only surmise
about, but which undoubtedly occurred during the 15-month period. This
report will focus on the likely influence of Margaret's environmental experiences.

The map of her known landscape expresses a considerable expanded
world (Figure 8.6a). She had moved into her new house only 3 months
earlier, but, not surprisingly, she was already able to map accurately the
elements around it (Cluster I). The second cluster of elements was also mapped positionally, though it was not even linked to the home. As far as I could
gather she had never walked to this town center area but had always been
driven there by her mother. An attempt to explain this in terms of the highly
"imageable" quality of the crossroads is made in a later section of this chapter
entitled "The Influence of Environmental Form."

Cluster III shows the route she has frequently taken on foot between her
old home and new home and vice versa; no doubt such two-way trips help
considerably with the common problem found in young children's mapping
of not being able to reverse their thinking in order to retrace a route.

The fourth cluster is an expression of Margaret's daily journey, sometimes
on foot with her brother, sometimes in her mother's car, to the High School
where she waits for the school bus. She made no attempt to express the
turns and different stretches of road on this trip probably because she had
traveled it so few times on foot since moving. Cluster IV also shows the

journeys to and from school. Margaret chose first to express the route via the mode she knows best, her mother's car, which she rode in from school throughout her preschool year. She then drew the route the bus would take coming from the elementary school to the high school, which is identical except for the last few hundred yards to her home. Except for the short strip of Factory Lane on which her new home stands, she expresses this journey as completely separate from the same journey to school taken in the school bus. In fact, she even crosses her bus journey road over her car journey road. This cluster was therefore scored at level two only.

This relationship between the level of spatial organization of an area and the type of locomotion used was common to almost all maps of children under 8 years of age. There were some exceptions, however, and these lead me to the hypothesis that the simple distinction between walking or cycling in comparison to being driven is not an adequate account of the influence of locomotion. The use of another child's map as an illustration suggests that the quality of the transportation mode may vary along a number of dimensions at once. Not only may kinaesthetic feedback be important in determining the degree of spatial learning during travel, but also the degree to which children's attention is drawn towards parts of an environment during travel and, probably even more important, the extent to which children are involved in decisions concerning the route to be taken (Acredolo, 1977; Herman & Siegel, 1978).

DAVY (6:11)

Davy's landscape model is extremely well-structured and extensive (Figure 8.7a). It is one of the only two models by 7-year-olds that are positional representations of the whole town. There are only two very minor errors. The majority of children are not able to demonstrate such an ability until 9 or 10 years of age.

The only two errors in the spatial relationships of the landscape model are the doctor's house, and around the library and church (Davy's old kindergarten). These buildings were accurately related with each other, but the cluster is incorrectly coordinated with the remainder of the map. The buildings are placed on the opposite side of the street, and inverted in sequence. This area lies beyond Davy's unaccompanied range. He had not visited the area on foot for over a year, when he had been accompanied to his old kindergarten in the church building. It is not surprising that these places are ordered topologically, remembered from the kindergarten free-periods spent on the front lawn of the library. The location of this region relative to the rest of his representation, on the other hand, was not difficult because of direct and frequent visual access to it from the familiar candy store in the center of town.

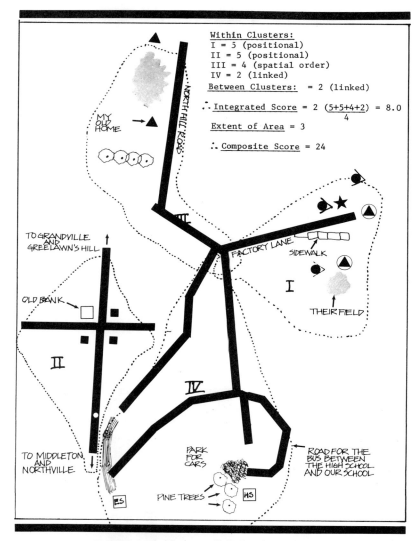

Within Clusters:
I = 5 (positional)
II = 5 (positional)
III = 4 (spatial order)
IV = 2 (linked)

Between Clusters: = 2 (linked)

∴ Integrated Score = 2 $\frac{(5+5+4+2)}{4}$ = 8.0

Extent of Area = 3

∴ Composite Score = 24

FIGURE 8.6a. *Margaret (6:3): Landscape model.*

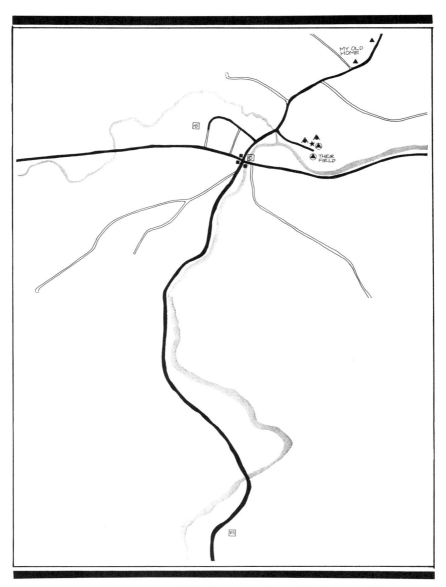

FIGURE 8.6b. *Margaret (6:3): Content analysis of landscape model.*

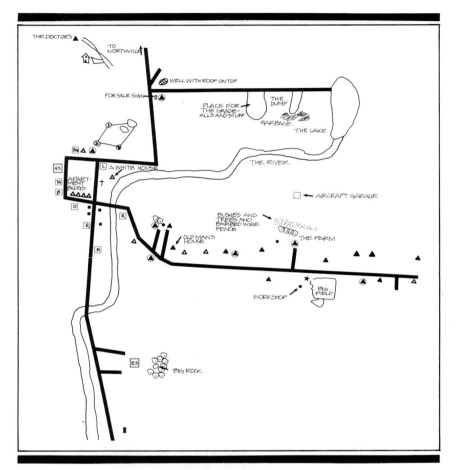

FIGURE 8.7a. *Davy (6:11): Landscape model.*

Two very large areas lie outside of the range that he has ever walked alone. The larger part of these areas have only been experienced from a moving vehicle: the journey from the town center crossroads to the school and to the town lake. An even more extraordinary quality of this map is the totally correct coordination of the river and the road network. This river cannot even be viewed from the road for most of its journey through the town, and has only been visited by Davy at two points: its end point at the lake, and in the center of town. Of the 80 children who constructed landscape models, only two—both boys of almost 10 years of age—were able to coordinate these two separate systems: that is, the roads and the river.

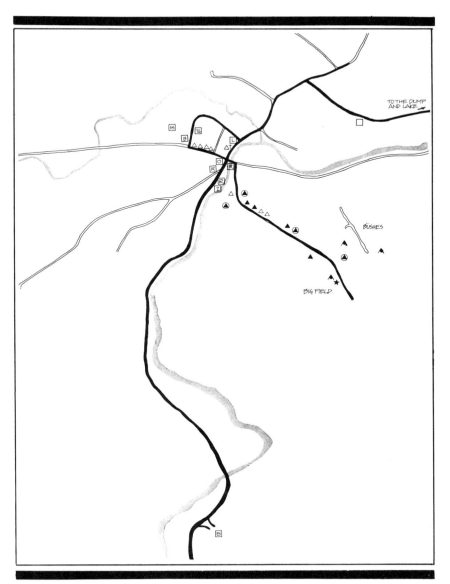

TO THE DUMP
AND LAKE

BUSHES

BIG FIELD.

FIGURE 8.7b. *Davy (6:11): Content analysis of landscape model.*

What conclusions can be drawn from this construction? First of all, it provides dramatic evidence that some children can produce "survey" type representations at a much earlier age than others. It also means they can go as far as inferring the location of places not experienced. But more important than how early a child constructs a map is the question of what factors influence the quality of a child's ability to represent the spatial organization of the landscape. Why should some children's model be so much better organized than those of others? I cannot comment upon the influence of any general level of cognitive level on children's constructions other than IQ (scores taken from existing school records), which showed an insignificant and much lower correlation with the children's integrated map scores than did age or the extent of a child's range of spatial activity. My explanation lies instead with the kinds of environmental experiences Davy has with the landscape, largely as a result of a conscious effort made by his parents to rear a child who is environmentally competent.

First of all, Davy does not just experience the town from a school bus or a family car, but also from the cab and from the open rear of his father's truck. The truck easily offers the most visibility. More important than this are my observations, supported by numerous comments from Davy's parents, that Davy's father shares the route he chooses to take and consciously develops skills of observation in his son while they journey to his work places together. Both of his parents talk with their children continually wherever they drive; they impart their curiosity about places. Similarly, when not driving, Davy's father emphasizes his son's ability to discover objects. This is part of his father's educational philosophy, one which can best be termed as an apprenticeship in practical education: Davy was being trained to be competent at hunting, finding objects and in using them resourcefully and in finding his way about. Such conscious training of abilities in children as part of distinct parental philosophies of practical education are an extremely important aspect of children's cognitive development which is often ignored by developmental psychology (for supportive theoretical literature see Vygotsky, 1978). In contrast to these focused and frequently punctuated trips with his father, is the school bus journey. The bus trip is most children's source of knowledge of this route and offers little opportunity for observation and reflection because of the high bus windows, crowding and socially complex conditions.

In summary, informal combination of data from a wide variety of observations, interviews, and tests indicate that some important suggestions of Lee (1963) and Appleyard (1970) can be extended. Specifically, spatial learning can be taken beyond the distinction of bodily movement versus being transported, and "passive" versus "active" involvement in navigation (i.e., directional decision-making). Experimental research has already begun to vary these conditions (Acredolo, 1977; Herman & Siegel, 1978). Hopefully it will investigate these conditions further, including having children direct their own exploration of the environment. In addition to other such minor points as the different visibilities from different types of vehicles, at least one possible major variable should be added to the research agenda: the effect of meaningful verbal annotations to places during travel. There is considerable recent experimental evidence to support the hypothesis that memory is improved when placed in contexts that are meaningful to the child.

The Influence of Environmental Form on Spatial Representations

In the earliest report of people's spatial representations of the geographic environment, *The Image of the City* (Lynch, 1960), the form or structure of the environment was found to have a dramatic effect upon people's ability to represent, or "image" it. Developmental psychologists investigating children's spatial representations have not focused on this issue, probably because of their different reasons for conducting research. Kevin Lynch's motivation was a desire to understand the "imageability" of cities in order to influence thinking about urban design and planning. Developmental psychologists have not usually made their purposes so clear, but they usually seem to be concerned with building theory on spatial representations and reference systems, occasionally with the claim that this might have some relevance to children's way finding. Not surprisingly, their discussions of spatial representations have been largely in terms of the cognitive abilities of the children, rather than such factors as the different demands and properties of the physical environment. No close analysis of the impact of environmental structure was made of my own data either, but some influences were so obvious that they could not be ignored.

Almost all of the children used the black cardboard-strip roads. In the less organized models, these were usually used to link objects together, whereas in the better organized models, the road structure was placed down prior to, or simultaneously with, the placing of objects. The children seemed to be using the roads and the angles they formed with each other as a reference system in the manner suggested by Piaget. The remarkable point is that the roads in one part of the town were so imageable that even the 5-year-old children were able to use them as a reference (e.g., Margaret, 5:0, see Figure 8.4a). It would seem that these crossroads are more imageable than other places, perhaps because they are symmetrical (the angles are equivalent) and such symmetry is more readily perceived and represented. Perhaps the traffic lights cause their car and school bus to stop frequently, allowing time to observe the scene. Additionally, the candy stores on three of the four corners make this one of the most highly valued places in town (Hart, 1979, Chapter 6).

As Lynch demonstrated long ago with the highly imageable Commons in downtown Boston, too great a reliance upon such a strong image can result in great distortion in a person's representation of the environment. Many children in Inavale imaged the crossroads so well that they modeled them even though they were unable to recall correctly how these crossroads related to other parts of the environment with which they were more intimately familiar. This resulted in maps with severe disjunctions or distortions. A good example is the model produced by Martha.

MARTHA (8:7)

Martha began by laying out the high "imageable" crossroads in the town center (Figure 8.8b). She then confidently filled in all of the details of East Main Street, which she knows so well because her free range embraces this area (Cluster I). In laying out this basic cross however, she incorrectly identified Snowdon Road as Plum Hill Road. Plum Hill Road actually lies between Snowdon Road and East Main Street, which it intersects obliquely. The effect of this single mistake is that she cannot integrate her otherwise well-known cluster number II. She has visited this second cluster occasionally, but not frequently enough for her to recognize her mistake. The third cluster is positioned correctly, even though it is not linked to the first cluster. The third cluster is also in the correct relative position but, as with most of the children in the younger grade levels, Martha is completely unable to integrate the school bus journey with the remainder of the model. One reason Martha may have had difficulty with this task is that she has lived in the town for only one year, just long enough to qualify for participation in this study. During this year she had made no walking or cycling trips, alone or with others, beyond the daily walk to the high school.

These observations suggest that the structure of an environment may have a considerable influence upon the ability of children to represent it. More specifically, some forms may be so much more "imageable" than others that they enable a child to use them as a reference for other places or objects in the environment. This may be an additional or alternative explanation for the high level of performance of children on the Hughes perspective task compared to Piaget's "three mountains" experiment (reported in Donaldson, 1978). Donaldson, in reporting Hughes' experiment, explains the child's greater ability to decenter is due to the fact that the task made more "common sense" to the child (see footnote 5). An alternative or additional factor may have been that in Hughes' experiment, the environment could be used as a perceptual support for constructing a reference system. Instead of having three different sized mountains as a reference, the children in Hughes' study had two walls which intersected each other to form a perfectly symmetrical cross. Although the cross could not be seen entirely from above by the child, it may be that it is easier to represent a cross and use it as a reference system than it is to represent the three mountains and use them as a reference system. Piaget has also argued that roads, rivers, and similar items, may be used as a reference system in the neighborhood modeling experiment (Piaget et al., 1960). Certainly this is an important factor to consider in future experimental research designs.

The Function of Place Naming in Spatial Representation

The place names used by children of 7 years of age and younger are largely functional descriptions of the environment such as Enid's "the house with the dog that bites" and the "snow slide to the school bus" (Figure 8.5). Similarly, when describing streets or regions the children use the names of children they play with such as "on Peter Scott's hill" or "it's down Joe Douglas' streetway." When talking with each other, children most commonly use such descriptors throughout their elementary school lives. When they use the more general descriptors in talking with adults, such as Plum Hill and North Hill, they frequently get mixed up.

The models produced by these children suggest that the landscape beyond their home and immediate vicinity does not initially consist of a stable set of places with an enduring set of functions, but rather, of different events, each occurring in a different place. There is little generalization concerning the various functions common to one place. For instance, Enid describes the town's recreation field as "the place where the fair is." As these children grow older they experience more events and through growing logical powers are able to associate these events with each other, to fix their occurrence in one place, and thereby to generalize about that place. Being able to apply general place names is no doubt an important development in the spatial representations of experienced places and even more so in inferring about places not directly experienced. The development of children's language needs to be built into future theory and research on the development of spatial representation.

I found that children did not seem to have much knowledge of, or interest in the world far beyond that which is experienced directly by them. Other than the frequently visited towns of Grandville and Middleton, virtually all places (as New York, Boston, or Washington) were equally as far or near to the children. These places lie in the "elsewhere schema" referred to by Howe (1931) and suggested by the writings of Lee (1963). Children frequently

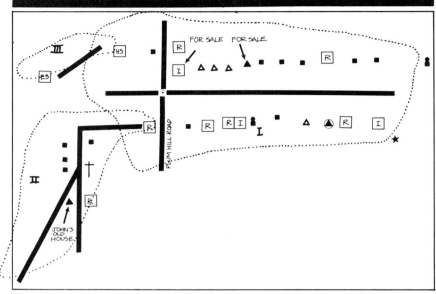

Within Clusters:

I = 5 (positional)
II = 5 (positional)
III = 2 (linked)

Between Clusters: 5

$$\therefore \text{Integrated Score} = 5 \; \frac{(5+5+2)}{3} = 20.0$$

Extent of Area   = 3

$$\therefore \underline{\text{Composite Score}} = 60$$

FIGURE 8.8a. *Martha (8:7): Landscape model.*

become very confused through the use of general names before they have grasped the concepts about place and place hierarchy. Danny, for example, thinks that New York City (and no doubt all cities) looks like the "Food City Restaurant" in town. While involved in the place recognition test in June, Johnny responded to the slide of the sandbox with: "Over that mountain is Washington, I know that." ("How?" I asked.) "Because my mother told me," he confidently responded. The following week, while chatting with him as he was building a town in the dirt of his driveway at home I asked him: "What is Inavale, a town or a state?" He responded: "A state I guess, because downtown must be the town." "O.K., is Inavale inside something else, like the United States?" "No," he explained, "because where the President lives is over the sandbank in Washington—you know, the sandbank across the

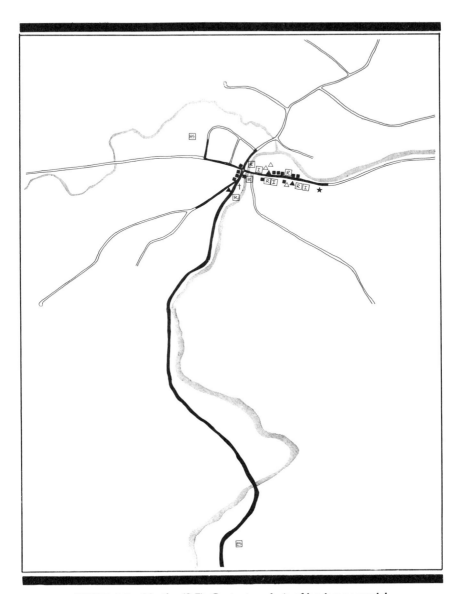

FIGURE 8.8b. *Martha (8:7): Content analysis of landscape model.*

street from us (his house)—and so that's the United States—that's what everybody tells me." A similar common error found was that most children think the small villages or even homes of their relatives are "New Hampshire," "Massachusetts," and so on.

The only spatial distinction the children seem to make is one of relative distance based on transport mode: California is farther away than Boston because you fly there. Combined with this lack of knowledge and interest in the relative location of places, there was a complete lack of differentiation between towns, cities, states, and countries: All were places "out there," though sometimes, especially when children had visited a place, they would have some idea of which direction it was; usually a place lay in the direction that their car left town.

That children throughout all of the elementary school grade levels were so confused about the geographic hierarchies of city, state, and nation should give us cause to pause. This was particularly true of children younger than 8 years of age, of course, because of the gradual development of their understanding of class inclusion. However, for 10-year-old children not to know whether or not their own state and the neighboring states are different regions, or if they include each other, can only be understood as the result of lack of information. Geographic or map education is given much less em- phasis in American elementary schools than in other nations. There is very little useful geographic information in the popular media and there are very few maps or atlases available in the average home. It is quite likely that we are all researching a population that is relatively illiterate in mapping.

The Effects of Externally Representing the Environment upon Children's Spatial Knowledge

It was clear to me from my place-recognition test that there was a much larger landscape that could be recognized but not represented. Furthermore, children referred to places lying off the photographs and gave me directions to these places even though they lay well outside the area they had modeled for me. In short, single external spatial representations must not be thought of as the same as a child's total ability to represent the spatial environment. The constructive act of mapping through modeling or drawing is probably very valuable in helping children to fix places mentally in relationship to each other. This was made particularly clear to me during the modeling exercise by the excited exclamations of second- and third-grade children as they discovered new relationships through the act of having to externalize them. This informal observation offers some support for the theory that toy play is important in mapping (Blaut & Stea, 1971). To account for their finding that children's mapping skills occur early, Blaut and Stea hypothesized that when children play with toys in the ground, they become familiar with important cognitive transformations in mapping, specifically, rotation in perspective, reduction in scale, and abstraction to iconic signs. I observed such mapping play in dirt all over the town as one of the most common play activities of children under 9 years of age. By concretizing intuitions of spatial relations in model form, and then physically manipulating them, children can improve their understanding of an area. I believe that most children in my research learned a lot about the spatial organization of their town through my so-called "eliciting" technique of modeling. This may explain why the children in the experiment by Hazen, Lockman and Pick (1978) could not infer what was on the other side of a wall but could model it; they improved their spatial understanding through the modeling task itself!

A very useful direction for future research in spatial representation would be interventional research, designed to explore ways of improving spatial cognition. We now need to know what children themselves want to learn about places, what place information they are trying to gather, for what purposes, how they are learning informally, and how this can be facilitated by education.

Summary of the Influence of Environmental Experience

In recognizing the theoretical strength of Piaget's work, Moore and I paid too much attention to the "stages" of intellectual development Piaget and his colleagues had laid out for us; we focused on extending these developmental sequences to large-scale spaces. Similarly, in most subsequent research, investigators have assumed that one can validly simulate large-scale environments in small-scale. They have used numerous, often ingenious, simulations of large-scaleness in carefully controlled laboratory environments. If one simply wished to generalize children's ability to represent the spatial configurations of a set of objects, it is acceptable to use a set of relatively meaningless objects in a laboratory setting. But if ones theory is interactional, it is not possible to generalize about the specific question of a child's ability to map large-scale environments solely with research using arbitrary, small objects within a manipulable space. We know that all normal preschool children will have had opportunities to spatially manipulate small objects freely. In contrast, we do not know if these same young children have had any experiences to manipulate (i.e., navigate through) the landscape freely. If they have not had any opportunity to manipulate at this geographic scale of environment, we may be simulating test situations that some children may have barely begun to face, whereas others may have struggled with them many times. In looking for interpretations of the data, it is not then sufficient to look into the experiment for possibly important variables or to the child for cognitive explanations. One must obtain some knowledge about the experiential variables and objective environmental variables which might explain children's different degrees of ability to "map" large-scale environments.

Recommendation for a Future Research Program

I retreated from an experimental research design because of the belief that the questions of our field had not yet been studied in their everyday, natural context. Descriptive, more ecologically valid research was needed. I now see the need to explore further some of the hypotheses generated by this more ecologically valid research. Developmental psychology has recently become aware of the very real problems of generalizing from laboratory research to children's cognition of geographic spaces (see particularly Acredolo, 1977, p. 8, and the conclusion of Herman & Siegel, 1978), and have begun to design most ingenious experiments to deal with the complex conceptual problems of geographic space representation and orientation.

It is time for us to develop a synthesis of our research designs; we need to investigate children's cognition in settings that are familiar to them and with tasks that are known to be meaningful to them. The unit of study in such complex ecological research must of course be individual children. We can ask the same children to represent the environment for different purposes (see Wapner, Kaplan & Cohen, 1976 for some attempts at this). We can also use a whole range of different media of representation to obtain a fuller account of the phenomena. In order to isolate the influence of cognition, independent cognitive tests could be given to the children. At the same time, important experiential measures can be collected such as extent and frequency of self-initiated free movement in the world and place recognition. Clearly this could be a fruitful area of collaboration for cognitive developmental psychologists, environmental psychologists, and perhaps those social psychologists who are beginning to understand the dynamics of family ecology and its impact on children's contact with the physical world.

The question of the selectivity of what children represent when they "map" the world for different reasons has not been a question for developmental psychologists, but it has been a question for planners geographers, and environmental psychologists who investigate children's spatial cognition. This question may have theoretical importance for developmental psychologists as well. In his study of "Why Buildings are Known," Appleyard found that "use significance" is more important than "visibility" of "physical form." If this is true, then the same is likely to be true of laboratory experiments. That is, features which are salient because of their usefulness may be more effective landmarks in orientation tasks than arbitrary features. Recent experimental research has investigated the effect of familiarity with landmarks, yet one landmark was still observed to be as good as any other landmark (Acredolo, Pick, & Olsen, 1975). Different landmarks may have different affective potential and these may themselves even be subject to developmental changes. This is the kind of question that is best explored naturalistically: What landmarks do children spontaneously use in the everyday environment? Answers to such questions can serve to improve experimental research designs.

Those of us investigating children's spatial representations have not been sufficiently concerned with questions of the utility of spatial representation to children. One unfortunate effect of our failure to consider carefully the values of spatial representation is that some other social scientists have assumed that we believe this is the only kind of spatial experience people have. This is made clear in the recent writings of some geographers who lay stress upon "existential space" or "lived space" (Relph, 1975; Seamon, 1979). I accept the notion that our individual spatial worlds change according to our acts and intentions, and that it is inadequate to recognize only an abstract world of spatial reflection. I also believe, however, that there are some relatively consistent qualities to the manner with which people represent to themselves the spatial relationship of objects and places in their world; this mapping of the world has considerable practical importance to them. I believe Jean Piaget and his colleagues have demonstrated that children, within our culture at least, do develop the ability to abstract qualities of the geometric spatial relationship of phenomena, and that this is important to their performance with the scientific and technical skills demanded by this culture. The mistake is to assume that such spatial cognition forms the whole of our spatial experience. It is important, then, to remember that we live and act in space, but we also often need to abstract ourselves from that being-in-the-world, in order to structure it so that we may more successfully locate ourselves and other phenomena within it.

But how accurately do children need to be able to represent the spatial properties of their environment? Most current research claims to be concerned with children's way-finding. But what kinds of representations are needed to successfully navigate through real environments? Perhaps we should try to answer this question before we sit down to discuss the finer points of children's performance in rather difficult, abstract, laboratory spaces. For example, in finding their way about their neighborhoods, children may use a great multiplicity of references that reinforce each other in an intuitive manner such as: "I can tell you which way to go when I am there," rather than using one or two key landmarks as we propose in our theories and research. Children may have a variety of representation and orientation strategies which are selected according to the particular task and the unique demands of the environment.[5] There is a real need for us to do more of this naturalistic research and thus to reduce the number of assumptions in the design of experiments. This may lead to some fresh ways to ask questions.

References

Acredolo, L. P. Developmental changes in the ability to coordinate perspectives of a large-scale space. *Developmental Psychology*, 1977, *13*, 1-8.

Acredolo, L. P., Pick, H. L., & Olsen, M. C. Environmental differentiation and familiarity as determinants of children's memory for spatial location. *Developmental Psychology*, 1975, *11*, 495-501.

Appleyard, D. Why buildings are known. *Environment and Behavior*, 1970, *2*, 100-117.

Blaut, J., & Stea, P. Studies of geographic learning. *Annals of the Association of American Geographers*, 1971, *61*, 387-393.

Donaldson, M. *Children's minds*. Glasgow, Scotland: Fontana/Collins, 1978.

Freeman, F. N. Geography: Extension of experience through imagination. *The psychology of common branches*. Boston: Houghton Mifflin, 1916.

Hart, R. A. *Children's experience of place*. New York: Irvington, 1979.

Hart, R. A., & Moore, G. T. *The development of spatial cognition: A review*. Worcester, Massachusetts: Graduate School of Geography, Clark University, Place Perception Research Report No. 7, 1971. (abbreviated versions in A. M. Downs, & D. Stea (Eds.), *Image of environment*. Chicago: Aldine-Atherton, 1973 and in W. M. Ittelson, H. M. Proshansky, L. Rivlin (Eds.), *Environmental psychology* (2nd ed.), New York: Holt, Rinehart & Winston, 1976.)

Hazen, N. L., Lockman, J. J., & Pick, H. L. The development of children's representations of large-scale environments. *Child Development*, 1978, *49*, 623-636.

Herman, J. F., & Siegel, A. W. The development of cognitive mapping of the large-scale environment. *Journal of Experimental Child Psychology*, 1978, *26*, 389-401.

Hughes, M. Egocentrism in pre-school children. Unpublished doctoral dissertation, Edinburgh University, 1977. Cited in Donaldson, *Children's minds*. Glasgow, Scotland: Fontana/Collins, 1978.

Howe, G. F. A study of children's knowledge of directions. *Journal of Geography*, 1931, *30*, 298-304.

Lee, T. R. On the relation between the school journey and social and emotional adjustment in rural infant children. *British Journal of Educational Psychology*, 1963, *27*, 100.

Lynch, K. *The image of the city*. Cambridge, Massachusetts: MIT Press, 1960.

Mark, L. S. Modeling through toy play: A methodology for eliciting topographical representations in children. In W. J. Mitchell (Ed.), *Environmental design: Research and practice*, (Vol. 1). Los Angeles: School of Architecture & Urban Planning, University of California, 1972.

Moore, G. T. Developmental variations between and within individuals in the cognitive representations of large-scale spatial environments. Unpublished MA thesis, Department of Psychology, Clark University, 1973.

[5] Research currently being conducted by Maxine Berzok at the City University of New York Graduate School Developmental Psychology Program adopts this perspective in an investigation of children's cognition of their daily school bus journey.

Piaget, J., Inhelder, B., & Szeminska, A. *The child's conception of geometry.* New York: Basic Books, 1960 (orig. 1948).

Relph, E. C. *Place and placelessness.* London: Pion Press, 1976.

Seamon, D. *A geography of lifeworld.* London: Croom-Helm, 1979.

Shemyakin, F. N. Orientation in space. In B. G. Ananyev *et al.* (Eds.), *Psychological Sciences in the USSR,* (Vol. 1). Washington: Office of Technical Services, Report 62-11083, 1962.

Vygotsky, L. S. *Mind in society: The development of higher psychological processes.* Cambridge, Massachusetts: Harvard Press, 1978.

Wapner, S., Kaplan, B., & Cohen, S. B. *Experiencing the environment.* New York: Plenum, 1977.

Commentary on Part III

9 On Mapping Researchers Mapping Children Mapping Space

ROGER M. DOWNS
ALEXANDER W. SIEGEL

Introduction[1]

The origins of this commentary are complex. It began with the Conference on Spatial Representation and Behavior across the Life Span: Theory and Application, which was the impetus for the present volume. At that time, Downs made comments in response to the papers presented by Hart and Siegel. The comments and the papers formed the basis for the chapters in this section of the book. Thus, this commentary is the creature of our collective second (and third) thoughts. We have tried to capture some of the excitement that emerged in listening to and discussing each other's work. To our pleasant surprise, there was a fascinating and unexpected convergence of ideas. On the surface, there was a considerable diversity of interests: Downs in the map-mapping distinction, Hart in a naturalistic study of landscape cognition, and Siegel in the problems of externalizing spatial knowledge. However, at a deeper level, there existed a shared belief that we need to ask better questions and find better ways of answering those questions.

In particular, we found ourselves grappling with some rather fundamental ontological and epistemological questions. It was these latter questions that were unexpected. Ironically, even the most cursory glance at the existing literature in cognitive mapping would indicate the improbability of such questions. The field has been characterized by a relatively innocent form of low-level empiricism, simple-minded data gathering and classification, co-existing with an abundance of speculative conceptual frameworks, each of which is

[1] We would like to acknowledge the helpful editorial comments of Lynn Liben and Nora Newcombe.

SPATIAL REPRESENTATION AND BEHAVIOR
ACROSS THE LIFE SPAN

grounded in what amounts to anecdote and common sense. This uncharitable (and extreme) assessment points to the unhappy divorce between data and theory, to the unawareness of the basic epistemological and ontological questions.

As we listened to each other at the conference and read the draft chapters, it became clear to us that the field of cognitive mapping could no longer accept the pursuit of innocent empiricism and speculative fancy. The fundamental questions that marked our separate starting points centered on three issues: (a) the nature and form of our explanations; (b) the purpose of our explanations; and (c) the nature of research design. The significance of these issues is best seen in the context of the conventional wisdom that has grown up around cognitive mapping. It is the conventional wisdom that has gone unquestioned; indeed, it is so seemingly obvious and commonsensical that it appears to be beyond question. However, until it is exposed and laid to rest, we cannot hope to make any substantial progress.

The Conventional Wisdom

Within the current body of work on cognitive mapping, there has emerged a conventional wisdom that has largely escaped our conscious attention. It is built around two motifs—the ideas of geometry and accuracy—and it has an associated language of expression. Thus, for example, we find Siegel arguing that: "Additional experience should *permit* children and adults *to scale and metricize* the distances between landmarks, resulting in *more accurate* route maps. . . . It seemed that even kindergarteners were *capable of using* metric distance relations between buildings and other features of the layout *to improve the accuracy* of their cognitive maps [italics added]." In a similar fashion, Hart argues that "Children at this level of development are able to build the 'model village' and the 'sand-box school environment' *taking into account the projective and Euclidian relations* of proportional reduction to scale, accuracy of distance, and metric coordinates [italics added]." These quotations exemplify the well-accepted tradition, which speaks of children "graduating" to "more sophisticated" levels of understanding: levels that have to be "attained" and that permit, for example, the "calibration" of metric distance judgments. To the extent that these desirable states have not been reached, then we as researchers must invoke judgments of "distortion" and "inaccuracy." We point out "arbitrary" things. Thus, cognitive performance is typically evaluated in terms of accuracy, and from the attainment of a given level of accuracy on a particular task, a particular level of competence is inferred or assigned.

Our writings, reflections, and discussions have led us to question this conventional wisdom as it applies to the attempts to understand the development of cognitive mapping. The origins of the belief that development is a process of graduation to something more sophisticated are to be found in the work of Werner, Piaget, and most other serious developmental theorists. But where is the empirical support for this belief? And what are the implications of this belief? For example, if the belief is translated to read: Development is progress in the sense of permitting better adaptation (ultimately a biological notion), then what is better adaptation? What is the criterion of adaptation; what do we mean by "better?" To what extent does this development-as-graduation belief constrain the construction of what we take to be legitimate questions and legitimate ways of answering such questions (White, 1977)? Are there alternative positions? Are there alternative motifs that can replace the ideas of geometry and accuracy? What languages of expression can we substitute?

Although we cannot pretend to have the answer to all of these questions, we do believe that they are indicative of the "better questions" that Siegel's title demands. Our arrival at these questions is the coincidental result of the choice of a similar starting point in the original presentations. Each of us began with a careful consideration of the meaning of accuracy. What is accuracy? What is it that is more (or less) accurate than what?

One thing is abundantly clear: Accuracy does not refer to spatial behavior. If we equate spatial behavior with the ability to navigate and move around in a large-scale spatial environment, then we must conclude that spatial behavior is incredibly accurate and thus well adapted. Children do not walk into things; they do not get lost with any noticeable frequency. They can explore their world in ways that can only be described as confident and creative. They show an acute awareness of the spatial limits within which they *can* range and within which they are *allowed* to range. (The latter may explain why they do not get lost.) Adults are no less successful in their spatial behavior. One can only be impressed with the fact that cities work: journeys to work, to shop, to recreation places do not go astray. People rarely get lost; what is more, they can adapt to changes in the spatial environment (traffic jams, street closures, snowstorms, etc.) and they can even make their way in novel environments.

Note the immediate problem that such a conception of accuracy causes us. Much of the behavior that we have associated with cognitive mapping is spatial behavior, operationally defined as spatial mobility. The conventional wisdom suggests that in order to understand spatial behavior, we must understand its immediate antecedents, cognitive mapping and cognitive maps. At the same time, if we accept the conventional wisdom, we find ourselves arguing that cognitive maps are distorted, inaccurate, unreliable, incomplete, and so on; everyone is familiar with this litany of characteristics. How can this be? How can we reconcile the apparent paradox between "accurate" spatial behavior (i.e., behavior that is competent, successful, and adaptive) and "inaccurate" cognitive maps? Are we forced to argue that adaptive spatial behavior is possible *in spite of,* rather than *because of,* these patently inaccurate cognitive maps? Or, more disturbingly, are we forced to accept a form of stimulus–response behavioral determinism: Adaptive spatial behavior is possible, in fact inevitable, because of the spatial properties of the environment? Neither position is acceptable nor necessary.

On Cognitive Maps as Representations

An alternative argument is that accuracy refers to the qualities and properties of cognitive maps as representations (or, as Siegel reminds us, "re-representations") of the real world. The value of this commentary rests on the elaboration of this seemingly trivial, naïvely obvious idea.

Given this position, we can again ask: What is accuracy? Clearly, agreement with an external standard. But what standard? Obviously, the real world. But from a constructivist point of view (Pepper, 1970; Reese & Overton, 1970), there is no such thing as *the* real world. From this perspective, reality is a construction by an individual and by a society. Jerison (1976) and von Uexkull (1957) have argued that different nervous systems create different realities (i.e., models of the world); Piaget (1971) and Bruner (1964) have argued that children of different cognitive-developmental levels construct qualitatively different models of the world; and Berger and Luckman (1967) and G. H. Mead (1934) have argued that different societies create different realities. Thus, at a number of levels—phylogenetic, ontogenetic, and sociocultural—there are multiple real worlds, each of which could potentially serve as a standard or benchmark against which to assess accuracy-as-agreement. Furthermore, even if consensus on a single standard of comparison were attainable, the amount of "inaccuracy" permissable is a function of the purposes for which the cognitive map is to be used (Wapner, Kaplan, & Cohen, 1973). The acid test is not agreement with the standard but the presence of adaptive (i.e., successful) spatial behavior.

Given that we wish to explore the properties and qualities (i.e., accuracy) of cognitive maps as representations, we are in essence arguing that cognitive maps are models of the world. And it is at this point that the conventional wisdom betrays us again. Implicitly, most geographers, urban designers, and cognitive and developmental psychologists have taken *the* (as in the obvious and the only) standard of comparison to be the cartographic map—the world according to Rand McNally. However, it is clear from the arguments in Downs' chapter that cartographic maps are also models of the world. By acknowledging what might be called *cartographic relativism,* we are forced to recognize that any map, be it cartographic or cognitive, is but one possible model of the world. Each map is *a* model of, not *the* model of the world.

From this perspective, cartographic maps are but one kind of model in which the real world is transformed into a two-dimensional, graphic product. Yet most of us (i.e., researchers) act and write as if *a* cartographic map is *the best* model of reality, in fact the *only* model of reality, and proceed as if a cartographic-map-in-the-head is the best of all forms of knowledge. But is it? Surely there are other models of the world, perhaps less elegant and cognitively economical than a cartographic map, that facilitate way-finding in new territory and ensure against getting lost in familiar territory?

A number of systems for successfully navigating extensive expanses of ocean have been well-documented (Gladwin, 1970; Lewis, 1972). The navigators using these cognitive systems (or models) do not need compasses, or cartographic maps, yet they rarely get lost. This simple example demonstrates that spatial behavior can be based on models of the world that are not cartographic, and that cognitive-maps-in-the-head need not be thought of in cartographic terms. As an obvious corollary, it follows that a cartographic map is not necessarily the best standard of accuracy.

In an early discussion by Trowbridge (1913), and in more recent discussions by Gatty (1958) and Lewis (1972), at least two kinds of navigational systems can be distinguished: home-centered and compass-centered. One can either orient oneself with respect to landmarks such as home or an island, or else by astronomically derived directions like north and south that "radiate out" from one's body.

The home-centered system is simple-minded and practical: It is a reliable, unembellished algorithm that ensures against getting lost. It contains built-in redundancy, and it is not very "pretty"—but it is safe:

> As early peoples ventured forth in search of food they maintained a constant anxiety about their home and would often look back to see where they were in relation to their point of departure. Each time they went out more territory would become familiar to them: and they would proceed further [Gatty, 1958, p. 46].

The compass-based system is more elegant but riskier:

> Compare this practical method [the home-centered system] with our complicated self-centre system in which man considers himself (wherever he is) as the centre. He divides the horizon into north, south, east, and west. . . . He involves himself in an intricate system of calculations, and, even with the aid of a compass, often loses his way. At each point when he stops to refer to the points of a compass, he may sever his connection with the previous place at which he did the same thing. All too easily, in this way, can he lose the thread which tied him to his original place of departure. [From *Nature Is Your Guide* by H. Gatty. Copyright © 1958 by Executors of the Estate of Harold Gatty and A. Fenna Gatty. Reprinted by permission of E. P. Dutton, p. 47.]

(There is also a mixed cognitive system—a 'local-reference" system—in which directions are related to some local prominent feature—a reef, a mountain, etc.)

Both the home-centered and the local-reference systems have built-in redundancy; thus, they have flexibility and permit the use of multiple problem-solving strategies. They are conservative: While being cumbersome, they minimize the possibility of getting lost. Note furthermore that the descriptions of these systems have much in common with the descriptions of those "immature" and/or "primitive" frames of reference attributed to younger children by Piaget, Werner, and others. Yet these "immature" or "primitive" systems serve a useful purpose and possess critical survival value (Fishbein, 1976).

As is often the case in contemporary discussions of development, competence is defined in "adultomorphic" terms. From this "adultocentric" perspective, thought starts out incompetent in the young child and is said to be competent when it becomes adult-like. We fear that the same kind of "adultocentric" error is being made in the conventional wisdom that equates spatial competence with compass-based navigational systems and carto-graphic-maps-in-the-head. Perhaps we can find out what children do, what their competencies in cognitive mapping are, *if* we consider that their models of the world are different from, rather than inferior to, the world according to Rand McNally.

How are we to address the accuracy issue in the light of this alternative argument? Now *what* does it mean to say that a child's cognitive map is inaccurate (and/or distorted)? Why, for example, is it inaccurate to produce a graphic representation with places, roads, and buildings "missing?" Such a judgment, based on the conventional wisdom, itself misses the point that car-tographic maps are themselves necessarily selective; they omit places and features by a process that is variously called abstraction or generalization. Such a process is dictated by the purpose of the cartographer, the choice of the spatial scale of the map, among other variables. Admittedly, the omissions are usually made in a consistent, explicit, and controlled fashion. But there is no reason to argue, a priori, that a child is not operating in a similar fashion (i.e., consistently, explicitly, etc.). Why is the product of the latter accorded the judgment, inaccurate? (We do recognize that a case is made in terms of adult intersubjective agreement as the basis for judgments of relative accuracy; however, this does *not* alter the basic thrust of our argument.)

The issue of cartographic relativism is a direct consequence of a careful reconsideration of the nature of models, an approach common to all three chapters. This reconsideration finds a second manifestation in Siegel's distinction between the nature of theories versus models. We are dealing with models of development and not with theories of how development "actually" occurs. These models are based on assumptions, and both models and assumptions must be evaluated in the light of heuristic utility. That we should find it necessary to state the obvious might be viewed with amusement. It might also be viewed as an unfortunate reflection on the lack of clarity that seems so characteristic of the conventional wisdom of cognitive mapping. A brief survey of some of the ramifications of the *"model-not-theory"* position is in order.

First, it is worth repeating the ubiquitous danger of what Hart calls an "adultocentric" view. Adultocentric is not a euphonious term; it is an effective term for the imposition of adult competencies on the representational products of children (Rommetveit [1977] calls it "negative rationalism"). It is a view consonant with the conventional wisdom: Children learn to produce "better" representations, that is, successively better approximations to the products of adult thought; this learning process follows a graduated and inevitable sequence. Adult modes of representation become desirable norms. This is not a necessary position. Even the most cursory acquaintance with the history of twentieth century art, with the evolution of representational and abstract art forms, is sufficient to disabuse one of such a notion. There is no single, obvious, "best" mode of representation.

Second, there is the necessity to distinguish between metaphors and analogies, an argument central to Downs' chapter. We can pursue this distinction in the following way. The conventional wisdom speaks of people using metric processes, traditionally thought of as based on a Euclidean geometry, in order to make distance estimates and to draw maps. Suppose we substitute an alternative formulation which begins with the idea of generating such estimates and maps. What if we argue that the child, or the adult, is operating *as if* he or she is a nonmetric multidimensional scaling (MDS) program? The basis of this analogical child is the process whereby the MDS program recovers metric relationships from nonmetric data (Shepard, 1974).

Is the "logic" of MDS applicable to cognitive mapping-as-a-representing process? Both computer program and cognitive process generate spaces—spatial models if you like. And at this point we are once again forced to consider the pervasive role of geometries and judgments about accuracy. For example, many MDS programs allow the researcher the option of specifying both the number of dimensions and the nature of the distance metric. This latter choice allows one to vary the geometry that is generated; Choose a Minkowski metric, an "r" value, of two and you have a Euclidean space. Numbers other than two generate families of non-Euclidean spaces with positive and negative curvature. Each geometry is a possible spatial model of the world. Does it make sense to conceive of cognitive mapping in an analogous fashion?

Representations are models. We, as researchers, can bring other spatial models (and other geometries) to bear on these representations in order to describe and interpret them. But we should be careful about the inferences that we draw if we get a "good" or, more likely, a "bad" fit between our spatial model and that of the person being studied. We most certainly can ask, what *if* the person operated *as if* a Euclidean geometry was being used? This is hypothetical thinking at its best. But when we find ourselves talking about projective versus topological spatial understanding, we should remember that these concepts refer to the understanding of geometries as used by the researcher and not necessarily to the geometries as used by (and hence understood by) the subject to generate responses. Again, we can speak about accuracies *if* we remember that response accuracies get generated from the particular geometric model, the *as if* model, that we, the researchers, have adopted. Perhaps the tenor of this argument is most succinctly expressed in the question: Who "has" the Euclidean geometry? (For a parallel argument, see Chapter 1 by Liben in this volume.)

From this discussion of models, geometries, and accuracy, we also find ourselves confronted with the question of the process of representation itself. (Our re-interpretation is nothing if not comprehensive!) How does representation take place? More particularly, why have we paid so little attention to this question? Let us begin with Siegel's distinction between knowledge and communication (see Chapter 7). It is true that "spatial knowledge must be distinguished from the communication of such knowledge via verbal description, in which developmental differences are already well-documented." We must be careful how we construe the implications of this statement. First, it applies to any and all media of external representation: verbal description, model building, graphics, photographic recognition tasks, and so on. Second, as Siegel also argues, one of the key problems is that of ways of externalizing spatial knowledge. It is unfortunately true that the only thing that we, as researchers, have access to are the external representations. However, it does us little good to speak of verbal or any other mode of communication as exercising a confounding effect. We can only study external representations directly; internal knowledge must be inferred carefully. And third, therefore, it follows that we must study modes of representation in and of their own right. For example, apart from the work on child art by people like Goodnow (1977), we know virtually nothing about developmental differences in graphics, cartographics, or model building. In this respect, Hart's detailed study of model building in children is a prime exemplar of work in an unexplored domain.

We must view modes of representation as languages for cognitive mapping, for externalizing spatial knowledge. Even as we do this, we must be careful about the interpretation of the representation process: Again the conventional wisdom can lead us astray. For example, Hart (Chapter 8) argues that: "As with all children of this age the journey to school is simply expressed as a short strip of road heading off in an arbitrary direction away from the place where the small 'school bus' (car) picks her up each day." Is this mode of representation arbitrary, or is it a creative convention? As adults, as researchers, we can point to the "inaccuracy" and the "inconsistency" of such a procedure. And yet whereas it does not fit the conventional cartographic map that we conceive to be the "accurate," standard model of the world, it does express meaning. An alternative interpretation is that the child has not yet learned to (or is it agreed to?) accept the limitations of conventional modes of representation. Thus part of what we take to be development may well be a process of explicit *self-limitation*. Development as *progressive attainment* is replaced by a view of development *as progressive acceptance of constraint*. Thus, the "cannot" in Hart's comment (Chapter 8) that: "children younger than eight years of age cannot (with rare exceptions) incorporate the school bus journey into their topographical representations. . . " might be changed to read "do not choose to." What they do not do is follow the "normal" dictates of cartographic convention. The irony of adopting such an alternative construction is highlighted by the suggestion in the conventional wisdom that the child is "freed" from the "limitations" of the early egocentric orientation system by graduation to a superior system. When it comes to evaluative judgments about representations, we should remember that the criteria underlying the judgments are relative ones.

If we reconsider work on cognitive mapping in the light of the preceding arguments, there is one characteristic of the empirical findings that is substantially ignored. One commonly finds, for almost any externalization procedure, significant individual differences in performance. These are manifested in relative success versus failure and, more important, in the strategies employed in the process of external representation. As we have reflected on such differences, it has become clear that they are perhaps one of the most significant of our findings; we cannot allow them to remain unremarked. (Wohlwill [Chapter 5 of this volume] makes a similar point.) They suggest a fundamental difference between *competence* and *performance*, between what one can do versus what one will do. And we can consider performance as interacting with those things that one is allowed to do. Thus, Siegel's concern with procedures of externalization emphasizes the effects of those things that one is allowed to do by the researcher: The dominant motif is thus the manipulation of the constraints of research design. Hart, on the other hand, is concerned with the effects of what parents will allow children to do: The dominant motif is thus the effect of spatial constraints (in terms of range and permission) on representations and spatial knowledge. Moreover, Hart shows how children respond to the active encouragement of parents; knowledge, as expressed in models, is determined by the nature and form of parental expectations.

These distinctions between "can do," "will do," and "are allowed to do" reflect significant differences in what we might call "research agendae." In understanding research agendae, it is useful to consider the critical issue of *representativeness of design* (Brunswik, 1956). We can use the differences between the research agendae of Hart and Siegel to illustrate a dialogue that centers on this issue.

First, both chapters acknowledge the problem of spatial scale versus spatial size (an issue discussed at length in Acredolo's chapter). Both opt for studies of large-scale space using procedures that generate small-scale representations of that space. Second, Hart and Siegel choose different basic research designs. The former opts for a naturalistic design, emphasizing "richness," whereas the latter chooses an experimental design, emphasizing "precision." Downs' chapter points to some of the differences in interpretation that follow from these choices. The essential nature of the choice is expressed in Siegel's comment (Chapter 7) that a slide presentation "is both an economical alternative to field research (and/or supplement to it), while having the advantage of permitting significant experimental control. . . . " It is crucial to see these choices as responses to a complex set of trade-offs and not as "right" or "wrong" in terms of the canons of research design. Third, Hart and Siegel handle the issue of experience in strikingly different ways. In general, Siegel is concerned in much of his research with the responses to controlled, limited, and experimenter-determined experience, whereas Hart emphasizes the obverse: uncontrolled, extensive, and self-determined experience.

The research agendae thus become expressions of what it is we are prepared to study; the specifics of the research design determine how this study is to be performed. We are again in the position of making an apparently obvious statement and yet it is one that has an immense bearing on how we see the evolving field of cognitive mapping. In essence, we are back to basic ontological and epistemological issues; moreover, we are forced to be explicit about these issues. Unless we are prepared to consider these issues, we cannot make sense of the field. The state of innocence that we spoke of in the introduction cannot be maintained: Innocence is not bliss.

As an example of where such considerations lead, let us focus briefly on distinction that Downs makes between macrospatial cognition and fundamental spatial relations. If this distinction is plausible, then we must re-evaluate the current body of empirical results. A concern with macrospatial problem solving would suggest the following: an emphasis on performance as "will do," an emphasis on performance in the light of "allowed to do" by spatial experience, appreciation of the constraints imposed by the particular problem that is posed and the range of ways in which the person is allowed to solve it, and so on. Hart argues that this concern with fundamental spatial relations should not be misconstrued: The danger lies in the word "fundamental." It is possible to argue that "fundamental" research has largely been concerned with abstract (read meaningless) sets of materials: Little reason is given (i.e., little sense of motivation or purpose) to manipulate them other than to satisfy the theoretical and practical needs of the experimenter. Siegel has a more graphic way of caricaturing work on competence: what the child can do if pushed to the wall or put into the "disaggregative" experiment typical of child psychology: 15 ft in front of a better mousetrap.

Our intent is not to end this commentary on an apparently frivolous note. We find ourselves in the position of arguing that we must ask better questions if we are to make progress in understanding cognitive mapping. One useful way to approach these questions is to list a series of methodological "trade-offs" that might act as organizing themes: performance versus competence, precision versus richness, holistic versus disaggregative, experimental versus naturalistic, representativeness versus rigor in design. These trade-offs give shape to the specific research paradigms and procedures that we choose. A second approach to asking better questions forces us to consider conceptual issues: the differences between theory and model, the metaphor–analogy distinction, the idea of cognitive mapping rather than cognitive maps, macrospatial cognition versus fundamental spatial concepts, representations and modes of representing and mapping. An explicit recognition of these methodological themes and conceptual issues must shape the research agenda; and will help to free us from the conventional wisdom that has stultified recent thought in the field of cognitive mapping.

References

Berger, P., & Luckman, T. *The social construction of reality.* New York: Anchor, 1967.

Bruner, J. S. The course of cognitive growth. *American Psychologist,* 1964, *19,* 1–15.

Brunswik, E. *Perception and the representative design of psychological experiments.* Berkeley: University of California Press, 1956.

Fishbein, H. D. *Evolution, development, and children's learning.* Pacific Palisades, California: Goodyear, 1976.

Gatty, H. *Nature is your guide.* London: Collins, 1958.

Gladwin, T. *East is a big bird.* Cambridge, Massachusetts: Harvard University Press, 1970.

Goodnow, J. *Children drawing.* Cambridge, Massachusetts: Harvard University Press, 1977.

Jerison, H. J. Paleoneurology and the evolution of mind. *Scientific American,* 1976, *234,* 90–101.

Lewis, D. *We, the navigators.* Honolulu: University Press of Hawaii, 1972.

Mead, G. H. *Mind, self, and society.* Chicago: University of Chicago Press, 1934.

Pepper, S. C. *World hypotheses.* Berkeley: University of California Press, 1970.

Piaget, J. *Biology and knowledge.* Chicago: University of Chicago Press, 1971.

Reese, H. W., & Overton, W. F. Models of development and theories of development. In L. R. Goulet & P. B. Baltes (Eds.), *Life-span developmental psychology: Research and theory.* New York: Academic Press, 1970.

Rommetveit, R. Psychology, language, and thought. Three lectures presented at Cornell University, Ithaca, New York, 1977.

Shepard, R. N. Representations of structure in similarity data: Problems and prospects. *Psychometrika,* 1974, *39,* 373-421.

Trowbridge, C. C. Fundamental methods of orientation and imaginary maps. *Science,* 1913, *38,* 888-897.

von Uexkull, J. A stroll through the worlds of animals and men: A picture book of invisible worlds. In C. H. Schiller (Ed. and Transl.), *Instinctive behavior.* New York: International Universities Press, 1957.

Wapner, S., Kaplan, B., & Cohen, C. B. An organismic-developmental perspective for understanding transactions of men and environments. *Environment and Behavior,* 1973, *5,* 255-289.

White, S. H. Social proof structures: The dialetic of method and theory in work of psychology. In N. Datan and H. W. Reese (Eds.), *Life-span developmental psychology: Dialectical perspectives on experimental research.* New York: Academic Press, 1977.

IV

Conceptualizing and Designing Spatial Environments

10 Self-World Relationships in Critical Environmental Transitions: Childhood and Beyond

SEYMOUR WAPNER
BERNARD KAPLAN
ROBERT CIOTTONE

Introduction

One need not be particularly perspicacious to note, in "environmental psychology" as in other areas of psychology, that a spatial conception like perspective or point of view plays a preeminent role. The perspective one adopts—tacitly or explicitly—governs the questions that become salient, the problems one poses, the methods that are employed to solve the problems, the data one considers relevant, and the interpretations that are made of the findings. Failure to take point of view into account leads to fruitless controversies. For this reason, we begin our chapter with a brief exposition of our perspective in approaching the general theme of this volume: *the representation and use of space.*

In line with our preceding remarks, it should come as no surprise that we believe that the orientation one adopts will even penetrate the way in which this seemingly neutral theme is construed, specified, and operationalized. Therefore, following the brief presentation of our point of view, we shall interpret the theme in our terms and give it a somewhat different twist from other perspectives on approaching this theme. We shall next apply our construal of the general theme to the specific topic, namely, "the representation and use of space" in critical transitions, in which it is assumed: (a) that "self-world" relations are disrupted; and (b) that attempts, variously successful, are made to reestablish some kind of "equilibrium" between the self and the nonself.

251

SPATIAL REPRESENTATION AND BEHAVIOR
ACROSS THE LIFE SPAN

The Perspective of Genetic Dramatism

We have long identified ourselves, and have been identified, with the organismic-developmental perspective, initially formulated by Heinz Werner (Werner, 1940, 1957; Werner & Kaplan, 1963; Werner & Wapner, 1952). For more than a decade, however (see Kaplan, 1966; Rand & Wapner, 1970; Wapner, Kaplan, & Cohen, 1973), we have tacitly incorporated, within this perspective, the essentially agenetic orientation of the literary critic, Kenneth Burke, as elaborated in his dramatistic model of human action in society (Burke, 1941, 1966, 1968, 1969a, 1969b, 1972). We are now in the process of trying, more fully and adequately, to integrate these two points of view in a unitary perspective, which, intramurally we have come to refer to as G-D, *genetic dramatism.*

Within this unitary perspective, we follow Burke in adopting the common sense assumptions that human beings are *agents* who undertake *actions* in their environments (or *scenes*) to achieve *purposes* or *goals*. In executing their actions (which are, to a remarkable extent, symbolic in character), humans utilize different *agencies* or *instrumentalities*.[1] We also adopt the widely accepted view that the character or nature of the agent, the nature of the settings in which the agent acts, the nature of the actions themselves, the nature of the goals for which action is undertaken, and the nature of the in- strumentalities for carrying out action vary in number and kind in the course of ontogenesis. It is also assumed that the *relationships* among these abstracted components of situations change in number and kind in the course of ontogenesis. The components and their interrelationships are also assumed to vary in different sociocultural settings, and with respect to the position of the agent in such settings. It is also expected that the ends or goals, actions, instrumentalities for effecting actions and achieving ends, will vary for agents of the same age, differing in status, character, state of con- sciousness, and so on.

Unlike those utilizing other perspectives, we regard *development* as analytically distinct from chronological sequence or ontogenesis. Although likely to be coordinated empirically with age changes, development for us consists of an increasing differentiation of purposes, the emergence of novel ends, and a corresponding articulation and specification of distinctive agen- cies for realizing these purposes. Correlative with the differentiation of goals and relevant agencies for their realization, there is, with development, an in- creasing hierarchic integration of purposes (ends) and instrumentalities (means).

[1] Burke's categories, of course, are closely linked to the basic categories of a good news reporter. To describe a situation or event adequately, a good reporter seeks to discover who (Agent), what (Act), where-when (Scene), how (Instrumentality), and why (Purpose, Goal).

By analytically distinguishing the *idea of development* from the *actualities of ontogenesis,* one can apply developmental analysis not only to ontogenesis (age changes), but also to pathological manifestations, to social organization and disorganization, to the processes involved in adaptation, maladaptation and readaptation operative in adults involved in life crises, and other situations. It should be especially noted that we do not identify development with change over time, but take the concept of development as a means of describing, assessing, and evaluating changes over time as well as differences between systems considered within a common "specious present" (see Kaplan, 1966, 1967).

It will be apparent that we include in our concept of development a normative component: We take developmental progression to be a desideratum. It is this normative component that leads us to focus on the conditions that facilitate and inhibit optimal development and to propose *strategies of intervention,* which will conduce to optimal development. Our position, thus, is in contrast with others who equate development with changes over the life span, and who are obliged, insofar as they are concerned with intervention, to invoke their own ends, extrinsic to their conceptions of developement, to warrant such intervention (see Louch, 1966).

Construing the General Theme

We turn now to our interpretation of the general theme: *The representation and use of space.* The way in which the theme is formulated suggests that representation, however conceived, is not one of the uses of space. This seems peculiar, since it is obvious that the child, as well as the adult, uses spatial locations, directions, and relationships to represent perceived or remembered states of affairs. The evidence of such an obvious counterexample suggests that *representation* was conceived by those who formulated the theme to have a special meaning. Correspondingly, *use* seems also to have been construed in a delimited and perhaps idiosyncratic way. Our guess is that representation was intended, and elliptically used, to designate so-called "internal representation" (see Moore, 1973, 1976; Moore & Golledge, 1976) something akin to what used to be called conception or thought, albeit more specified, and regarded as a linguistic or quasi-linguistic code. Use on the other hand we take as having been used to refer to practical action in the world. One would be said to "represent" space in thinking about the locations, directions of movement, and relationships among people and things. One would be said to "use" space in moving from one position to another "in space" or in "dividing space" as one might do in a house or office, and so on.

The term *representation* has been used in diverse contexts and with dif-

ferent meanings (see Bernheimer, 1961; Pitkin, 1972). The different meanings may be related to each other only by "family resemblance" (Wittgen-
stein) or may be ultimately subsumable under a generic concept (Pitkin). In
any case, it would be presumptuous and vain to cavil about the correct
meaning of the term. As shall become clearer, we take "representation" to
mean something other than "internal codification"; its paradigmatic realization is in the depiction in some public domain (or medium) of something
which one sees, remembers or imagines or something about which one
thinks.[2]

We also give the term *use* a wider scope than we take to be intended in
the formulation of the theme. There are many uses of space—pragmatic-
practical, aesthetic, religious, interpersonal. We also use space for the
representation of states of affairs perceived, remembered, or contemplated.
Our construal of the theme therefore reduces to *the uses of space*, representation being understood not as opposed to the use of space but subsumed
under the use of space.

Excursus on the Uses of Space

In discussing the "uses" of space, one is confronted with the same kind of
dilemma that obsessed Augustine in the examination of time. One can easily
say about "space" what the good Saint observed about "time":

> For what is space? Who can easily and briefly explain it? Who even in thought can
> comprehend it, even to the pronouncing of a word concerning it? But what in
> speaking do we refer to more familiarly and knowingly than space? And certainly
> we understand when we speak of it; we understand also when we hear it spoken of
> by another. What, then, is space? If no one asks me, I know: If I wish to explain to
> him who asks, I know not [Augustine, *Confessions*].

We have no intention here of grappling with the problem of metaphysics
or ontology that so beset Augustine. Until and unless we are pressed, we
shall use the term *space* in the various and variously related ways in
which it is used in everyday and professional discourse. To facilitate our brief
sketch here of the "uses of space," and, moreover, to link the present discussion to the theoretical perspective we seek to advance, we shall talk about the
uses of space in terms of the categories advanced by Kenneth Burke (1969a)
in his *Grammar of Motives*.

[2] We acknowledge that a drawing or utterance is to be taken as a representation only when
there is an "intention" to represent (see Anscombe, 1938; Louch, 1966). How this intention is
established is, of course, a difficult issue to resolve; fortunately, it is beyond the scope of this
chapter.

Let us briefly recall these categories: Agent, Act, Scene, Agency or Instrumentality, and Purpose or End. It seems to us that in unreflective considerations of the uses of space, most of us are inclined to take space principally as the scene(s) of action(s). This holds not only for the proverbial man or woman in the street, but also for child psychologists, environmental psychologists, geographers, and so on. It is our intent to show that space is also used or experienced in terms of the other categories just mentioned. We will start with the familiar space as scene and then consider in turn space construed in terms of the other components.

One cannot do anything in a physical way without using space as a *setting, medium,* or *scene.* An infant moving its arms uses space; an infant seeking the mother's breast uses space; a toddler staggering and stumbling from one place to another uses space; a child playing around the house or going to school uses space; an adult, walking, jogging, or driving to work, uses space. Even as we toss and turn in sleep, we use space. In all of these uses, of course, "space" is subsidiary rather than focal, tacitly there rather than explicit (cf. Polanyi, 1966). One incidentally and inevitably uses space to execute actions. To be sure, the use of space as scene of action generally implicates agents and purposes as well as action. Spaces are typically scenes for agents engaged in actions for the realization of certain ends.

One must and should, of course, distinguish the settings of action for infrahuman animals from the settings for human beings. One may indeed reserve the term *scene* solely for the settings or milieus of human action. The space in which human beings carry out their various actions is already socioculturally structured. And this socially structured space is "regionalized." By this we mean that certain physical expanses are set aside, are bounded, are circumscribed, and culturally invested with certain rules, regulations, customs, properties, inhibitions, restrictions, and so on. The regions we refer to, of course, may range from an international community to a nation, to a state, to a neighborhood, to a home, to a room and even to an illusory closet in a room. Such "culturalized regions" may and do easily cut across "natural divisions" and areas, established by physical-geographical phenomena such as mountains, rivers, and canyons.

One need not elaborate the fact that access to certain regions or places may be prohibited; access to other regions or places may be limited solely to those who have a specified achieved or ascribed status. Certain actions are allowed only in certain places and not others. The quality, direction, and speed (or rate) of locomotion is regulated. One recognizes, or in the process of socialization is gradually taught to recognize, through both rewards and punishments, these sociocultural "facts." In line with wide-spread usage and directly in accord with Burke's conception of "symbolic action," we simply emphasize here that human beings *use,* that is, live and act, principally in symbolic spaces or scenes. Their action is regulated primarily by the symbolic values and norms invested in such scenes (see Altman, 1975; Burke, 1966; Goffman, 1963, 1967; Hall, 1959).

Let us consider, next, *space as Agency or Instrumentality*. Here we refer to the use of physical expanses defined as regions or areas that are used as means or instrumentalities for accomplishing certain ends. Consider, for example, the classic film, *The Hunchback of Notre Dame*. Recall how the hunchback, fleeing from those who would harm him, runs into the Church as an instrumentality of refuge, as a means of protection. The Church serves as a "sanctuary." This is a striking illustration of the way in which "space" is used as an instrumentality in the course of maintaining or achieving a certain self-world relationship. One can easily find an enormous number of illustrations of the same kind of "use of space" in a moment's reflection on one's own experience. We all know of individuals, some of them ourselves, who use their offices as a refuge from various impingements coming from their surroundings. This is a sanctuary of a different sort. E. T. Hall (1959, 1969), Erving Goffman (1963, 1967), and others have highlighted how space is used as a symbolic instrumentality to exhibit one's status, one's identifications, one's personal relations to others, and so on. The phenomena are obvious, and by now, banal. Here again, our purpose in stressing these obvious facts is to highlight that spatial expanses construed as "instrumentalities" comprise one class of the uses of space.

Next consider *space as Agent*. In habitual and automatized transactions with the environment, the agent-character of a spatial expanse is not likely to be noted. However, one need merely imagine being on a desert, or lost in a forest, to realize how mere expanse or spatial interval may become experientially transformed into an anthropomorphized entity, an agent operating to block us from a desired goal: one who works its, his, or her will to thwart our purposes. This class of uses of space is perhaps more likely to be neglected by certain scientists governed by a geometric-technical orientation to the world than by those who focus on experiential aspects of existence (see Ittelson, Franck, & O'Hanlon, 1976; Koffka, 1935; Lewin, 1935; Merleau-Ponty, 1962; Werner, 1940).

We now turn briefly to *space as Purpose or Goal*. One can easily bring to mind individuals who make it one of their chief goals in life to accumulate as much "space" as possible. Perhaps all of us, at one time or another, have been motivated to secure a certain segment of space almost as an end in itself: as if, in the absence of such possession of a space, one would be rootless and homeless—totally without orientation or self-definition. One needs a room of one's own.

Finally, we may mention *space as Act*. Surely, one can conceive of several kinds of actions that are defined essentially by aspects or features of spatiality. If I engage in the physical act of distancing myself from another, I am clearly using properties of space qua action. Sometimes, of course, in the very same "animal act" of distancing myself from another, I may also be engaged in a symbolic action, using movement in space to symbolize my attitudes and sentiments toward that other. One may also use relative location—for example, above, below, side by side—to symbolize status relations, prestige seeking, superiority, or subservience. Aficionados of motion pictures may recall here the spatial choreography between Chaplin-Hitler and Oakie-Mussolini in *The Great Dictator*.

The discussion thus far should suffice to provide a global idea of how many of the uses of space would be conceived and illuminated through even a superficial application of Burke's *dramatistic perspective* or, more exactly, of the categories of his *Grammar of Motives*. Although we do not have the time here to undertake a much deeper application of this perspective, it is useful to take some space to show how the Burkean approach prompts one to look at the very constitution of objects and artifacts as *symbolic spatial entities* and to analyze the relations between such entities and the sociocultural regions that they occupy, and into which they are placed. This brief discussion will be seen to have considerable bearing later on on our understanding of the uses of space, including spatially constituted objects in critical transitions.

Save for poets, lunatics, and lovers, most adults engaged in transactions with the environment regard objects in terms of their functional values; they rarely consider the aspects of spatiality that enter into the constitution of the natural objects and cultural artifacts that surround them. If they incidentally take some notice of shape and organization, it is unlikely that they will consider these features as pertaining to space. Yet, clearly, all objects are spatial entities. Those objects, which we as humans construct, require considerations of space: positions, locations, directions of parts in relation to other parts and to the whole. We simply call attention to this fact without dwelling on it. Rather, we wish to emphasize here that the manner in which cultural objects are spatially structured varies in different societies and in different regions within a society or subgroup of a society.

There are not the same kinds of spatial structures in the bathroom as in the kitchen, in the playroom as in the bedroom. There are not the same kinds of spatial structures in areas set aside as residential as there are in areas that are reserved for the marketplace or for recreation. It is not only that *regions* are demarcated and distinguished socioculturally, but the spatial objects that occupy regions are differentiated in their spatial shape and these differentiations are determined, in very large part, by social and individual purposes. Just as the various macroregions may be seen as instrumentalities for the realization of specific functions, so the objects within such regions are constructed in ways that relate to their social and individual functions. Here again, of course, in the human domain, symbolism and symbolic action play a preponderant role: The same physical structure (entity, object) may, in one scene, function as an ashtray, in another as a work of art (cf. Siegel, 1975).

We see, then, even in this cursory treatment, that space can be used in an enormous variety of ways—which are at least roughly subsumable under the dramatistic categories elaborated by Kenneth Burke. But where does *representation*—one part of the general theme of this volume—enter (to use a spatial metaphor)? One must of course distinguish here the "use of space to represent" and the "representation of space and spatial relations." Consider quickly, the *use of space to represent,* and typically, to represent a variety of phenomena that are typically taken to be nonspatial in character. We have already illustrated the manner in which so-called physical space and spatial dimensions and properties—location, relative position, direction, size, shape, expanding and contracting, thickening and thinning, verticality and horizontality, and even a tilt toward diagonality, the concave and convex, divergency and convergency, the smooth and the rough, the open and the closed, and many others (see Roget's *Thesaurus*)—come to be used to symbolize or represent an enormous variety of conceptions pertaining to all kinds of relations between human beings and nature, human beings and each other, human beings and the Cosmos. As Ernest Bevan pointed out some years ago (*Symbolism and Belief*), many of the expressions for the Supreme Being (the Ultimate Agent) are simply linguistic designators of "what's up there above." And we all know that the place below can easily represent the horrors of the Scene of Hell. We need not go further through the litany: Space—spatial relations and properties—can be used to represent Agents, Acts, Scenes, Agencies, and Ends, and all the variety of relations among these dramatistic components.

Now, let us consider the other linkage between representation and space: the representation not of nonspatial phenomena of culture and cosmos, but, rather, the representation of so-called realistic or perceptually given spatial relations, dimensions, and properties: the actual interval between two objects, how close, how far; the relative position of parts of the body, one's own or another's; the spatial arrangements of rooms in a house, buildings on a campus, houses, offices, bars, and banks in a city; and so on. Here, we are principally concerned not with hypothetical covert processes of codification in mind or brain, but with the use of various public media—language, gesture, drawings, paintings, sculpture, music, and so on, as agencies or instrumentalities for rendering or re-presenting various spatial relationships open to the examination of others. The media, then, are the means, agencies or instrumentalities for realizing, *in their own terms and with regard to their own distinctive properties,* the re-presentation of realistic space. Of course, the representations are sometimes instrumental as in entertainment or pedagogy, sometimes intrinsic as in artistic work.

So much, now for the *uses of space,* including representation, from the Burkean dramatistic perspective. We turn next to a schematic attempt to show how we are trying to interweave the dramatistic point of view with the organismic–developmental one. After this brief treatment, we shall talk about transformations in self–world relationships, with emphasis on the various uses of space in critical environmental transitions. Finally, we shall present some examples of empirical studies, for those who may have found our exposition thus far too elevated or too debased, too broad or too narrow, too deep or too shallow.

Dramatism and Development

We have already referred to general characteristics of the organismic-developmental approach. We here attempt, again in a cursory way, to interweave this approach with the Burkean perspective to demonstrate how an integral *genetic-dramatism* might lead one to deal with the uses of space in critical transitions throughout the life cycle. A big order, of course, and we can only provide the appetizers here.

According to the Wernerian perspective, at primitive levels of development, syncretic fusions prevail: With regard to the Burkean categories, this would entail that there is relatively little differentiation among the analytically abstractable components of situations. Agent, act, agency, scene, and end are intermeshed. It is only for purposes of clarity in exposition, therefore, that one may refer to fusions between agent and act, agent and agency, agent and scene, and so on, when, in fact, all the components are interpenetrated with each other. Specifically, this means that when one talks about, for example, an agent/scene fusion, one might well use the same illustration to exemplify an agent/agency fusion, since scene and agency are not clearly differentiated from each other in primitive levels of functioning.

To take such an illustration: a schizophrenic patient, mentioned by Harold Searles, could not distinguish herself from the chair on which she sat; from one point of view, the chair might be considered as the scene; from another, as an instrumentality for the function of resting. Such phenomena, of course, are not peculiar to pathology. Young children may maintain their rudimentary sense of self in their crib only when in bodily contact with their "security blanket." Is the blanket a scene or is the blanket an agency? Again, in some elderly people, one finds an enormous difficulty in disentangling self from habitual contexts of action and from the instrumentalities they have persistently employed in executing these actions in their customary scenes. Without such scenes and instrumentalities, they may undergo a sense of loss of self, depersonalization, depression, and so on, as if they are no longer the same agent in the absence of their habitual surroundings and instruments of action.

Also at primitive levels of functioning, somewhat beyond the states of syncretic fusion, one would, from a developmental perspective, expect a seemingly antipodal set of phenomena: the isolation of the components without appropriate integration. An agent in a certain scene, with its own sociocultural demands may experience himself or herself as unrelated to what is going on, as having a sense of not-belonging, as being unable to fit in. This is the sense of "what am I doing here?" For various reasons, one may be unable to adapt one's self to the demands of the various sociocultural scenes in which one is expected to operate.

Such phenomena are, of course, typically found in pathological cases, in part, it may be, because the individual is fused with some imaginary scenes and preoccupied with actions in such scenes and cannot meet the demands of the new sociocultural contexts. One finds the same kind of phenomenon in "we normals" under conditions of obsessions, which preoccupy us and therefore preclude our integration in the scenes of our "real social life." One is elsewhere when one should be here. Similar phenomena are surely found also among children: Engaged with their imaginary playmates, engrossed in the process of identifying with television characters, they may easily be alienated from the demands made upon them to accommodate themselves to the scenes imposed by insensitive or unsympathetic adults who insist on their adaptation to the demands of everyday sociocultural life. Again, one finds the isolation of agent from scenes-agencies in elderly people who are obliged to move to new surroundings when their selves are still attached to, or fused with, now anachronistic scenes.

We could, of course, elaborate and exemplify fusions and isolations with respect to the relationships of each of the dramatistic components to each other. We hope, however, that we have said enough here to indicate, without such elaboration and illustration, the general lines along which this could be done: agents fused with action or isolated from their actions; agents fused with end or isolated from their ends—without hope, goal, or cause; act fused with scene or isolated from and inappropriate to the scene. Once again, one could easily draw examples from all phases of the life span, from pathology, from so-called normal adults in various states, and, as we shall show, from situations of critical transition, in which self-world equilibrium is radically disrupted.

It is important next to contrast these more primitive levels of functioning with higher, more advanced, levels of functioning. In order to do this fully, we would have to go into a detailed discussion of something we have not yet touched on; namely, internal distinctions within each of the generic categories. We would have to talk about different levels within the general agent component, within the general scene component, and so on. Clearly, the young child qua agent is not the same kind of agent as the normal adult. Clearly, the settings or scenes in which the child or psychopathological individual operates are not the same, either in variety or abstractness, as the scenes in which the adult acts. Clearly, the acts of a child, the acts of which a child is taken to be capable, are not commensurate with the variety and kinds of acts that a normal adult can presumably execute. Again, it is clear that the young child does not possess the variety and range of instrumentalities that are available to the adult. Finally, the ends we usually attribute to a child, even though some of them may persist throughout life, are surely not coextensive with the range of purposes presumably governing the actions of normal adults.

To do justice to the different levels of agent, agency, scene, act, and end, therefore, one should—and intramurally we do—use different designators. For example, within the category of agent, we distinguish respondent, actor, and person. Correspondingly, within the category of scene we distinguish ambiance, milieu, and scene proper. With regard to the category of ends, we draw a distinction among drives, motives, and values.

It is important to mention that there is an organic or reticulate relationship among the different components and hence among stages or steps within the various components; that is, a correspondence occurs. If an agent operates in terms of stimuli from the surrounding environment (*ambiance*) or in terms of peremptory internal stimuli (*drives*), the agent will necessarily function as a *respondent*. If the agent, on the other hand, operates in terms of higher order values, and uses environmental properties as agencies to make novel instrumentalities, the agent is, in our terms, a *person*. With regard to this point, it should be stressed that any one of us—presumptively normal adults—may operate in ambiances at certain times, in milieus at others, and in *scenes proper* at still others. Drives may sometimes override motives or values, sometimes be subordinated to them. We are, then, now respondents, now actors, now persons. One is no more likely to be a homogeneous, one-level agent than the environment in which one lives or acts is homogeneous and unitary.

Although we have thought it important to allude to the refinements of our perspective, we shall, in the present context, stay principally with our generic categories: agent, act, scene, agency, and purpose. How are these related to each other at the more advanced developmental levels of functioning? As far as possible, we shall orient our discussion toward the themes of this volume: namely, the representation and use of space.

It is posited that at higher levels of development—indeed what legitimates talking about higher levels of development—is the differentiation of the different components and the hierarchic integration of the components. The integration is governed by the higher levels of purpose, namely values or long range goals, and it is with respect to such values that individuals select scenes of their actions and utilize the properties of such scenes to secure or invent instrumentalities for the realization of actions relevant to the values. Few of us, of course, as we have noted earlier, function uniformly at these higher levels; inner and outer circumstances often lead to "regressions" to lower levels of functioning. Here we stress the ideal: At such ideal higher levels, then, an autonomous agent chooses certain values, selects or helps to construct sociocultural scenes in which those values can best be realized; and utilizes or constructs instrumentalities, which will enable the execution of actions consonant with those values.

Such agents or persons, freely and with full responsibility for their actions, may use "realistic" or "physical" spaces as the scenes for acts, as acts themselves for the expression of certain values, as instrumentalities or the source of instrumentalities for the execution of action, as goals (e.g., conquest of space). In sum, such persons are capable of using space in the widest range of ways, and have the individuality and flexibility to shift from one to another of these diverse ways in accord with their higher values. Moreover, such persons can use spatial properties to represent or symbolize the most diverse kinds of phenomena in the most diverse domains; and also have the capacity to represent or symbolize spatial properties and relations through diverse media. The emphasis, throughout, is on autonomy, flexibility, and stability of the agent qua *person*. Agents, functioning at the highest levels use space developmentally; they are not used by it, or subjected as a respondent to it. This does not mean that there cannot be a voluntary "surrender," a controlled "regression in the service of the ego," so to speak. But that is the decision of the autonomous agent.

Obviously, this is an idealization and a caricature. It requires much qualification and elaboration. But we trust that it will serve the purpose of contrasting the more primitive levels of functioning with the highest one, the one that might obtain, perhaps if we were not—human, alas, all too human. It is this perturbation that results in our exposure at various times during the life span to critical environmental transitions. Such transitions disrupt the ideal equilibrium or harmony in which the autonomous agent engages freely in all the uses of space. They lead, in our view, to a breakdown in agent-scene relationships, which prompt regressions of various sorts in the uses of space until a new equilibrium is established.

Critical Environmental Transitions

Having now, albeit schematically, presented and partially illustrated the perspective of genetic dramatism, we turn to the application of this point of view to the phenomena of *critical transitions*. The notion of critical transitions must be contrasted with that of an ideal self-world equilibrium or harmony: a situation in which the agents, experiencing themselves as distinct entities are governed by ends that are not in conflict, but hierarchically organized, and who have or can have available the instrumentalities for acting in the world so as to achieve such ends. Such an ideal self-world harmony is, of course, a fiction. We are constantly exposed to changes in internal and external conditions demanding an awareness of obstacles and a need for changes in functioning; we all have experiences of rapid shifts in demands from the environment. We are always, thus, in some kind of transition (Wapner, 1977, 1978; Wapner, Cohen, & Kaplan, 1976; Wapner, Kaplan, & Cohen, 1973).

We mark off such normal conditions of transition that do not disrupt the dynamic equilibrium from what we call critical or radical transitions. In the latter instance, something happens in the agent, in the environment, or in the interface between both, which radically ruptures the harmony and leads to a sense of disequilibrium. One cannot, of course, give an exhaustive enumeration of such critical transitions. But a few illustrations may suffice to convey the range of phenomena we subsume under this rubric: forced migration, obliging one to leave the locus of one's habitual action; the loss through death or separation of someone very intimate; the abandonment by another; the obligation to leave a well-known and familiar environment for one that is alien; the obligation to retire from one's job or vocation; the sudden upheavals in familiar scenes of action occasioned by natural catastrophes; psychotic episodes that disrupt one's relationships with the environment. These are the kinds of phenomena to which we refer when we talk about critical environmental transitions. Ultimately, of course, it is the experience of the agent that determines whether a transition is radical or not.

One cannot, at this point, say that the same kinds of changes take place with respect to the uses of space under all of these conditions of radical transition. That is, of course, a topic for sustained systematic investigation. But let us assume in a provisional way, that there are commonalities in all of the previously mentioned critical environmental transitions.

To provide an illustration of what occurs in such transitions—with regard especially to the uses of space—we shall consider the well-worn topic of an outgrown romance, in which one of the participants experiences himself or herself as "abandoned." We use this illustration, first, because it is one with which we here are all ostensibly familiar; and second, because one does not usually reflect on what happens to "space" under such circumstances, such a radical transition.

With such a transition, the whole organization, uses, and representation of space, including one's own relations to the other objects in the environment and to one's own body as a spatially constituted entity, undergo remarkable and profound transformations. Regions to which one formerly had almost automatic access are no longer available, and become dynamized entities which forbid one's entry; that is to say, they may function as a *counteragent or antagonist,* with which one struggles. The various objects in the environment and the relations among them take on different saliencies and experiential relevance. The very objects participating in the scenes of the former relationship, are now experienced as fused with those scenes and may even become instrumentalities either to evoke the former scenes or to be expelled in vainly seeking to abolish them from one's life and mind. Again, one may try to flee from the customary scenes of the former life: by distancing one's self physically and psychologically—there is here a regression to psychophysical undifferentiatedness—from the places of one's pain. Here we have space used qua action, both physical and symbolic. In the concurrent and alternating attempts to try to reestablish a self-world harmony, one may take as one's end the search for and finding of "the place" which will enable one, once again to function as an autonomous person, not subject to the promptings of environmental stimuli or to the involuntary intrusions of internal "stimuli"—obsessions, peremptory drives, transient and conflicting motives, and so on.

We must not, of course, neglect the body-self facet of the self-world relationship during such a radical transition. One may experience the bodily organization as disturbed in various ways, ranging from derealization or hypochondriasis to a sense of bodily shrinkage. One may take certain parts of the body or arrangements of parts of the body as inimical, and, in pathological instances, may even try to destroy parts of the body as if they were demonic agents of one's distress. Of course, all of this change with regard to the body is deeply connected with one's attitude to the self: In such instances, however, one is again regressed to a psychophysical undifferentiatedness, in which self and body are fused. Much more could be said about the body-self pole, but what we have just said should suffice.

In all of these instances, where space takes on these different characteristics, we are typically not dealing with an autonomous person, but with a respondent, pushed by peremptory drives or transient and conflicting motives, or moved by sign-stimuli in the ambiance or in milieus that trigger off responses. The agent does not voluntarily adopt these uses, but is seized by them.

There are many other critical transitions in which the disruption of self-world relationships does not lead to such a sense of overwhelming loss or to such pervasive effects as we have just discussed. It is our belief, nevertheless, that in such transitions, there are at least attenuated manifestations of all of the phenomena we have mentioned. For example, children who immerse themselves in the home environment and use spaces and places there mainly as scenes of action, may, in being obliged to go to school, take the school setting as a threatening agent from which they must flee; they may search for regions there as instrumentalities of refuge or sanctuary, and so on. They may also suffer from formerly nonexistent bodily aches and pains and manifest bodily disturbances. The disruption occasioned by being forced to go to school may also penetrate other domains of the children's world. In another place, we shall seek to exemplify and document this contention in much greater detail.[3]

Empirical Studies

We turn now to the long delayed section on empirical investigations. First, let us note that we deal here only with studies done at Clark University. Second, almost all of these studies were carried out before our present framework had been given the degree of articulation that we trust it now has; therefore, some protocols and findings have been subjected, post hoc, to kinds of analyses they may not have had when they were initially carried out. Third—and this will be obvious—the studies deal mainly with transitions of a far less radical character than those we have just discussed; indeed, most may be taken to deal not with critical transitions at all, but only with those kinds of momentary disequilibria to which even the most ideally integrated person is subject. Fourth—and this again will be obvious—the studies are concerned only with circumscribed facets of agent's action in sociocultural scenes.

Despite these caveats and qualifications, we treat these studies here because we believe they will serve to illuminate the ways in which our *genetic-dramatistic orientation* leads us to examine how agents use space, including the use of space in instrumental acts of representation. Indeed, in

---

3 We have not, in this chapter, surveyed and incorporated the range of empirical and experimental literature consonant with our perspective. We recognize that there have been many studies, done by others within other frames of reference, which can fit easily into our formulation, and do much to enrich it.

this section, we shall deal mainly with *the representation of spatial relations* between objects, and between self and objects, by agents of various ages and/or in various states symbolizing situations, under diverse natural or experimental conditions.

The studies we discuss below may be grouped under five headings: (a) purely ontogenetic studies of the representation of spatial relations among objects; (b) microgenetic studies of spatial representation; (c) ontogenetic and microgenetic studies of the representation of space; (d) the nature and role of the representation of space in adults intermittently deprived of an habitual instrumentality for orienting one's self in various scenes; and (e) the representation of spatial relations among objects by adults obliged by external agents to move to new scenes of action.

The first inquiry, an *ontogenetic* study of nonverbal representation of spatial relationships, does not bear on the issue of critical transitions at all (Rand & Wapner, 1970). Subjects of various ages were asked to depict, via a medium of representational drawing, a situation in which a person is looking for a lost penny. Two-hundred and twenty-eight subjects, 19 boys and 19 girls in each of six age groups from 7 to 16, were asked to draw two pictures: "themselves looking for a lost penny in the grass" and "themselves standing in the grass."

We limit ourselves here to a discussion of drawings by subjects of different ages with respect only to the "lost penny" situation. The youngest children either represented themselves in the grass or the penny in the grass, but not both even in juxtaposition (Figure 10.1). At a later stage, there was the representation of both *agent* and more articulated *scene* (i.e., the penny was depicted), but there was no explicit representation of agent's *action*, and no indication of any *goal* of action (Figures 10.2, 10.3). A more advanced step is manifested when there is a greater articulation of the agent; that is, where the agent's attitude is, at least globally depicted although the action of looking is not yet expressed, the agent juxtaposed to the penny is represented as crying, sorrowful, and so on (Figure 10.4). At still later stages, the agent is represented in a posture to suggest some kind of looking (Figures 10.5-

FIGURE 10.1. *7-year-old. (Adapted from Rand & Wapner, 1970.)*

FIGURE 10.2. *7-year-old. (Adapted from Rand & Wapner, 1970.)*

FIGURE 10.3. *7-year-old. (Adapted from Rand & Wapner, 1970.)*

FIGURE 10.4. *7-year-old. (Adapted from Rand & Wapner, 1970.)*

FIGURE 10.5. *11-year-old. (Adapted from Rand & Wapner, 1970.)*

FIGURE 10.6. *11-year-old. (Adapted from Rand & Wapner, 1970.)*

FIGURE 10.7. *7-year-old. (Adapted from Rand & Wapner, 1970.)*

10.11), to highlight the act of looking, which may be difficult within the medium of drawing, some subjects elongated the arm of the agent (look-ing-searching) or turned the fingers into a rakelike object (Figures 10.12-10.15), thereby doing something akin to what Freud has discussed in his treatment of the "regard for representability" in the *Interpretation of Dreams:* That is, unable to depict "looking," the subjects seemingly transform

FIGURE 10.8. *9-year-old. (Adapted from Rand & Wapner, 1970.)*

FIGURE 10.9. *11-year-old. (Adapted from Rand & Wapner, 1970.)*

FIGURE 10.10. *13-year-old. (Adapted from Rand & Wapner, 1970.)*

FIGURE 10.11. *15-year-old. (Adapted from Rand & Wapner, 1970.)*

FIGURE 10.12. *7-year-old. (Adapted from Rand & Wapner, 1970.)*

FIGURE 10.13. *13-year-old. (Adapted from Rand & Wapner, 1970.)*

FIGURE 10.14. *14-year-old. (Adapted from Rand & Wapner, 1970.)*

FIGURE 10.15. *13-year-old. (Adapted from Rand & Wapner, 1970.)*

FIGURE 10.16. *16-year-old. (Adapted from Rand & Wapner.)*

that notion into the related idea of searching, and this transformation allows them to represent the "generic" or "more global" act in a more commodious way. Finally, there are those drawings in which the agent's goal-directed action in the scene is more or less clearly depicted including a representation of an action-specific instrumentality, namely, a searchlight (Figure 10.16).

In sum, this study suggests that in the ontogeny of the representation of situations, there is an increasing integration of differentiated components: agent, scene, act, goal, and instrumentality. Not surprisingly, the ontogenetic sequence conforms in the main to the ideal developmental sequence.

The second study we shall discuss deals with the microgenesis[4] of spatial representation in a situation that might be said to border on a critical transition: individuals voluntarily moving into a new and unfamiliar scene. Specifically, freshmen entering a small university campus were asked, over

[4] *Microgenesis* is used here to refer both to methods for investigating, and findings resulting from, changes in a complex process within an individual of roughly constant age. The time-scale considered in microgenetic studies may vary from the seemingly instantaneous formation of a percept or thought to the kind of 6-month period of progressive formations considered here.

a 6-month period, to make a number of sketch maps of the setting into which they had come and to which they were in the process of adapting. Once again the instrumentality of representation of spatial relations was nonverbal.

A set of six sketch maps made by one subject is shown in Figure 10.17. Visual inspection will show a development in the internal structure of the sketch map representations. Analysis of the six sketch maps made over the 6-month period by 17 subjects was undertaken with respect to four issues: number of on-campus buildings; number of correctly articulated forms; number of streets; and the veridicality (or distortion) of "real" spatial relations among the buildings. The findings clearly demonstrated that, with progressive exposure to a scene, young adult (or older adolescent) individuals represent the spatial relationships constituting a scene in an increasingly differentiated and integrated manner.

This particular inquiry also throws some light on the factors entering into the initial objects chosen for representation on sketch maps, and the manner in which objects are added to subsequent sketch maps. We shall not discuss these issues here, but refer to the paper dealing with the entire study (Schouela, Steinberg, Leveton, & Wapner, 1980).

The next study we discuss deals with both *ontogenetic and microgenetic* changes in nonverbal representation of spatial relations. Here again, the subjects had been translocated to a new and unfamiliar environment; the subjects were four American children—ages 4½, 6½, 9, and 10—who accompanied their parents to Holland.[5] These children drew sketch maps of the town they visited for a 9-month period. The sketch maps were drawn during different periods of their stay. Although there were as many as 22 maps drawn by some of the children, we here consider only the maps drawn soon after initial entry, the maps drawn after approximately 2 months in residence and the maps drawn after approximately 6 months in the novel environment.

Microgenetic changes are evident in the sketch maps of all four children. Consider the 4½ year old (Figure 10.18). In the initial map, global undifferentiated blobs are used to represent some objects like cows; there is no evidence of the coordination or integration of spatial regions. Nor is there any depiction of actions or transactions within the scene. In the intermediate map, the form of the objects constituting the scene is more articulated; moreover, there are representations of a few connecting links between regions. In the sketch map for the sixth month, there is a much greater articulation of the objects constituting the scene and a greater degree of integration among the object-representations.

One will note that the 6½-year-old starts at a more advanced level (Figure

[5] We thank Dr. David Stevens of Clark University who provided us with the drawings by his four children.

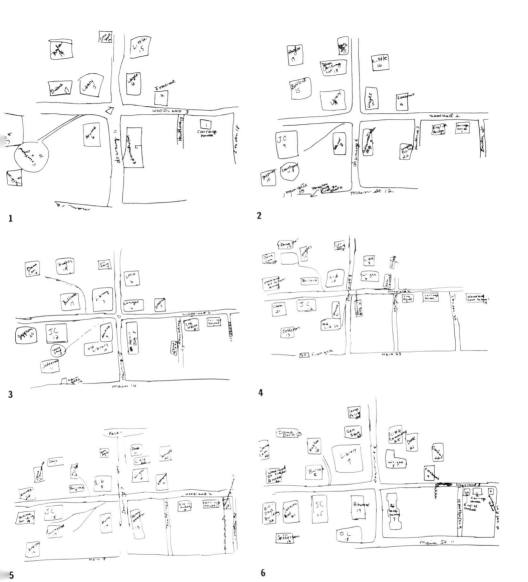

FIGURE 10.17. *One subject's sketch maps showing development of cognitive organization of an environment over a 6-month period. (Adapted from Schouela et al., 1979.)*

10.19) than the 4½-year-old, and progressively articulates, differentiates and integrates the scene well beyond the level reached by the younger child. Again, the same may be said for the 9-year-old (Figure 10.20) vis-à-vis the 6½-year-old. And once more, one can see a comparable phenomenon for the 10-year-old (Figure 10.21). Thus, both microgenetically and ontogenetically, with regard to sketch map representations of an environment, one witnesses the progressive differentiation of a scene into distinct objects with their spatial interrelations becoming more and more integrated.

The fourth study we mention here—a microgenetic one—seeks to stimulate a critical transition, albeit in an attenuated way. In this study, carried out with college student subjects, the agents were intermittently deprived of an essential instrumentality in one's normal orientation to and organization of the world: Namely, they were blindfolded, and thus deprived of sight in their explorations of a small experimental room. In this inquiry, 10 agents were allowed 10 30-second trials to explore the room. After each trial, the blindfold was removed, and the agents asked both to describe verbally and to draw a picture of the room explored under the adverse conditions: Thus, two different media of representation were employed. Here we note that analysis of the drawings and verbalizations of the agents indicated a microgenetic shift in the nature of the representations from: (a) a more functional to more geometric spatial organization of the scene; (b) a more global and diffuse organization to a more articulated and integrated one; and (c) a more topological to a more metric structuring of spatial relationships among the objects constituting the scene (for details, see Follini, 1966).

A second part of this inquiry was directed toward the role of different modes of representation in facilitating action in a scene, under the condition of experimental deprivation of a fundamental instrumentality. Twenty-five agents explored the room, in the manner just described. But here, one group of agents provided both drawings and verbal representations; one group just drew a map between trials; a third group provided only verbal descriptions; and a fourth group engaged in ostensibly irrelevant arithmetical problem-solving. There was some evidence that those who represent spatial relations in any medium between trials manifest a more highly organized conceptual structurization of the scene than those who do not engage in representational activity. On the other hand, there was no evidence that those who "know" more about the structure of the scene are better able to act practically within the scene (i.e., get from one place to another blindfolded) than those who do not represent the scene either verbally or pictorially. At least as far as this study goes, it suggests that higher lever conceptual activity need not be integrated with practical action in a situation.

The final set of studies to be discussed here deals with situations that are much closer to what we mean by "critical or radical transitions" than those

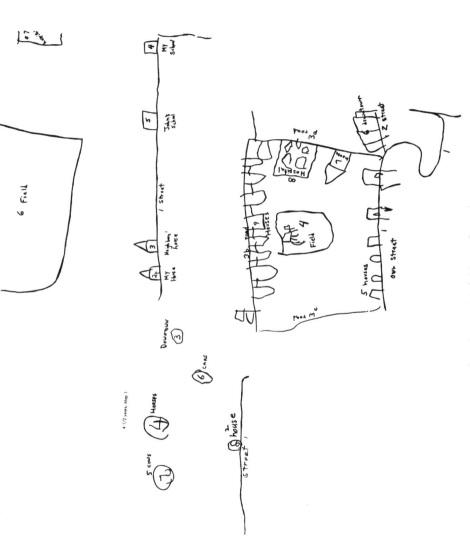

FIGURE 10.18. Sketch maps for 4½-year-old child over 6-month exposure to new environment.

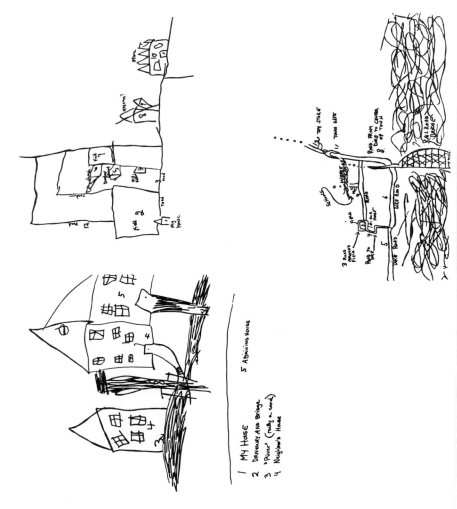

FIGURE 10.19. Sketch maps for 6½-year-old child over 6-month exposure to new environment.

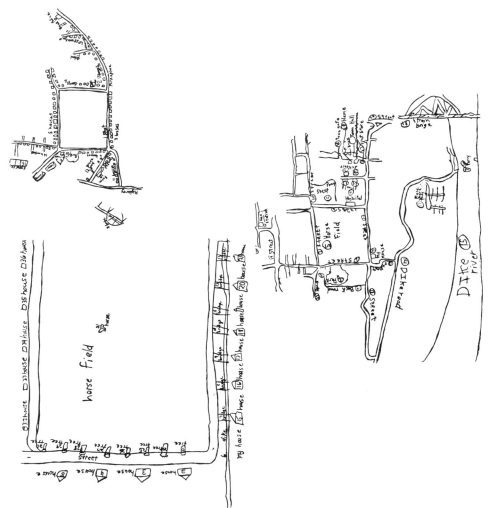

FIGURE 10.20. *Sketch maps for 9-year-old child over 6-month exposure to new environment.*

277

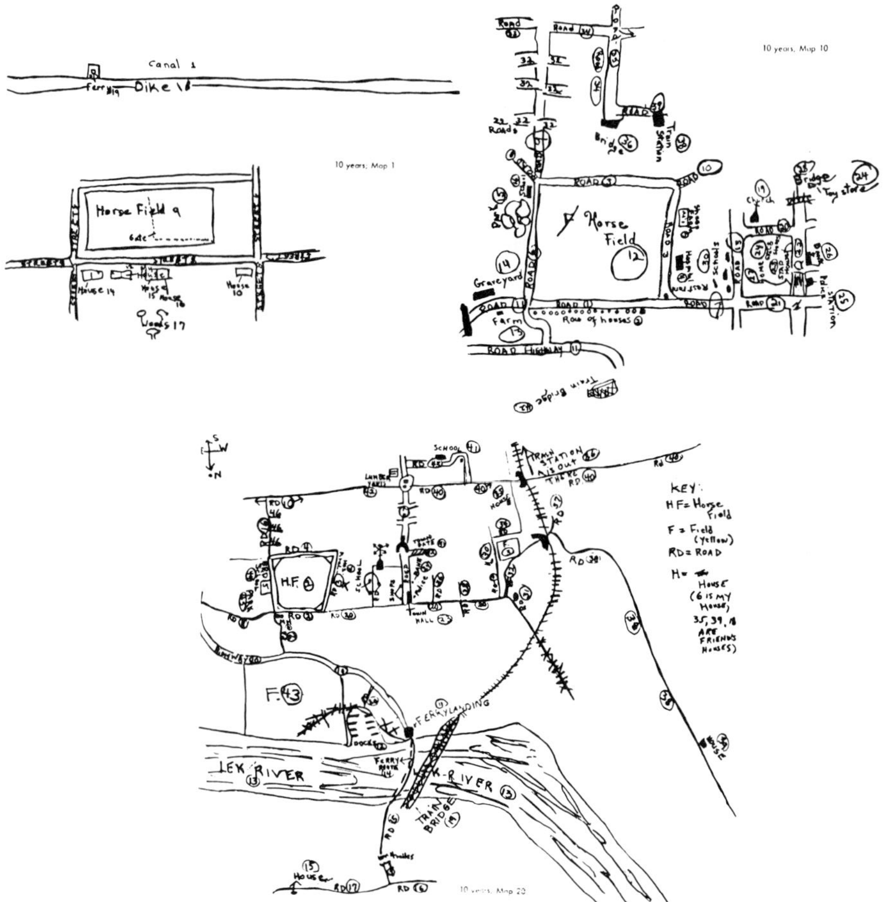

FIGURE 10.21. Sketch maps for 10-year-old child over 6-month exposure to new environment.

treated thus far. One inquiry, done only in a preliminary way, concerned the ways in which elderly individuals, obliged to go to an old-age home sought to cope with the radical change in scene. The second inquiry, carried out far more fully and comprehensively, concerned the ways in which various members of a "therapeutic community"—schizophrenics, antisocial personalities and staff members—coped with a relocation of their "community" —the shift to a new scene of action (Demick, 1977; Demick & Wapner, 1978).

In the study of relocation to an old-age home (Schmitt, Redondo, & Wapner, 1977), an attempt was made to examine how elderly people, obliged to go to nursing homes, coped with the transition to the new scene and from the habitual old scenes of their action. The main finding of relevance here is the fact that those individuals who brought with them various objects from the habitual scenes—pictures, rocking chairs, mementos of various kinds—seemed to exhibit a better adaptation to the new scene than those elderly agents who went without such "transitional objects." These "transitional objects" apparently enable one to integrate the older scenes with the new one, providing a bridge between the two worlds.

In the inquiry into the relocation of the therapeutic community, the various groups and the members constituting them were assessed, over a 2-month period, with regard to "experience of self," "experience of environment (or scene)," and "experience of self-environment relationships." These assessments were made on four occasions: (a) 3-4 weeks before the move; (b) 2-3 days before the move; (c) 2-3 days after the move; and (d) 3-4 weeks after the relocation.

Consider some of the findings. First, with regard to the agents themselves: Estimations of head-width revealed that both patient groups were affected by the process of relocation, but in different ways; the schizophrenics showed an increase in apparent head-width immediately preceding relocation. This overestimation of head-width remained constant until the final assessment period when there was a return to the initial level of overestimation. On the other hand, the antisocial agents manifested a decrease just before and just after relocation, making estimates closer to their actual head-width (see Demick, 1977; Demick & Wapner, 1978). Without going into an interpretation of these different outcomes, one may make the general remark that transition induces changes in the experiences of self at least in those agents who have no say in the move.

With regard to the familiar habitual scene of action, as relocation approached, the schizophrenics manifested strikingly less accurate and detailed verbal representations of their habitual scenes of action, something which did not occur in the antisocial group. Finally, the schizophrenic agents typically demonstrated a greater "closeness"—one might say, *fusion,* with their habitual scenes as the time for relocation became imminent.

So much for our report of some studies. We can see, now, with all the proverbial advantages of hindsight, and through the lenses of our new genetic-dramatistic perspective, many things that might have been introduced in our naturalistic and experimental inquiries, many analyses that might have been done. But this is not the place to elaborate our plans for systematic inquiry in the future.

Conclusion

Our chapter is already far too long. Our conclusion, therefore will be limited to a summary of what we have tried to do here: (a) present the outlines of a new perspective, genetic-dramatism, which weds the organismic developmental approach to the dramatistic one; (b) show schematically how this perspective influences the manner in which one examines the uses of space, as manifested in overt action and as experienced in feeling, perception, and thought; (c) indicate and illustrate how we use the phrase "critical environmental transitions"; and (d) present findings from some empirical studies that reveal in a modest and partial way, various substantive and methodological features of genetic-dramatism.

Acknowledgments

This chapter is a joint effort. Nevertheless, it should be noted that the three authors contributed differentially to the various aspects of the chapter. Kaplan has been mainly responsible for the exploitation of Burke's work and the attempts to integrate Burke and the organismic-developmental perspective, working here closely with Wapner. Wapner and Ciottone have taken on the principal responsibility for the incorporation of empirical research on the issues of transition, only a portion of which is discussed and elaborated in this chapter. Kaplan, with Wapner, accepts the responsibility for the style and shape of the chapter.

References

Altman, I. *The environment and social behavior: Privacy, personal space, territory, crowding.* Monterey, California: Brooks/Cole, 1975.
Anscombe, G. E. M. *Intention.* London: Blackwell, 1938.
Bernheimer, R. *Nature of representation.* New York: New York University Press, 1961.
Bevan, E. *Symbolism and belief.* Boston: Beacon Press, 1950.
Burke, K. *Philosophy of literary form.* Baton Rouge: Louisiana Press, 1941.
Burke, K. *Language as symbolic action.* Berkeley: University of California Press, 1966.
Burke, K. *Counterstatement.* Berkeley: University of California Press, 1968.

Burke, K. *Grammar of motives.* Berkeley: University of California Press, 1969. (a)

Burke, K. *Rhetoric of motives.* Berkeley: University of California Press, 1969. (b)

Burke, K. *Dramatism and development.* Barre, Massachusetts: Clark University Press with Barre Publishers, 1972.

Demick, J. *Effect of environmental relocation upon members of a psychiatric community.* Unpublished MA thesis, Clark University, 1977.

Demick, J., & Wapner, S. *Effects of environmental relocation upon members of a psychiatric community.* Manuscript submitted for publication, 1978.

Follini, M. B. *The construction of behavioral space: A microgenetic investigation of orientation in an unfamiliar locality.* Unpublished MA thesis, Clark University, 1966.

Goffman, E. *Behavior in public places.* Glencoe, Illinois: Free Press, 1963.

Goffman, E. *Interaction ritual.* New York: Doubleday Anchor, 1967.

Hall, E. T. *Silent language.* New York: Doubleday, 1959.

Hall, E. T. *Hidden dimension.* New York: Doubleday Anchor, 1969.

Ittelson, W. H., Franck, K. A., & O'Hanlon, T. J. The nature of environmental experience. In S. Wapner, S. B. Cohen, & B. Kaplan (Eds.), *Experiencing the environment.* New York: Plenum, 1976.

Kaplan, B. The study of language in psychiatry: The comparative-developmental approach and its application to symbolization and languague in psychopathology. In S. Arieti (Ed.), *American handbook of psychiatry, Vol. III.* New York: Basic Books, 1966.

Kaplan, B. Meditations on genesis. *Human Development,* 1967, *10,* 65-87.

Koffka, K. *Principles of Gestalt psychology.* New York: Harcourt Brace, 1935.

Lewin, K. *A dynamic theory of personality.* New York: McGraw-Hill, 1935.

Louch, A. R. *Explanation and human action.* Berkeley: University of California Press, 1966.

Merleau-Ponty, M. *Phenomenology of perception* (translated from the French by Colin Smith.) London: Routledge & Kegan Paul, 1962.

Moore, G. T. *Developmental variations between and within individuals in the cognitive representation of large scale environments.* Unpublished MA thesis, Clark University, 1973.

Moore, G. T. Theory and research on the development of environmental knowing. In G. T. Moore & R. G. Golledge (Eds.), *Environmental knowing.* Stroudsberg, Pennsylvania: Dowden, Hutchinson & Ross, 1976.

Moore, G. T., & Golledge, R. G. *Environmental knowing.* Stroudsberg, Pennsylvania: Dowden, Hutchinson & Ross, 1976.

Pitkin, H. F. *The concept of representation.* Berkeley: University of California Press, 1972.

Polyani, M. *The tacit dimension.* New York: Doubleday Anchor, 1966.

Rand, G., & Wapner, S. Graphic representations of a motivational act: An ontogenetic study. *NAEA Studies in Art Education,* 1970, *12,* 25-30.

Schmitt, V. L., Redondo, J. P., & Wapner, S. *The role of transitional objects in adult transition.* Manuscript in preparation, 1977.

Schouela, D. A., Steinbrg, L. M., Leveton, L. G., & Wapner, S. Development of the cognitive organization of an environment. *Canadian Journal of Behavioural Science,* 1980, *12,* 1-16.

Siegel, D. *Aesthetic and practical apprehension of different types of objects in a display versus a practical setting.* Unpublished MA thesis, Clark University, 1975.

Wapner, S. Environmental transition: A research paradigm deriving from the organismic-developmental systems approach. In L. van Ryzin (Ed.), *Proceedings of the Wisconsin Conference on Research Methods in Behavior-Environment Studies.* Madison: University of Wisconsin, 1977.

Wapner, S. Some critical person-environment transitions. *Hiroshima Forum for Psychology,* 1978, *5,* 3-20.

Wapner, S., Cohen, S. B., & Kaplan, B. (Eds.), *Experiencing the environment.* New York: Plenum Press, 1976.

Wapner, S., Kaplan, B., & Cohen, S. An organismic-developmental perspective for under-
    standing transactions of men-in-environments. *Environment and Behavior*, 1973, *5*,
    255-289.
Werner, H. *Comparative psychology of mental development*. New York: Harper, 1940; 2nd
    edition, Chicago: Follett, 1948; 3rd edition, New York: International Universities Press,
    1957.
Werner, H. The concept of development from a comparative and organismic point of view. In
    D. B. Harris (Ed.), *The concept of development: An issue in the study of human behavior*.
    Minneapolis: University of Minnesota Press, 1957.
Werner, H., & Kaplan, B. *Symbol formation*. New York: Wiley, 1963.
Werner, H., & Wapner, S. Toward a general theory of perception. *Psychological Review*, 1952,
    59, 324-338.

11 A Cross-Cultural and Dialectic Analysis of Homes

IRWIN ALTMAN
MARY GAUVAIN

Introduction

This chapter analyzes the home, which is an important environmental setting that has received relatively little attention in psychological research. Although considerable research is available for a variety of institutional settings such as prisons, schools, and hospitals, it is difficult to find systematic programs of environment-behavior research on the home as a social-psychological setting. However, this is not to say that homes have been ignored by other disciplines. For example, interior designers have traditionally examined interior spaces—contemporaneously and historically. Many geographers and landscape architects have studied exteriors. Architects and architectural historians have accumulated bodies of knowledge about design features of homes across cultures and throughout history. Anthropologists often buttress ethnographic analyses with descriptions of settlements and dwellings; archeologists map out community and housing patterns as essential facets of their work.

We will address two aspects of home environments that complement current knowledge: (*a*) the home in relation to certain social–psychological dimensions; and (*b*) the home as viewed from a cross-cultural, comparative perspective. Specifically, this chapter proposes a dialectically oriented conceptual framework for analyzing social–psychological features of homes. The basic idea is that homes reflect the dialectic interplay of *individuality* and *society,* such that there are forces for people to be linked with, and influenced by, the larger community and, at the same time, to be separate from and independent of societal influences. We also propose that the individual/society dialectic is manifested in two subordinate dialectic opposi-

283

SPATIAL REPRESENTATION AND BEHAVIOR
ACROSS THE LIFE SPAN

tions that appear in home design and use, namely, identity/communality and accessibility/inaccessibility. The second goal of the chapter is to apply this dialectic framework to the comparative cross-cultural analysis of homes. In so doing we hope to illustrate the possibility for systematic analysis of similarities and differences among cultures in the design and uses of dwelling spaces. Aside from Rapoport's analysis (1969a) of homes in relation to environmental factors such as temperature and climate, technology, resources, and cultural variables such as religion and social structure, systematic comparisons of homes across cultures are rare indeed.

The first sections of this chapter describe dialectic dimensions for the analysis of representations and use of space in homes, and features of our cross-cultural approach. The main body contains an analysis of spatial aspects of homes from a sample of cultures, in terms of locations and exteriors, thresholds and entranceways, and layout and use of interiors. The last section discusses application of the analysis to future research on homes.

The Idea of Dialectics

The concept of dialectics has a long, complex, and controversial history in Western and Eastern philosophy, and we do not intend to offer a complete explication of its qualities. The interested reader is referred to several excellent sources for further information about dialectical thinking in philosophy (Adler, 1927, 1952) and in relation to psychological phenomena (Rychlak, 1968, 1976).

There have been several historical uses of dialectics: as a method, as an ideology, and as a "world view." One traditional application of dialectics has been as a method of reasoning. Some ancient Greek philosophers, notably Socrates, deliberately sought out opposing points of view to any stated position, based on the logic that consideration of such alternatives would result in better understanding of an issue. Our interest here, however, is not in dialectics as a method of reasoning.

Another use of dialectics has been in relation to political and other ideologies. Some dialecticians, notably Marxists, see the clash of materialistic processes as eventually resulting in an ideal political system—a classless society. Some critics state that Marxian dialectics is not Socratic in form because it initially presumes a desired outcome. And, in ancient Greece sophistry was criticized because it involved the use of dialectical reasoning to achieve a preconceived outcome (Adler, 1952). As such, sophistry, and perhaps Marxism, does not involve a free and open clash of oppositional ideas; instead, they may constitute ideological, biased uses of "pure" dialectical principles. In any case, our interest is not in the ideological realm of dialectics, whether it be political or theoretical.

An additional conception, and the one we will emphasize, is of dialectics as a "world view" or set of assumptions about the functioning of the physical and psychological world. Although dialectic world views have appeared throughout history and in different cultures, three general features that occur in many such conceptions will guide our thinking:

1. The world, universe, and human affairs involve various oppositional tensions. Some of these are in the physical realm, such as fire and water, earth and heaven, and day and night. Others are in the social realm, such as harmony and conflict, selfishness and altruism. These oppositions are in dynamic relationships, with one pole of the opposition dominating at one time, and the other dominating on other occasions, although neither completely or totally suppresses the other. In ancient Chinese philosophy, such oppositional processes were imbued in the constructs of Yin and Yang (Wilhelm & Baynes, 1967). Yang forces were creative, aggressive, domineering and "male" qualities, whereas Yin forces were recessive, passive, and "female." In more modern philosophical thought, Hegel's conception of the clash of ideas as involving a thesis, an antithesis, and eventual resolution in the form of a synthesis of oppositions is an exemplar of the concept of a dialectical opposition.

There are many uses of this facet of dialectics in psychological theories, although we do not often think of them in this way. For example, Freud's concepts of the primal, self-gratifying *id* in continual conflict with the symbol of society, the superego, portrays a dialectical idea of personality (Rychlak, 1968). The *ego*, as mediator and resolver of the id–supergo conflict, is analogous to Hegel's synthesis of a thesis and its antithesis. Simmel (1950) also described social relationships as involving an interplay of various oppositional processes, such as intimacy and trivia, harmony and conflict, closeness and distance, subordination and superordination. In developmental psychology, the Piagetian concept of adaptation, composed of assimilation and accommodation, has a quality of dialectical opposition. Assimilation involves the child's incorporating new experiences into an existing mental scheme or personal framework. But there is also a simultaneous process of accommodation, where the qualities of the environment often contribute to a change in the child's mental scheme. Thus, for Piaget there is a continual oppositional interplay between stability and change in the child's conception of the world.

2. A second feature of dialectics that we will adopt is that oppositional processes function as a unified system. Oppositional poles help define one another, and without such contrasts neither would have meaning. The

physical concept of day is given meaning by its opposite, night, and vice versa. Thus, homogeneity without contrast could not be distinctive or unique. So it is that Simmel (Wolff, 1950) hypothesized that both harmony and conflict are essential to human relationships, each serving to define and lend meaning to the other, and each functioning with the other as part of a total system. So, the unity of opposites within a superordinate system is an important quality of our approach. We will describe homes as partly reflecting both the unique identity of its occupants as well as their communality with the broader culture, with each serving as aspects of a unified dialectic system.

A related point is that we conceive of a range of possible relationships between oppositional processes. Thus, one culture may reflect far more communality than identity. There is no implication that a dialectic system strives toward a universally optimal level of relationship, or that it moves in the direction of balance, consistency, homeostasis, or equality of oppositions. Dialectic systems can have a variety of relationships between opposites, and there is no theoretical or philosophical reason to assume that a particular relationship between opposites is best or ideal. Thus, an equal balance between identity and communality is not necessarily better than an unequal relationship between these processes.

The only requirement for preservation of dialectic systems is that there must always be some minimum amount of either opposition. Without the barest evidence of an opposition there would be, by definition, no system. So, while the relative strength of oppositional forces may vary widely, a minimum amount of each force must be present to keep the system intact.

3. A third feature of dialectic systems is that the relationships between opposites are dynamic; changes occur over time and with circumstances. Sometimes changes occur on a short-term basis; sometimes they appear over the long term. Sometimes the shifting relationships between opposites occur on a cyclical basis; sometimes they are sequential and cumulative. Cyclical relationships are exemplified by day-night and seasonal cycles, where opposite poles shift back and forth in the strength of their relationship to one another. Sequential or cumulative changes involve the Hegelian idea of a thesis and antithesis being resolved by a synthesis that incorporates the opposites into a new phenomenon.

Although it is central to dialectic philosophy, several factors make it impossible for our analysis to emphasize the dynamic, changing character of homes. First, ethnographic material does not usually provide information about changing aspects of homes. Second, communality/identity and accessibility/inaccessibility features of homes are relatively stable and usually only change on a long-term basis.

This brief discussion of dialectics can not be comprehensive. It is, in a sense, an operational definition of key features of dialectic thinking that we have adopted as a heuristic device to understand some social-psychological features of homes better.

Dialectic Dimensions of Homes

An assumption of our analysis is that homes mirror a wide variety of environmental and cultural influences, and that dwelling forms gradually evolved in response to a variety of interactive forces. Thus, the Eskimo igloo is an adaptation to the harsh Arctic environment, with its construction from ice and snow blocks and its circular shape, its below-ground and compartmented tunnel entranceway, and its raised interior (Cranstone, 1972; Rapoport, 1969a). The traditional Pueblo Indian community of the Southwestern United States reflects the influence of the physical environment, with its terraced, modular living units yielding shade and interior cool places (Rapoport, 1969b). Cultural factors are evident in the organization of the Pueblo dwellings around a community plaza and their grouping along matriarchal lines. Homes are tangible reflections of cultural adaptations, practices and beliefs.

In particular, we will suggest that dwellings reflect the degree to which cultures and their members must cope with common dialectic oppositions, namely, individual needs, desires, and motives versus the demands and requirements of society at large. Individual forces relate to the attempt of people to be unique and distinct—independent and free of the influences of others. These forces are associated with the satisfactions of individuals, and their families or primary reference groups. At the same time, there are forces operating to make the person part of and at one with society; to facilitate his or her identification with the community; and to increase susceptibility to influence and dependence on the larger community.

Several aspects of the individual/society tension fit with general features of dialectics described earlier. While societies probably vary in the extent to which individual versus societal forces predominate, we expect that both forces will exist to some extent in all cultures. Thus, according to dialectic philosophy, it is not likely that one will find a viable culture in which there is total control of the lives of individuals, nor is it likely that one will find a society with absolutely total individual freedom. Thus, we assume that all social systems involve the interplay of some level of individual and societal oppositional forces.

In addition, as in the case of general dialectic philosophy, we do not assume that social systems strive toward perfectly "balanced" relationships between individual and societal forces. A great range of possible relationships exist, any of which may be quite viable, as long as some amount of both oppositional processes exists in the system. Thus, unlike physiological homeostatic systems (Cannon, 1932) or some psychological systems (Lewin, 1936), we make no assumption of the desirability of exact equality of opposing forces.

Finally, also in accord with general dialectical reasoning, we assume a dynamic and changing relationship between individual and societal forces. Thus, by virtue of external and internal factors (political, economic, social, and environmental), there are likely to be shifting emphases of individual versus societal forces, on both a long- and short-term basis. Even in the last few decades the American culture has witnessed changing economic and political emphases on the "rights of individuals" versus the "rights of society." We expect, of course, that cultures will show differential rates of change in the relationship between the oppositions of individuality and society, but the essential point is that dialectic processes are dynamic and are subject to changes in the relative strength of oppositional poles.

The individuality/society dialectic has many specific forms, aspects of which have been researched in social psychology, although not within a dialectic framework: for example, independence (individuality) versus conformity (society); competition (individuality) versus cooperation (society); self-gain (individuality) versus altruism (society). We propose that homes in a variety of cultures reflect in their design and use two specific aspects of the general individuality/society dialectic: (a) identity/communality; and (b) an openness/closedness, or accessibility/inaccessibility.

Identity/Communality Dialectic

The home depicts the uniqueness and individuality of its occupants, that is, their personal identity as individuals and as a family, along with their ties, bonds, and affiliations with the community and larger culture of which they are part. Identity has often been used to describe modern American suburban homes, where people are depicted as searching for dwellings to meet their particular individual and family needs, where they display their status, and where they decorate homes so as to make themselves distinct from others—and perhaps even to be better than others. Cooper (1976) emphasized the identity facet of homes in our society:

> As we become accustomed to, and lay claim to, this little niche in the world, we project something of ourselves onto its physical fabric. The furniture we install, the way we arrange it, the pictures we hang, the plants we buy and tend, all are expressions of our images of ourselves, all are messages about ourselves that we want to convey back to ourselves, and to the few intimates that we invite into this, our house.
>
> In the contemporary English speaking world, a premium is put on originality, on

having a house that is unique and somewhat different from others on the street, for the inhabitants who identify with these houses are struggling to maintain some sense of personal uniqueness in an increasingly conformist world. On the other hand, one's house must not be too way-out, for that would label the inhabitant as a nonconformist, and that, for many Americans, is a label to be avoided [p. 437].

In this statement, in spite of its emphasis on personal identity, Cooper suggests that the display of uniqueness operates within the bounds set by community norms. Thus, American suburban homes do not have backyards facing the street; house colors fall within an acceptable range; and, although interiors may vary a great deal, they also fall within appropriate bounds defined by the culture.

In summary, we will use a sample of cultures to illustrate how family dwellings simultaneously reflect the personal identity of occupants and their bonds with the larger community and culture. Furthermore, we expect to find that cultures vary in the extent to which their homes emphasize one or the other side of the identity/communality dialectic, although both identity and communality should be present to some extent.

Accessibility/Inaccessibility Dialectic

A second facet of the individuality/society dialectic involves the degree to which homes emphasize the openness or closedness of occupants to outsiders. This dialectic draws on recent theorizing about privacy as a boundary regulation process (Altman, 1975, 1976, 1977). According to Altman, privacy is a dialectic boundary process whereby a person is differentially accessible or inaccessible to others, depending upon the relationship and other factors. This framework also states that privacy is regulated by a range of behavioral mechanisms that function in profiles or patterns. These mechanisms include verbal and paraverbal communications, nonverbal behavior, and environmental behaviors such as personal space and territoriality. To illustrate these concepts, Altman (1977) showed how cultures provide vehicles for people to regulate openness and closedness, and that what differs among cultures are the particular verbal, nonverbal, and environmental behaviors by which accessibility is achieved.

We will propose here that the home also serves as a behavioral mechanism that is used to regulate openness/closedness in its location, exterior, threshold and entranceway, and in its interior design and use. Once again, we will assume that the home serves both poles of the accessibility/inaccessibility dialectic, perhaps to different degrees in different cultures.

Obviously, there are many oppositions that might be applied to the analysis of homes, as additions or substitutes to those we selected. We chose the accessibility/inaccessibility dialectic because of our previous theoretical work on privacy regulation and the potential for bridging those ideas. In another analysis we used the identity/communality dialectic to describe small communities and large cities, cross-culturally and historically (Altman & Chemers, 1980). Again, this dialectic seemed as if it would apply nicely to homes as well as to communities. Finally, our judgment was based on intuition; after scanning a variety of ethnographic material, we concluded that the accessibility/inaccessibility and identity/communality oppositions appeared in many cultures.

Our proposed dialectic dimensions are also compatible with some recent empirical research on the psychological meaning of homes to American children (Hayward, 1977a,b). Of nine psychological dimensions identified in this research, a number seem to reflect identity (the home as a place to personalize, a symbol of the self, a base of individual activity, a locus of one's heritage or childhood), or communality (a setting reflecting relationships with family and with neighbors and the community.) Certain of these and other dimensions identified by Hayward also relate to accessibility or inaccessibility, such as the home as a place of refuge and a place to be alone. Thus, the idea of the home in relation to identity/communality and accessibility/inaccessibility is not inconsistent with people's perceptions of the psychological significance of their dwellings.

Strategy of Analysis

The goals of this chapter are explicitly heuristic and hypothesis-generating, rather than offering decisive tests of an explicit framework. With such a perspective we adopted an exploratory strategy of analysis in relation to the following: (a) a cross-cultural approach; and (b) features of homes to be analyzed. One feature of our analysis was to use a cross-cultural or comparative perspective. Cross-cultural comparison offers a number of benefits (Whiting, 1954). By applying concepts to a range of cultures one increases the possibility for assessing the generalizability of propositions. Furthermore, the study of different cultures can be a source of new ideas. Another advantage of a comparative approach is that it facilitates examination of one's own culture from a broader perspective. Finally, a comparative approach is intrinsically valuable in its attempt to examine similarities and differences among cultures of the world.

But there are also potential difficulties with this approach (Altman, 1977; Brislin, 1980; Triandia, 1980). Generalizable comparative studies require representative sampling from a broad range of cultures. Given our exploratory goals, this criterion was not wholly met, yielding a possible selection bias. In addition, one is sometimes faced with interpretation of gaps in ethnographic materials. For example, does the absence of information about decorations on entranceways to homes mean that there were no such decorations—or does it mean that the ethnographer did not attend to such decorations? Finally, there are difficulties in attributing meaning to certain cultural practices. How does one decide if a given design characteristic relates to an identity/communality dialectic, or to aspects of the political, economic, or other systems of a culture?

Many of the points raised above are captured in the idea of cross-cultural research as attempting ideally to achieve "emic" and "etic" orientations to other cultures. An etic orientation involves, in part, the establishment of universal principles of behavior across cultures. In seeking broad generalizations one usually applies a general theoretical idea to account for the behavior of people in other cultures. In addition, one's own views or cultural perspective may influence interpretation of the behavior of other people. While the search for general principles of human behavior is important, a solely etic approach can yield a distorted understanding of another culture, since one's own theoretical or value system is selective in what is examined and how events are interpreted. Therefore, cross-cultural researchers also call for a complementary emic approach to comparative analysis of cultures. An emic orientation attempts to understand a culture on its own terms, and in relation to its unique beliefs, attitudes, and values, without imposing external values on that culture. Of course, a totally emic orientation is also unsatisfactory. If every culture were treated as totally unique and if all understanding were completely culturally specific then it would be impossible to describe similarities and differences among cultures in a systematic and generalizable way. The ideal, therefore, is to balance emic and etic orientations in order to capitalize on the strengths of each perspective.

A significant component of our analysis is etic, as we apply the dialectic oppositions of identity/communality and accessibility/inaccessibility to the homes of other cultures. However, we have attempted to be responsive to emic considerations, by being open to the possibility that cultures will show unique residential characteristics on these polarities and by allowing for the possibility that other dialectic oppositions might apply.

One of our primary ethnographic sources was the *Six Cultures* series. These studies were quite useful because of their systematic and common ethnographic format. From these materials illustrations were drawn from Tarong, a kin-based barrio in northern Luzon in the Philippines (Nydegger & Nydegger, 1966); Taira, a Japanese hamlet on the northeast coast of Okinawa (Maretzki & Maretzki, 1966); Juxtlahuaca, a Mixtecan barrio in central Mexico (Romney & Romney, 1966); a Gusii community in the hills of the South Nyanza District of Kenya (LeVine & LeVine, 1966); and the village of Khalpur, India, in the foothills of the Himalayas (Minturn & Hitchcock, 1966). Other illustrations are drawn from a variety of ethnographic sources. For example, Faegre (1979) provided information on the living environments of the north African Berbers, Tuaregs, and Bedouins, as well as the nomads of central and northern Asia, Persia, Lapland, and North America. Still further illustrations are derived from our own observations, experiences and travels in the United States, Scandinavia, and elsewhere.

A second procedural issue concerned the parts of the home to be analyzed. We decided to subdivide the home into three general parts:

1. *Location and exterior:* This refers to the placement of a home on a plot of land, its relationship to roads and to other dwellings, and general features of the exterior of the dwelling.
2. *Entranceway and threshold:* This area of dwellings has had considerable religious, mythological, and social significance, and therefore seemed to be worthy of special attention.
3. *Interior layouts and use:* The interior of the home is a complex place with many subareas. However, given our limited goals, we treated the interior as a broad category.

Identity/Communality of Homes across Cultures

Location and Exterior of Homes

In many cultures, houses are situated in accordance with environmental, climatic, cosmological, and religious influences. Eskimo igloos are often positioned parallel to the wind (Rapoport, 1969a); Bedouin tents of the Middle East are usually pitched facing either east toward Mecca or south so that the back wall is set against the northern winds, with the men's side of the tent facing the holy eastern direction (Faegre, 1979); the *tipis* of the American Plains Indians were usually pitched with the opening facing east because of the religious significance of the rising sun and because the wind on the plains blew from west to east (Faegre, 1979; Fraser, 1968). On the other hand, the siting of the suburban American home usually seems to be relatively unaffected by environmental, climatic, or religious factors. American homes are positioned in every conceivable relationship to wind, sun, and the weather. Perhaps the ability to ignore climate and environment is associated with technology in the form of air conditioning, heating, lighting, and climate control. However, our goal is to explore the idea that the location and positioning of homes in the American suburban culture and elsewhere may be related to dialectic forces associated with identity/communality and accessibility/inaccessibility of people to one another.

American middle-class suburban tract homes are usually located in the middle or rear part of a lot, with some separation, in the form of a lawn, between the home and a public street.[1] In many respects the location of the home and certain features of the front and exterior present to others the unique, idiosyncratic, and individual qualities of the residents. For example, landscaping the front yard is a traditional American vehicle for achieving individuality and uniqueness; enormous amounts of time, energy, and money are invested in the cultivation of grass and shrubbery in a never-ending cycle of fertilizing, watering, and cutting. In addition, Christmas lights and decorations are displayed in the front; the upkeep and personalization of the front is carefully done; trash and gardening equipment are usually stored in the rear; vegetable gardens rarely appear in the front yard, and so on.

The identity theme is also reflected in new suburban communities, where homes are often initially quite similar in design. Very quickly homes are repainted in different colors; decorations and facings that have no functional value are added to the exterior; and landscaping is individualized. Is as much initial effort devoted to the rear of homes? We think not, except for the tendency to demarcate boundaries by fences and shrubbery.

The fronts of American homes and yards not only express identity, but they also depict the bonds of a family with the community (see Figure 11.1) This is especially evident in formal and informal projects that often involve whole streets and communities. Some neighborhoods are lawn- and shrubbery-oriented, and people engage in cooperative planting projects, sharing of tools, and garden and lawn contests. Other communities are oriented toward redecorating the fronts of homes, Christmas lighting contests, or construction of decks and carports. Thus, the exterior of the home and the lot not only permit American suburbanites to achieve identity and uniqueness, but they also facilitate the display of community ties.

In some cultures, bonds with the community are evident in the clustering of dwellings around a central courtyard or plaza. Pueblo Indians of the southwestern United States live in terraced dwellings that are stacked on top of one another in a modular, apartment-like fashion (Rapoport, 1969a,b). Residential units are part of a single structure that faces a central plaza. Work, community activities, and religious events take place in the plaza, and the overall design of the pueblo reflects the unity of the residents with the community. At the other extreme, homes in parts of the Middle East and Asia portray low community identity. Homes often present a blank wall to public thoroughfares. The absence of windows and a bare wall that serves as the back of the dwelling suggest little communality with the public at large or even with immediate neighbors. In essence, dwellings are turned inward, facing a central courtyard used by an extended kin group or a single family.

In general, there is evidence for both identity and communality in the

[1] Analyses of middle-class homes are based on our own informal observations and experiences with a limited range of such dwellings.

FIGURE 11.1. *Front facades of American suburban homes with plantings, grillwork, decorations, awnings, and other displays. (Photographs by Jim Iloste.)*

FIGURE 11.1 *(cont.)*

homes of other cultures. In Tarong, a kin-based hamlet in northern Luzon, Philippines, houses face onto a common yard shared by a kin group (Nydegger & Nydegger, 1966). Positioning a house away from the yard would be considered antisocial and would deprive occupants of social interaction. People are proud of their shared yard, they sweep it thoroughly and keep materials and tools neatly arranged under their houses. As such, the residents of Tarong express their involvement with, and pride in, the community. However, the uniqueness and identity of a family is often reflected in the construction of individual homes. Although size is dictated almost solely by number of occupants, the quality of construction materials directly reflects a family's wealth.

As another example, nomadic North African Berbers pitch their tents in a sacred order—the *douar*, or circle—around which related families gather (Faegre, 1979). Wealthier and more important families have larger and more elaborate tents, thereby reflecting status and personal identity. Regardless of its size, however, the front of each tent faces the center of the douar, where the mosque tent is located. The mosque tent serves as a religious school and as a sanctuary for visitors. Side by side here, we see evidence for both identity and communality in the location and exterior qualities of homes.

Another example appears in the community design of the South Nias villages of Indonesia (Fraser, 1968). The chief's home is located at the upper end of the village and the commoners' dwellings are situated at the lower end, in accord with their conception of the universe as having an "upper world" and an "underworld." Furthermore, all dwellings face one another in a row, and in the center of the single street is a community plaza. The plaza is a sacred place, and is chosen by the religious leader as a central site around which the rest of the village is built. So, communality is represented in overall village design and in the location of dwellings. But so is individual identity. For example, the chief's dwelling is the largest and its exterior is richly decorated. And, although most other homes are similar to one another, individualized totems and markers in front of dwellings reflect the unique qualities of their occupants. We see again the interplay of identity and communality with respect to location and general exterior.

A similar pattern appears with respect to the exterior of homes. Certain nomadic tribes of Central Asia live in domelike structures called *yurts* that are covered by layers of felt (Faegre, 1979). These self-supporting structures have a woven tension band of felt tied around the top of the dwelling. Some yurt dwellers weave intricate patterns on the band to denote a particular family, thereby reflecting their unique identity. Tribes also decorate their yurts differently from one another. For example, the Kirgiz design includes a brown felt trim that is sewn to the border of a white felt cover, whereas the Uzbek yurt is covered with a black felt roof with white bands. Thus, the exterior facade of the yurt communicates both attachment to the larger community, and individual uniqueness (see Figure 11.2).

Another example comes from the Bedouin nomads of Saudi Arabia and other parts of the Middle East (Dickson, 1969; Faegre, 1979). These people live in tents made of large strips of cloth woven from goat hair or wool. Communality and identity are reflected in several ways on the exterior of the Bedouin tent. Although the number and name of each strip is always the same from group to group, the length of the strip depends upon the importance and status of the individual owner. The strips have designs that are associated with a particular tribe or clan, but they also reflect the unique talents and embellishments of the women who weave the material. In addition, the *qáta*—a curtain that separates women's and men's areas of the tent—contains elaborate woven designs. The front of this curtain extends

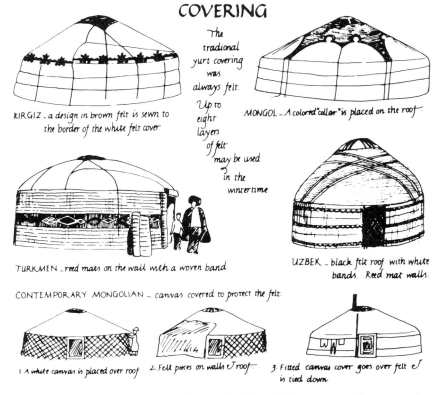

FIGURE 11.2. *Decorative coverings of yurts for different tribal groups. (Illustrations from* TENTS: Architecture of the Nomads *by Torvald Faegre. Copyright © 1979 by Torvald Faegre. Reprinted by permission of Doubleday & Company, Inc.)*

beyond the tent opening and is positioned to face outward for all to see. Its design also has both tribal patterns and the unique ideas of its female weavers. Here again, there is the interplay of both identity and communality in the exterior of dwellings.

One final example comes from the fronts of homes in the old section of Bergen, Norway, a traditional fishing port, where homes are built of wood, are of similar style, and face directly onto narrow streets. It is common for front windows to display attractive white lace curtains, crystal or glassware, statues, flowers, and other decorative items. Home after home has a similar display, perhaps reflecting community norms. However, one also sees considerable individualization of exteriors. Houses are painted different colors, some have ornate trimming around windows, the curtains are made of different fabric and have different designs, and front windows differ in what specific items are displayed.

In summary, the positioning and general exteriors of homes in a variety of cultures reflect simultaneously identity or uniqueness, and the bonding of people with the larger community. However, the examples presented above also suggest that cultures differ in the relative strength of identity or communality in home exteriors. Given the limitations of our data, it will be necessary for future research to describe more precisely the differences among cultures in the relative balance of identify and communality in homes.

Entranceways and Thresholds

Throughout history thresholds and entranceways have had mythological and religious significance. Raglan (1964) noted, for example, that gateways and entranceways to the palaces of the rulers and to religious places often symbolized the boundary between the secular-profane world and the sacred-holy world. In many religious buildings, particularly Renaissance cathedrals, statues of religious figures surround entranceways, whereas gargoyles, the figurative representations of evil, are placed outside the church to symbolize their exclusion from the sacred interior of the church.

According to Raglan (1964), thresholds to homes have also assumed a sacred quality, as if they too were a separation between the "cold cruel world" and the warm protective haven of the home. Even today, many Jews affix a *mezuzah* or paper scroll to the doorway of their homes and, upon entering, a pious Jew will touch the mezuzah in recognition of the sacred and holy quality of the place. Raglan observed that Teutons, Finns, Syrians, Egyptians, Persians, and members of other cultures have held the belief that one must never step on the threshold of a home, but must always step over it. The reasons for such practices are numerous and include beliefs that spirits, souls, fairies, deities, or mysterious beings live under the threshold.

Other people simply believe that it is "bad luck" to step directly on a threshold. Carrying a bride across the threshold to a new home also suggests the symbolic importance of the entranceway to a home.

On the whole there are few religious or cosmological values regarding entranceways or thresholds in the suburban American culture. Of course, the decoration of front doors at Thanksgiving, Halloween, or Christmas may symbolize earlier religious and cosmological values, but many such practices now have a secular and commercial basis. However, the American threshold and entranceway seem to reflect the dialectic interplay of identity/communality. For example, one is apt to find several indicators of uniqueness and identity at the entrance to a suburban home in the form of carefully landscaped pathways, lamp posts, decorative nameplates, elaborate doorknobs, knockers, lighting fixtures, large and elaborate doors, and sometimes a family initial decoratively scrolled on a storm door. At the same time, entranceways and thresholds also reflect community ties of the family with its neighbors and friends. The care with which entranceways are treated symbolizes respect for visitors, who usually enter a home through its most important front door, whereas the family often uses side and rear entrances (Altman, Nelson, & Lett, 1972). Furthermore, the entranceway may be lighted at night, there is often a "welcome" mat at the doorway, and sometimes there are special decorations to symbolize the hospitality of the family toward friends and the community. Thus, the threshold of the American home simultaneously reflects identity and communality.

Thresholds and entrances to homes occur in different configurations across cultures. For example, thresholds in family compounds in India and Mexico extend forward into the public domain and they often have a visible barrier, such as a gate or courtyard door, which sharply separates public and family spaces. Even in parts of the United States and Europe, in congested suburbs and cities, fences, hedges, and gateways are used to extend the threshold and to distinguish clearly the boundaries of the home from the community.

Entranceways to yurts, the dwellings of some Asian nomadic tribes described earlier, clearly depict the identity/communality dialectic. The door, originally made of felt, was often elaborately decorated with detailed appliqué designs, and served as an important status symbol (Faegre, 1979). In more recent times, wooden doors have been used frequently and many are finely carved or are paneled. On the communality side of the dialectic it is considered impolite to step on the threshold or to touch the tent ropes when entering a yurt. This custom emphasizes the importance of the entranceway to the family and reinforces a community belief that the dwelling is a symbolic representation of the universe. As such, the yurt threshold conveys the sanctity of both its inhabitants and of the community as a whole in relation to the universe.

The entranceways of Bedouin tents (Dickson, 1969) reflect communality in their common design and use of space. For example, the men's area is always located on the eastern side of the tent and is separated from the women's area by a qáta (dividing curtain). It is customary for male visitors to approach the tent on the men's side, so as to avoid seeing the women. Identity is shown by the elaborately decorated and individually woven qáta which faces outward for all to see, and by a handmade and uniquely decorated type of camel saddle that the women display in front of their area to show their talents.

The Tlingit Indians of the northwestern American continent place carved totem poles with figures of animals, humans and mythological creatures in the front of their dwellings, often near entranceways (see Figure 11.3). In some cases, the entranceway itself may contain detailed carvings. The figures on totems can represent symbolic and historical events unique to the life of the dwellers, indicating personal identity, and they also often portray events that apply to the clan or larger culture, thereby signifying communality. So, totem poles and entranceways simultaneously depict both aspects of the dialectic.

Finally, homes in Bergen, Norway, exemplify the same point with respect to thresholds and entranceways. Communality is reflected in the fact that most people decorate their entranceways with large carved doors, shiny brass knockers and door handles, stone or wood carvings on the doorframes, and have potted plants and flowers flanking the entranceway and steps leading up to the main door. Identity is evident in the fact that people decorate and arrange their front area displays in rather different ways, with individualized flower arrangements, different types of door panelling and knockers, etc. (see Figure 11.4).

In summary, the entranceways and thresholds of homes in a variety of cultures depict the indentity/communality dialectic, in much the same way as do the location and exterior of homes.

Interior of Homes

Individuality is a pervasive feature of American homes. People seek out spatial arrangements that are distinctive vis à vis their neighbors and that satisfy their individual family needs. Uniqueness is also reflected in the specialization of room functions, with different rooms used for cooking, eating, sleeping, entertaining, and relaxing. In fact, a family's identity is often symbolized by the number and variety of rooms in its home. Furthermore, parents and children usually sleep apart, with parents occupying a larger, more elaborate sleeping room. It is also a practice for American suburbanites to decorate bedrooms in ways that display the sex, interests, and individu-

FIGURE 11.3. *Front facade of North American Tlingit Indian home with carvings of animals, humans, and mythical figures (National Museum of Man, National Museums of Canada).*

FIGURE 11.4. Front facades and doorways of nineteenth century Danish homes with elaborate archways and doors, window decorations, and displays. (Photographs by Irwin Altman.)

FIGURE 11.4 (cont.)

ality of the occupants (Brown, Vinsel, Foss, & Altman, 1978; Rheingold & Cook, 1975). Individuality of family members is also evident in the primary users of certain rooms, for example, a father often has a special room such as a study or workshop that he controls and that he may decorate or personalize (Altman *et al.*, 1972).

The decor and furnishings of American homes also symbolize the desire of occupants to differ from others. Many people organize the interior decor of their home around an ethnic or national theme, such as, Chinese, Danish modern, French Provincial, or American Colonial. Furthermore, considerable time, energy and money is spent in decorating and cleaning the home, so as to present the image of order, friendliness, and uniqueness of the family's home environment.

The other side of the dialectic, communality, is also present in homes both in relation to family members and in respect to outsiders. Not only are there places that distinguish the individuality of family members from one another, but there are also communal areas where members come together as a family unit: for example, the dining room, kitchen, or family room. Sometimes family areas have decorations that display the family as a unit; in the living room or family room one might see photographs of family members and relatives. Such places illustrate the uniqueness of the family to outsiders, but they also portray the bonds of family members with one another.

The interior of the American home also illustrates a family's ties with the community. For example, the role of societal norms is shown in the use of rooms for generally accepted functions. American suburbanites do not usually sleep in kitchens or dining rooms, nor do many people sleep in a single room. Furthermore, while considerable variation in decor is permissible, most middle-class homes have similar furnishings and arrangements. For example, Altman *et al.* (1972) found that the typical American living room not only contained chairs, lamps, and sofas, but it was quite common to have a grouping composed of a sofa, a coffee table, one or more end tables and lamps, all arranged as a central unit. People also use certain places when entertaining outsiders. For example, living rooms and formal dining areas are used for special guests, not only to enable the family to present itself as a unique entity, but also to symbolize the importance of the guest to the family.

Although size, arrangement, decor, and use of homes differ cross-culturally, identity and communality are evident in the interiors of homes of many cultures. In the village of Tarong in the Philippines (Nydegger & Nydegger, 1966), floor plans of homes are similar in the number and orientation of rooms, and even in the placement of bamboo-shuttered corner windows. Furthermore, most households have the same amount and types of furnishings. So, communality is strong. Individual wealth and personal identity, however, are indicated by the quality of interior furnishings and, even though decorations in the main living room are limited, it is very important to a Tarongan that this place be attractive and comfortable, since this is where guests are served. This area of the home is analogous to the American living room and is also a place of individual pride. Walls often have a mirror and photographs of weddings, funerals, and family members. Some homes also display school and baptismal certificates, calendars, political posters, and even magazine photographs of movie stars, politicians, and other famous people. Therefore, along with communality there is evidence of displays of individual identity in the Tarongan home.

In some communities, where homes are quite similar and reflect community norms, there are often subtle details that portray a family's uniqueness. Families in Juxtlahuaca, Mexico (Romney & Romney, 1966) live in similar one-room houses made of adobe. The interiors of some houses, however, are plastered and painted white, with a strip of color painted around the bottom. While this adornment is minor compared to the elaborate decor of American homes, it nevertheless is an expression of family identity and is especially significant since community bonds are so pervasive in home design and in other household practices.

The Japanese hamlet of Taira (Maretzki & Maretzki, 1966) has two types of houses: one is simple and small; the other is larger and more elaborate. However, the basic floor plan of both types is uniform. In spite of such communality, families express individuality by unique decorations of walls. Some families put up paintings or scrolls, others use pictures from magazines and newspapers, and still others have pictures of Japanese royalty or scenic pictures of Japan.

In another context, Dickson (1969) noted how the interior layouts of Bedouin tents are identical. The men's part of the tent, where guests are entertained, is always at the eastern end. Although it is common to have carpets and pillows on the floor, a fireplace in the center, and the man's camel saddle displayed prominently, identity is apparent in the elaborateness of the area and its decor, which reflects a man's wealth. The women's area is at the western end of the tent and is used to store food and cooking utensils. Even though women rarely see visitors and are usually working inside the tent, their decorated saddles are placed in a prominent position so as to be seen by passers-by (see Figure 11.5). So, even in nomadic communities, one sees peoples expressing community bonds and individual uniqueness through the vehicle of the home environment.

A similar pattern occurs among the Tuareg, a nomadic people who dwell in the southern Sahara Desert. Most Tuareg skin tents are similar in color and shape, with low flat roofs to withstand sandstorms (Faegre, 1979). But, inside the tent one finds "another world." Almost every interior surface of the Tuareg tent is decorated. The roof seams are sewn with fringes and bits of

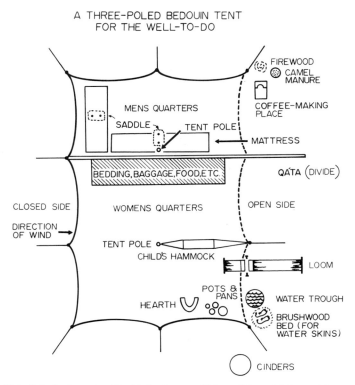

FIGURE 11.5. *Interior layout of the Bedouin tent. (Adapted from Dickson, The tent and its furnishings, 1969.)*

leather that flutter in the wind, giving the roof an appearance of being in constant motion. Wall mats have richly woven patterns; the bed, which is in the middle of the floor space, is carved with detailed designs; cushions are decorated with colorful patterns.

Through its interior adornments, the Tuareg tent epitomizes the blend of individual expression and community bonds. The women of this culture are skilled artisans, and the entire interior of the tent exhibits their work. The fact that all the women work at adorning their tents suggests the community's acknowledgment of the importance of the inside of the tent. Yet, within such displays of communality, one sees the unique skills of individuals presented in tangible form.

For many American families, the living room is as close to being a sacred place as one will find in the home. Although it does not usually have altars, religious objects or shrines, the living room is sacred in a psychological sense and often serves as a symbol of the family's status and values. It is usually centrally located, is readily accessible to the front door of the home, and is a place where guests are entertained. Considerable resources are expended in decorating this room, and it displays the unique tastes and resources of the family. Yet, on the communality side, families usually adhere to norms regarding the use of this setting, and also decorate it within socially acceptable bounds.

In some cultures, similar areas have been set aside to express the sanctity and uniqueness of the home and family. These areas often contain home altars or shrines and often abide by community customs regarding placement and decorations. In Taira, Okinawa (Maretzki & Maretzki, 1966), all houses have ancestral shrines in the second room of the eldest son's home. Shrines have photographs of dead relatives, as well as other personal belongings, such as letters, money, and keepsakes. During religious holidays, red hibiscus flowers, the color of the dead, are placed on the shrine. In homes in Tarong, Philippines (Nydegger & Nydegger, 1966), the shrine is usually located in the bedroom, but it is always at one end of the house and is positioned at right angles to the ridgepole of the dwelling. It may consist of only a candle and a colored lithograph of a favorite saint or the crucifixion, or it may be quite elaborate. In Juxtlahuaca, Mexico (Romney & Romney, 1966), every house has an altar in the main room. It is always raised off the floor and decorated with flowers and an incense container, and often serves as a knick-knack shelf. Objects adorning it vary from house to house, and usually include prints or pictures of saints, candles, gourds, stones, and odds and ends. So, although there are many community norms that affect the placement, decoration, and use of shrines in family homes, there is also considerable variation that reflects personal uniqueness.

This section of the chapter described how a variety of cultures reflect the identity, distinctiveness, and uniqueness of homes, along with communality, bonding, and ties of people to their neighbors, community, and culture. The existence of the communality/identity dialectic is reflected in different facets of dwellings—location, exteriors, entranceways and thresholds, and interiors. In addition, the examples suggest that cultures differ with regard to: (a) the relative importance of communality and identity; and (b) the specific mechanisms for displaying identity and communality.

Accessibility/Inaccessibility Dialectic

As discussed earlier, the global individuality/society dialectic has at least two facets: an identity/communality dialectic and an openness/closedness or accessibility/inaccessibility dialectic. This latter dialectic refers to the process of privacy regulation (Altman, 1975, 1977; Altman & Chemers, 1980a,

1980b). According to Altman, people or groups make themselves differentially accessible to others; on some occasions there are forces toward openness and on other occasions there are forces toward closedness. And, people use a variety of mechanisms to regulate their accessibility to others: verbal, paraverbal, nonverbal. and environmental. We will treat the home as a particular type of privacy regulation mechanism in relation to locations and exteriors, entranceways and thresholds, and interiors.

Locations and Exteriors of Homes

On the one hand, the readily visible front yard of American homes makes accessible part of the American family's life and values, as displayed in their lawn, shrubbery, landscaping, and general exterior. It is a common practice for passers-by and neighbors to look at one another's yards and homes; in so doing they probably often make inferences about a family and its values. In this way the lot and front of the home are public display areas. Yet the home is located toward the middle or rear of the lot, somewhat separate and private from public thoroughfares. Furthermore, there are strong norms not to walk or even enter yards without permission. So, simultaneous with the openness and accessibility of family homes there is an element of separation and inaccessibility. Compare this with parts of Canada and England (Cooper, 1974), where many homes are blocked from view by high shrubbery, trees and fences in the front yard, and where there is often a sharp demarcation between public thoroughfares and private property. Similarly, homes in the Middle East and elsewhere often present a blank wall to public thoroughfares, and information about family life is almost totally inaccessible to passers-by. Thus, the siting, location, and front yard practices of American homes convey a simultaneous blend of openness and closedness.

In many respects the rear area of the American suburban home has been a place for the family to avoid contact with outsiders. Some backyard areas are only large enough to accommodate a small patio or garden; others have full-scale recreational and garden settings with swimming pools, barbecue areas, and vegetable gardens. Regardless of size the rear areas are often treated as the personal domain of the family. The rear area is rarely visible from the public street and it is usually not near the main threshold of the home. Frequently the rear area of a home is physically separated from public view through the use of high fences or hedges that surround the yard. Some suburbs even have houses located on adjacent lots in such a way as to prevent neighbors from seeing into one another's yards. A similar practice occurred in fourteenth-century Moslem communities in West Africa (Prussin, 1974). Building codes required that entranceways to homes on either side of a road could not be directly across from one another, in order to prevent people from seeing into one another's homes. In addition, windows of upper stories had to be positioned so that people would not be able to see into neighboring dwellings.

Accessibility and inaccessibility occur in a variety of forms in other cultures. Among the Nyansongo of Kenya, homestead separation and autonomy are highly valued, and neighbors are treated with suspicion (LeVine & LeVine, 1966). Homes are organized around kinship groups that have their own land and cattle, and are separated from other clusters of homes by boundaries, hedges, and trees. Individual homes within the group are dispersed to ensure separation, but the network of paths in the cluster makes it easy to get from one house to another. However, paths between homestead groups are less accessible. From the yards of each homestead cluster one can see and be seen by passers-by on the main road and one can watch people of another cluster on the opposite hill. Thus, some accessibility exists, while the overall design of the community ensures residential separation.

In Tarong (Nydegger & Nydegger, 1966), a community described previously, neighborhood living groups are connected by footpaths, making homes readily accessible to almost anyone in the community. However, the paths near houses are under the control of residents and passers-by are obliged to greet the houseowner by requesting the right to pass. Thus, there is simultaneous access of homes along with individual ownership and the right to inaccessibility.

As another example, during the hot summer months nomadic Bedouins of the Middle East pitch their tents close together around limited water sources and leave the tents completely open, yielding close contact among neighbors. However, it is also customary to hang up wall curtains for privacy and to keep out wind and sand during stormy weather. An additional privacy mechanism concerns rules about exposure of women to male outsiders. A visitor must approach from the front and always on the men's or eastern side of the tent. Women then have an opportunity to avoid being seen or to adjust their facial veils (Dickson, 1969; Faegre, 1979). Furthermore, when male visitors are served food, supplies are passed by the women over the tent divider without the women being seen (Cole, 1975).

In the small Okinawan hamlet of Taira, houses are so close that neighbors can hold conversations without leaving their homes (Maretzki & Maretzki, 1966). Furthermore, houses are easily accessible from the street and there are no formal rules about trespassing, so that people freely cross each other's property. Yet, some privacy is achieved since homes are often surrounded by trees, hibiscus hedges, and fences. In addition, there are strong norms regarding personal property and stealing is almost unheard of in the community. Even in this extremely open community, mechanisms exist to permit control of access to individuals and to their homes.

Similar mechanisms have also evolved in certain Sea Dayak communities of Indonesia (Patterson & Chiswick, 1980), where many families live in a communal dwelling. In front of family apartments are a covered public gallery and an open deck that extend along the entire length of the long house. These areas are used by everyone, yielding extensive social contacts among residents. Yet, there are compensatory practices whereby people can regulate their dealings with others. For example, whenever possible, relatives occupy adjoining apartments, which permits people to regulate at least part of their daily lives in relation to outsiders. And, kinship ties are somewhat fluid, so people are relatively free to come and go as they choose. In addition, the deck and gallery are used differently during the day and evening. Although readily accessible during the daytime, gallery and deck areas become the territorial domain of apartment residents during the evening hours.

These illustrations portray a variety of ways in which people throughout the world have situated their homes so as to regulate their accessibility and inaccessibility to others. We cannot, on the basis of available information, describe the total range of home location and siting mechanisms used in different cultures, given our dependence on ethnographic material that was often collected for other purposes. Nor can we yet quantify the extent to which different cultures emphasize one or the other pole of the accessibility/inaccessibility dialectic; this remains a task for future research.

Thresholds and Entranceways

As discussed earlier, thresholds and entranceways often have had religious or mythological significance, and sometimes represent the interface of the personal life of a family and the public world of a society. On the one hand, the home represents independence, security, and the rights of the dwellers as individuals, whereas the outside world often involves public control over persons. As such, the entranceway and threshold can be viewed as points of opposition on the individuality/society dialectic, specifically in terms of the accessibility or inaccessibility of people to one another.

In the United States, visitors rarely cross the threshold of a home unless they are invited to do so. There is a strict norm in American suburban society that people "respect one another's privacy" and that entering another's home without permission is a serious violation of cultural norms. Inviting or not inviting entry to a home therefore serves as a clear indicator of the occupants' desire for more or less contact.

The doorway assumes differential importance in other cultures, depending on time of day. In the Colville Lake community of northwestern Canada, inhabited by the Hare Indian tribe (Savishinsky, 1974), house doors are never locked during the day and people freely enter one another's homes without knocking or asking permission. A similar practice occurs in the Javanese culture studied by Geertz (cited in Westin, 1970). However, at night, the doors of Colville Lake houses are locked, curtains are drawn, and the absence of chimney smoke is a signal not to disturb the household.

Similar dynamics occur in several cultures. For example, in the village of Khalapur, India, members of the Rajput caste exhibit a blend of openness and closedness in relation to thresholds, entranceways, and their general living environment (Minturn & Hitchcock, 1966). Men's and women's quarters are physically separated, sometimes by large distances. Men's houses are typically located on a platform, away from pathways, and a roof porch is used for sleeping. Even though the platform can be seen by outsiders, it is a private place that is used primarily by the occupants and their friends and kin.

Among the Rajput, women live in secluded kin groups, in courtyard areas surrounded by walls, with only a single entranceway into the courtyard. Except for the general entranceway there are no windows or openings to individual dwellings that face the outside community. Instead, each woman sleeps and sometimes eats in a small cubicle that opens onto the courtyard. Daily activities take place in the courtyard, so that women are continually observed by others. However, they achieve inaccesibility in their cubicles and in the courtyard by a variety of mechanisms. For example, eating takes place alone, either in a cubicle or in a corner of the courtyard, where it is perfectly acceptable to turn one's back to others while eating. So, the small cubicle represents a place with a boundary or threshold rarely crossed by others.

Another example is from the village of Tarong in the Philippines (Nydegger & Nydegger, 1966). Here, the front porch of the home serves as a focus of daily activity, and it is in constant use by family, neighbors, and visitors. The porch is approximately 5-6 ft off the ground and is reached by a bamboo ladder. In the evening or when no one is home, the ladder is pushed away from the porch, thereby discouraging visitors. Thus, the ladder, a formal entranceway or threshold, provides cues to the community regarding the accessibility of a family to outsiders. A similar practice was exhibited by the Iroquois Indians of the United States, who wrote an extensive political constitution and code of personal behavior (Parker, 1968). One of their laws stated

> Certain signs shall be known to all people of the five nations which shall be noted that the owner or occupant of the house is absent. A stick or pole in a slanting or leaning position shall indicate this and be the sign. Every person not entitled to the house by right of living within upon seeing such a sign shall not enter the house either by day or night, but shall keep as far away as his business shall permit [p. 57].

In Juxtlahuaca, Mexico, a smiliar cue at the entranceway to a house com-

municates family accessibility (Romney & Romney, 1966). In this community, kin groups live together in a compound that consists of dwellings surrounding a common courtyard. Individual homes have small boards or fencelike
partitions for doorways. These are open during the day, but at night or when
the family is away the partition is raised, reflecting the inaccessibility of the
family to outsiders.

As shown these illustrations of thresholds and entranceways depict an
open-closed dialectic process. In the next section we examine ac-
cessibility/inaccessibility in the interior design and use of dwellings.

The Interior of Homes

In a variety of ways the American suburban home involves an interplay of
accessibility and inaccessibility. For example, family members usually have a
primary territory (Altman, 1975), such as a bedroom, over which they have
considerable control. Doors can be closed to avoid contact; people do not
usually intrude into others' spaces without permission; and there are strong
norms about ownership and privacy (Altman et al., 1972).

The home is also used to regulate contacts with outsiders. In an analogy
with the theatre, Goffman (1959) used the idea of "front regions" and "back
regions" in homes. Front regions are like being on stage, where actors present images they wish to convey to an audience. So it is in homes, where
visitors are presented with certain styles of behavior by their hosts and where
guests are restricted to certain parts of the home, such as the living room,
guest bathroom, or the family room. Back regions of the home, such as
bedrooms, are often unavailable to outsiders. These rooms are typically
remote from public places and are often located in the rear or on the upper
level of multistory homes. In bedrooms, people dress and groom in order to
present themselves in accord with some appropriate role. The back region,
hidden from guests, may be a shambles and not at all congruent with the actors' on-stage presentation; clothing and accessories may be strewn all over,
beds unmade, and disorder reigning.

There are examples from several other cultures that illustrate how homes
are organized into front and back regions. Errington (1978) noted that the
front area of the Buginese house was a public place where guests were entertained. The rear door and rear area were used by family members, and the
front and rear areas were separated by a partition of woven cane or rattan
and sometimes even had a sign above the doorway to the rear that essentially stated, "off limits to guests." Gulick (1969) found a similar division in
the homes of a Lebanese village. Here, the rear quarters were separated
from the front by tall cabinets and curtains and, once again, guests were not
permitted access to the back region. And, in Taira, Okinawa (Maretzki &

Maretzki, 1966), the living room was located in the front of the house and could be opened to the outside by sliding panels along the entire front wall. However, even the simplest houses had a thin wall which separated the rear bedroom and kitchen areas from the front area. Finally, Alexander (1969) described homes in Peru as having a systematic gradation of accessibility. Formal guests were either kept at the front door or were permitted entry to the formal parlor, whereas friends were permitted to use the more informal living areas, such as the kitchen.

In the case of American suburbia, the living room is usually accessible to visitors. With its rich decorations and formal qualities the living room is an important display area for adult visitors. For many American families the living room is as close to a sacred, front region as one will find in the home—although it rarely contains religious objects or shrines. The living room is usually located centrally, readily accessible to the front door of the home, and often faces the public street. Congruent with the stereotype of "Suburbia, U.S.A.," the living room sometimes has a large "picture" window that permits the family to have a view and also allows passers-by to glimpse into the best room in the house. As such, this room serves a two-way communication function, perhaps a reflection of both the identity/communality and accessibility/inaccessibility dialectics.

In some cultures, where extended families share a dwelling space and where contact with others is extensive, there are mechanisms that allow for control of social contact. In the Bedouin tent, the men's and women's sides are divided by a decorated curtain, the qáta. The men's section occupies approximately one-fourth to one-third of the eastern end of the tent and all male activities typically occur there. The women work in their section, which is further subdivided among wives, so that a woman controls her area (Cole, 1975). Male guests and older sons sleep in the men's section or outside the tent. Through these practices the accessibility of women to men outside their conjugal unit can be controlled.

Among the Nyansongo of Kenya (LeVine & LeVine, 1966) there are many proverbs indicating the importance of regulation of accessibility/inaccessibility: for example, "He who enters doors will be found with a swollen intestine," and "Homesteads are secret hiding places." In that polygamist community, the homes of co-wives are separated from one another by at least one agricultural field to reduce dissension. Inside the dwellings wives have a secluded area where the wife cooks and where the husband, wife, and small children sleep. The house also has a public area that the husband uses to entertain guests and to store personal possessions. There is a separate entrance to the public room that keeps outsiders away from the wife's area. Thus this culture has an interior design that helps regulate the social accessibility of homestead members to others, especially wives.

Among the Hare Indians, extended families share a house, which has only a single large room (Savishinsky, 1974). There is little opportunity to avoid others, yet there are rules that govern interaction. For example, family members rarely use each others' sleeping areas and the articles used to personalize these areas are never removed by anyone except the owner. Thus, by strict respect for personal territories some control of self-other accessibility is achieved. Similar practices occur in many communal living societies (Altman, 1977).

Savishinsky also described the long-term living arrangements of this community as reflecting an interplay of separation/relation, or openness/closedness. Part of the year, people live in the village, but during a yearly hunting season, small family groups disperse and are isolated from others. Savishinsky noted that people often grew weary and tense with one another's company after being at the village for several months and seemed to long for the solitude of the wilderness. Yet, after being on the winter hunt for a while, people began to look forward to returning to the village and to contacts with others. Both situations apparently became stressful after a while and each was anticipated and sought on a cyclical basis. Thus, a dialectic interplay of accessibility/inaccessibility characterized social relationships. A similar process appears in other cultures, including the Pygmies of Africa (Turnbull, 1968), who live in larger and smaller groups on a periodic basis.

Taken together, the illustrations of home siting and location, exteriors, thresholds, and interiors indicate how the dwelling is used to regulate the openness/closedness of residents. Thus, not only does the home serve as a vehicle for expressing the self as an individual and in relation to the community, but the dwelling serves as an important vehicle for people in cultures around the world to regulate their openness and closedness to others.

Perspectives and Future Directions

The guiding theme of this chapter is that cross-cultural and dialectic perspectives offer a useful approach to understanding homes and dwellings. This section discusses potential benefits and limitations of this approach and then considers directions for future research.

Cross-Cultural and Dialectic Analysis

As noted earlier, a cross-cultural perspective offers an opportunity to increase our understanding of homes. It provides access to a great variety of house forms and living arrangements, and thereby facilitates an appreciation of the range of dimensions of residential living. Furthermore, a comparative approach permits a perspective and detachment that can free one from the biases of one's own culture. A cross-cultural approach to homes also highlights the transactional unity and inseparability of people, places, and environments (Altman & Chemers, 1980a,b; Ittelson, 1980). In addition, it permits an evaluation of the generalizability of hypotheses and theories over a range of settings. Finally, cross-cultural analysis facilitates the generation of new hypotheses that might not be evident from the study of a single culture.

But cross-cultural analysis has its problems and dilemmas. As discussed earlier, establishment of general principles of home design and use requires a theoretical framework that applies to more than one culture (an etic orientation), yet there is some danger of forcing an etic theoretical perspective on another social system. Thus, it is also necessary that a culture be studied from the perspective of its own value system (an emic orientation). As discussed by cross-cultural researchers (Triandis, 1980; Brislin, 1980), one must adopt balanced etic and emic orientations, to minimize their individual limitations and to capitalize on their respective strengths.

There are several specific problems with the approach taken in this chapter. First, our analysis did not include a random or systematic sample of cultures. Instead, we selected cases on a more or less expedient basis, although we attempted to choose diverse cultural groups. Second, we conducted an "armchair" anthropological analysis and relied on written accounts of home design and use. Obviously, a great deal is missed when cultures are not visited first hand. And, it is often the case that the use and design of homes may not have been central to a given ethnographer's interests. As such, we were not able to assess the thoroughness of reports about home designs, or the relevance of material to our theoretical framework. Another problem concerns the difficulty of interpretation of materials. Does a particular home design reflect family social structure, economic values, religious values, or the dialectics discussed in this chapter? Having limited experience with a culture increases the possibility of erroneous interpretations.

Our analysis also involved a dialectic orientation. This approach recognizes the complexity of the homne in relation to culture and the environment, and it also treats the dwelling as part of a unified system of interactive forces. In addition, our approach to dialectics allows for variations among cultures and changes over time within cultures, without the implication of an ideal or universal relationship between variables. Thus, one might trace changes in homes over long periods of time in relation to identity/communality and accessibility/inaccessibility, to see shifting strengths of polar opposites as a culture evolves. Or, it is theoretically possible to compare cultures on the relative strengths of various oppositional processes. So, a dialectic perspective, given its emphasis on complexity, unity, and change, seems well suited to a cross-cultural analysis of homes.

But there are also dangers to a dialectic orientation. First, although the term has been used throughout history, there is no consensus about its meaning and use. One must sift through philosophical writings to select, as we have done, a set of features that applies to a given problem. As such, it is necessary to develop an "operational definition" of the concept. In so doing, however, one necessarily emphasizes certain features of dialectics and ignores other features.

Another issue concerns the selection of dialectic dimensions. How does one know which ones to use? To what extent do selected oppositions have subordinate or overlapping dimensions? Our choice of the individual/society dialectic and its two subordinate dialectics of identity/communality and accessibility/inaccessibility was based on an intuitive analysis of research and theory on homes in relation to social-psychological processes. Thus, one must be alert to the possible use of other dimensions to fully understand homes. Another difficult issue concerns the quantification of dialectic processes. How does one measure empirically the identity or communality of parts of a home? How does one calculate the actual strength of oppositional forces? Although we do not have answers to these theoretical and methodological questions, they need to be addressed in the future if the present strategy is to be useful.

Directions for Future Research

Social-psychological research on homes is sorely lacking, whether one adopts a cross-cultural and dialective perspective or not. Within the orientation of this chapter there are four types of research that can be pursued: descriptive research, diagnostic research, theoretical research, and applied research.

DESCRIPTIVE RESEARCH

While scattered information about homes is available in a variety of fields, data have not been collected in a systematic fashion, nor has research been sensitive to the dialectic dimensions of identity/communality and accessibility/inaccessibility. Descriptive studies are needed to catalog indicators of dialectic processes in homes of different cultures. Methodological techniques are also required to quantify oppositional processes and the relative strength of opposites. By so doing one can "score" aspects of homes within and across cultures on their degree of openness/closedness and identity/communality. What is called for here is extremely complex; yet it is crucial to build a bank of descriptive information about homes.

DIAGNOSTIC STUDIES

Individuals, families, and cultures exhibit many changes over time. Sometimes changes occur developmentally, such as stages of infancy, childhood, adulthood, and later years. Children grow, mature socially, and eventually go off on their own; people move to new environments; family members die; and extended kin groups come to live in a family dwelling. Cultures also undergo changes, sometimes slowly and sometimes suddenly, as in cases of forced resettlement of people by virtue of government policy, or rapid introduction of advanced technology.

Diagnostic questions relevant to social change are numerous. Are there aspects of design and use of homes that differentiate successful and unsuccessful adaptation to new circumstances? Do successful people, families, and cultures adopt particular coping mechanisms, in the form of home design and use, that distinguish them from those who exhibit maladaptive behavior in new settings? In what ways do familial and social changes catalyze upheavals in the identity/communality and accessibility/inaccessibility dialectics that existed prior to the changing circumstances? Do different characteristics of dialectic dimensions in the home contribute to successful or unsuccessful adaptation to new settings?

THEORETICAL RESEARCH

There are several facets of our approach that give rise to basic theoretical questions. For example, how do homes in different cultures vary in the relative strength of polar oppositions on various dialectic dimensions? In what ways do other aspects of a cultural system tie in with home design and use vis à vis these dialectic dimensions? Are there cases of extreme strength of certain oppositional processes and how do these relate to the viability of a family or culture?

An even more fundamental set of questions concerns the relative "amount of variance" accounted for by the proposed dialectics. Are some dialectic oppositions more important than others? Are there other dialectic dimensions that should be used to study homes? Our proposal was exploratory, and it may be that additional or alternative dimensions may be appropriate to an analysis of homes.

Another set of theoretical questions relates to the socialization process. How are children socialized into the use of the identity/communality and accessibility/inaccessibility processes? When does it happen? What form does it take? Is attention given equally to teaching children how to cope with individuality/communality and with accessibility/inaccessibility, or is one or the other dialectic differentially emphasized? Is more emphasis placed on one or the other of these dialectics at different stages of socialization? By tracking the socialization process in terms of these dimensions, we may not only learn about the mechanisms of socialization, but we may gain insight into a culture's view of the importance of various dialectic oppositions at different stages of development.

A related issue for families and cultures pertains to the pattern of response to normal life-cycle changes and to broader cultural changes. To what extent does the adaptive or maladaptive family or culture emphasize adjustments to one or the other dialectic and to various poles of such dialectics? Is there an orderly process of adjustment to life-cycle or cultural changes in terms of these dialectics?

APPLIED RESEARCH

Finally, there are a variety of applied research topics that can be studied from a cross-cultural and dialectic perspective. In what ways should the design of homes in our own and in other cultures be guided by the dialectic processes discussed in this chapter? Specifically, in instances of planned environmental change is it possible to create alternative designs for housing according to these dimensions that will enhance adaptation to new circumstances and ameliorate life crises? Are there educational and training programs that can be developed in connection with environmental design programs to heighten sensitivity to these dialectical processes?

It is fitting that this chaper ends with research questions for the future, rather than with detailed studies and hypotheses. So it is that the approach proposed in this chapter should be viewed as primarily illustrative and heuristic. Our goal was to explore the possibilities and potentialities of a cross-cultural dialectic analysis of homes, and not to demonstrate unequivocally its worthiness.

Acknowledgments

We are indebted to Lynn Liben, Nora Newcombe, and Barbara Rogoff for their comments on earlier versions of this chapter.

References

Adler, M. J. *Dialectic*. New York: Harcourt Brace, 1927.
Adler, M. J. (Ed.), *The great ideas: A syntopicon of great books of the western world*, Vols. I and II, Chicago: Encyclopedia Britannica, 1952.
Alexander, C. *Houses generated by patterns*. Berkeley: Center for Environmental Structure, 1969.

Altman, I. *The environment and social behavior.* Monterey, California: Brooks/Cole, 1975.

Altman, I. Privacy: A conceptual analysis. *Environment and Behavior,* 1976, *8,* 7-29.

Altman, I. Privacy: Culturally universal or culturally specific? *Journal of Social Issues,* 1977, *33,* 66-84.

Altman, I., & Chemers, M. M. Cultural aspects of environment-behavior relationships. In H. C. Triandis & R. W. Brislin (Eds.), *Handbook of cross-cultural psychology, (Volume IV.).* New York: Allyn & Bacon, 1980, pp. 335-393.(a)

Altman, I., & Chemers, M. M. *Culture and environment.* Monterey, California: Brooks/Cole, 1980.(b)

Altman, I., Nelson, P. A., & Lett, E. E. The ecology of home environments. *Catalog of Selected Documents in Psychology.* Washington, D. C.: American Psychological Association, Spring 1972.

Brislin, R. W. Cross-cultural research methods, strategies, problems, applications. In I. Altman, A. Rapoport & J. Wohlwill (Eds.), *Environment and culture. Volume 4, Human Behavior and Environment.* New York: Plenum, 1980, pp. 47-82.

Brown, B., Vinsel, A., Foss, C., & Altman, I. Privacy management styles and prediction of college dropouts. Paper presented at American Psychological Association, Toronto, Canada, 1978.

Cannon, W. B. *Wisdom of the body.* London: Kegan Paul, 1932.

Cooper, C. The house as a symbol of the self. In H. Proshansky, W. H. Ittelson, & L. G. Rivlin (Eds.), *Environmental psychology.* New York: Holt, Rinehart & Winston, 1976, Pp. 435-448.

Cole, D. P. *Nomads of the nomads.* Chicago: Aldine, 1975.

Cranstone, B. A. L. Environmental choice in dwelling and settlement: An ethnographical survey. In P. Ucko, R. Tringham, & G. W. Dimbleby (Eds.), *Man, settlement and urbanism.* London: Duckworth, 1972, Pp. 487-504.

Dickson, H. R. P. The tent and its furnishings. In A. Shiloh (Ed.), *Peoples and cultures of the Middle East.* New York: Random House, 1969, Pp. 136-152.

Errington, S. The Buginese house. Unpublished manuscript. Unviersity of California, Santa Cruz, 1978.

Faegre, T. *Tents: Architecture of the nomads.* New York: Anchor Books, 1979.

Fraser, D. *Village planning in the primitive world.* New York: Braziller, 1968.

Goffman, E. *The presentation of self in everyday life.* New York: Doubleday, 1959.

Gulick, J. The material base of a Lebanese village. In A. Shiloh (Ed.), *Peoples and cultures of the Middle East.* New York: Random House, 1969, Pp. 79-98.

Hayward, D. G. An overview of psychological concepts of home. Paper presented at Environmental Design Research Association, University of Illinois, Urbana-Champaign, Illinois, 1977.(a)

Hayward, D. G. Psychological concepts of home among urban middle class families with young children. Ph.D. dissertation, City University of New York, 1977.(b)

Ittelson, W. H. Knowing and doing in the environment. Paper presented at the Conference on Spatial representation and behavior across the life span: Theory and application. Pennsylvania State University, University Park, Pennsylvania, May, 1980.

LeVine, R. A., & LeVine, B. *Nyansongo: A Gusii community in Kenya.* New York: Wiley, 1966.

Lewin, K. *Principles of topological psychology.* New York: McGraw-Hill, 1936.

Maretzki, W., & Maretzki, H. *Taira: An Okinawan village.* New York: Wiley, 1966.

Minturn, L., & Hitchcock, J. T. *The Rājpūts of Khalapur, India.* New York: Wiley, 1966.

Nydegger, W. F., & Nydegger, C. *Tarong: An Ilocos barrio in the Philippines.* New York: Wiley, 1966.

Parker, A. C. Constitution of the five nations league. In W. N. Fenton (Ed.), *Parker on the Iroquois.* Syracuse: Syracuse University Press, 1968.

Patterson, A. H., & Chiswick, N. R. Privacy and the environment of the Sea Dayaks (Iban): A cross-cultural report. Paper presented to the Environmental Design Research Association (11), Charleston, South Carolina, March, 1980.

Prussin, L. Fulani architectural change. Paper presented at the Conference on Psychosocial Consequences of Sedentarization, Los Angeles, U.C.L.A., 1974.

Raglan, L. *The temple and the house.* London: Routledge & Kegan Paul, 1964.

Rapoport, A. *House form and culture.* Englewood Cliffs, New Jersey: Prentice Hall, 1969. (a)

Rapoport, A. The Pueblo and the hogan: A cross-cultural comparison of two responses to an environment. In P. Oliver (Ed.), *Shelter and society.* London: Barrie and Rockliffe, 1969, Pp. 66-79. (b)

Rheingold, H. L., & Cook, K. V. The contents of boys' and girls' rooms as an index of parents' behavior. *Child Development,* 1975, *46,* 459-464.

Romney, K., & Romney, R. *The Mixtecans of Juxtlahuaca, Mexico.* New York: Wiley, 1966.

Rychlak, J. F. *A philosophy of science for personality theory.* Boston: Houghton Miflin, 1968.

Rychlak, J. F. (Ed.), *Dialectic: Humanistic rationale for behavior and development.* Basel, Switzerland: S. Karger, 1976.

Simmel, G. In K. H. Wolff (Ed.), *The sociology of Georg Simmel.* New York: Free Press, 1950.

Savishinsky, J. S. *The trail of the Hare: Life and stress in an arctic community.* New York: Gordon & Breach, 1974.

Triandis, H. C. (Ed.), *Handbook of cross-cultural psychology. Volumes 1-5.* Boston: Allyn & Bacon, 1980.

Turnbull, C. M. The importance of flux in the hunting societies. In R. B. Lee & I. DeVore (Eds.), *Man the hunter.* Chicago: Aldine, 1968, Pp. 132-137.

Westin, A. *Privacy and freedom.* New York: Atheneum, 1970.

Whiting, J. W. M. Methods and problems in cross-cultural research. In G. Lindzey & E. Aronson (Eds.), *Handbook of social psychology, Volume II.* Reading, Massachusetts: Addison-Wesley, 1968, Pp. 693-728.

Wilhelm, R., & Baynes, C. F. *The I Ching: Book of Changes.* Princeton, New Jersey: Princeton University Press, 1967.

12 Spatial Ability, Environmental Knowledge, and Environmental Use: The Elderly[1]

DAVID A. WALSH
ISELI K. KRAUSS
VICTOR A. REGNIER

Contemporary literature in a number of disciplines has shown an increase in research that examines the use that people make of their environmental space. Psychologists have begun to explore the development of cognitive abilities that are essential for learning and using spatial information. Architects and urban planners have been reporting investigations of the use that people make of urban environments. Many conferences and published volumes have proposed interdisciplinary approaches to work in these areas (cf. Downs & Stea, 1973; Pastalan & Carson, 1970; Windley, Byerts, & Ernst, 1975). This chapter reports the design of an interdisciplinary research project now in progress at the Ethel Percy Andrus Gerontology Center at the University of Southern California and some results that have emerged from the project. This project represents a combination of the research interests of psychologists and urban planners and is designed to explore the variables that influence how elderly adults use their urban neighborhood environments.

Figure 12.1 presents an outline of the major components of the project with directional arrows that symbolize the focal issues that have been explored. The first question concerns the relationship between an individual's knowledge of a neighborhood environment and the degree to which the services and facilities of that environment are used. The second question concerns the relationship between an individual's spatial-cognitive ability and his or her knowledge of the neighborhood. The third is the relationship between

[1] The research reported in this chapter was supported by a National Institute of Mental Health reseach grant (5 RO1 MH 29277) awarded to the authors. Additional support was provided by a Research Career Development Award (5 KO4 Ag 00017) granted to David A. Walsh by the National Institute on Aging.

321

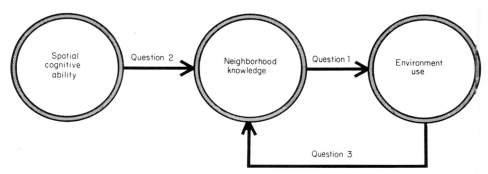

FIGURE 12.1. *The major research components and their hypothesized interrelationships.*

an individual's use or exposure to a neighborhood and knowledge of that neighborhood. To address these issues it was necessary to collect a wealth of information from the same individuals regarding their use and perception of their neighborhood environments, their knowledge of those neighborhoods, and their ability to acquire information about novel environments. The following sections describe the approach to these questions and the results that are emerging from this investigation.

Environmental Use

Neighborhood Selections

Two neighborhoods within the Los Angeles standard metropolitan statistical area were selected for sampling. A concern for the identification of elderly age-concentrated communities led to a procedure that utilized three variables at the census tract level for selection. The 1970 Census tract variables of the percentage of adults 60 years or older (60+); density 60+ (people per acre); and the percentage of 60+ living under the poverty level were each rank ordered. Tracts were assigned scores according to their decile ranking. The highest scores were arithmetically combined to isolate two large census tract clusters of low-income, high-density elderly populations. Figure 12.2 locates these two neighborhoods within the context of Los Angeles County.

The lower-income variable was utilized in the selection procedure in order to identify environments that could be subject to physical design or social service interventions. Thus, the implications of our research relate directly to environments where interventions such as design changes would be justified. The following sections briefly describe some of the attributes of the selected neighborhoods.

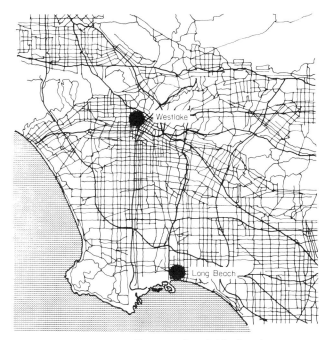

FIGURE 12.2. *Two sample neighborhoods.*

WESTLAKE NEIGHBORHOOD PROFILE

The Westlake district of the City of Los Angeles is located adjacent to the west edge of the downtown area. Westlake was developed around the turn of the century fulfilling the role of a vacation mecca for easterners visiting Southern California for reasons of health and relaxation (McWilliams, 1973). The housing stock reflects this earlier role, having a disproportionately high number of small studio and one-bedroom apartments. Older hotels, many of which have been recycled for retirement living, are distributed throughout the district.

The Westlake neighborhood is an older district built physically close to the original downtown core. It thus has environmental qualities that are substantially different from other neighborhoods. It contains the highest residential density of any area in the City of Los Angeles—along with the highest percentage of deteriorated or substandard housing.

Older people and transients have traditionally been attracted to this district because the smaller size, low-cost housing stock was not attractive to low-income families. Density mapping of the concentrations of persons over 60 verify that this district also has the highest concentration of elderly in the City of Los Angeles. The neighborhood is convenient for older residents as it contains a large urban park with senior citizen activities, numerous lower-cost retail stores, and the highest density of public transit service excepting the downtown.

It is not an area without problems. The recent move of undocumented aliens and Mexican and Oriental immigrants into the area has caused numerous conflicts. Rental levels have increased dramatically as older residents on fixed incomes compete with newcomers for the limited housing opportunities. Crime rates have increased along with traffic accidents as the area has become more congested.

Finally, expansion pressures from downtown retail offices and businesses have stimulated the demolition of older residential buildings and replaced them with high-rise office structures or parking lots. This trend has resulted in the steady erosion of an already limited housing stock. As evidence, the number of residential demolitions has outpaced new construction during the last 15 years. The Westlake district is a neighborhood in transition providing convenience along with problems to its older population.

LONG BEACH NEIGHBORHOOD PROFILE

The Long Beach neighborhood located adjacent to the Pacific Ocean and including the older downtown portions of the City of Long Beach shares a similar developmental profile with the Westlake neighborhood. Developed primarily between the years of 1905-1920, this area contains many wood-frame stucco apartment buildings from this era.

The Long Beach earthquake of 1933 has also influenced the physical profile of the city. Many unreinforced masonry structures were destroyed during this disaster, while older loosely constructed frame structures survived. The recent replacement of public buildings such as the city hall and the Veterans' building has given the downtown a more contemporary image.

The original Long Beach residents were transplanted midwesterners, many of whom came from Iowa. Older grand homes were constructed reminiscent of those left by this group in the Midwest. During the 1930s and 1940s these homes were subdivided into smaller rental units. The social homogeneity of the population combined with the more intimate physical scale of the city has allowed a politically active and responsive relationship to grow between older people and city government.

The selected neighborhood is the central business district of the City of Long Beach and includes census tracts with the highest concentration of low-cost rental housing. Many of the residents of this district have lived in Long Beach most of their lives. The census tracts surrounding the downtown business stores and offices contain the highest density concentrations of population. The older residents of this neighborhood share many of the same amenities and problems as Westlake residents. Social services, health services, public transportation, and convenience to downtown shopping are positive features of the neighborhood. Increases in crime, deteriorated, poor-quality housing and municipal plans for the redevelopment of downtown have reduced the quality of downtown living by discouraging reinvestment and attracting transients.

Neighborhood Specification

The census tract identification procedure isolated two community areas of approximately 4 square miles that were used for sample selection. Each neighborhood was scrutinized by an extensive auto trip through the area, noting major streets, landmarks, and the visual homogeneity of surrounding residential areas. A Lynchian analysis (1960) was conducted of each neighborhood using secondary indicators gleaned from relevant city planning documents in combination with windshield survey notes.

This analysis documented in Figure 12.3 provided a systematic visual inventory of significant landmarks, nodes, districts, edges, and paths. Heavily trafficked streets, tall buildings, major commercial centers, socially or physically homogeneous residential areas, physical barriers, street-grid changes, and important intersections are noted on the maps. This analysis, in combination with census tract statistics, suggested the borders of a smaller 2-square-mile-sampling district located inside the larger areas. It was from these smaller districts that our samples of older respondents were selected.

SAMPLE SELECTION

One hundred and one older people were selected randomly from each neighborhood; the sample universe was painstakingly developed from a building-by-building survey of each block of the sampling district. Research assistants attempted to identify all persons 60+ for each building or residential unit in the sample area from interviews with housing managers and neighbors. This list identified approximately 5000 elderly individuals from each neighborhood by address. Utilizing a random number strategy, 101 respondents were selected from throughout the neighborhood. Table 12.1 contains descriptive demographic data detailing characteristics of the population selected.

Both neighborhoods contain high percentages of low-income respondents who have lived in the neighborhood for a considerable number of years. The Westlake sample has a higher percentage of male respondents. Sample summaries also show Westlake respondents to be lower in average income, health, and age. The range of Long Beach respondents with regard to income and years in the neighborhood was much greater than for Westlake respondents.

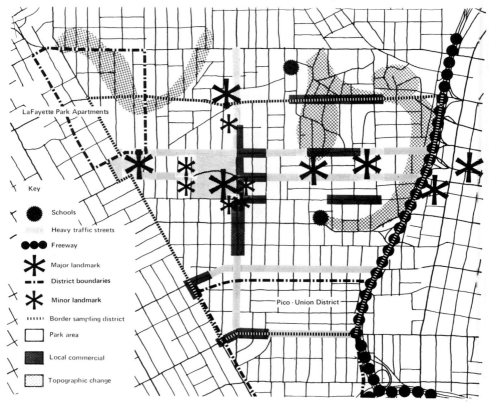

FIGURE 12.3. Westlake and Long Beach Lynchian maps. (Long Beach map appears at top of facing page.)

TABLE 12.1.
Respondent Characteristics

	Westlake	Long Beach
Male	47	37
Female	54	63
Years in neighborhood	17.20	19.37
Income	$250-333[a]	$334-416[b]
Health	10.59[b]	10.65[b]
Age (average)	71.31	73.33

[a] Income shown is for single person living alone; income was approximately 50% higher for family.

[b] The health ratings are a composite score based on self-reported medical history for major physiological systems. The range of scores is from 7-28, with a score of 7 representing perfect health.

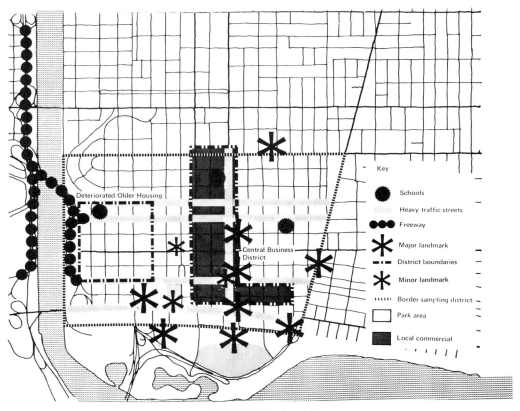

FIGURE 12.3. (cont.)

Environmental Use

Research questions raised in the introductory portions of this manuscript suggest that the use of neighborhoods may have a significant impact on the neighborhood knowledge of older respondents. This portion of the study investigates the activity interface between respondent and neighborhood. Figure 12.4 details the relationships to be tested and data gathered in this portion of the study.

The concept of neighborhood use is operationalized by a combination of four measures: pedestrian paths, behavioral settings, self-reported use of 32 categoric goods and services, and a diary of reported trips outside of the dwelling unit during a monthly period (subsample $n = 60$). Two measures of neighborhood perception were collected. The first portion of the interview schedule asked the respondent to identify his or her *neighborhood* by drawing a line around that area on a scaled map of the community (1 inch equals

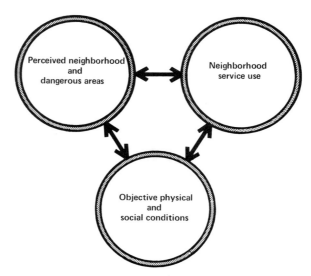

FIGURE 12.4. *Environmental use data set relationships.*

650 feet). The second measure required the subject to outline unsafe or dangerous areas on the base map. Ten social and environmental measures aggregated at the city block level are collected in map form to document their distribution throughout the neighborhood.

The relationships among these variables will help to resolve the following questions:

1. Do neighborhood-outline maps and use patterns from a sample of respondents show avoidance of areas that contain high distributions of negative environmental and social qualities?
2. How do neighborhood areas defined by the respondents relate to goods and services trip-making patterns?
3. Are dangerous and unsafe areas defined by the respondents coterminous with negatively rated social and environmental profiles?

Use Patterns Data Collection and Aggregation

The four profiles of neighborhood use were collected using three techniques: map identification, diary, and self-reported service use. Information on self-reported use of 32 services was collected during an interview. Respondents were asked to identify how often per month they used common retail stores and services; the exact location of the stores and services; and the mode of transit they used to get there. A subsample of 60 respondents was studied further. Specifically, a follow-up diary was collected for a 30-day period containing information about where they traveled outside of their dwelling unit. In addition to frequency, location, and mode data, the diaries detailed the times of trips made during the day; compound trips during a single day; and whether or not the respondent was accompanied by a companion. Cross tabulations of service destination by transit use, distance from residence, and frequency of use describe various dimensions of the use of goods and services.

One index describing the number of destinations visited on a monthly basis was calculated and correlated with knowledge and spatial abilities measures. This index is referred to as the *service-use frequency* for each respondent. Another measure of service use is the length of trip to each destination utilized. Summing the total monthly distance traveled and dividing by the number of trips taken, an average "service radius" was calculated analogous to the concept of "home range [Lewin, 1936]."

Consensus map distribution of all monthly trips is created by placing on a single map the total number of trips made by respondents to service destinations throughout the neighborhood. This consensus service-use map thus shows neighborhood locations with high and low levels of utilization.

Pedestrian path and behavioral setting data were collected from respondents by asking them to locate on the map where these activities took place. Thus, consensus maps identify the most commonly traversed pedestrian paths, as well as places in the neighborhood where older people go "to spend the time of day relaxing or meeting friends."

Neighborhood Cognition Data Analysis

Each respondent was asked to identify "his/her neighborhood" and portions of the surrounding area they consider to be dangerous or unsafe. Calculations of neighborhood size, configuration, and position with regard to the respondent's home, describe basic characteristics of the neighborhood maps. Similar comparisons and aggregations are performed with unsafe areas. In addition to categorizing basic characteristics of the maps, a single-consensus neighborhood map is derived by coding each respondent's neighborhood outline map into a synagraphic computer program. The program calculates consensus by establishing a three dimensional array. Two dimensions of the array define the east–west, north–south dimensions of the neighborhood categorizing the neighborhood into 50 × 60 ft rectangular plots. The third dimension of the array calculates the number of individuals who selected each small plot as a part of his or her neighborhood. The same program is utilized to establish a consensus map of dangerous and unsafe areas.

Social and Environmental Profile Data Analysis

Ten variables were gathered from secondary sources; they define specific social and environmental attributes that are believed to affect the use and cognition of the surrounding neighborhood. The variables include the following: street crime, residential crime, land use, traffic flows, traffic accidents, public transit, topography, fires, density 60+, and density under 18 (18-). Street crime, residential crime, and traffic accidents are aggregated by location specifically for people over the age of 55. Density 60+ population and 18- density are taken from 1970 U.S. Census block statistics.

Each variable is mapped by dividing the variable range into three equal levels and plotting areas of high, medium, and low concentrations. Thus, the residential crime map, for example, is configured to define three levels of victimization. Areas that contain the highest density concentrations are given the darkest shade; the medium-density areas a lighter shade; and the low-density areas no shade. Each map is available for visual comparison with neighborhood-outline maps and use patterns. Thus, configurations, densities, and overall shape provide the dimensions for comparison. A SYMAP consensus map of environmental and social qualities is also constructed, which adds together each separate map combining all values associated with a particular geographic rectangle of the neighborhood. The same grid pattern used for the neighborhood-outline consensus map is also used for this map. The result is a representation that combines the best and worst rated features of the environment to create a consensus map of the most positive and negative areas of the neighborhood.

Analysis and Findings

Data regarding service use in the Westlake neighborhood have now been analyzed for 100 respondents. Westlake sample respondents averaged approximately 1.8 destinations per day. Tables 12.2-12.7 detail selected characteristics of service use for Westlake respondents. The services listed in each table are taken from the listing of 32 possible destinations.

Broadly characterized, over two-thirds of the 32 goods and service trip destinations are accessible by walking. Auto access (as a driver or passenger) and bus access in that order are the next most popular transit modes. Service use outside of the neighborhood is very low. Even though the Westlake neighborhood has excellent public transportation, fewer than 16% of all monthly trips are taken outside of the neighborhood. Community residents are very strongly oriented to the local neighborhood and make most of their shopping trips within the local environment.

Table 12.2 rank orders the eight services utilized by the greatest number of respondents. These eight services account for slightly less than 50% of

TABLE 12.2.
Services Utilized by Greatest Number of Westlake Community Residents

Number of respondents	Destination	Number of monthly trips	Percentage of total trips
88	Supermarket	796.9	14.7
82	Bank	167.1	3.1
79	Pharmacy	201.6	3.7
78	Physician	75.8	1.4
75	Beauty/barber	104.4	1.9
72	Variety store	193.4	3.6
72	Small grocery	941.1	17.3
69	Department store	146.2	2.7
Total		2626.5	48.3[a]

[a] Includes rounding error

monthly trips to all goods and services. Although the number of trips to each individual service are not consistently high, over 68% of our sample respondents patronized these services.

Table 12.3 rank orders the eight service destinations that received the greatest number of trips. These destinations account for slightly more than 70% of all monthly trips. This table repeats the small grocery, pharmacy, supermarket, and variety store destinations reflected in Table 12.2. However, park, liquor store, restaurant, and luncheonette are included in this table.

Tables 12.2 and 12.3 utilize slightly different criteria in suggesting the relative importance of particular services for neighborhood support. Table

TABLE 12.3.
Services Receiving Greatest Number of Average Monthly Visits

Percentage of total trips	Destination	Number of respondents	Number of monthly trips
17.3	Small grocery	72	941.1
14.7	Supermarket	88	796.9
10.9	Restaurant	66	591.1
8.3	Park	53	448.9
8.1	Luncheonette	46	440.8
4.4	Liquor store	26	239.9
3.7	Pharmacy	79	201.6
3.6	Variety store	72	193.4
70.9[a]	Total		3853.7

[a] Includes rounding error

12.4 isolates four services that are utilized by a high percentage of respondents who make a low number of monthly trips. These destinations are most likely to be last in rank orderings of service trips. Over 69% of respondents utilize these services from nearly once to slightly more than twice a month.

Table 12.5 lists four services that are utilized by a low percentage of respondents. These individuals, however, make a high number of monthly trips to these destinations. These stores and services could be considered "life enhancing" because they support a significant amount of activity for a smaller subset of the sample population. These services are visited from once to twice per week by less than 26% of the sample.

Table 12.6 rank orders the seven destinations that attract the highest number of neighborhood-bound trips. At least 80% of the respondents use these services within the target neighborhood. Only one of these destinations (small grocery), however, accounts for a high percentage of total trips. These trip destinations are significant in that they describe services older people are likely to rely on within comfortable walking distance of their residences.

Table 12.7 rank orders service destination for which at least 50% of the

TABLE 12.4.
Services Utilized by High Number of People Making a Low Number of Monthly Trips

Number of respondents	Trips per respondent per month	Destination
69	2.19	Department store
82	2.04	Bank
75	1.39	Beauty/barber
78	.97	Physician

TABLE 12.5.
Services Utilized by Low Number of People Making a High Number of Monthly Trips

Number of respondents	Trips per respondent per month	Destination
26	9.23	Liquor store
13	9.11	Bar
25	4.72	Bakery
20	3.53	Filling station

TABLE 12.6.
Percentage of Sample Utilizing Services Within Boundaries of Sampling District/Neighborhood

Percentage of respondents	Destination
100.0	Bar
100.0	Liquor store
96.2	Small grocery
88.6	Dry cleaners
86.6	Variety store
82.0	Beauty/barber
80.3	Pharmacy

TABLE 12.7.
Percentage of Sample Utilizing Services Outside Boundaries of Sampling District/Neighborhood

Percentage of respondents	Destination
100.0	Department store
80.8	Clothing store
79.4	Church
56.7	Supermarket
54.6	Movies
52.2	Physician

sample travels outside of the neighborhood (as defined in Figure 12.5) to access. In the case of the department store, outside-the-neighborhood trips are necessary because this service is not included within neighborhood boundaries. However, for the remaining services adequate opportunities exist for neighborhood-bound patronization. The supermarket, which is a highly utilized popular destination, is located outside of the target neighborhood for 56% of the sample. These nonneighborhood based services stimulate trips outside of the local familiar neighborhood and might be considered prime candidates for special transportation services.

Consensus Neighborhood Outline Maps

Figure 12.5 displays the consensus configuration of the Westlake neighborhood outline maps. Although each individual's defined neighborhood was unique in size and configuration, this consensus analysis demonstrates that certain portions of the surrounding environment are held in high consensus as "the neighborhood." The highest number of overlapping map configurations are located near the center of the neighborhood. The

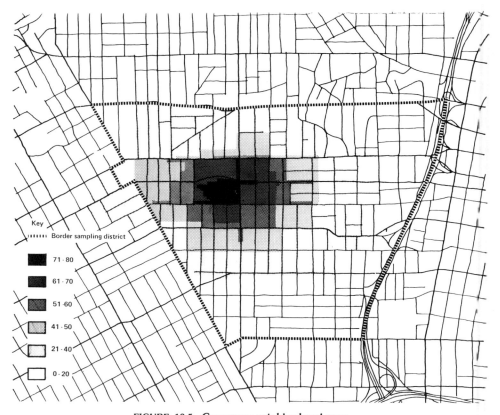

FIGURE 12.5. *Consensus neighborhood map.*

intersection of Wilshire and Alvarado was defined by 80% of the sample to be a part of "their neighborhood." Each level displayed in Figure 12.5 represents decreasing consensus. The zone of highest consensus includes between 71% and 80% respondents. It includes the southern portion of MacArthur Park along with short extensions of the primarily commercial Wilshire, Alvarado, and Seventh Streets. Zone two expands to include the remainder of the park, the commercial center of the neighborhood, and a small portion of the residential neighborhood directly south of the park. Zone three expands east, west, and south, including most of the commercial area along Wilshire, Seventh Street, Sixth Street, and Alvarado. Zone four expands in all cardinal directions to include areas east to Hoover, west to Union, south to Ninth Street, and a small area directly north and east of the park. Zone five continues expansion in a concentric pattern stretching to in-

TABLE 12.8.
Comparison of Neighborhood Consensus Zones with Location of Destinations

Consensus levels	Number of respondents	Percentage of study area	Percentage of total use units
1	71-80	2.71	19.6
2	61-70	6.29	9.9
3	51-60	7.31	5.6
4	41-50	13.82	25.2
5	21-40	29.24	18.2
Neighborhood		40.63	6.2
Map		—	13.5
In city		—	1.8
Total		100.0	100.0

clude residential areas north and south of the park, and commercial areas east and west of the park.

Consensus Map Comparison with Use Patterns

Comparisons of the Westlake service destinations with the consensus configuration of neighborhood maps demonstrate the importance and salience of these neighborhood areas. Table 12.8 relates the consensus levels from Figure 12.5 with the location of service use destinations. Zones one and two of the consensus map account for the destinations of slightly less than 30% of all monthly trips, even though they define only 9.0% of the land area of the neighborhood. A closer examination of levels one through four reveals that slightly more than 60% of total monthly trips to the 32 most popular service destinations are located within 30% of the neighborhood, an area of approximately 60 square blocks. This comparison suggests that consensus neighborhood outline maps provide an accurate indicator of areas that are valued for the retrieval of supportive goods and services necessary for independent living. Furthermore, consensus maps may reveal portions of the neighborhood that are salient to the greatest number of individuals. Further data analysis comparing neighborhood cognition and use configurations with objective characteristics of the environment is planned.

Environmental Knowledge

How well the elderly know the neighborhood may, in part, determine their use of services available in the neighborhood. The converse may also be true in that use of available services may, in part, determine how well the neighborhood is known. A basic premise of the study was that neighborhood knowledge and use are correlated and interdependent. An elderly individual with limited experience in an area may be reluctant to seek out a new shopping area where prices are lower than in a small, local store. Another individual who needs a particular service may become familiar with other services available along the route and may then be more willing to travel that path on other occasions. An individual with a highly organized spatial concept of an area may make better use of the area than someone with a limited geographical concept of the area. Knowledge of the neighborhood and the basic ability to acquire and use new spatial knowledge may also be interdependent. An individual with high-level spatial skills might be better equipped to learn and remember locations of services than would a person with poor spatial skills.

So that these relationships might be tested, two methods of assessing spatial knowledge of neighborhood were selected from among the many possible methods. Hand-drawn maps and relative distance judgments were selected because they provide very different estimates of neighborhood knowledge. Subjects themselves decide what information to include on the hand-drawn maps; the inclusion of information therefore is determined by subjective factors and reflects each individual's knowledge store, assessment of the requirements of the situation, and ability to record information. The distance judgments measure provides precise estimates of relative distances between known landmarks, which could be compared against actual distances.

In a pilot study, respondents had been asked to define "neighborhood." Responses tended to be idealistic rather than descriptive. Picket fences, friendly, supportive neighbors, and other remembered or wished-for features were most frequently mentioned. The concept of "the neighborhood" we used was based on three factors: (a) it should include "home"; (b) it should be familiar; and (c) many critical services should be obtained within its boundaries. Since the concept of neighborhood elicited by the pilot questioning was so different from the researchers' familiar, use-oriented concept, a detailed definition of neighborhood was avoided in the interview portion of the larger study. Instead each individual's "neighborhood" would be inferred from the information recorded on the hand-drawn maps, cartographic maps, and through answers given in the interview.

Hand-Drawn Maps

Hand-drawn maps were collected before neighborhood-use measures so as not to influence unduly the content of these maps. They were instructed to "draw a map of your neighborhood, that is, the area where you live, are familiar with, and know well" and to include "home" on the map. Just as each individual would interpret "map" somewhat differently, we expected "neighborhood" to have a different meaning for each individual. The instructions were minimal, so that the content would reflect each individual's concept of "neighborhood." After finishing the map each subject was asked to indicate north on the map. The maps were drawn on 17½ square-inch paper, which provides an automatic carbon copy on an underlying page. After 2 min, the first carbon was removed and a second one put in its place. Six minutes later the second carbon was replaced by a third. The total time allotted for this map exercise was 14 min.

OVERALL IMPRESSIONS

Compared to maps collected from younger groups the maps of our elderly sample were frequently limited in scope, disorganized, and minimally complex. Factors other than cognitive abilities could account for the poor quality of the maps. Motor difficulties present in many of the samples, poor drawing skills, concern over task requirements, and low motivation to complete the task conceivably could have contributed to the poor quality of many maps. However, as in other areas of cognitive abilities in the elderly, the range of map skills and knowledge represented on the maps was very wide. The enormous variety of maps drawn would seem to indicate that no one's concept of neighborhood was prohibited by the minimal instructions.

Many maps included little more than the street on which the subject's home was located and one or two identifiable structures. Some of the maps were at least as informative as many cartographic maps. A few maps indicated previous structures as well as the buildings that replaced them, providing an interesting time perspective. Personal comments about aspects of the neighborhood and personal activities were frequently included. Some "maps" were little more than verbal descriptions of problems in the neighborhood (crime, litter, etc.) and a few were pictures of what might be seen from an apartment window. Samples of maps are found in Figure 12.6. Approximately half of the subjects finished their maps within the first 8 min and some within 2 min. Others stated that the allotted time was not enough to include everything they would like to have had on their maps.

HAND-DRAWN MAP ANALYSES: EXISTING SCHEMES

Several schemes for the qualitative analysis of hand-drawn maps have been reported and widely cited (Appleyard, 1970, 1976; Ladd, 1970; Moore, 1976). Although these schemes have elicited great interest, their use beyond the study for which they were developed has not been commonplace. Since evaluating the quality of the maps drawn by our

(A)

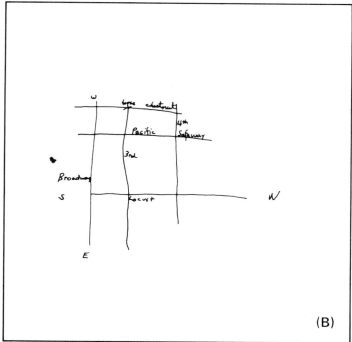

(B)

FIGURE 12.6. *Examples of hand-drawn maps of elderly individuals. (See also maps on facing page.)*

1. Pine Ave as my shopping district
   for dry goods and appliances
2. Pacific Ave as the Local Bus
   route for interchange
3. Long Beach Blvd. and the main
   artery of traffic to Los Angeles
4. From Anaheim to Ocean and
   Long Beach Blvd to Magnolia
   as being a neighborhood
   composed of business, churches,
   residences and City Hall Complex
   housing our main Library
5. Benefitted by two major Supermarkets

6. Having a Downtown Neighborhood
   Center interested in many areas of service
   and aid.

7. A quiet area providing recreation
   facilities and Low Cost housing
   For all ages.

8. An area well furnished with
   easily accessible Public transportation.

9. A well keep area in need of better
   Lighting on some streets

10. A very friendly atmosphere and one of
    co-operation between neighbors

11. An extremely integrated area with
    Little controversy about the racial
    or ethnical background of any resident.

(C)

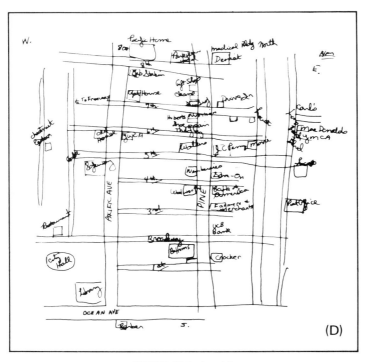

(D)

FIGURE 12.6. *(cont.)*

respondents was a critical part of our research we decided to try some of the available schemes to see if they would be useful in distinguishing among the maps drawn by elderly individuals. Although the scheme developed by Moore (Hart & Moore, 1973; Moore, 1976) was designed for use with children's maps, Ladd's for use with teenagers and Appleyard's with adults, they incorporated elements we expected to find in the maps we had collected.

Ladd's scheme distinguishes among maps that are pictorial, those that are schematic, those resembling a map and those resembling a map with other identifiable landmarks. Moore's scheme, based on Piagetian and Wernerian developmental models, categorizes maps into groups reflecting increasingly higher conceptual levels along four dimensions. The lowest level maps are characterized as undifferentiated concrete egocentric, the second as differentiated and partially coordinated into fixed subgroups, and the highest as operationally coordinated and hierarchically integrated. Appleyard's scheme originally outlined in 1970 and revised in 1976 provided for two successive categorizations of maps. Maps are described as either sequential or spatial and as corresponding to one of four types, ranging from completely fragmented to highly organized within sequential or spatial categories.

In our attempts to apply these schemes to our maps, we encountered several difficulties. Some of the maps were so primitive that they did not appear to fit into the schemes at all. Some were too limited in area to meet the requirements for the most highly organized maps although they were well organized within the limited area represented. The major difficulty with the Moore scheme was that any given map might be categorized at a particular level on one dimension and at another level on a second dimension. We were forced to disregard evidence of high levels of conceptualization in one characteristic if most of a map represented lower levels of conceptualization. Appleyard's scheme was not appropriate for our investigation because it had been developed for populations and geographical areas considerably different from the samples and areas we were studying. Furthermore, his methods of structuring a city may reflect more about the area being described than about the cognitive processes involved in constructing a map representing the area. The areas included in many of our subjects' maps were not extensive enough to allow a determination of the particular method of structuring a city these individuals were employing. Ladd's categories appeared to be the most appropriate for our maps since on intitial inspection there appeared to be an appropriate category for each map. On reflection, the differences between the highest two categories did not distinguish among our most highly structured maps.

Nevertheless, the maps were rated according to the Ladd and the Moore schemes by three raters, each of whom rated 66 or 67 maps for each district according to both schemes. Thus, two raters scored each map. Ratings were analyzed to provide reliability figures for each scheme. Pearson correlations ranged from .46 to .59 for the Ladd ratings and from .43 to .85 for the Moore ratings.

Because of low inter-rater reliabilities and because of the difficulty experienced while attempting to classify the maps according to schemes developed for very different age and geographic groups, another scoring system is under development. Whereas neither the reliability nor the validity of the scheme is yet established, potential components have been identified and can be described.

HAND-DRAWN MAP ANALYSES: PROPOSED SCHEME

The major characteristic of the proposed scheme distinguishing it from previous schemes is that each map may be scored according to several criteria, rather than identifying each map as being representative of *only one* particular category. In devising a new scheme, the first task was to determine what quantitative and qualitative information a "good" map might contain. A priori decisions were made to include such information as size of area represented, amount and type of information, accuracy of the representation, the presence of specific personal information, the presence of general orientation information, and the level of organization of the representation. Scores for each of these variables may be determined, either by simple counts or by ratings. A composite score will be computed to indicate that the separate scores may then be combined so that a single number representing several kinds of information may be obtained. This index may be used to indicate the overall complexity of the map while the component scores may be used individually. Table 12.10 summarizes the proposed components. Each map has been scored for accuracy, extent of area included, amount of informational content including both absolute number of streets and places and the place-to-street ratio. These analyses will be discussed individually.

NEIGHBORHOOD SIZE

The size of the area represented was determined by noting the streets used as the map boundaries and measuring the area represented on cartographic map in square centimeters. In some instances distances were estimated. The average hand-drawn neighborhood size was about 92 acres or approximately 1/7 square mile. Two hand-drawn maps and their extents as outlined on cartographic map may be compared in Figure 12.7. The hand-drawn maps were smaller in the size of the area represented than the areas indicated by the subjects to represent their neighborhoods on the cartographic maps (Krauss, Awad, Ohta, & Regnier, 1978). The sizes of the neighborhoods represented on the two maps were correlated ($r = .36$, $p < .001$) as were size of neighborhood on the hand-drawn map and level of service use ($r = .18$, $p < .01$). Stepwise multiple regressions (Table 12.9) indicated that amount of driving and ease of walking significantly predicted neighborhood size on the hand-drawn maps ($R = .28$, $p < .01$). District, service use, education, health, sex, and age did not add significantly to the predictive value. Men who walk easily were more likely to use neighborhood services ($R = .46$, $p < .01$). The other predictor variables just mentioned did not add significantly to the prediction.

ACCURACY

Accuracy of the hand-drawn maps was rated on a scale of 1 (least accurate) to 10 (more accurate) by two raters. The most accurate maps were

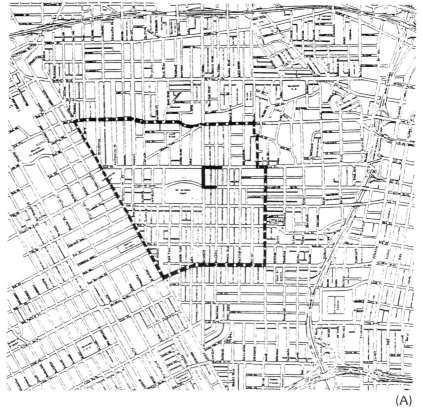

(A)

FIGURE 12.7. *Extent of neighborhoods as represented on three hand-drawn maps. (See also maps on facing page.)*

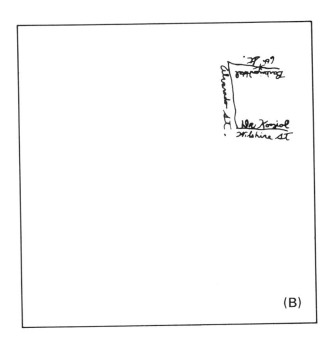

(B)

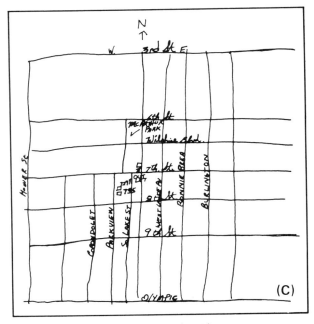

(C)

FIGURE 12.7. *(cont.)*

TABLE 12.9.

Multiple Regression Analysis for Knowledge of the Neighborhood Variables

Dependent variable	Predictors	Multiple R	R square	R square change	F^a	p^b
Size of neighborhood indicated on hand-	Drive	.22	.05	.05	10.12	.01
drawn map (N = 202)	Walk	.28	.08	.03	6.06	.05
Service use (N = 202)	Sex	.32	.10	.10	19.36	.01
	Walk	.40	.16	.06	12.07	.01
	Age	.44	.19	.03	6.61	.05
	HDSQC^c	.46	.21	.02	4.77	.05
Accuracy (N = 202)	Sex	.16	.03	.03	5.13	.05
	Health	.22	.05	.02	5.12	.05
	District	.27	.07	.02	4.82	.05
ALSCAL III	Education	.30	.09	.09	12.37	.01
stress values (N = 126)	Health	.35	.12	.03	3.92	.05

^{a} F when entered

^{b} p is the value of added variable.

^{c} HDSQC is neighborhood size for hand-drawn map.

likely to show several major landmarks and major streets in correct orientation relative to each other. The least accurate maps showed streets that should be parallel as intersecting, streets in incorrect order, landmarks in the wrong section of the neighborhood, and so on. Maps rated as intermediate in accuracy may have had one area fairly correctly depicted but in an incorrect orientation with respect to the other areas, or may have had several inaccuracies in one part of the neighborhood but not in another. The general rule was to judge the degree of accuracy of the information presented without regard to missing information, complexity, or size of map area.

Differences of opinion of three or more rating points were discussed to determine the reason for the discrepancy, and new scores assigned. Misplacement of a major street could lead a rater to orient the map incorrectly, or similarly, a mirror-image map if not detected as such could appear entirely wrong. Correlations between the two sets of ratings were .82 for Westlake and .89 for Long Beach. The ratings were then averaged to arrive at a single accuracy index.

Healthy males living in Long Beach were likely to have the most accurate maps as shown in Table 12.9 (R = .27, p < .05). Levels of education, age, size of neighborhood, driving frequency, and ease of walking did not add significant variance. Very little of the total variance is accounted for (.07); however, we expect that spatial abilities as measured in the laboratory perspective-taking studies will account for substantial additional variance. Those data are not yet available for analysis.

It is not immediately clear why neighborhood size and accuracy of maps are predicted by different variables. Subsequent analyses including ability factors may clarify the relationship between the two indices.

CONTENT

Each map was scored for the number of streets with labels identifying them, streets drawn but without identification labels, and labels indicating the presence of streets even though the streets were not drawn. These three indices were combined to provide a single composite index of the number of streets. The maps were also scored for the number of structures (residential, core service, life-enhancing, other commercial, social service, natural or aesthetic and residual) whether labeled, unlabeled, or represented by labels only. Counts were tallied for the total map and for the successive 2, 6, and 6-min carbons. To determine whether an individual relied more on streets or structures to describe the neighborhood, a ratio score was devised that could be used to compare the three carbons for each individual as well as to compare individual's maps with each other. With the place to street ratio score (PSR) defined as $\dfrac{places}{places\ +\ streets}$, we were able to infer what organizing principles our respondents used in drawing their maps. Some individuals began with an overall street grid in the first 2 min and then filled in the grid with various structures. Others worked from one smaller area including both streets and buildings or landmarks and then moved to other areas. Still others filled in a fairly detailed central area and moved outward in concentric circles as they progressed through the task. For those individuals working for more than 8 minutes the mean ratio (PSR) was .55 and showed an increasing linear trend through the time sequence with successive ratios of .27, .57, and .75 $(F(1, 71) = 110.25, p. < .001)$. We interpret this to mean that in general, most people began their maps with some sort of street grid or pattern and then filled in the pattern with landmarks and a few more streets.

Frequency counts of the streets on the maps indicated that most streets were labeled with an average of 5.65 labeled streets per map but some streets were not labeled ($\bar{X} = 1.14$) and some street.labels appeared with no streets ($\bar{X} = .40$). Frequency counts of places and buildings indicated that core services were most frequently noted with an average of 1.48 labeled service structures and labels with no structures ($\bar{X} = .56$), followed by residences ($\bar{X} = 1.11$), and residential labels ($\bar{X} = 1.08$). The elements least likely to be included were natural or aesthetic landmark elements such as parks, lakes, the ocean, trees, and statues, with an average of .25 such elements per map. This finding leads us to question the importance of natural and aesthetic aspects of the neighborhood for our subject samples. In future analyses we will look at the relationship between the place to street ratio and life experience factors, spatial abilities, and service use.

Maps will also be scored for the presence of personal and general references. Some maps express no more than the individual's daily routine and provide little or no general orientation for the area as a whole whereas others are completely impersonal. Each map will also be scored for the level of organization represented, that is, fragmented, partially organized either in small areas or overall, and fully organized. There will also be a category for maps with no organization such as verbal maps. Once a map has been scored according to each of these categories and dimensions, a multivariate complexity score may be obtained. The more information a map includes, the more highly organized and the larger the area covered, the higher the complexity. To summarize, each map will be scored according to three rated variables (accuracy, personal–general orientation, and level of organization) and three variables based on frequency counts (size of area represented, content units, that is, streets and places, and place to street ratio). The complexity score will reflect size of area, content units, PSR, and level of organization, although other combinations will also be tested.

The score representing the complexity of a map may be used to relate the neighborhood representation to cognitive ability and neighborhood service use information. Of course, any one or any combination of the component scores could be used in a similar fashion, with the result that little or no information is lost. We hope that the multivariate aspects of the scheme will make it an accurate and useful scheme for the analysis of hand-drawn maps of elderly and nonelderly groups. Examples of highly complex and very simple maps are found in Figure 12.6 along with an example of a verbal and a pictorial map.

Relative Distance Judgments

A simple procedure was developed to obtain an estimate of distance judgments, which we felt would reflect the accuracy of the underlying cognitive representation. The respondents inspected 10 photographs of landmarks selected as being generally recognizable in a pilot study and indicated on a scale of 1–5 how familiar they were with each landmark. Then the subjects were presented with plastic discs 3.7 cm in diameter, each of which was numbered and labeled to correspond to the landmark photographs. The task required placing the discs representing the recognized buildings on a large sheet of paper in such a way that the distances among the discs represented the relative distances among the actual neighborhood landmarks. When all the discs were placed, the interviewer noted the placements by marking a point on the underlying paper through a small hole in the center of each disc.

This method offers several advantages over the frequently used paired-comparison method of estimating relative distances. That measurement process may require hundreds of consecutive comparisons over several sessions (Golledge & Spector, 1978) to determine all of the relative distances. Such a procedure would impose an immense burden on our elderly subjects and would add unnecessarily to the amount of time needed for the interviews.

The disc placement data were analyzed by ALSCAL III, a multidimensional scaling program (Takane, Young, & V. de Leeuw, 1977). Based on Euclidian distances, ALSCAL III uses an alternating least squares principle to compare individual subjects' placements to the target placements. The disc placements are rotated and contracted or expanded to a point of best fit with the target matrix. ALSCAL III provides an index of stress for each set of points, which was then used as a dependent variable. The technique, however, does not distinguish between a correct placement and a mirror-image or rotated placement.

Stepwise multiple regression analyses with ALSCAL III stress levels as the dependent variable indicated that higher levels of education and good health were the primary predictors of landmark placement $(R = .35, p < .01)$. Only the data for the 126 subjects with no missing placements were used (see Table 12.9). Factors such as ease of walking, higher service use, amount of driving, sex, years in the neighborhood, income, and age did not contribute significant predictive value (Krauss, Awad, & McCormick, 1978). Perspective-taking abilities, rotation abilities, memory for places, and ability to learn new environments undoubtably contributed to the ability to make accurate relative distance judgments; some of these relationships are discussed in the final section of this chapter.

Although the ALSCAL III technique does not provide for statistical testing of placements between two groups or between obtained and target matrices, a recent advance in scaling methodology (Ramsay, 1977) will allow us to

TABLE 12.10.

Components of Qualitative Hand-Drawn Map Scoring Scheme

Variable	How obtained
Extent of neighborhood	Measured on cartographic map in cm
Total map elements	Tallied
Place to street ratio	Places/places + streets
Level of organization	Rated (0-3)
Accuracy	Rated (1-10)
Personal orientation	Rated (0-3)
General orientation	Rated (0-3)

determine whether two groups differ significantly in their placements or whether the placements of any group differ significantly from actual landmark location. At this point it is safe to say that certain life factors, which differ widely among elderly individuals, do predict how well one is able to locate landmarks relative to each other.

The knowledge of the neighborhood data as analyzed to date may be summarized quite briefly: There is little consistency in the factors found to predict size of the neighborhood represented on the hand-drawn maps, accuracy of the representation, or goodness-of-fit of the landmark placement. Two indices of mobility predicted size of the neighborhood indicating that the greater the ability to move around in and out of the neighborhood, the greater the area included in the map. Very different factors predicted the accuracy of the representation of the neighborhood: Males in good health and living in Long Beach drew the most accurate maps. Good health also contributed to the accuracy of landmark placement, but education was the more powerful predictor. When knowledge of the neighborhood and personal background variables were used to predict the level of service use, sex, walking, age, and size of the neighborhood were the most powerful predictors. Service use was also predicted by the number of landmarks recognized well enough to include in the landmark placement.

In later phases of the project, personal background factors, knowledge of the neighborhood variables, and spatial ability will be used to predict service use. Not until all the data are utilized will the relationship among the segments become clear.

Assessing Spatial Abilities in the Laboratory

One of the earliest concerns in the conceptualization of the project was whether individual differences in spatial cognition that may be associated with aging could account for any of the variance in neighborhood service use. We have operated under the assumption that knowledge of a neighborhood layout would be a mediating factor between cognitive ability and service use. It was hypothesized that high-ability individuals would have greater knowledge and more capacity to utilize that knowledge in navigating the environment than would low-ability individuals. It was recognized from the start that many factors other than cognitive ability alone might account for a large portion of the variance in neighborhood knowledge. For example, the tenure of an individual in a neighborhood might outweigh individual differences in spatial ability as it affects the acquisition of environmental layout information. Furthermore, an individual's knowledge of the neighborhood may have been acquired at an earlier age, one at which the subject had cognitive resources that are no longer available. The loss of these resources might discourage individuals with sound knowledge of the neighborhood from venturing about in that space if they experienced frustrations in utilizing previously acquired knowledge. These concerns led to the development of a series of laboratory tasks designed to assess the ability to acquire and manipulate spatial information about a novel urban environment.

One of the main research questions of interest was the effectiveness of different procedures for acquiring new spatial information. The typical pattern of exposure that most adults experience when encountering a new environment is a surface level view of that environment. Frequently, our first exposure to a new city consists of an auto or walking tour of the space. Through the assistance of Donald Appleyard and his colleagues at the Environmental Simulation Laboratory at the University of California at Berkeley, we simulated a surface-level trip through an imaginary city constructed as an architectural model. The video display simulates an auto trip through the neighborhood. Color video equipment was used in the filming. This 20-min trip through the nine-block urban area serves as one of the two conditions of information exposure now being used in laboratory assessments of spatial ability. Figure 12.8 shows one interior view of the model photographed at the Environmental Simulation Laboratory. A second

FIGURE 12.8. *Surface-level view of the interior of the urban model. (Photographed at the Environmental Simulation Laboratory, University of California at Berkeley.)*

condition allows subjects to view the urban model. Figure 12.9 shows the size and structure of the urban model used. Half of the subjects from each neighborhood participate in each viewing condition. The latter condition allows subjects to spend 2 min and 15 sec viewing the architectural model from each of eight points separated by 45° angles. We are examining the effect of these two viewing conditions on two measures of spatial ability.

The first measure is designed to assess how accurately subjects can place the location of major landmarks (distinctive buildings). After subjects have been exposed to the urban environment through one of the procedures described above, they are presented with a 3-foot-square sheet of paper containing an outline of the model street grid and 10 miniaturized model buildings. The subject's task is to place each building at its correct location. Following this measure we have collected another landmark placement measure that is similar to the disc placement measure described in the earlier section of the chapter on environmental knowledge. Subjects are presented with a large blank sheet of paper and asked to place 10 discs corresponding to the 10 buildings placed earlier. We are collecting this information in order to determine if there is some unique variance associated with placing the discs rather than the model buildings.

FIGURE 12.9. *The urban model and perspective-taking experimental set-ups.*

Our second dependent measure was designed to assess subjects' ability to manipulate spatial information cognitively. The task we have chosen for this purpose is a form of the perspective-taking task developed by Piaget and Inhelder (1956) and modifed by Coie, Costanzo, and Farnill (1973). Figure 12.9 shows the experimental apparatus. The subject is seated in front of the nine-block architectural model. The task is to decide if each of 156 slides is a correct portrayal of the model as viewed from one of the eight positions around the model. In addition to the correct/incorrect decisions, subjects are required to report their confidence in each decision. The whole experimental procedure is under computer control, and the subject's response time for every decision is recorded, in addition to the correctness and confidence of these responses.

The test slides are of five types. One-fifth of all slides are correct views of the model as seen from one of the eight test positions. The remaining slides contain one of four error types: (a) the slides are mirror images of the correct views; (b) they reverse the foreground/background relationships between buildings; (c) they reverse both the foreground/background and left/right relationship between buildings; or (d) they present the view the subject sees from the sitting position (egocentric slides) rather than the view indicated for testing on that trial.

The experimental procedure is quite simple for the subjects. Each trial begins with a warning tone that is the signal to begin looking for one of the eight indicator lamps to light. These lamps are positioned at points around the model separated by 45° angles. At the moment one of the lamps lights, a shutter opens displaying one of the 156 test slides on the projection screen facing the subject and located at the opposite end of the model. The subjects' task is to decide if that slide is a correct view of the model as seen from the indicated position. When a decision is reached, the subject presses one of two telegraph keys indicating the judgment. One of three keys on an adjacent panel is then pressed to indicate the confidence in the prior decision ("very certain," "fairly certain," or "guessing"). Each test slide remains visible for a maximum of 10 sec, but disappears as soon as the subject makes the initial response regarding its correctness. The sequence in which the test positions and test slides are presented is chosen randomly by the computer and every subject receives a unique random order. Thus, the perspective-taking task allows us to assess how accurately and quickly subjects can imagine and identify an urban skyline from various locations.

In addition to the experimental assessments described previously, we have administered some other standardized tests of spatial ability to our subjects during the laboratory data collection phase of our research. The two measures are the figure rotation subtest of the experimental edition of the Adult Mental Abilities Test (Schaie, in preparation), adapted from the

Primary Mental Abilities test (Thurstone & Thurstone, 1949) and an adaption of the Building Memory test published by the Educational Testing Service (ETS). A final spatial measure assesses how accurately subjects can identify the point in an unfamiliar building hallway where an experimenter dropped a pencil during an earlier tour (Acredolo, Pick, & Olsen, 1975).

Findings

Data from 50 subjects have now been collected and examined. The manipulation of viewing conditions has been found to have a statistically significant effect on the accuracy with which subjects can place the distinctive landmarks ($t(48) = 4.82, p < .001$). The data from these 50 subjects show the average centimeters of error in placing the miniaturized buildings is 34.1 cm following the video presentation of the spatial layout as compared with 22.8 cm of error when subjects view the model directly. This difference provides support for the idea proposed by Downs and Stea (1973) that macrospatial cognition is a more difficult mode of cognitive operation than microspatial cognition. Macrospatial cognition involves the storage, retrieval, and integration of spatial information over time, whereas microspatial cognition involves the perception of the interrelation of spatial elements and their relative locations in a single glance. Thus, the finding that subjects are less accurate in placing the location of landmarks following the video condition suggests that the memory and synthesis demands of the task are more difficult for our elderly subjects than the cognitive demands of the model viewing condition. The disc placement measure shows some further support for this finding.

The ALSCAL III index of stress showed that the disc placements of subjects who viewed the surface level video presentation were less consistent with the actual locations of these buildings than were the placements of subjects who viewed the model directly (stress values, .53 and .46, respectively), and this difference was statistically significant ($t(52) = 3.67, p < .001$). These findings are also consistent with the idea that viewing the spatial layout of our imaginary city in a single glance is more effective for acquiring accurate relative distance information than is a surface level exposure that requires the sequential integration of spatial information over time. The intercorrelation between the landmark and disc-placement measures is high and positive ($r = .62, p < .002$) and suggests they measure similar cognitive abilities.

The perspective-taking performance of 50 subjects has also been analyzed at this time. The materials and methodology were developed (*a*) to provide a laboratory task for assessment of the ability of our older samples to manipulate complex spatial information cognitively; and (*b*) to investigate the effects of a variety of experimental variables on life span differences in these cognitive processes. The effects of the viewing condition have also proved important for the perspective-taking measure ($F(1,46) = 5.82, p < .01$). This result is not difficult to understand when one considers the experimental arrangement. The subjects are seated in front of the model during this task and are not allowed to move from their seat position. Subjects who viewed the model from all positions thus have some memory of the model view from each "to-be-tested" perspective. Thus, it is not surprising that subjects who initially viewed the model from each perspective are more accurate in identifying test slides than those who viewed the model from a surface-level vantage point. However, there was no significant interaction between the viewing condition and slide type effects.

The results of the perspective-taking task show that the older subjects tested are least sensitive in detecting the egocentric slide types ($Ag = .52$). (Ag is a nonparametric signal detection measure computed from the error and confidence data: It measures the area under the receiver operating characteristic curve. Perfect error detection would result in an $Ag = 1.0$.) Sensitivity for detecting errors in the recognition slides increases, in order, for the mirror image (left–right reversal) slides, front/back slides and front/back–left/right slides ($Ag = .56, .69, .70$, respectively). The effect of the slide factor is statistically significant ($F(3,138) = 17.6, p < .001$). The reaction time data collected for the perspective-taking task provide some confirmation for the pattern of results found for the error detection data. The longest response times were found for correctly recognizing mirror image slides (5.07 sec). Correctly detecting the left/right–front/back slides and the front/back slides required similar response times (4.12 sec and 4.10 sec, respectively). The primary difference between the response time data and the error detection data is the result for egocentric slides. Whereas the detection sensitivity for these slides was lower than for all other slides, the response time for the correct identifications of this slide type was most rapid (3.34 sec). The effect of slide type on the response time measure was also statistically significant ($F(4,184) = 18.06, p < .001$).

Taken together, the results from the error detection data and response time data show that subjects from our samples are best able to detect errors in front/back relationships and have greater difficulty detecting left/right errors. The results for the egocentric errors are somewhat puzzling. These slides depict what the subject is seeing from his seated position. Yet, detection sensitivity is low for this slide type whereas response times are rapid. This anomaly can be explained as follows: The subjects' task is to minimize response time and maximize accuracy in deciding if the test slide matches the test position. In carrying out this task the subjects must ignore the visual array before them and attend to or "imagine" the unviewed test position. Note that the egocentric slides exactly match the subjects' view. Failure to suppress the information the subject sees from consideration in making the match decision will lead to mistakes in responding to this slide type. On the other hand, if subjects detect the match between the test slide and their view of the model they can immediately eliminate it from further consideration if some other test position has been indicated for that trial. This ad hoc explanation is quite consistent with the rapid response times for correctly eliminating egocentric slides on such trials.

Relationships among Spatial Ability, Environmental Knowledge, and Environmental Use

The previous sections of this chapter have outlined the variables that have been collected in the environmental profile, neighborhood knowledge, and spatial abilities components of our project. This final section outlines some of the correlational analyses concerning the relationships between spatial ability, neighborhood knowledge, and service use.

The first set of correlational analyses examines the relationship between spatial ability and environmental knowledge. As discussed earlier, one of the questions central to the project was whether spatial ability contributed significantly to the knowledge that older adults have of their neighborhood. It was assumed that a host of factors, such as tenure in a neighborhood, availability of transportation, and physical mobility, is likely to contribute importantly to the variance in neighborhood knowledge. However, it was expected that spatial ability would be an important variable in predicting neighborhood knowledge and some of the simple correlational analyses are quite encouraging. Substantial correlations have been found between spatial ability and the accuracy with which subjects can locate major neighborhood landmarks.

For a sample of 31 subjects, performance on standardized paper and pencil tests correlated highly with accuracy of locating neighborhood landmarks ($r = .57$, $p < .001$ with the ETS building memory test, $r = .47$, $p < .001$ with the Figure Rotation Test of the Adult Mental Abilities Test). Some substantial correlations have also been discovered between performance on the experimental tasks designed to assess ability and the measures of the subjects' knowledge of their neighborhood layout. For example, the sensitivity of detecting perspective errors correlates $- .41$ with the accuracy of locating neighborhood landmarks (i.e., the higher the error detection sensitivity, the lower the stress (error) in a subject's landmark placements). The speed with which subjects make perspective decisions also correlates with the landmark-stress index ($r = - .39$, $p < .03$), with the faster subjects showing less error in their placements. Furthermore, the stress measure collected on subjects' ability to place landmarks correctly from our urban model correlated significantly with the accuracy of their hand-drawn maps $(r = -.25, p < .03)$. Thus, the results for 50 of the subjects completing the laboratory ability assessment phase of our research show that even within a narrow age range, sufficient variation in individual spatial ability exists to predict knowledge of neighborhood layout. These varied analyses indicate that spatial ability is indeed related to knowledge of the neighborhood as was predicted at the outset of the study.

A second set of correlational analyses was carried out to examine the relationship between spatial cognitive ability and neighborhood use. Using a sample of 50 subjects, a number of important relationships were uncovered. For example, the performance of subjects in the perspective-taking task (Ag), who had viewed the video presentation, correlated significantly with the service radius index $(r = +.41, p < .03)$. This correlation shows that subjects who were more accurate in perspective taking traveled a longer average distance to retrieve goods and services. We also found a statistically reliable correlation between the accuracy of placing landmarks from our model environment and the total distance subjects traveled per month $(r = -.22, p < .05)$; the more accurate subjects, with lower stress scores, traveled the greater distances. These analyses suggest that cognitive-spatial ability plays a measurable role in determining the neighborhood use level of older adults in an urban environment.

A third set of correlational analyses examined the relationship between neighborhood knowledge and neighborhood use. Although many other analyses remain to be completed, the significant simple correlations that have emerged to date are surprisingly few. Among the largest correlations found is the relationship between the rated accuracy of subjects' hand-drawn maps and the size of their service radius index $(r = .20, p < .08)$. Although this correlation suggests that subjects who draw more accurate maps also travel farther to recover neighborhood goods and services, the correlation is of borderline significance and accounts for only about 4% of the variance. A more promising indicator of the relationship between knowledge and use is the negative correlation between the number of discs representing landmarks the subjects were unable to place and the use of services $(r = -.38, p < .001)$. The more landmarks the subjects were unable to identify, the fewer services they used, indicating that greater knowledge of landmarks in the neighborhood is related to greater use of the available services. The combination of personal background factors such as sex, walking, and age and the knowledge factor of size of the neighborhood represented on the hand-drawn maps predicted service use to an even greater extent $(R = .46, p <$

.05). We are optimistic that knowledge will provide an even more important predictor of neighborhood use when it is considered in similar multivariate predictor analyses planned for the future.

The findings we have reported suggest several implications for service agencies. Planners and architects involved in modifying or creating environments for the elderly should be aware that the more knowledge neighborhood residents have of the area in which they live, the greater their use of that neighborhood is likely to be. Some very basic spatial abilities are also related to the use of services as well as to the knowledge of the neighborhood. Unless measures are taken to inform residents of available services, these services, however useful, may be underutilized. At the same time, the needs of residents with poor spatial abilities must be considered so that appropriate training interventions can be used to maintain their independence in the community by assuring access to needed goods and services. By increasing knowledge of the neighborhood without taxing poor ability to acquire and use spatial information, agencies devoted to serving the elderly will be able to serve their intended functions with enhanced probabilities of success.

This work also advances the urban design theories of planners and architects such as Lynch (1960) who have developed approaches that seek to integrate data regarding the cognition of the environment into city-planning analysis methods. Their major precept is that imageable, legible environments are far more important than stylistic treatment or French Renaissance street patterns in the design of physically pleasing and stimulating urban places. This research brings their concerns a little closer to application by (a) dealing with a subpopulation group who have in some cases limited competence and are therefore more dependent on the clarity of the physical environment; and (b) gathering behavioral data, along with physical design elements, in order to understand better the complex relationship between use, spatial ability, and knowledge of the environment. The clearer specification of these relationships can only enhance the design process.

References

Acredolo, L. P., Pick, H. L., Jr., & Olsen, M. G. Environmental differentiation and familiarity as determinants of children's memory for spatial location. *Developmental Psychology*, 1975, *11*, 495-501.

Appleyard, D. Styles and methods of structuring a city. *Environment and Behavior*, 1970, *2*, 100-118.

Appleyard, D. *Planning a pluralist city*. Cambridge, Massachusetts: MIT Press, 1976.

Cliff, N. Orthogonal rotation to congruence. *Psychometrika*, 1966. *31*, 33-42.

Coie, J. D., Costanzo, P. R., & Farnill, D. Specific transitions in the development of spatial perspective-taking ability. *Developmental Psychology*, 1973, *9*, 167-177.

Downs, R. M., & Stea, D. Cognitive maps and spatial behavior: Process and products. In R. Downs & Stea (Eds.), *Image and environment: Cognitive mapping and spatial behavior*. Chicago: Aldine, 1973.

Golledge, R. G., & Spector, A. N. Comprehending the urban environment: Theory and practice. *Geographical Analysis*, 1978, *10*, 404-426.

Hart, R. A., & Moore, G. T. The development of spatial cognition: A review. In R. M. Downs & D. Stea, (Eds.), *Image and Environment: Cognitive mapping of spatial behavior*. Chicago: Aldine, 1973.

Krauss, I. K., Awad, Z. A., & McCormick, D. J. Accuracy of landmark relative distance judgements in two elderly groups. Paper presented at the annual meeting of the Gerontological Society, Dallas, 1978.

Krauss, I. K., Awad, Z. A., Ohta, R. J., & Regnier V. A. Neighborhood imagery and service use among the urban elderly. Paper presented at the annual meeting of the American Psychological Association, Toronto, 1978.

Ladd, F. C. Black youths view their environment: Neighborhood maps. *Environmental Behavior*, 1970, *2*, 64-79.

Lewin, K. *Principles of topological psychology*. New York: McGraw-Hill, 1936.

Lynch, K. *The image of the city*, Cambridge, Massachusetts: MIT Press, 1960.

Moore, G. T. Theory of research and the development of environmental knowing. In G. T. Moore and R. Colledge (Eds.), *Environment knowing: Theories, research, and methods*. Stroudsburg, Pennsylvania: Dowden, Hutchinson & Ross, 1976.

McWilliams, C. *Southern California: An island on the land*. Santa Barbara: Pepperdine-Smith, 1973.

Pastalan, L. A., & Carson, D. H. *Spatial behavior of older people*. Ann Arbor: The University of Michigan Press, 1970.

Piaget, J., & Inhelder, B. *The child's conception of space*. London: Routledge & Kegan Paul, 1956.

Ramsay, J. O. Maximum likelihood estimation in multidimensional scaling. *Psychometrika*, 1977, *42*, 241-266.

Takane, Y. Young, F. W., & de Leeuw, J. Nonmetric individual differences multidimensional scaling: An alternating least squares method with optimal scaling features. *Psychometrika*, 1977, *42*, 7-67.

Thurstone, L. L., & Thurstone, T. G. SRA *Primary Mental Abilities Test*. Science Research Associates, Chicago, 1949.

Windley, P. G., Byerts, T. O., & Ernst, F. G. *Theory development in environment and aging*. Washington, D.C.: The Gerontological Society, 1975.

Commentary on Part IV

13 Spatial Representation and the Environment: Some Applied and Not Very Applied Implications

ARTHUR H. PATTERSON

The marked diversity of the chapters discussed here prevents considering them with regard to any single overriding point. The individual chapters approach representation from both applied and theoretical perspectives, and thus have implications for both applied researchers concerned with environmental design, and theoretical researchers concerned with spatial representation. This applied and theoretical distinction in the use of space is similar to the dual use of representation offered by Piaget (1951). He viewed representation used in the sense of knowledge (cognitive representations) as "conceptual representation," and representation used in the sense of symbolizing absent realities (re-presentation) as "symbolic representation."

For example, Chapter 12 of this volume by Walsh, Krauss, and Regnier deals with the external event of re-presentation (the drawing of maps) in an effort to elicit design implications. In order to interpret those maps, however, Walsh *et al.* find it necessary to consider the internal, or conceptual representation process. Wapner, Kaplan, and Ciottone, on the other hand, begin Chapter 10 with conceptual representation (for them, representation of the meaning of the environment), but then turn to symbolic representations (e.g., drawings) to show how the conceptual representation affects the use of space. Finally, in Chapter 11, Altman and Gauvain analyze extant environmental behavior, which has implications for both conceptual and symbolic representation.

It is apparent that these chapters transcend any simple applied–theoretical dichotomy. Rather, they raise issues that range well toward both ends of an applied–theoretical continuum. Furthermore, all three chapters move past the traditional approach to cognition of objects (the environment) as distinct from observers, and appear to embrace Ittelson's (1973) definition of en-

361

vironmental cognition, where the person is an interactive part of the environment.

Nowhere is this more clear than in Altman and Gauvain's chapter, which explores the dialectic interplay of society and the individual as reflected in the home. This chapter differs from the others in this section (and from the others in this volume) in that first the environment is analyzed, and then cognitive and affective states are subsequently inferred from that environment. That is, the arrangement of the home (environment) is viewed as representing those cognitive/affective states.

Thus, for example, according to Altman and Gauvain, the landscaping of the front yard can be used for achieving individuality. But the residents who landscape in order to show individuality must be basing their behavior on some cognitive representation of what spatial arrangement (environment) indicates individuality; they may even rely on some symbolic representation (in the sense of symbolizing some absent reality) as they try to produce that spatial arrangement. This may be even more apparent in the case of *selecting* a home. Cooper-Marcus (1974) suggests that people frequently select a house as a basic symbol of "self." This would clearly require some cognitive representation of what environment best symbolizes the self.

Scale

Another interesting variable reflected across these three chapters concerns the scale of the environment (either represented or, in this case, analyzed). If we consider a continuum of scale from small, such as a table, to large, such as the universe, it is apparent that research on spatial representation, including the chapters in this volume, tend to cluster at the small end. However, even at this end of the continuum, there are interesting differences in the relative size of the environments considered. The scale of the Altman and Gauvain chapter is relatively small (a home), and is at times quite small, such as when discussing a portal.

Walsh *et al.* deal with the relatively large scale of neighborhoods, with streets and buildings conceptualized and re-presented. Wapner *et al.* deal with environmental transitions, which can range from as large a scale as changing cities (or countries) to as small a scale as a new room (in a house or school). In fact, scale can even cease to be meaningful in the Wapner *et al.* chapter, as in their example of a psychotic episode that disrupt one's relationship with the environment.

The relationship of scale to spatial representation and behavior raises several interesting empirical questions. For example, are large and small scale environments conceptualized and re-presented in the same ways (as with a city as opposed to a room)? Similarly, as scale clearly affects behavior (one uses and moves about a room differently than one uses and moves about the world), does it also affect the relationship of use and representation? Or, perhaps most important, what is the meaning of scale to the individual? More research in which scale is manipulated is clearly needed.

Environmental Meaning

Turning more directly to the chapter by Wapner *et al.*, there is an interesting point of overlap with the Altman and Gauvain chapter in their treatment of the meaning of the environment to the observer-user. In discussing the dialectic dimensions of the environment, Altman and Gauvain refer to the psychological meaning of the home. Wapner *et al.* similarly are concerned with the meaning of the environment, although from a far different perspective. In what they term their "genetic-dramatist" approach, Wapner *et al.* consider the environment's emotional meaning to the observer. It is this consideration of meaning in representation (e.g., the environment as agent, act, scene, etc.) that the authors apply to the use of space, here specifically in critical environmental transitions.

Wapner *et al.* discuss the nature of space, a topic largely left untouched in the other chapters. This is valuable, for throughout the spatial representation literature one finds "space" largely undefined (see Liben, Chapter 1 this volume). Thus, space is a building in some chapters, the area between buildings in other chapters, and the relative orientation of objects in yet others. Although there is a commonly accepted architectural definition of space as that which is enclosed by design, Wapner *et al.* present a stimulating approach for spatial representation research in that space is not bounded by any physical constraints.

Instrumentality of Space

Recognizing the typical use of space as a scene for action (perhaps more typically called a "setting"), Wapner *et al.* also present space as an agency or instrumentality. The example they use of the Hunchback of Notre Dame's seeking refuge in a church may remind one of Altman and Gauvain's presentation of the dialectic opposition of accessibility/inaccessibility. That is, Altman and Gauvain are concerned with environmental (spatial?) arrangements, which convey that a home is accessible or not. Wapner *et al.* are here concerned with a space (environment?) serving to provide refuge through conveying inaccessibility to the Hunchback's pursuers. Perhaps most simply, it is possible to state that Altman and Gauvain's emphasis is on the environment, and subsequently the environment's social-psychological meaning to the user, whereas Wapner *et al.* emphasize the meaning of the environment (e.g., space) to the user, and subsequently how that meaning affects the use of the environment.

In an allied work Altman (1975) presented a theory of privacy that can illustrate how spatial arrangement can be used to convey meaning, which then affects other's use of the environment. Altman viewed privacy as selective control of access to one's self. Among other mechanisms, he offered personal space and territoriality as means of increasing or decreasing one's achieved level of privacy. Thus, if a person desires more (or less) privacy than he or she has achieved, that person may increase (or decrease) his or her personal space "bubble" or territorial range. The use of personal space or territoriality serves as a self-other boundary control mechanism, which conveys to others how much social interaction is desired. Space, or spatial arrangements in the case of territoriality, are thus imbued with meaning, which affects the behavior of those in that environment.

Age Related Issues

Although many developmental approaches to understanding spatial representation and behavior (this volume included) emphasize studies of children, Wapner *et al.* use examples from childhood to old age. Although this life-span approach by definition has ontogenetic value, it is particularly useful here, for it allows some comparison with the Walsh *et al.* chapter, which exclusively considers spatial representation and behavior of the elderly.

Wapner *et al.* present in Chapter 10 an example of elderly people undergoing forced relocation to an "old-age home." The authors note that the generally negative effects of this environmental transition were somewhat ameliorated by the bringing of personal objects (such as chairs and pictures) to the new scene. These objects were interpreted as providing "bridges" between the old and new scenes, which resulted in better adaptation to the new scene. The relatively small size of these objects (easily transportable personal items) again points to the importance of exploring the role of scale in spatial representation and behavior. Also, their use ties into other studies of environmental change in the elderly.

Hunt and Pastalan[1] have conducted a series of studies of the effect of forced relocation to nursing homes among the elderly, with an emphasis on

---

[1] This work is part of an as yet unpublished series of studies by Michael Hunt and Leon Pastalan at the Institute of Gerontology of the University of Michigan.

365

the beneficial effects of preexposure to the new environment. Initially, elderly were taken for "get acquainted" visits to the home. However, the cost and physical limitations (often the poor health of the older person—the reason for the relocation in the first place) led them to investigate the use of models to simulate a visit to the home. Preliminary work has indicated a significant reduction in the negative effects of forced relocation, perhaps by the forming of a sort of bridge (after Wapner *et al.*) from the old to new environment.

Perceived Environmental Control

The bringing of personal objects into the new environment may not simply be a matter of easing the transition by connecting the old and new settings. Bringing the objects could possibly be perceived as indicating some environmental control in that setting. Recent studies of environmental control in the elderly (e.g., Langer & Rodin, 1976; Schulz, 1976) have found increased health and morale among those elderly people who perceived themselves as having some degree of control over their environment. For example, a study of territorial behavior in elderly homeowners found less fear of crime in those who were territorial than those who were not (Patterson, 1978). Here "territorial behavior" was the active manipulation of the environment so as to mark the home as being under the territorial influence of the resident, combined with attitudinal expressions of territoriality. The results were interpreted as indicating that it was perceived control of the environment that mediated fear of crime. Thus, the relationship of perceived control to spatial representation and behavior becomes salient, especially among the elderly where there is an apparent loss of some control with aging. Interestingly, the Wapner *et al.* chapter notes that although a person functioning at the highest level of development *uses* space, and is not used *by* it, inner and outer circumstances often lead to "regressions" to lower levels of functioning.

Consideration of the Walsh *et al.* chapter may begin with noting that this chapter differs from the other two in that it does not deal with change. The Wapner *et al.* chapter is concerned with environmental transitions (among the elderly and nonelderly), and the Altman and Gauvain chapter deals with the dynamic nature of the relationship among opposites to consider change over time and with circumstances, while the Walsh *et al.* chapter examines representation and use in the existing neighborhood of the elderly.

There is an irony here, for the very dialectic interplay of forces for people to be linked with society and, at the same time, to be separate from society discussed by Altman and Gauvain contribute to the nature of the environments considered by Wapner *et al.* and Walsh *et al.* That is, there exists a life-span developmental process by which children are brought into the society, and by which elderly are disengaged (or parted from) the society. Perhaps the salient point is that there are strong age-related environmental roles, and that these may be reflected in spatial representation and behavior.

Problems of Application

Walsh *et al.* take an explicitly interdisciplinary approach to an applied problem: Their study is designed to provide information that can be used for environmental interventions. As of yet, however, the question as to how to derive those interventions from a mapping task has not been sufficiently answered. But, by focusing on neighborhood *use* in the representation task, the authors appear to be moving in the appropriate direction. There is a distinction in the use of representation, analogous to that of Piaget (1951) presented above, which may be of use here. Kaplan (1973) views mental representations as helping people search for and comprehend environmental information critical to location and orientation decisions, whereas Kosslyn (1975) views mental representations as maintaining some approximate isomorphic correspondence to the actual physical structure of the information in the environment.

The applied, yet exploratory nature, of the Walsh *et al.* chapter requires the authors to deal with both of these meanings of representation simultaneously. Thus, the elderly are asked to represent their environment (neighborhood), and the resulting maps are studied for their correspondence to the neighborhood (Kosslyn's use of representation), while parts of the mapping process are used simultaneously to infer behavior based on location and orientation decisions (Kaplan's use of representation). The route to environmental interventions based upon spatial representation research is thus not a direct one. (As an aside, this use of "route" and "direction" to a cognitive goal is discussed by Wapner *et al.*)

An interesting finding of this chapter is that neighborhood use, as measured through self-report of service use and trips, is correlated with the neighborhood map. Similarly, neighborhood use is correlated with spatial ability (as measured in a laboratory task), and spatial ability is correlated with the orientation of neighborhood landmarks. However, the correlational nature of the data leaves the questions: What is the causal direction? Does use of the neighborhood lead to improved maps of the neighborhood? Does spatial ability lead to improved maps of the neighborhood (orientation of landmarks, in this case)? Does spatial ability lead to increased use? Or, do better maps lead to increased use; do better maps lead to better spatial ability; and does increased use lead to better spatial ability?

Obviously, there are interdependent and reciprocal relationships here. Walsh et al. note this interdependence, but are not able to empirically ascertain the nature of the relationship. There is a suggestion to the causal direction in the belief of Piaget and Inhelder (1956) that activity in space is necessary for spatial representation. This would indicate that neighborhood use must precede the neighborhood map (with the obvious exception of the case where one consulted other maps before entering into the neighborhood). Thus we are at an initial stage, and the subsequent causal relationship of use and map (and spatial ability) remains unexplicated. This appears particularly important where environmental intervention can occur at the level of modifying neighborhood use, providing spatial information, training spatial ability, or actually changing the environment. The particular costs and benefits associated with these strategies would certainly be affected by the precise nature of the above relationships.

Application to the Elderly

Walsh et al. employ laboratory tests of spatial ability in an effort to understand the mapping and neighborhood use of their elderly respondents better. However, a review of spatial abilities of the elderly by Evans (1980) presents evidence that elderly are less proficient in orientation processing than are young adults. The elderly were less accurate on perspective-taking tasks (such as the Piagetian three mountain problem), and had higher error rates and slower reaction times on spatial memory tasks. This would appear to indicate that there may be aspects of mapping that are specific to elderly, and not typical of spatial representation in younger adults or children. For example, would the spatial abilities of the elderly require different cues than necessary for younger adults for the eliciting of spatial behavior? Similarly, are the familiar aging related sensory losses important to spatial representation and behavior? These questions, and others of this type, would bear on any environmental interventions based upon this type of research.

Comparison to nonelderly would also be valuable with regard to spatial behavior. The data by Walsh et al. in Chapter 12 on service use (e.g., 1.6 service trips a day) could be potentially more informative if placed in context with the nonelderly. In the case of service trips, one would have a tendency to predict that they would be important in value and frequency to the elderly. But there would certainly be other spatial behaviors which might have counterintuitive implications. An example of this would be recreation behavior. In a study of fear of crime and recreation behavior in urban elderly, Godbey, Patterson, and Brown (1979) predicted that fear of crime would adversely affect use of public recreation services. However, the data revealed that those elderly who partook of public recreation services had a significantly higher fear of being victimized than those who remained at home. Although plausible hypotheses for this outcome abound (e.g., increased exposure to potential victimization), the fact remains that it was those elderly with a fearful cognitive representation of the environment who were venturing about in it.

In a similar vein, Walsh *et al.* found that the elderly were most likely to place core services on their maps, and least likely to include natural elements, such as trees, lakes, and parks. Would this be the result of some spatial representation process unique to the elderly, as compared to, for example, children. As with the above questions, there is a need here for empirical inquiry.

It is worth considering, however, whether this finding might be an artifact resulting from the study's emphasis on the use of services. Supporting this would be the strong "consensus maps," which contained the areas where services were obtained. Lawton (1977) states that services to the elderly are the most salient single aspect of the older person's environment aside from his or her home; he labels this the "resource environment." He considers the resource environment to be the "social space" of an older person and has extensively reviewed the studies that have investigated this area. Lawton concludes that (among other factors) the proximity and salience of the resource to the older user mediates use of that resource.

Given this emphasis on proximity and salience, Chapter 12 by Walsh *et al.* appears to raise stimulating questions with regard to the functional significance of the spatial representation of the elderly. If services are very important to the elderly, and use of those services is mediated by proximity and salience, the way in which those services (or at least their locations) are conceptually represented clearly plays a role in that mediating process. Knowledge of this relationship could be used as an intervention point for applied work such as facilitating use of services by the elderly.

Conclusion

Although varying in their theoretical and applied intents, all three chapters have offered valuable contributions in both areas. Just as important, the chapters raised questions with regard to spatial representation and behavior, which, when answered, will have implications for both theoretical and applied work.

References

Altman, I. *The environment and social behavior.* Monterey: Brooks/Cole, 1975.

Cooper-Marcus, C. The house as a symbol of self. In V. Lang *et al.* (Eds.), *Designing for human behavior.* Stroudsburg: Dowden, Hutchinson, and Ross, 1974.

Evans, G. W. Environmental Cognition. *Psychological Bulletin.* 1980, *88*, 259-287.

Godbey, G., Patterson, A. H. & Brown, L. The Relationship of crime and fear of crime among the aged to leisure behavior and use of public leisure services. Washington: The Andrus Foundation, 1979.

Ittelson, W. H. Environmental perception and contemporary perceptual theory. In W. Ittelson (Ed.), *Environment and cognition.* New York: Seminar Press, 1973.

Kaplan, S. Cognitive maps in perception and thought. In R. Downs and D. Stea (Eds.), *Image and environment.* Chicago: Aldine, 1973.

Kosslyn, S. M. Information representation in visual images. *Cognitive Psychology*, 1975, *7*, 341-370.

Langer, E., & Rodin, J. The effects of choice and enhanced personal responsibility setting. *Journal of Personality and Social Psychology*, 1976, *34*, 191-198.

Lawton, M. P. The impact of the environment on aging and behavior. In J. Birren & K. W. Schaie (Eds.), *Handbook of the Psychology of Aging.* New York: Van Nostrand Reinhold & Company, 1977.

McGee, M. G. Human spatial abilities: Psychometric studies and environmental, genetic, hormonal, and neurological influences. *Psychological Bulletin*, 1979, *86*, 889-918.

Patterson, A. H. Territorial behavior and fear of crime in the elderly. *Environmental Psychology and Nonverbal Behavior*, 1978, *2*, 3, 131-144.

Piaget, J. *Play, dreams and imitation in childhood.* New York: Norton, 1951.

Piaget, J., & Inhelder, B. *The child's conception of space.* London: Routledge & Regan Paul, 1956.

Schultz, R. Effects of control and predictability on the physical and psychological well-being of the institutionalized aged. *Journal of Personality and Social Psychology*, 1976, *33*, 5, 563-573.

Conclusions

14 Spatial Representation and Behavior: Retrospect and Prospect

NORA NEWCOMBE

Spatial representation and behavior have been studied for a wide variety of reasons and from many different disciplinary perspectives, including those of philosophy, psychology, anthropology, geography, architecture, and urban planning. The chapters in this volume represent only some of these disciplines, but even so, the range of problems, populations and methodologies is great. It is therefore somewhat surprising to find that several themes emerge as important issues touched on in one way or other throughout the book. In this concluding chapter, I will attempt to present four issues, which seem to me to run through the chapters, and to discuss briefly how these bear on the agenda for future research.

Spatial Representations and Spatial Behavior

Beginning with Liben's introduction (Chapter 1), the question of the relationship between spatial representations and spatial behavior appears repeatedly in this volume. How can spatial behaviors be used to make inferences about spatial representations? Conversely, how do spatial representations influence spatial behavior? And, indeed, is there a valid distinction to be made between behavior and representation?

The representation/behavior terminology is a variety of the competence/performance distinction made in psycholinguistics (Chomsky, 1965) and is plagued with the same difficulties linguists and psycholinguists have found in using this seemingly clear concept (e.g., Greene, 1972). For those using this distinction, any particular spatial performance or behavior, whether locomotion and way-finding or map-drawing and model-building, is

373

SPATIAL REPRESENTATION AND BEHAVIOR
ACROSS THE LIFE SPAN

assumed to be related to an underlying spatial competence. Part of this competence is what is often termed a spatial representation, or a cognitive map. The observed behavior cannot, however, be a simple revelation of spatial competence; it is also affected by various performance factors, such as the memory load of a particular task, understanding of what is asked, or motivation to perform well. Making inferences about the nature of spatial representations, given this view, requires a complex process of analysis of the various spatial behaviors thought to provide evidence about the nature of the representations, so that due allowance can be made for the performance factors associated with each particular task.

Various opinions of how such an analysis is properly done exist. In the introductory chapter of this volume, Liben reminds us of one viewpoint in discussing the traditional Piagetian distinction between sensorimotor or practical space and representational or conceptual space. In Piaget's view, acting in space (moving around the environment and interacting with objects) is not indicative of cognitive level. In other words, not all spatial behaviors are indicative of spatial competence for Piaget; behaviors must be divided into the sensorimotor and the conceptual. Drawing, modeling, and perspective-taking are among the activities considered conceptual and thus indicative of cognitive level or competence.

This is, of course, partly true by definition; Piaget is in a sense free to divide behaviors in any way he chooses, and to give the resulting categories different labels—as long as everyone is clear about the basis for division and the meaning of the constructs. But such an exercise is not important or useful unless the distinction captures an important criterion of difference. At first blush, the Piagetian distinction seems commonsensical, but it quickly leads to a variety of problems. In a chapter on systems of reference, Piaget and Inhelder (1948/1967) write that "the kind of drawings which children produce between the age of 4 and 8, showing chimneys perpendicular to sloping roofs and men at right-angles to hills they are supposed to be climbing . . . suggests that the child has a long way to go in passing from a postural or sensori-motor space to a conceptual one.[p. 379]" But many people would immediately object that perhaps the problem is not conceptual, that children simply have difficulty in drawing what they see. Kosslyn, Heldmeyer, and Locklear (1977) support this point by demonstrating that children can recognize correct representations of what they are unable to draw. Furthermore, in evaluating children's drawings, we have also the problem discussed by Downs and Siegel (Chapter 9 of this volume) that considering as "correct" the perspective drawing endorsed by post-Renaissance western art is perhaps to ignore that other principled renderings of space exist.

Siegel's view of the competence/performance, representation/behavior issue is based on these kinds of objections to many tasks used to investigate spatial knowledge. In his discussion of efforts to "stalk the elusive cognitive map," he adopts the position that we ought to try to find methods of simplifying task demands as greatly as possible, in order to allow subjects to display their competence (to externalize their cognitive maps) as fully as possible. He is troubled by the story of Buffy, the kindergartener whose model of her classroom was in complete disarray, and who was yet able to navigate the classroom in day-to-day activity. The cognitive map of her classroom, which might be inferred from her everyday action, was quite different from that which might be inferred from her modeling. Thus, Siegel implicitly advocated considering locomotion and action with objects as behaviors on a par with modeling or other conceptual tasks, different primarily in that the former have minimal performance factors interfering with our view of competence.

A third position represented in this volume addresses the representation/behavior issue by claiming that it has been improperly formulated. Wapner, Kaplan, and Ciottone, in Chapter 10 write that representation and behavior should not and indeed cannot be distinguished as they are in the title of this book. Rather, representation is one of the many possible uses of space, and producing representations is one, among many, of spatial behaviors that we may study. Downs in Chapter 6 adopts a similar position in his discussion of maps as metaphors. He prefers to speak of mappings rather than of maps to stress the point that creating a repesentation (whether purely internal or externally observable) is a form of activity, always influenced by the purpose of creating the representation and the forms available for its creation. According to Downs, dependent variables in studies of cognitive maps need therefore to be conceptualized also as independent variables. All techniques for externalizing cognitive maps require different activities and these cognitive processes are deserving of research in their own right. A particular technique is not necessarily better or worse than another, that is, not more or less revealing of the map in the head.

In Chapter 1, Liben attempts a reconciliation among these points of view by suggesting that there are three senses of "representation," which need to be carefully distinguished. "Spatial products" is the label she gives to external representations, such as maps, models, and verbal descriptions; these can be of interest in their own right as well as be viewed as clues to internal representations. She uses "spatial thought" to refer to internal representations that are consciously accessible and which may (or may not) have the analogue or imagistic format suggested in slightly different research by Shepard and by Kosslyn. "Spatial storage" is closest to the general term "competence," and refers to hypothesized representations, not consciously accessible, but thought by the outside observer to exist, in some unknown format, because observed behavior is compatible with the person (or animal) "having" such a model. That is, the organism behaves "as if" such a model were present.

The distinction between "spatial thought" and "spatial storage" is an important one, which may resolve much confusion. The distinction involves at least three separate dimensions, which it may be useful to distinguish. The first concerns the format of the representation, whether analogue or propositional. This dichotomy has a long and vexed history in psychology; Anderson (1978) suggests that the question may not be answerable, because appropriate format-process pairs can always be invented to explain any observed behavior. Thus, the first distinction may be difficult to use, although it has intuitive appeal, and some writers have more optimism than Anderson concerning the possibility of deciding empirically how knowledge is represented (Hayes-Roth, 1979; Pylyshyn, 1979). A second distinction involves whether knowledge is consciously available. Here again, the contrast has intuitive appeal, but it is difficult, as Liben acknowledges, to work with empirically.

A third basis for a distinction involves the nature of the evidence required to make a claim concerning what a given piece of data shows about an organism. Some evidence is sufficient only to make an "as if" statement: The organism is behaving as if such-and-so were the case about what it knows. In some cases, this is as far as we can go. But in other cases, additional evidence strengthens the case; an organism capable of symbolic behavior can indicate verbally, by using maps, models, and so on, the nature of the representation it believes it has about a spatial environment. When this coincides with the inferences one would draw on the basis of observation of action, one is in a position to make a stronger "as if" statement: More than one type of spatial behavior is "as if" a certain representation existed. If accessible symbolic knowledge and the evidence of action do not coincide, a quandary remains. Is introspection wrong, or impossible to manifest because of difficulty producing spatial products? Or is there some other explanation for the observed action patterns, some more parsimonious reason for the organism behaving as it does?

The dichotomy between representation and behavior is a difficult one to work with in part because it raises the whole issue of the appropriateness of mentalism. If all we can observe is behavior of various sorts, what use is it to postulate the existence of unobservable mental entities? In what sense can we claim that one behavior is a better guide to an unobservable mental entity than another? An extreme logical positivist answer to the problem of how to stalk the cognitive map is that one should not. One should simply identify as clearly as possible the various spatial *behaviors* of interest, and study each as a topic in its own right; their definitions would be purely operational and the relationships among them matters for empirical discovery. None of the authors in the present volume, however, adopts such a position and it is interesting to explore why not. Why is it necessary to postulate the existence of some mental entity, however mysterious its nature and however misleading the metaphor of it as a map may be?

This question may be addressed more starkly if we consider the literature on the spatial behavior of animals. The term "cognitive map" was used by Tolman (1948) to describe the behavior of rats in mazes. The rats had learned a right-angled path from a start box to a goal box. This was then blocked, and the rats were allowed to choose an alternate path from among various arms arrayed in sunburst fashion. The majority of rats chose the arm oriented in the direction of the goal box, and Tolman concluded that this showed that the rats "understood" the spatial relation between the start and the goal without having directly experienced it.

Olton (1979) has criticized the logic of the Tolman experiment but has demonstrated, using other kinds of mazes, that rats are able to learn such general principles: "Go to the center of the maze" or "Go to the top of the maze," which seem to require the rats to understand their present spatial position within an overall representation of the maze. Menzel (1973, 1978) has demonstrated mapping abilities in chimpanzees by carrying chimps on a circuitous path around a compound and allowing them to observe the hiding of food in 18 locations. When the chimpanzees were released from a holding cage and allowed to search for the food, they not only remembered the locations fairly well, retrieving 12 pieces of food on the average, but they followed economical routes in their search, organizing their action to avoid redundancy. Wild orangutans have shown similar capabilities and their ability to plan foraging routes seems vital to the ability of these large animals to survive on a diet of fruits (MacKinnon, 1978).

Following shortcuts, planning routes, and locating detours are thus the spatial behaviors that have led students of animal behavior to posit the existence of "cognitive maps." No animal psychologist has, however, devised a way (yet) by which even a chimpanzee can draw a sketch map or rank order locations for multidimensional scaling (although Menzel [1978] does call for research on chimpanzees' ability to learn spatial information from pictorial or maplike representations). Thus, it seems, using Liben's terminology, that we are dealing in the case of animal research with "spatial storage," with the claim that actions in space are conducted "as if" an organism were in possession of certain facts. The fact that observation of action alone, in the case of animals, can lead to data seeming to require postulation of a cognitive map, should lead to rejection of the idea that data regarding action *necessarily* bear only on a kind of knowledge called sensorimotor knowledge. The two forms of knowledge seem distinguishable only on the basis of whether or not the knowledge is tacit or conscious. It seems more defensible to me to adopt the position of Wapner *et al.* and Downs: that is, representing space is an activity like any other; to answer questions about the nature of representation, we must rely on information regarding a variety of behaviors. No one behavior is the royal road to knowledge of spatial representations.

Piaget has rightly drawn our attention, however, to the fact that many actions do *not* provide evidence of spatial competence. Standing upright is regulated by vestibular and motor pathways, for instance, and presumably has a large innate component. Thus it surely does not indicate understanding of verticality. Likewise, Buffy may well avoid the walls and furniture of her classroom by direct reaction to her perception of solid objects in her way. Actions regulated by built-in circuitry or as responses to environmental stimuli certainly do not necessarily provide information about cognitive maps, although they are helpful in allowing people to move about their environment (and may ultimately allow the construction of overall spatial representations).

Evidence that Buffy can plan routes, detours, and shortcuts in everyday behavior in her classroom or school would, however, be persuasive as evidence that her knowledge is inadequately revealed by the modeling task and that performance factors have interfered with demonstration of competence. It should be remembered, however, that reducing task difficulty (load factors) to facilitate examination of competence can be problematic. For one thing, it is not very easily accomplished. Almost any task involves *some* performance factors. For instance, Siegel comments that multidimensional scaling may well misrepresent knowledge: rank ordering to the "nth" item is certainly not a task generally undertaken in everyday life and subjects are prone to take "nonrandom walks" in making such judgments, telling the experimenter what is closest to the object they have just mentioned rather than what is eighth closest to what is supposed to be their reference point.

This point is substantiated by Liben and Newcombe (1980). Rank-ordering data collected by Kosslyn, Pick, and Fariello (1974) suggested that preschool children judge distances to be longer when locations are separated by either transparent or opaque barriers, whereas adults distort only across opaque barriers. This suggests either that functional distance is more important in children's than in adults' spatial representations, or perhaps that children organize representations into "local subspaces" and have trouble integrating these subspaces. What Liben and I showed was that these results can be replicated using a rank-ordering task as the dependent variable, but that a different picture of developmental change emerged when a distance-estimation task was used instead. We do not take this as evidence that either technique is better than the other. Neither has a claim to be considered a more valid guide to internal representation; each tells us something about how knowledge of space can combine with the different mental processing required by the different tasks to produce judgments.

One implication of the foregoing discussion is that past conclusions about spatial competence may need to be modified by considering more carefully the exact nature of the task (i.e., the reasoning called for.) An example is Blaut and Stea's (1971) rather global assertion that preschoolers demonstrate basic competency in mapping behavior when they demonstrate their ability to identify features on aerial photographs. Acredolo reminds us in Chapter 3 of this volume that mapping can be defined as the lawful reduction of a large to a small space. An area viewed from a plane is thus a small-scale rather than a large-scale space. When children show that they can recognize features of such already produced translations, they demonstrate competence in the same sense as children recognizing drawings did in the study by Kosslyn *et al.* (1977).

Blaut and Stea did not test the ability to make a map, specifically because they lacked the means to control performance factors such as "motor skills, hand-eye coordination, and familiarity with tools and medium [p. 390]." They did report, however, that some map-making skills could be taught to first-graders. The Blaut and Stea demonstration of early competence in mapping seems to demonstrate an early competence in recognizing miniaturized and rotated physical features, but recent work by Bluestein and Acredolo (1979) shows that while 3-year-olds can interpret cartographic symbols as representing objects in space, the ability to superimpose a map on a space, to use a map to learn about spatial relations, is not present, but undergoes development during the 3-5-year age range. Thus, a finer analysis of what is involved in the Blaut and Stea recognition task led to new data on both what does and what does not develop in mapping skills in preschoolers.

In summary, arguments have been presented in this section that spatial representations are necessary postulates in the study of spatial behavior, but that their nature can be inferred only by careful process analysis of the various tasks which might be used to look at them. Simple rules for choosing tasks, such as "action does not count" or "always trust the simpler task" will not suffice. In the next section, the question of how to value (in practical terms, how to score) the data resulting from these tasks will be considered.

Accuracy

A second issue that emerges in these chapters is the issue of the validity of scoring responses to mapping tasks as more or less "accurate." Downs raises this point in Chapter 6 of this volume when he argues that the "world according to Rand McNally" is a convenient fiction and that those who believe that there is "something out there" that either a physical or a cognitive map can render more-or-less well are naïve realists. The naïve realist response to this criticism might well be that it verges on solipsism; if we cannot know the

"something out there" with any certainty, we also cannot be certain we do
not know, and thus the argument is logically contradictory.

It seems to me that the essential issue raised by Downs of which investigators need to be aware is not solipsistic but rather that people choose
representational systems to achieve various ends; they are willing to accept
various kinds and degrees of error in their representations in order to achieve
these desirable ends, for instance, representing the globe on a two-
dimensional surface. There are two related points to be made here. One is
that many notational systems generally exist, which can represent the same
physical information; for instance, elevation information can be represented
by colors on a map, by lines joining points of equal elevation, by shading and
hachuring, or by three-dimensional modeling. In this example, all four
systems are conventional and well-recognized; none is more "correct" than
another, although the first two are digital and the last two are analogue
systems (cf. Goodman, 1968). But it is possible that when we look at maps
or models produced by people not familiar with conventions that they will
use notational systems of their own invention. These could be equally sensi-
ble, systematic, or useful as the more familiar ones, but could go unrecog-
nized by an investigator. We can recall in this connection Goodnow's (1972)
discussion of "rules and tricks of the trade" in musical notation. Goodnow
found that children often chose ways of representing rhythms unfamiliar to
adults and liable to be unnoticed and considered incorrect by psychologists;
however, these ways are just as valid and reasonable as more conventional
methods once noticed.

A second point about choice of representational systems is more related to
the theme of Downs' Chapter 6, and is also touched on by Wapner, Kaplan,
and Ciottone in Chapter 10 and by Altman and Gauvain in Chapter 11.
It is not only possible that the same information can be represented using different notational sysems, but also that different metrics or scaling rules may
be more or less appropriate in different contexts. The appropriate metric may
not always be obvious at first glance, or obvious to an outside observer. An
example from psychophysics is that intensity as measured in physical units
does not correspond one-to-one to psychological intensity, or loudness,
which is therefore measured in decibels. In the spatial domain, distance in
feet or miles, angular displacement and so on may be useful metrics for some
problems, but perhaps primarily for those that do not involve emotional
meaning. Wapner *et al.* point out that emotional associations can structure
spatial perception so that places close at hand, if alien or forbidden, may
seem subjectively distant. In a smilar vein, Altman and Gauvain point out
that cultural rules of accessibility may mean that the practical distance between two points is often not the same as the distance-as-the-crow flies. It
does not seem best to characterize such facts as showing that personal or

cultural meanings induce inaccuracy or distortion in cognitive maps. Rather, a different metric is being used to capture a different kind of information about spatial relationships.

The basic message that I take from all this is that the metrics that people actually use to structure space should be of interest, rather than characterized simply as "error" and thrown in the rubbish heap of the error term. The fact, for instance, that many people show noncommutativity in making distance judgments (distance from A to B not equal to distance from B to A) does not show necessarily that those people are illogical or have disjointed cognitive maps. Noncommutativity may also be taken to show that the rules people use for making such judgments are not geometric in a simple and familiar way. The rules also involve factors such as familiarity and attractiveness (Stea, 1969). Similar problems of noncommutativity appear in human judgment of nonspatial relationships as well (Tversky, 1977) and formal models (i.e., geometries) of the processes involved in these judgments can be formulated.

Decalages and Developmental Sequence

If the study of development is to be more than the description of change at the most microscopic level (e.g., Gesell's catalogue of the average age of occurrence of specific motor behaviors), then we must strive to make observations that allow for inductive generalization and that lead us to postulate the existence of more generalized abilities or understanding underlying behavioral observation. Piaget's *structures d'ensemble* are the most highly formalized such description, but non-Piagetian developmental psychologists perform a similar act of generalization when they speak, for instance, of "attachment" instead of crying-when-mother-leaves or "metamemory" instead of predicting-what-is-harder-to-remember. The status of such generalizations becomes problematic, however, when one is faced with exceptions to the proposed rule. Piaget calls exceptions to his proposed stage descriptions "horizontal decalages." Flavell (1971) has discussed in lucid detail the difficulties of assessing the existence and extent of horizontal decalages due to the difficulty of being sure that the measures used to test supposedly correlated tasks are of equivalent difficulty.

Most of the authors in this volume who deal with developmental data do not adopt stage theories. But they do look for sequences in the development of spatial cognition; in fact, Pick and Lockman state explicity that this is their strategy. But what are we to conclude when similar logical competencies are identified at different ages or when similar sequences of development are identified in quite different age ranges? One example of such a decalage is discussed by Pick and Lockman: Infants' spatial knowledge in the object–body domain appears to develop in advance of logically analogous knowledge in the object–object domain. A second example can be taken from the work of Acredolo: 3- and 4- year-olds exhibit an egocentrism, or place rather than response learning, under certain conditions—a mode of response not found, under certain different experimental conditions, for 9-and 11-month-old infants.

The central issue in considering such apparent anomalies is the degree to which problems we have analyzed as formally similar are in fact psychologically similar. That is, there is no decalage problem—no problem of sequences out of synchrony—if our logical description of the underlying ability allowing for solution of different problems has been in some way mistaken. (This is really the same argument as that made before in the first section of this chapter on spatial representations and spatial behavior.) One clear illustration of the point can be taken from the program of research by Huttenlocher and Presson (1973, 1979) on perspective-taking and mental-rotation problems. The original observation that led to these studies was of a decalage between children's ability to solve perspective-taking problems (to indicate how an array would look to a person viewing it from another position) and their ability to solve mental-rotation problems (to indicate how an array would look if it were rotated). Although the tasks are formally similar in that in both cases a viewer looks at an array and is asked about the appearance of the array given a changed relation between viewer and array, the former are much harder than the latter and children are much older before they are able to perform perspective-taking without errors.

In the 1973 paper, Huttenlocher and Presson suggested that this was due to the fact that instructions were interpreted literally: Either imagine yourself moving or imagine the array moving. Imagining the self moving was suggested as more difficult and thus developmentally later. In the 1979 paper, this hypothesis was rejected because further data showed that viewer rotation was *not* always more difficult than array rotation; in fact, it was *easier* if questions asked about specific items ("which figure is in back following the change?") rather than about the overall appearance of the array. The results were explained by hypothesizing that arrays are coded with respect to the larger spatial framework of the room in which they are located rather than merely being coded internally, each item in respect to others. Both children and adults, it was argued, code this way, and both age groups follow the task instructions using similar strategies. Huttenlocher and Presson then postulated that "the simplest explanation for age-related improvements in the ability to solve Piagetian perspective problems is that there are increases in capacity of various processing components (e.g., working memory) [p. 392]."

The hypothesis that small-scale spatial arrays are often coded with respect to the larger spatial environment is supported by Acredolo's and by Siegel's discussions in this volume; the lesson that studies of small-scale spatial cognition cannot be considered as carried out in a vacuum is a clear and important one. But for the present discussion of decalages there is a more important point: A careful and differentiated process analysis of the two tasks involved in the apparent decalage reveals the underlying dissimilarity as well as the similarity in the mental steps by which they are solved. In this case, the differences discovered were integrated within a *quantitative* account of developmental change. In other cases, a more refined analysis of tasks might reveal the existence of performance factors, which could account for the asymmetry in age at onset while still preserving a stage theory of development.

One approach to decalages is thus to assume that they are ultimately explicable by identification of the crucial differences between tasks that are formally similar. Another approach is to argue that even without such differences, changes in problem context may lead to failure to generalize knowledge demonstrable in another problem context. In research on mathematical problem-solving by tailors in Liberia, for instance, Jean Lave (1977) has found that the tailors are able to solve problems concerned with tailoring, but not problems requiring identical mathematical operations presented in a school context. Conversely, Liberians with formal schooling but without tailoring experience did adequately with school problems, but had difficulty with tailoring problems. It is possible that the appreciation of formal similarity among problems in different contexts is a late-appearing feat, a form of metaknowledge, and that prior to this achievement, the problems are not psychologically similar. The implication of this idea for stage theories of development is disturbing: Our descriptions of underlying competence may well be overly general and abstract, and lines of development may be much more specific and context-bound than we have assumed.

Much more work on these issues needs to be done in the area of spatial cognition. For instance, Pick and Lockman note that the fact that Acredolo's 3-year-olds in one experiment showed egocentric responding in learning a location whereas infants in another experiment showed allocentric responding could be due to at least two factors: the distinctiveness of marking in the room and whether the change of position was active or passive. Greater distinctiveness would facilitate spatial coding, and, in line with this, infants showed allocentric responding in distinctive landmark conditions, whereas preschoolers showed egocentric responding in undifferentiated contexts. It is puzzling, however, that activity would also seem to favor spatial memory, as has been shown by Feldman and Acredolo (1979), but it was the preschoolers who were active, whereas infants were moved from place to place.

Again we see that the issue of factors moderating performance on formally similar tasks is a crucial one for the study of developmental sequence and stage.

Environmental Cognition and Spatial Abstraction: The Relevance of Multidisciplinary Perspectives

To this point, we have discussed some important issues that arise in the study of spatial representation and behavior, but without considering the field as a whole, or the mutual relevance of the different lines of research being pursued from different perspectives. As Liben pointed out in her introduction, investigators differ not only in what kind of spatial representation they wish to study, but in whether they are primarily concerned with how people get around their spatial environments and how they arrange and use them *or* whether they are primarily interested in spatial abstraction and people's notions of space in general. In disciplinary terms, the former tends to be the concern of environmental and social psychologists, architects, planners, and geographers, and the latter the concern of cognitive and developmental psychologists and philosophers.

The question arises: Do the students of these different content areas really have much to say to each other, and, if so, what? For instance, in the context of this volume, what does the person interested in sequences in the early acquisition of spatial frames of reference, as studied by Acredolo and by Pick and Lockman, have to learn from a piece as purely social and environmental as that of Altman and Gauvain? Vice versa, does the reader of Chapter 11 by Altman and Gauvain, interested in the dialectical relation of individual and society and how this relation is reflected in the decoration and placement of home environments, have anything of relevance to learn from the cognitive developmentalist?

Viewed narrowly, the answer would be no; the immediate research projects in which such individuals are engaged tend not to be affected by the others' work. But one of the wider themes of this book is that all of these lines of research can (and need to) be seen as related. They are relevant to different parts of Liben's Figure 1.2; all contribute to better understanding of the *system* of interrelationships of cultural and individual history, individual characteristics, environmental characteristics, and spatial activity and representation.

In the present volume, there is a great deal of interest in the influence of individual characteristics on spatial activity and representation. All of the chapters, with the exception of Chapter 11 by Altman and Gauvain, deal with this aspect of the system, although they focus on different individual characteristics: Chapter 2 by Pick and Lockman, and Chapter 3 by Acredolo on age, cognitive stage, and knowledge; Chapter 4 by Harris on sex as a variable through which we may look at cognitive style, spatial ranges, emotional expectancies, genetic differences, and hormonal differences; Chapter 7 by Siegel and Chapter 8 by Hart again on age, stage, knowledge, and range; Chaper 10 by Wapner, Kaplan, and Ciottone on age, stage, and knowledge; Chapter 12 by Walsh, Krauss, and Regnier on age (on a different end of the life span), physical status, experience, and ability. Other chapters concern other parts of the system. Interactions between individual characteristics and characteristics of the physical environment are of concern in the three chapters in Part III, and to a lesser extent, in most of the other chapters. The last three chapters make especially clear that environmental cognition involves the imposition of meaning—socioemotional as well as cognitive—on the spatial structure of the environment, and the reciprocal effect of such environments on individuals and their spatial representations and activities.

Considering the chapters in the context of the system outlined by Liben allows us to examine further what lessons people interested in apparently disparate topics can learn from each other. In sections on accuracy and its meaning by Downs, and Downs and Siegel, and as just discussed, we have already made the point that judgments of inaccuracy or distortion in cognitive maps may arise from failure to acknowledge the role of emotional and cultural meaning in structuring such maps; or, if it is acknowledged, failure to consider it a *legitimate* metric for use in representation. This is a clear example of how a researcher concerned with spatial abstraction could benefit from considering research in the field of environmental use.

Other examples arise in this volume as well. One is Downs and Siegel's discussion of the danger of "adultocentric" definitions in developmental studies in Chapter 9. "Adultocentric" refers at least partly to adult dimensions of socioemotional meaning, as well as to adult height, cognitive stage, and spatial range. Thus, a landmark for an adult is not necessarily important from a child's perspective (e.g. a bar, an insurance office) nor are children's landmarks necessarily important to adults (e.g. a tree good for climbing, an empty lot used as a playground). Remembering this can allow us to reconcile seemingly contradictory findings. Hart reports in Chapter 8, for instance, that children seem to adopt different landmarks from those used by adults to organize their models of their home environment. This is in accord with the "adultocentric" argument, but apparently at variance with Siegel's conclusion that children in his route-learning task did no better when given landmarks chosen by children than when given landmarks chosen by adults.

The crucial difference between these paradigms appears to lie in the extent to which they involve socioemotional meaning; in the Siegel situation, all subjects are learning about unfamiliar territory. Thus, what constitutes a "good landmark" is defined by physical characteristics such as distinctiveness and discriminability. Adults could be expected to choose such landmarks with greater consistency, given their greater metamnemonic knowledge and task orientation. But landmarks in Hart's situation are defined by patterns of use, and use and experience can be expected to differ considerably for people of different ages.

As a third example of how the study of environments is important to those interested in spatial abstraction, recall Acredolo's (1979) finding that infants' use of egocentric frames of reference is markedly lower in their homes than in either an unmarked laboratory or a differentiated but unfamiliar office. The relevant variables here remain to be discovered, but the phenomenon is obviously one that cannot be ignored by those interested in "pure" spatial abstraction.

What of lessons learned in the reverse direction, by students of the environment from those interested in spatial abstraction? People working on environmental use and way-finding should be interested to learn from Walsh, Krauss, and Regnier in Chapter 12 that substantial correlations exist between spatial ability, as assessed by psychometric tests and by laboratory tasks, and some measures of environmental knowledge and use. The implication is that understanding of individual cognitive characteristics is necessary to the study of social patterns of environmental use. (Of course, for correlations causality can be reversed, so another implication is that patterns of environmental use need to be studied more carefully by those interested in spatial ability and abstraction, as Wohlwill reminds us.)

People interested in way-finding might profit from research on spatial abstraction by adapting paradigms from cognitive psychology to the study of cognitive processes during way-finding. Hart has done this to an extent in looking at children's models from a different perspective than that of Piaget, and Siegel by studying memory for spatial routes in various laboratory situations. What might be done further along these lines is, for example, to examine how cognitive stage determines natural way-finding: Are preschoolers who use allocentric frames of reference better able to follow directions, or do children who have difficulty with Hazen, Lockman, and Pick's (1978) inference questions have trouble planning detours? Furthermore, knowing more about how people think about their environment (spatial abstraction) might well help us to understand what they like and do not like about their surroundings, why they use space in certain ways and not in others, and so on. For instance, do people personalize their dwellings, as discussed by Altman and Gauvain, at least in part because they feel more comfortable and less likely to be lost and disoriented in a differentiated landscape?

Conclusion

The contributors to this volume share many concerns and interests. In this conclusion I have been able to write at length about only four issues: (a) the relationship of spatial representation to spatial behavior; (b) the use of "accuracy" as a dependent variable in studies of spatial cognition; (c) the worrisome problem of apparent decalages in development of spatial abilities; and (d) the mutual relevance of different disciplines interested in space. Many other themes could have been identified as well. For instance, the authors share an interest in the effect of activity and experience in an environment on spatial representation: Walsh et al. found large correlations between use of space and various measures of accuracy of sketch maps; Wapner et al. illustrated the effects of experience on children of different cognitive levels with their description of successive maps drawn by children in a family newly gone to Holland; and Hart emphasized the range children are allowed to walk or bike unaccompanied as a factor explaining the nature of their town models. Differential spatial experience is also considered by Harris as a potential source of sex differences in spatial ability; the importance of this factor has been strongly argued elsewhere by Saegert and Hart (1978). Wohlwill in Chapter 5 reminds us that much more work on actual environmental experience remains to be done.

At some point, however, commentary must stop and work of another kind begin. We hope that this volume has served to provide an overview of current thinking about spatial cognition; if it also serves as a stimulus to thought and research, which will solve the problems raised here, it will have served its purpose.

Acknowledgments

I would like to thank Roger Downs and Lynn Liben for discussion of the ideas in this chapter.

References

Acredolo, L. P. Laboratory versus home: The effect of environment on the 9-month-old infant's choice of spatial reference system. Developmental Psychology, 1979, 15, 666-667.

Anderson, J. R. Arguments concerning representations for mental imagery. Psychological Review, 1978, 85, 249-277.

Blaut, J. M., & Stea, D. Studies of geographic learning. Annals of the Association of American Geographers, 1971, 61, 387-393.

Bluestein, N., & Acredolo, L. Developmental changes in map-reading skills. *Child Development*, 1979, *50*, 691-697.

Chomsky, N. *Aspects of the theory of syntax*. Mouton, 1965.

Feldman, A., & Acredolo, L. The effect of active versus passive exploration on memory for spatial location in children. *Child Development*, 1979, *50*, 698-704.

Flavell, J. H. Stage-related properties of cognitive development. *Cognitive Psychology*, 1971, *2*, 421-453.

Goodman, N. *Languages of art*. Indianapolis: Bobbs-Merrill, 1968.

Goodnow, J. Rules and repertoires, rituals and tricks of the trade: Social and informational aspects to cognitive and representational development. In S. Farnham-Diggory (Ed.), *Information-processing in children*. New York: Academic Press, 1972.

Greene, J. *Psycholinguistics: Chomsky and psychology*. Harmondsworth, England: Penguin, 1972.

Hayes-Roth, F. Distinguishing theories of representation: A critique of Anderson's "Arguments concerning mental imagery." *Psychological Review*, 1979, *86*, 376-382.

Hazen, N. L., Lockman, J. J., & Pick, H. L., Jr. The development of children's representations of large-scale environments. *Child Development*, 1978, *49*, 623-636.

Huttenlocher, J., & Presson, C. Mental rotation and the perspective problem. *Cognitive Psychology*, 1973, *4*, 279-299.

Huttenlocher, J., & Presson, C. C. The coding and transformation of spatial information. *Cognitive Psychology*, 1979, *11*, 375-394.

Kosslyn, S. M., Heldmeyer, K. H., & Locklear, E. P. Children's drawings as data about internal representations. *Journal of Experimental Child Psychology*, 1977, *43*, 191-211.

Kosslyn, S. M., Pick, H. L., & Fariello, G. Cognitive maps in children and men. *Child Development*, 1974, *45*, 707-716.

Lave, J. Tailor-made experiments and evaluating the intellectual consequences of apprenticeship training. *Quarterly Newsletter of Institute for Comparative Human Development*, 1977, *1*, 1-3.

Liben, L. S., & Newcombe, N. Barrier effects in the cognitive maps of children and adults. Paper presented to the Southeastern Conference on Human Development, Alexandria, Virginia, April, 1980.

MacKinnon, J. *The ape within us*. Holt, Rinehart and Winston, 1978.

Menzel, E. W. Chimpanzee spatial memory organization. *Science*, 1973, *822*, 943-945.

Menzel, E. W. Cognitive mapping in chimpanzees. In S. H. Hulse, H. Fowler, & W. K. Honig (Eds.), *Cognitive aspects of animal behavior*. Hillsdale, New Jersey: Erlbaum, 1978.

Olton, D. S. Mazes, maps, and memory. *American Psychologist*, 1979, *34*, 583-596.

Piaget, J., & Inhelder, B. *The child's conception of space*. New York: Norton, 1967 (Originally published in 1948).

Pylyshyn, Z. W. Validating computational models: A critique of Anderson's indeterminacy of representation claim. *Psychological Review*, 1979, *86*, 383-394.

Saegert, S., & Hart, R. The development of environmental competence in girls and boys. In M. Salter (Ed.), *Play: Anthropological Perspectives*. Cornwall, New York: Leisure Press, 1978.

Stea, D. The measurement of mental maps: An experimental model for studying conceptual spaces. In K. R. Cox & R. G. Golledge (Eds.), *Behavioral problems in geography*. Evanston, Illinois: Northwestern University Press, 1969.

Tolman, E. C. Cognitive maps in rats and men. *Psychological Review*, 1948, *55*, 189-208.

Tversky, A. Features of similarity. *Psychological Review*, 1977, *84*, 327-352.

Author Index

Numbers in italics refer to the pages on which the complete references are listed.

Subject Index

397